NARCISSISM AND SUICIDE IN SHAKESPEARE AND HIS CONTEMPORARIES

Narcissism and Suicide in Shakespeare and his Contemporaries

ERIC LANGLEY

OXFORD

UNIVERSITY PRESS

OXFORD

UNIVERSITY PRESS

Great Clarendon Street, Oxford OX2 6DP

Oxford University Press is a department of the University of Oxford.
It furthers the University's objective of excellence in research, scholarship,
and education by publishing worldwide in

Oxford New York

Auckland Cape Town Dar es Salaam Hong Kong Karachi
Kuala Lumpur Madrid Melbourne Mexico City Nairobi
New Delhi Shanghai Taipei Toronto

With offices in

Argentina Austria Brazil Chile Czech Republic France Greece
Guatemala Hungary Italy Japan Poland Portugal Singapore
South Korea Switzerland Thailand Turkey Ukraine Vietnam

Oxford is a registered trade mark of Oxford University Press
in the UK and in certain other countries

Published in the United States
by Oxford University Press Inc., New York

© Eric Langley 2009

British Library Cataloguing in Publication Data
Data available

Library of Congress Cataloging in Publication Data
Data available

Typeset by SPI Publisher Services, Pondicherry, India
Printed in Great Britain
on acid-free paper by the
MPG Books Group, Bodmin and King's Lynn

ISBN 978-0-19-954123-2

3 5 7 9 10 8 6 4

for
R. F. L.
and
B. H. L.
here is of all the very this

Acknowledgements

During the years it has taken to write this book, I have had the good fortune to work alongside wonderfully generous and encouraging colleagues, too numerous to all identify individually, at the Universities of Leeds, York, St Andrews, Sheffield, and at UCL. Thanks especially go to Paul Hammond, under whose assured and reassuring supervision this project began, and whose support remains much appreciated, as well as to all those in the School of English at Leeds, particularly David Lindley, Martin Butler, and the much missed Sally Dawson. Many debts (of friendship not least) have been accrued while teaching at St Andrews: the enthusiasm and support of Neil Rhodes and Lorna Hutson has proved inspirational and invaluable. I have been extremely fortunate as a teaching fellow to have taught at such welcoming and sympathetic institutions and it is the enlightened attitude of each Head of School and every colleague that has made this book possible.

I owe an incalculable debt to my former and current students, whose collective interest and insight is in some way evident on every page. One representative student must symbolically stand in on behalf of the rest: James Page, a student I tutored in the first seminar I ever taught and whose off the cuff comment initiated almost a decade of my work. To all, heartfelt thanks.

Many friends have discussed aspects of this book with me—Alex Davis, Sarah Dillon, Andrew Elliott, Bridget Escolme, Chris Jones, Robert Jones, Tom Jones, Donovan MacAbee, Margaux Poueymirou, David Stirrup and the overeducated allotment holders of Plot 69B to name but a few—and many more have suggested things to read or quotations to include. Particularly productive lines of enquiry have been suggested by Chris Boswell, Rebecca Calcagno, Susannah Gebhardt, Nasser Hussain, Tim Langley, Marcus Nevitt, and Jeremy Prynne. Especial thanks to Stewart Mottram with whom I have enjoyed countless conversations (making my 'aberrations obvious'): a perfect career companion, advisor, and friend.

This work has been enormously benefited by the comments of two anonymous readers at OUP; the intellectual generosity of the responses and the challenges they posed provided much needed provocation, encouragement, and correction. Thanks also to Jacqueline Baker, Bonnie Blackburn, Keira Dickinson, Andrew McNeillie, and Elizabeth Stone at the Press.

Thanks also to my parents, Roger and Barbara, to whom this book is dedicated, and to Ruth, Tom, and Holly. Finally, I cannot thank Gillian Roberts enough; she has read every page, clarified my thinking, supported me throughout, and makes all possible, enjoyable, and worthwhile.

An earlier version of sections from Chapter One has appeared in *Forum for Modern Language Studies*, 44/1 (2008). I am grateful to the publishers for permission to reuse this material.

Contents

Abbreviations

All quotations from Shakespeare are drawn from the New Cambridge series.

TGV	*Two Gentlemen of Verona*
Tim.	*Timon of Athens*
Tit.	*Titus Andronicus*
Tmp.	*The Tempest*
TN	*Twelfth Night*
TNK	*The Two Noble Kinsmen*
Tro.	*Troilus and Cressida*
Ven.	*Venus and Adonis*
Wiv.	*The Merry Wives of Windsor*

Introduction

> Narcissus so himself himself forsook,
> And died to kiss his shadow in the brook.
>
> (*Ven.* 161–2)

'Himself himself forsook': this tiny and tidy display of Shakespearean rhetorical ingenuity encapsulates much of what follows. Suggesting the mirrored surface of Ovid's pool, reproducing the shadow or reflection of Narcissus' face on the water's surface, the neat economy of a single word in tight repetition discloses the self-enclosed and self-perpetuating dynamic of narcissistic fascination. The reflection of 'himself' against 'himself', an interaction admitting no difference or threatening alterity, speaks both of the immaculate self-absorption of the narcissist and of the fragility of a purely self-constituted subjectivity. 'Narcissus so himself himself forsook': the moment of self-referential isolation is simultaneously an act of self-destruction.

> *Suicide* (from *sui*) the slaying or murdering of himself; self-murder.
> *Suist* (from *sui*) one that loves himself, a selfish man.[1]

As he stares into his reflection, the self-immersion of the Ovidian youth is revealed as suicidal: 'to love one's self alone is to turn the self upon the self murderously and without pity'.[2]

This book is about early modern literary narcissists and self-murderers. During its course, these two groups will be shown to have mutual affinity both in the nature of their impulses towards self-assertion and absorption,

---

[1] T[homas] B[lount], *Glossographia; or, A Dictionary* (London, 1661), s.v. 'Sui-'.
[2] Arthur Kirsch, 'Macbeth's Suicide', *ELH*, 51 (1984), 269–96 at 293.

and in the very specific vocabularies of their expression on the Shakespearean stage and more generally in early modern texts (whether poetic, dramatic, literary, or non-literary). Together, the suist and the suicide share an analogous or complementary function in the development of early modern aesthetic, philosophical, and theological discourses concerning self-awareness and ownership. They stand as negative exemplars of excessive self-subjection and self-involvement, as advocates of gratuitously isolationist self-sufficiency. Proffered in indictment of what is perceived of as a classically informed inclination towards systematized introspection, reflection, and self-scrutiny, the suicide and the narcissist are cautionary figures of immoderate individualism. For those who resist an increasingly prevalent rhetoric of interiorized authority, these suicentric figures offer an opportunity for censure as the period renegotiates its intellectual commitment to reflexive models of self-knowledge and consciousness; they are the easily identifiable representatives of extreme self-ishness, reprimanded for being precursors to, harbingers or evidence of, an ever more articulated and rhetorically articulable introjected geminative subject. While period thought contests the ethics of self-scrutiny, these two too selfish subjects become freighted with particular philosophical significance; competing attitudes towards ipseic autonomy (self-ownership, assertion, affirmation, and even formation) are made visible in the various treatments of these figures.

Variously, through examining the features of dramatic suicide oratory, exploring rhetorical figures habitually associated with depictions of narcissism, or revealing the discursive characteristics of the early modern suicide debate, I seek to demonstrate the peculiar function of these two uniquely introspective figures in early modern explorations of subjectivity. The diverse representations of these two seemingly contrasting yet inherently comparable figures—both simultaneously self-productive and destructive—provide touchstones, lodestars, and litmus tests for the period's divergent attitudes towards the self-aware subject. My subject, therefore, is the character who loves himself or who kills himself, who acts upon himself either with self-directed adoration or self-destructive violence. My subject is the subject whose subject is himself.

As the study progresses, it becomes increasingly evident that these sixteenth- and seventeenth-century conceptions of subjectivity are characteristically predicated upon systems of reciprocity, reflection, and a governing foundational structure of mutuality: so, we will meet lovers, each a 'mine' to one another, whose love provides a model of shared identity; we will meet friends, each a 'second self' to one another, whose amity provides an ideal of psychic support; we will meet penitents, one eye on the divine, in whom God provides a vital and revitalizing introjected presence. As Charles Taylor suggests in his *Sources of the Self*—a discussion that will be returned to at critical moments throughout this study—there is, in these models of reciprocation, a sense 'in which one cannot be a self on one's own':

I am a self only in relation to certain interlocutors: in one way in relation to those conversation partners who were essential to my achieving self-definition; in another in relation to those who are now crucial to my continuing grasp of languages of self-understanding.[3]

An essayist like Montaigne or Bacon would concur that the friend acts as one such interlocutor; a sonneteer like Spenser or Sidney may understand the beloved in similar fashion; while, for poets and theologians such as Milton, Herbert, or Donne, God is the defining, subjecting presence. Conversely, the ultimately unattainable or self-defeating objective for narcissist and defiant self-slaughterer alike is to find a way in which one *can* be a self on one's own, in which one *could* depend only upon oneself and therefore assume ownership of one's own actions and ends: I am a self only in relation to myself.

Crucially, it is still within the context of a sense of mutually constructed individuality, reliant upon interlocution and relation, that the self-reflections of the narcissist and the self-destruction of the self-slaughterer must be read, not as entirely inexplicable antitheses to the norm, or exceptions to an ontological rule, but as uncannily extreme examples. Indeed, they are exceptional only in the extent of their conformity to what become increasingly involved and shockingly tight dynamics of reciprocation (eye to reflected eye, knife to throat). So Taylor regretfully explains in relation to modernity that 'culture has developed conceptions of individualism which picture the human person as, at least potentially, finding his or her own bearings within, declaring independence from the webs of interlocution which have originally formed him/her, or at least neutralizing them'; likewise in early modernity, that

---

[3] Charles Taylor, *Sources of the Self: The Making of the Modern Identity* (Cambridge, 1989), 36.

declaration can naively seek to deny those predicating structures of reciprocation, to declare an impossible independence from dynamics of mutuality but only by locating an interlocutor within.[4] My broad conception of ontological development during this period would chart how that formative reliance upon relation, response, and interlocution so fundamental to early notions of the subject (precisely 'subjected to/by/via an other') might be appropriated and introjected by an aggressively self-subjecting individual: response to oneself (mis)understood as a fragile alternative to response to alterity. Therefore even the declaration of independence is dependent upon the rhetorical and ipseic structures of response: the narcissist reciprocates, himself to himself, and the self-slaughterer responds, himself against himself, both figures appropriating an available ontological rhetoric of response and still working within its logic. To be explicit, this is not to reawaken that bogeyman of 1980s literary criticism—disinterring the bones of a well-buried 'bourgeois subject of liberal humanism'—but to acknowledge a period preoccupation with private agency while understanding even the most introspective individual as indivisible from the available structures of dialogic ipseity: I will requisition Donne's resonant construction, 'this dialogue of one'.[5] Even a narcissist still requires an interlocutor, but thinks he finds it in the entwine of 'himself himself'; the suist and the suicide both speak their monologues in these dialogic terms.

Suicide and narcissism repeatedly figure as both apotheosis and nadir of the impulse towards mutuality: so, amorous verse that advocates the echoes and mirroring of coupled erotic exchange must, however, suppress the latent narcissine potential in such reflection, and somehow learn to condone the frequently suicidal narrative conclusions; so, friendship essays advocate the near perfect reciprocation of an *alter idem* but must suppress the self-serving potential of such a relation, and somehow promote the self-sacrifice crucial to friendly interaction; so, penitential verse that advocates self-scrutiny must suppress the self-absorption such attention involves, and somehow promote a language

[4] Taylor, *Sources of the Self,* 36.
[5] John Donne, 'The Ecstasy', in *The Complete English Poems,* ed. A. J. Smith (Harmondsworth, 1971), 74.

of self-denial and martyrdom that can sound disconcertingly similar to the suicidal conclusions that the church condemns. In short, this study suggests that the self-slaughterer and the narcissist epitomize the reflective subject, rehearsing threateningly self-reliant renditions of the prevailing ipseic and ontological model. Reciprocation, mutuality, reflection: all are enacted alone, between himself and himself, between myself and myself, between active self (viewer/murderer) and passive subject (image/victim), with an anti-social autonomy that cannot and does not remain uncensored.

Taylor understands that 'to study persons is to study beings who only exist in, or are partly constituted by, a certain language'.[6] Accordingly, the objective of my study is to listen for this language, to hear a 'self [that] is both made and explored with words', and discern the rhetoric and grammar of its constitution.[7] The challenge faced by a study of historical subjectivity is to avoid the anachronisms that result from potentially ahistorical assumptions, where the temptation to 'discover' aspects of modernity lying latent in early modernity too easily leads us to read for proto-Freudianism, clumsily articulated predictions of our contemporary condition, or echoes of ourselves. Accordingly, Jonathan Sawday has emphasized 'the problem posed by language itself' and, alongside other etymologically aware literary critics (Patricia Parker, Peter Stallybrass, Katherine Eisaman Maus, and Jeffrey Masten among others), has sought to excavate sixteenth-century sense from beneath layers of historical rewriting; 'the rich, post-Freudian vocabulary of self-reflection upon which we now draw', Sawday cautions, 'is, by definition, of relatively recent origin'.[8] With the intention of hearing an early modern voice more clearly, part of the aim of this study is to identify an earlier grammar of self-reflection, a rhetoric that pre-dates Freud and need not be read in a Lacanian mirror, and consequently

---

[6] Taylor, *Sources of the Self*, 35.
[7] Ibid., 183.
[8] Jonathan Sawday, 'Self and Selfhood in the Seventeenth Century', in Roy Porter (ed.), *Rewriting the Self: Histories from the Renaissance to the Present* (London, 1997), 29–48 at 29. See Katherine Eisaman Maus's justification for her study of the 'rhetoric of inwardness' or ' "inwardness topos" ', in *Inwardness and Theater in the English Renaissance* (Chicago, 1995), 26; 15.

seeks to understand Narcissus before Narcissism, reflexive self-formation before the *stade du miroir*. Shadi Bartsch writes in *The Mirror of
the Self* that

incorporating the work of Lacan into this study would have given rise to a
volume very different from the one I have produced. It would have had to
situate the Lacanian response to psychoanalysis in a world unfamiliar with
this kind of analysis...overlay[ing] the Lacanian phallus...on the ancient
phallus.[9]

While my period is early modern not early Roman, like Bartsch I
hope to avoid 'reading [period texts] *for us*', simply to find 'how
modern practice repeats-with-a-difference some very old problems
and prejudices'; like Bartsch, 'I prefer to cling to the illusion that
I am reading these elements...*for them*'.[10] I too concede the self-
delusion involved in reading *for them*, but find this a productive
naivety, at least permitting the attempt to excavate a period conception
of the narcissist: much of what follows has Lacanian resonance, antici-
pating and ultimately informing post-Freudian ipseic models, but I am
reluctant to approach the early modern text merely as embryonic or
anticipatory.[11] Lynn Enterline, whose *The Tears of Narcissus* is an
exemplary work of psychoanalytically informed literary criticism and
who brilliantly negotiates the interaction of modern and early modern,
begins her work with the acknowledgement that 'the very psycho-
analytic theory sometimes invoked to describe the genealogy of modern subjectivity warns one to be wary about claims of likeness—or

---

[9] Shadi Bartsch, *The Mirror of the Self: Sexuality, Self-Knowledge, and the Gaze in the
Early Roman Empire* (Chicago and London, 2006), 13; see also Maus, *Inwardness and
Theater*, 31. Liz Oakley-Brown productively examines how Lacanian paradigms relate to
the Ovidian original and its early translations, and I recommend her work to those who
regret the comparatively untheorized discussion I am offering. See 'Translating the
Subject: Ovid's *Metamorphosis* in England, 1560–7', in Roger Ellis and Liz Oakley-
Brown (eds.), *Translation and Nation: Towards a Cultural Politics of Englishness* (Clevedon, 2001), 48–84.

[10] Bartsch, *The Mirror of the Self*, 13.

[11] The rhetoric of the 'preposterous' could, for example, be requisitioned as antici-
pation of Lacan's 'anticipated belatedness' or as a correlative of a 'future anterior'
grammar of subjection. See Samuel Weber, *Return to Freud: Jacques Lacan's Dislocation
of Psychoanalysis*, trans. Michael Levine (Cambridge, 1991), 16; Jacques Lacan, *Écrits*,
trans. Alan Sheridan (London, 1977), 86.

claims of difference—in any subect's story about its own origins': 'I can no more step outside the collective fictions of self-representation than any other critic' should be the opening admission in any study of the represented subject.[12]

I examine two heavily censured geminative subjects. The rhetorical structure of nascent 'radically' introspective identity is as much delineated by its detractors as its proponents, producing an interiority mapped out by censure; it is condemnation of self-constitution that cements the rhetoric of reflection as the dominant rhetorical structure of ipseic experience. Consequently, the narcissist and suicide provoke approbation that, paradoxically, provides a vocabulary, a rhetoric, a grammar of self-reflection, suistic gemination, independence (hanging on oneself). Renaissance theological responses to narcissist and suicide alike make evident how the Christian imperative towards self-denial is brought up hard against an often ethically incompatible classicist sensibility, sanctioning self-ownership or destruction. The sixteenth- and seventeenth-century interaction with classical treatments of suistic subjects reveals the complex negotiation at the heart of that Renaissance aspiration and intent, dictating that aspects of the renascent must be reinterred (while suicide may be wonderful drama for the playwright, it is catastrophe for the preacher). Christianity approaches suicide and suism as opportunities to delineate and insulate itself from aspects of its classical inheritance, yet theological or moral calls for self-trial and self-denial legitimate introspection and articulate, hence perpetuate, that which they condemn.

'Narcissus so himself himself forsook, | And died to kiss his shadow in the brook': within a turn of phrase, a rhetorical sleight, we can see the reflective construction and destruction of a self-idolizing literary subject, and see an instance of a much larger and widespread conception of reciprocal identity: this, the self-absorbed subject, is 'the ground-worke of my booke: It is then no reason thou shouldest employ thy time about so frivolous and vaine a subject'.[13]

---

[12] Lynn Enterline, *The Tears of Narcissus: Melancholia and Masculinity in Early Modern Writing* (Stanford, 1995), 13. See also, for his discussion of the subjectivity effect, Joel Fineman, *Shakespeare's Perjured Eye: The Invention of Poetic Subjectivity in the Sonnets* (Berkeley, 1986).

[13] Michel de Montaigne, *Essais*, trans. John Florio (London, 1613), sig. A5^v.

1. THE CASE OF SIR GEORGE RODNEY

Retir[ing] to an Inn in the Town, [he] shut himself up in a Chamber, and wrote a large paper of well-composed *Verses*, to the *Countess* in his own blood (strange kind of *Composedness*) wherein he bewailes and laments his own unhappiness; and when he had sent them to her, as a sad *Catastrophe* to all his *Miseries*, he ran himself upon his *Sword*, and so ended that life which he thought death to injoy.[14]

We begin here because, unlike much of what follows, this is something near to 'real'. In a work that deals with the figures and motifs of love poetry, with the rhetorical habits of dramatic suicide oratory, and the loaded vocabulary of pulpit preaching, it is easy to feel inured to the actuality of Renaissance suicidal experience. Perhaps we recall Dryden's critique of Ovid's elaborate rhetorical strategies, the 'glittering trifles' of his 'conceits and jingles':

Would any man who is ready to die for love, describe his passion like Narcissus? Would he think of *inopem me copia fecit* and a dozen more such expressions poured on the neck of one another, and all signifying the same thing? If this were wit, was this a time to be witty, when the poor wretch was in the agony of death?[15]

The 1601 poetic dialogue between Sir George Rodney and Frances Howard, Countess of Hertford, was given final punctuation by Rodney's actual suicide. Expressing himself in the recognizable language and rhetoric of the literary self-slaughterer, Rodney first adopts the verbal figures of an aesthetic archetype, then carries them through. Somewhere, in the literary and suicidally literal activity of George Rodney, poetic trope became tragic reality: he says 'myself my self must kill' and then does so.[16] Dryden's '[w]ould any man who is ready to die for love,

---

[14] Arthur Wilson, *The History of Great Britain: Being the Life and Reign of King James the First* (London, 1653), 258.

[15] John Dryden, 'Preface to Fables Ancient and Modern', in *Of Dramatic Poesy and Other Critical Essays*, ed. George Watson, 2 vols. (London, 1962), ii. 279.

[16] George Rodney, 'Sir George Rodney before He Killed Himself', in Donald W. Foster, '"Against the Perjured Falsehood of Your Tongues": Frances Howard on the Course of Love', *ELR*, 24 (1994), 72–103, l. 3.

describe his passion like Narcissus?' is answered in the affirmative by Rodney, perhaps peculiarly, and with some undoubted pathos, 'witty on his death-bed' after all.[17]

Part of the work of this study is to chart this specific reflexive 'myself my self' construction as it appears in the Renaissance's literary representations of suicide, a point of textual focus in which the larger dynamic of paradoxical self-assertion and self-denial is played out, allowing self to turn on self in a moment of absolute sufficiency and ultimate negation. I move from narcissism, where the self-lover's self-involvement is concomitant with his self-destruction, to suicide, where the self-loather both takes his time, asserts his agency, and takes his life, asserting nothing. This book examines moments of potential self-fulfilment— often their failure, occasionally their success—but always searches for the elusive moment of complete independence, where self exists only in relation to self, where myself acts upon myself, himself reflects himself, herself loves herself, or, as in the case of George Rodney that follows, where I loathes I. This small linguistic habit is the hook for much of what follows, and its first occurrence is suitably in the words of a self-murderer who clearly felt the figure, realized its efficacy, or at least was compelled to adopt the language of the suicidal role he was about to play.

Rodney begins with a plea for tragic reciprocity:

> My heart shall bleed as fast as thine [eyes] shall weep.
> For if, in shedding tears, thou dost not feign,
> With drops of blood I'll pay thy tears again,
> To make our sorrows somewhat like abound,
> That as thine eyes, so may my heart be drowned.[18]

In the early months of 1601, the West Country gentleman followed the recently married Countess to her husband's Wiltshire estate, and, having taken a room in the local inn, set about winning back his disdainful former lover. One hundred and forty-two lines of stock Petrarchan verse, apparently written in the significantly younger suitor's own blood, sought to persuade his '[s]weet poison, precious woe, infectious jewel', the 'fair and cruel' Countess, to pity his lovelorn

---

[17] Dryden, 'Preface', 279.
[18] George Rodney, 'Elegia', in Foster, '"Against the Perjured Falsehood"', ll. 8–12.

state (ll. 33; 35). Bearing 'defiance in her beauty', clouding his hope with her 'disdain', the Countess with her 'barren heart' conforms to a familiar model of love-lyric paradox: enticing yet cruel, beautiful enough to enflame Rodney's passion, cold enough to break his heart (ll. 32; 82; 28). And in return, in a calculated Petrarchan manoeuvre, the poet reins her in with words; she, who is beyond his actual possession, becomes his in verse, made to play muse in his aesthetic.

I shall be dealing in figures of reciprocation: verbal mirroring, echoes, rhetorical structures of repetition. Here Rodney, swapping his heart's blood for his mistress's tears, in what he acknowledges to be a near-mercantile exchange—talking of 'pay', of 'audit', and 'interest'—explicitly writes the unwilling Countess into his apparently loving model of reciprocation: he 'shall' give this; she 'shall' return that (ll. 15–16). Loving mutuality insists that 'my' and 'thy' interact in tight entwine, and that 'our' grows from their interplay; lovers are always 'somewhat like' each other, and the ocular progression from 'thine eyes' to 'my heart' locks couples into an erotic pattern of give and take that becomes the governing dynamic for a generation of love poets. Arthur Wilson's commentary on the incident mentions that Sir George had 'good hopes from her fair *Eyes*',[19] but Rodney sees what 'danger lies | In [their] bright shining rigor' (ll. 61–2). These eyes 'wound with being looked on' and the 'seer | Still is more bound' into the visual exchange (ll. 63; 64), but these stock complaints never quite efface the underlying truth that he still is the seer, the looker on, and only bound according to the logic of the male lyricist, a logic that insists on interaction, any interaction, any model that binds, that recaptures his lost Countess. Shakespeare's Venus will play the game of courtship with similar tactics.

My discussion of the epyllion tradition—*Venus and Adonis* and *Hero and Leander* being its best-known representatives—focuses on the verbal figures of repetition that instil this governing tenor of mutuality, and in doing so considers the position of the single self in these patterns of reciprocation.[20] Put simply, mutuality is seen to implicate self-effacement; coupling comes at the cost of self-sufficiency. Running concurrent with a movement towards loving reciprocation is, by necessity,

---

[19] Wilson, *The History of Great Britain*, 258.
[20] Christopher Marlowe, *Hero and Leander*, in *The Poems*, ed. Millar Maclure (London, 1968).

an increasing acceptance of the inadequacy of the single self. Indeed, Rodney's text is dominated by this tendency. There is something self-defeating in a love that impels him to castigate his worthless state: 'I am no baron's son, nor born so high. | Would I were lower (so I were not 'I')' (ll. 56–7). This is, by nature, self-destructive: 'For too too well my fortunes make me know | My hapless love must work my overthrow' (ll. 17–18). In the repetition—I . . . I . . . I . . . I—we see the first incremental tumble of an increasingly devalued self-signifier: first built up to a surfeit, a state of 'too too' much, then overthrowing itself through its own excess. This is a love that undoes itself, an 'I' that would not be 'I'. This self-defeating model is his poetic motif, until almost every recourse to the 'I' is a refutation, every mention ('And I') becomes an opportunity for self-renunciation ('mean in rank I know I am'; l. 53):

> In love, I ('I'? but O, that word, I fear,
> Is hateful still, both to thy heart and ear!) (ll. 50–1)

When she answers, the Countess mimics his self-defeating repetition—'Poor is that part of beauty I enjoy | If, where it wins one, one it must destroy'—clearly exasperated by this model of destructive passion.[21] These are suicidal signs.

But Rodney's 'I' is also insistent, near narcissine:

> How well I could with air, chameleon-like,
> Live happy still by gazing on thy [cheek],
> In which (forsaken man) methinks I see
> How goodly love doth threaten death to me. (ll. 43–6)

Just as his love overthrows itself, it also feeds itself. We are perhaps reminded of Cleopatra's description of Pompey, whose erotic death comes from fixing his gaze on her brow (*Ant.*, I. v. 32–5), a gaze that Jonathan Gil Harris describes as 'self-scrutinizing' and 'obliquely but suggestively aligned with that of Narcissus'.[22] Rodney's 'death', at this juncture in the answer-sequence, could be read as similarly erotic (a sexual dying), but the context of the work instils a gruesome kind of

---

[21] Frances Seymour, 'The Answer of the Countess of Hertford to Sir George Rodney's Elegy', in Foster, ' "Against the Perjured Falsehood" ', ll. 9–10.

[22] Jonathan Gil Harris, ' "Narcissus in thy Face": Roman Desire and the Difference it Fakes in *Antony and Cleopatra*', *SQ*, 45 (1994), 408–25 at 411.

literalism, this seeming to be a young man with a tendency to literalize poetic tropes. '[He] read so many books that he became a sign, a sign wandering through [the] world': like Don Quixote, as Michel Foucault describes that meta-fictional figure, Rodney reveals a deep dependency upon literary forms, becoming 'a letter that has just escaped from the open pages of a book. His whole being is nothing but language, text, printed pages, stories.'[23] If there is pathos, it is founded here; the Countess understandably reads his verse as just another Petrarchan display ('Poorly, methinks you strive to play the poet'; l. 122), but he hardly seems to realize the distinction between poetry and reality: 'I am too deeply wounded to live long' (l. 124). The poetic erotic standard is sexually symbolic—'I die when I love you'—but Rodney, literally, just dies. Perhaps we read the 'wound' as sexual (if this were Shakespeare, if this Spenser), but Rodney actually bypasses that regulation reading; if he says 'wound', he means it.

No surprise then that the Countess, clearly a better 'reader', alive to what she must assume to be a translatable metaphoric display of poetic conceit, rebuffs him, unpicks his poetic language, refuses to play the part ascribed to her:

> Small cause have I, the owner, to rejoice,
> That cannot take free passage in my choice
> But, for the fruitless painting of my cheeks,
> Must even become a slave to what it likes
> Or be termed 'cruel', or (which is much worse)
> Of death and bloodshed undergo the curse! (ll. 11–16)

She frees herself precisely by throwing back the stock motifs, returning the 'cheek' he gazed upon, repudiating his conception of her as the painted lady ('thy face far differs from thy mind!').[24] She sees how his depiction had conceptually imprisoned her, not in a role she is 'like' but rather that he 'likes'. One by one, unloading his epithets—refusing 'cruel'—she builds towards an exasperated challenge to his pseudo-desperate conventions:

> So if one desperate in madness do it,
> (Not yielding) are we accessory to it?

---

[23] Michel Foucault, *The Order of Things* (Abingdon, 2002), 53; 51.
[24] Rodney, 'Elegia', l. 42.

> Is bondage then the happiness attends
> On those whom everyone for 'fair' commends? (ll. 17–20)

Setting herself '[a]gainst the perjured falsehood of your tongues' (l. 62), Frances refuses to be written, choosing to be '(Rather than fair, in thralldom) brown, and free' (l. 22), slipping from the construction of femininity. She sees her role in the youth's poetic affections as merely 'beauty's mirror', reflecting 'your own error', simply a surface in which Rodney, a man for whom '*seem*, not *is*, hath most dominion', reflects his own desires, 'guided by [his own] heart'.[25]

It is this impulse of near-narcissism, a love almost entirely sufficient in itself, that easily comes to assume a self-murderous quality in a transformation that enacts the movement of my study from self-love to self-slaughter; 'Herein my griefs and I shall well agree: | I'll bury them as they have deaded me.'[26] Trying to make her reciprocate, Rodney seeks to enforce their mutuality. But failing that, he has taken an inward turn and found this reciprocation within. His grief and he well agree, interaction being now entirely buried within himself: he burying it; it deadening him. Rodney's opening poem makes clear why this study has to work through narcissism to arrive at a discussion of suicide, both self-love and self-slaughter being impulses of self-absorption, both of self-destruction, both unsettlingly commonplace in what purport to be poems directed towards a beloved other. In its second half, my discussion will deal with this internal doubling, a felt duality that facilitates suicidal actions of complete self-sufficiency for Shakespeare's separated lovers, resolute Romans, and the tragically isolated.

And for a moment the Countess entertains concern: 'die as poets do', she cautions, 'in sighs . . . in sonneting *ay-mes*, | With such-like pretty deaths, whose trim disguise | May batter yielding hearts and blind soft eyes' (ll. 135–8), appreciating the potential for genuine self-harm in Sir George's 'frantically enflamed' passion (l. 42). But, in the manner of Shakespeare's Rosalind (*AYL*, IV. i. 75–85), 'No, no', she rationally reassures herself,

> I never yet could hear one prove
> That there was ever any died for love.

---

[25] Seymour, 'The Answer', ll. 23–6; 66.
[26] Rodney, 'Elegia', ll. 113–14.

>   Nor would I have you be the man begin
>   The earnest dare to such a sportive sin. (ll. 139–42)

'For that', she concludes, 'would prove a laughter for an age, | Stuff for a play, fit matter for a stage' (ll. 143–4). Unfortunately, as Foster remarks: 'In wooing his lovely mistress, Rodney took his language from Petrarchan verse, his manners from French romances, and his hopes and dreams from romantic comedy—and when she finally jilted him, he took his cue from Italian tragedy.'[27] Stuff for a play, cues from Italian tragedy: the Countess and the critic read Sir Rodney alike. And his response is in the trim disguise of complaint lyric, of love sonnet, not a thought in it unique, not a turn of phrase that may not be found frequently amongst the texts I shall go on to analyse. Rodney, perhaps more than the Countess, is limited by his mode of expression, his identity fashioned by the poetic vocabulary of the roles available to him; like Quixote, he is 'made up of interwoven words'.[28]

But—

>   What shall I do that am undone?
>   Where shall I fly, myself to shun?[29]

—his sixteen lines of eight couplets are remarkable for the concentrated density of these linguistic figures of self-deconstruction. So this 'I' is undone, 'myself' is shunned; in his first couplet, Rodney announces this undoing of the single state, an unpicking that occurs even on the level of sign so a distinction is made between the referent of 'I' and 'myself'. The 'I' can somehow shun 'myself'.

Rodney continues:

>   [Ay] me . . . (l. 3)

It is amazing that, considering the Countess's express mockery of 'sonneting *ay-mes*', Rodney should in response employ (twice) the exact phrase. In 142 lines, Rodney had not used the expression. Then, *after* the Countess has ridiculed the phrase, in only sixteen lines he uses it here in line 3, and then again in line 13. This is provocatively wilful.

[27] Foster, '"Against the Perjured Falsehood"', 85.
[28] Foucault, *The Order of Things*, 51.
[29] Rodney, 'Before He Killed Himself', ll. 1–2.

Foster calls it an allusion to the Countess's poem, and, working on this premiss, surely Rodney implies, precisely by referring to that passage of 'The Answer' that most aggressively attacked his aesthetic posturing, that while he knows he sounds contrived, he cannot get beyond this language. And, despite the importance I attach to it, it is difficult to establish a definitive reading of this admission. Perhaps (and this is what Anne Ferry argues that Renaissance sonneteers attempt), he redeems language, filling empty words full of genuine emotion, elevating 'loving suicide' from romantic trope to actual felt reality, using tired cliché in a way that reclaims, reanimates the convention.[30] Maybe 'ay-mes' really do denote his self-disgust, disappointment, or whatever it is he feels here. Maybe, to use the Renaissance phrase, these figure forth. So, this language is full, fertile, signifying.

Alternatively, perhaps this is a simple admission: he cannot get beyond this language. Read Foster's summary again, this time with pathos, because these roles—the Petrarchan sonneteer, the French romantic, the Italian tragedian—have materially (in its modern critical sense too) defined him, delineated his responses. So, read 'ay me' as a quiet plea: he knows she knows the phrase is trite, but he has no other mode of expression. And suddenly, these lines and sentiments seem confining. He says he finds it written in the stars, but his destiny is less astrological than poetic.[31] They are 'starry letters' he beholds 'writ in skies above', his fate 'enrolled' in the heavens, and the connotations of writing are more pertinent than he imagines, as it is letters—literary form, poetic models—that ultimately determine his death. Like Quixote at his lowest ebb and aware of his textually determined state, Rodney authenticates the fiction that writes him:

If he is to resemble the texts of which he is the witness, the representation, the real analogue, Don Quixote must also furnish proof and provide the indubitable sign that they are telling the truth, that they really are the language of the world. It is incumbent upon him to fulfil the promise of the books.[32]

---

[30] Anne Ferry, *The 'Inward' Language: Sonnets of Wyatt, Sidney, Shakespeare, Donne* (Chicago, 1983).
[31] Ibid., 6–7.
[32] Foucault, *The Order of Things*, 52.

As authentication of complete resemblance, as a furnishing of proof, a guarantee of truth, and as fulfilment of his inherited promise, the final recourse of this poetic lover is the act of suicide: 'myself my self must kill'.[33] 'We shall demonstrate intense love joined to deep despair', Erasmus has wittily instructed all scorned lovers: 'We shall try by turns moaning, flattery, and despair.'[34] 'With great show of humility we shall beg that she will at least resign herself to being loved', but Rodney, his desperate plea for reciprocation finding no kind response, has arrived at Erasmus's 'last resort': 'We shall add that if this request is not granted, we are resolved to cut short a cruel life by whatever means possible':[35]

> That I (poor I!) must die for love.
> 'Twas not my love deserved to die—
> O no, it was unworthy I.
> I for her love should not have died,
> But that I had no worth beside.
> [Ay] me.[36]

He has remained 'faithful to the [poetry] that he has now become'.[37]

In an ipseic or ontological move that will be discovered throughout this work, George Rodney attempts to isolate the I, and so separate out his unworthy self, dividing *myself* from *my self*. Rodney's identity is, he announces, entirely comprised of his love of her; he is, in these terms, beyond himself, beside himself. Consequently each declaration of self is quickly followed by a renunciation. But, in the alliterative escalation, the internal rhyme relations dictated by the insistence of 'I . . . I . . . die . . . die . . . I. | I . . . died . . . I . . . beside. | [Ay]' forge, through extended assonance, through the visual bonds of ploce, hooks of anadiplosis between the lines, a network of self-signification, a kind of web of 'I'. Indeed, 'her love' is the central absence in these lines (either that which he lacks, or even more interestingly, 'her love' is merely shorthand for 'my love for her', in which case she figures at an even further remove).

---

[33] Rodney, 'Before He Killed Himself', l. 3.
[34] Eramus, 'The Letter of Friendship', in *Collected Works*, ed. J. K. Sowards, 40 vols. (Toronto, 1985), xxv. 203–5 at 204.
[35] Ibid.
[36] Rodney, 'Before He Killed Himself', ll. 8–13.
[37] Foucault, *The Order of Things*, 53.

There is quite literally almost nothing beside the *I*. This is all 'I', and yet rejects 'I'. This is the paradox of self-slaughter, an action of ultimate agency and negation, a kind of radical involvement in oneself, which destroys the self. Self-loving and self-loathing, Rodney has cast himself in the role of love-poet, rejected and introspective, and the characteristic declarations of suicidal intent that the role entails are precisely what seem to dictate his final 'most desperate attempt'.[38]

2. MYSELF MYSELF

The figure of repetition that George Rodney employed in stating 'myself my self must kill' has a definite place in the imaginative lexicon of a dramatic self-murderer or poetic narcissist where self-reflection is a constant keynote: 'Thus the ofte repeatyng of one worde, doth muche stirre the hearer, and makes the worde seeme greater, as though a sworde were ofte digged and thrust twise, or thrise in one place of the bodie.'[39] Thomas Wilson, requisitioning the impact of violence, effaces the distinction between the power of a word and that of an action. Although words can only gesture ('seeme'), acting at one remove ('as though'), there is a palpable desire to fashion, through the machinations of rhetoric, an energetic, effective, and affective language. This language, while being a 'learned, or rather an artificiall declaration of the mynde', can still 'stirre the hearer', seem greater, and convey something every bit as tangible as the dig and thrust of a sword.[40]

What is an overtly linguistic trick, two pronouns placed in unusual proximity, can therefore be read as an attempt to capture the violence of self-destructive action. Replicating violent action in linguistic aggression, the figure captures a sense of impropriety or indecency peculiarly apt for a discussion of the disgraceful act of suicide. In the period's rhetorical handbooks there is a governing sense of propriety, a belief in the civilizing function of fitting language and apt expression. Consequently, there is a concomitant fear of rhetorical excess, of gratuitous display where, for example, a figure of repetition may be deemed not

[38] Wilson, *The History of Great Britain*, 258.
[39] Thomas Wilson, *The Arte of Rhetorike* (London, 1553), 204.
[40] Ibid., 1; 72.

'figuratiue but phantastical', and rather than being used 'to a purpose, either of beautie or of efficacie', a rhetorical conceit may be seen as 'a very foolish impertinency of speech'.[41] There is an underlying moral tenor to the rhetoricians' discussions, and a sense of moral indignation in their treatment of self-slaughter's characteristic rhetorical motif.

Wilson's description of the violence of repetition comes in his discussion of what he calls the 'Doublette': 'when wee rehearse one and the same worde twise together. Ah wretche, wretche, that I am.'[42] Puttenham describes a less compressed form of ploce or 'the Doubler' as a 'speedie iteration of one word' with the intermission of one or two words: his example is Walter Raleigh's 'Yet when I sawe my selfe to you was true, | I loved my selfe, bycause my selfe loved you.'[43] The language of amorous verse comes dangerously close to disclosing an underlying impulse of narcissism, and accordingly the proximity and interplay of personal pronouns in the frequent employment of ploce or 'the Doubler' mimics the discordant self-absorption of the poet. In his description of the related figure of symploche, Puttenham notes how repetition can seem to 'wrap vp the verses by reduplication, so as nothing can fall out', displaying the rhetorician's characteristic tendency to approach the line from a mimetic, pictorial perspective.[44] The 'myself myself' construction wraps the verse so tightly in reduplication that it will come to stand as an extreme example of both literal and figurative self-sufficiency or self-absorption.

This closer repetition is what Puttenham defines as epizeuxis, 'the Underlay or Coocko-spel', where 'ye iterate one word without any intermission':

for right as the cuckow repeats his lay, which is but one manner of note, and doth not insert any other tune betwixt, and sometimes for hast stammers out two or three of them one immediately after another, as *cuck, cuck, cuckow*, so doth the figure *Epizeuxis*...without any intermission at all.[45]

---

[41] George Puttenham, *The Arte of English Poesie* (London, 1589), 168.
[42] Wilson, *The Arte of Rhetorike*, 203.
[43] Puttenham, *The Art of English Poesie*, 168.
[44] Ibid., 167.
[45] Ibid., 168.

Normally, when rhetoricians describe the figure they have it as a form of amplification, a passionate redoubling of a word for 'greater vehemency', used 'chiefelye when our affections be much moved'.[46] But Puttenham cites amongst his examples, ascribing it as his favourite, this from Raleigh: 'With wisdomes eyes had but blind fortune seene, | Than had my looue, my looue for euer beene.'[47] This is closer to what John Smith describes as anadiplosis or 'Reduplication', where the 'figure of the first clause is repeated in the beginning of the next': 'With death, death must be recompensed.'[48] Here, the figure does not entail an escalation of passion but allows a complicated grammatical telescoping, effectively dividing a single quality into two discrete elements. This, as we have seen in the verse of George Rodney, is particularly apt in a suicidal context, allowing the self to occupy both subject and object positions as it enacts violence upon itself: 'I will', says Henry Chettle's Mathias, 'revenge myself upon myself.'[49]

Equally, the figure is employed to denote a certain self-reliance: 'There's nothing left | Unto Andrugio, but Andrugio.'[50] Language becomes the site for potentiality affirming reflection—'Myself myself, will dare all opposites'—presenting a defiantly inclusive identity. These examples are from John Marston's *Antonio* plays:

> Well, ere yon sun set I'll show myself myself,
> Worthy my blood.[51]

Cicero identifies this reiterative construction as *geminatio verborum*, a verbal twinning or doubling, and Jeffrey Masten has demonstrated persuasively how gemination, or self-doubling, is fundamental to period

---

[46] Henry Peacham, *The Garden of Eloquence* (London, 1577), sig. J.iii.[r]. See John Smith, *Mystery of Rhetoric Unveiled* (London, 1665), 80; Angel Day, *The English Secretorie* (London, 1614), 85.

[47] Puttenham, *The Art of English Poesie*, 167.

[48] Smith, *Mystery of Rhetoric*, 92; 93.

[49] Henry Chettle, *The Tragedy of Hoffman*, ed. J. D. Jowett (Nottingham, 1983), II. III. 854. For extended discussion of the function of self-slaughter in the revenge-tragedy tradition, see Rowland Wymer, *Suicide and Despair in the Jacobean Drama* (Brighton, 1986).

[50] John Marston, *Antonio and Mellida*, ed. W. Reavley Gair (Manchester, 1991), III. I. 60–1.

[51] Ibid., III. I. 77; ll. 114–15.

conceptions of individuality.[52] That 'individual' literally means 'in-divisible' (developing from its original Trinitarian context where 'an indivisible unitie' has tripartite structure) is indicative of how integral interaction is to the period's conception of subjectivity. Throughout my study, I will demonstrate how rhetorical gemination mimetically mani-fests structures of ipseity formation, enacting self-reflection, self-relation, and interaction.[53] Ipseic vocabulary is characterized by this subsumed sense of response—from in-dividual to al-one—and similarly 'self', the reflexive pronoun, only expresses identity predicated upon mutuality ('auto' meaning 'same'); Michel Foucault describes how seemingly au-tonomous individual self depends on a 'dialectical movement', becoming, as in the case of both narcissist and suicide, all-one with its indivisible self.[54] Discussing 'the ways in which rhetoric generates logical categories that represent and create opportunities for individual agency', Marshall Grossman argues that the 'subject is inscribed *in* a set of linguistically determined rhetorical configurations', and accordingly the preposterously involuted indivisibility of the suicidal or narcissine subject is articulated in this radically compressed geminative structure.[55]

Paradoxically, it is this language of self-assertion or definition that unravels in reflective repetition. 'Myself myself' empties value from the sign instead of internally redoubling worth; 'myself' is simultaneously empty (prior to being shown 'myself'), and valuable (the second 'myself' which will be shown to the first). This seemingly cyclic chronology of presenting 'myself [to] myself', echoed in 'nothing left | Unto Andrugio but Andrugio', shows both a line and its depicted state of selfhood to be caught within expression, trapped in complex linguistic circuitry, where full and empty signs circulate around each other (nothing can 'fall out' of this linguistic cycle). Likewise, showing the valued 'myself' to the empty 'myself' presumes to re-create some significant self, yet the interplay of

---

[52] Cicero, *On the Ideal Orator (De oratore)*, ed. and trans. James M. May (Oxford, 2001), 3. 54. 206; see Jeffrey Masten, *Textual Intercourse* (Cambridge, 1997), ch. 2.

[53] Thomas Wright, *The Passions of the Minde in Generall* (London, 1630), 217–18; see Raymond Williams, *Keywords: A Vocabulary of Culture and Society* (Bungay, 1976), s.v. 'Individual'; Patricia Parker, *Literary Fat Ladies: Rhetoric, Gender, Property* (London, 1987), 69–73.

[54] Michel Foucault, 'Technologies of the Self', in Luther H. Martin, Huck Gutman, and Patrick H. Hutton (eds.), *Technologies of the Self* (Amherst, 1988), 16–49 at 25.

[55] Marshall Grossman, *The Story of All Things: Writing the Self in English Renaissance Narrative Poetry* (Durham, 1998), pp. xvi; 25.

identical terminology and the negative tenor of 'nothing left' merely speaks of isolation. Marston's *Antonio* plays are ultimately driven by an impulse dictating that 'blood cries for blood, and murder murder craves', and rhetorical gemination is ultimately associated with this all-encompassing destructive logic of revenge.[56] The cyclic pattern of the figure has become self-devouring, murder craving murder craving murder. So, we have a figure suiting expressions of self-assertion which allows such assertions to be undercut with the suggestion of self-destruction.

This brings me, following the lead of Patricia Parker, to invoke a second complementary rhetorical definition:

Prepostere: com. *Preposterous, unorderlie, wrong overthwart, altogether from the purpose.*

Preposterer. *To place or set preposterously; to disorder, to turn arsivarsie; to put the cart before the horse.*[57]

As Parker explains, the word 'preposterous' comes from *posterus* (after or behind) and *prae* (in front or before), combining to give a sense of 'back for front', or, as Cotgrave has it, 'arsiuarsie'.[58] The pre-post-erous, otherwise known as '*Hysteron proteron*, when that is laste sayde, that was first done', or '*Hysterologia*... the last first', is a figure that, in its inversion of making 'the last done which should have been first', puts, as almost all the rhetoricians remark, the cart before the horse.[59] This reversal of the usual order, this grammatical impropriety, is 'from the purpose', 'disorderly, untoward, contrary to due outcourse'.[60] As Shakespeare uses the term, Parker demonstrates, 'it involves not just verbal but also social or hierarchical reversal [figuring as] the marker of the unnatural as well as the reversed', and 'it therefore stands as the inverse of orders claimed to be "natural & necessary"'.[61] No surprise,

---

[56] Marston, *Antonio and Mellida*, III. i. 216.

[57] Randle Cotgrave, *A Dictionarie of the French and English Tongues* (London, 1611), s.v. *préposterer*.

[58] Patricia Parker, *Shakespeare from the Margins: Language, Culture, Context* (Chicago, 1994), 21. See Lee A. Sonnino, *A Handbook to Sixteenth-Century Rhetoric* (London, 1968), 145–6.

[59] Peacham, *The Garden of Eloquence*, sig. F.iiii.[r]; Smith, *Mystery of Rhetoric Unveiled*, 203; Richard Huloet, *Abecedarium Anglicolatinum* (London, 1552).

[60] A. Day, *The English Secretorie*, 82; J. B., *An English Exposition* (London, 1616), s.v. 'Preposterous'.

[61] Parker, *Shakespeare from the Margins*, 21.

then, that Shakespeare's festive world is governed by a preposterous dynamic: 'those things do best please me', Shakespeare's embodiment of green-world anarchy announces, 'that befall prepost'rously' (*MND*, III. II. 120–1). Within this environment, the head-over-heels condition of young lovers is expressed 'very preposterously' (*Wiv.*, II. II. 189) in involuted grammatical construction, signalling a congruence of emotional and rhetorical topsy-turviness. Sometimes the excitingly dissident potential of preposterous inversion is requisitioned for the articulation of forbidden desires or otherwise unspoken sexual practices; Parker sees how the geminatio trope, in its occlusion of difference and the lexical homogeneity of its response, provides a keynote figure for representations of homoeroticism. And more broadly, Jeffrey Masten demonstrates how the ipseic structures of indivisibility suggested by the etymological structures of 'individual' are exemplified in the mutual identities of homosociability and formative male friendship.[62] The rhetorical and psychological geminative doubling involved in loving amity and homoerotic desire is integral to period conceptions of socialized subjectivity, and a sense of masculine indivisibility is a widely available ipseic blueprint for a Renaissance in-dividual.

Iago's machinations, turning black to white as he serves his turn upon the tumbled mind of Othello, are suitably described as preposterous (I. III. 62; 321), providing a vicious variant of comedic disorder. Joel B. Altman describes the 'preposterous' as bordering on 'linguistic viciousness because it effects a dislocation between the natural order of things and its representation in speech', and Parker acknowledges 'much darker structural analogues to this trope'.[63] Accordingly, I suggest an extra dimension to this figure of preposterousness, seeing its characteristic disruption of linear order—its confusion of 'succession and following', and its viciousness—at work in the reiterative constructions 'myself my self must kill', and 'I'll show myself myself'.[64] Both suicide and narcissist demonstrate the preposterousness of self-gemination: 'Did you ever see | A Wretch', asks the Ovidian youth, 'that lov'd prepost'rously like me?'[65]

---

[62] Joel B. Altman, '"Preposterous Conclusions": Eros, *Enargeia*, and the Composition of *Othello*', *Representations*, 18 (1987), 129–57, 133; Parker, *Literary Fat Ladies*, 70.

[63] See Masten, *Textual Intercourse*, ch. 2.

[64] Parker, *Shakespeare from the Margins*, 21.

[65] 'Book Three', in *Ovid's Metamorphosis: Translated by Several Hands*, trans. Pittis and Bridgwater (London, 1697), 137.

If, as Altman describes, rhetoricians attribute 'visual, tactile, and spatial qualities to aural phenomena', here the word undoes itself in uncomfortable proximity, celebrating 'the plasticity of language [and] one's ability to move it around in some kind of aural space that may be perceived tactilely and visually'.[66] By splitting the single self into two halves, and facilitating violent action back upon the self, this suicidal gemination precisely threatens an 'unnatural' inversion, where subject acts upon object, and yet the object is subjected. The preposterous construction upsets the grammatical rules, here defined by John Brinsley, who states that '1 Wordes must bee placed in order . . . according to the plaine and proper nature of the speech' so '2 The word gouerning or directing [is] to be placed before those which it gouerneth or directeth'.[67] Brinsley's sense of grammatical propriety is clearly disturbed by this arsiuarsie inversion of logical sequence, a complaint suggestively close to John Donne's description of self-slaughter that 'we can not properly worke upon our selfes, because in this act, the same party must be *Agent* and *patient*, and Instrument'.[68] The self-slaughterer, becoming, as John Sym says in his attack on suicide, '*active* and *passive subject* of his own *action*'[69] and, as in the case of George Rodney, becoming active and passive subject of his own utterance, is caught within a paroxysm of chronology, where action acts back, where a word is trapped in grammatical crisis. That 'himselfe should kill himselfe' is preposterous.[70]

This rhetorical motif, itself a concentrated grammatical suicide, is the self-slaughtering keynote of this work, its preposterous dynamic appearing time and again throughout the Renaissance portrayals of suicide. Equally, in the late 1500s, gemination appears in another guise, in poetic treatments of narcissism, the archetype of preposterous and improbable desire: the hysteron proteron is, as Altman explains, 'not simply a verbal scheme but a way of knowing, of behaving, and of representing . . . it is informed by an economy of desire that is, in the

---

[66] Altman, 'Preposterous Conclusions', 133.
[67] John Brinsley, *Ludus Literarius; or, The Grammar Schoole* (London, 1612), 98.
[68] John Donne, *Biathanatos*, ed. Ernest W. Sullivan II (London and Toronto, 1984), 2. 6. 4.
[69] John Sym, *Lifes Preservative Against Self-Killing; or, An Useful Treatise Concerning Life and Self-Murder*, ed. Michael MacDonald (London, 1988), 54.
[70] Ibid., 49.

deepest sense, improbable'.[71] It is this impossible economy where the subject seeks confirmation of itself via dialogic interlocution that drives Renaissance depictions of desire, and which is articulated with such preposterous economy in the related impulses of narcissism and self-murder:

You hate and love beautiful men at the same time; you hate them as thieves and murderers; you are also forced to love and revere them as mirrors sparkling with the heavenly glow. What can you do, O wretch? When to turn, you do not know; alas, O lost soul, you do not know. You would not want to be with this murderer of yourself, but you would not want to live without his blessed sight. You cannot be with this man who destroys you, who tortures you. You cannot live without him, who, with wonderful enticements, steals you from yourself, who claims all of you for himself. You want to flee him who scorches you with his flames. You also want to cling to him. . . . You seek yourself outside yourself, O wretch.[72]

How much more wretched when you burn with your own narcissistic flame, revering yourself in your own mirror, or become murderer of yourself, stealing you from yourself? This is the torture, Renaissance writers insist, that awaits those who turn and seek themselves inside themselves, claiming themselves for themselves.

---

[71] Altman, ' "Preposterous Conclusions" ', 134.

[72] Marsilio Ficino, *Commentary on Plato's* Symposium *on Love*, trans. Sears Jayne (Dallas, Tex., 1985), 129.

PART I
NARCISSISM

1

Visions of Narcissus

> In ample stories written tis,
> Who list but for to minde it;
> How loved *Narcissus?*
> Go look and you shall finde it.
> This Eccho was a Nymph most chaste,
> Alack, the more the pitty,
> She should be so, and should not reape:
> What follows in my Ditty?
> *Narcissus* was but young, I wisse,
> But yet of perfect feature,
> And had enough to satisfie
> A reasonable creature.[1]

The myth of Echo and Narcissus was the first of Ovid's tales to be independently published in English translation (T. H.'s Fable of *Ovid Treting of Narcissus* in 1560), and its central characters, the selfish youth and selfless nymph, are among the most prominent of the period's literary classical archetypes.[2] A 'multivalent myth', its exploration of themes of vanity, disdain, or individualism, and its easy applicability for didactic purposes, make the Ovidian episode a standard reference point in both verse and drama, employed to caution against pride, to demonstrate the dangers of introspection, to chastise the disdain of an unwilling beloved,

---

[1] John Day, *The Knave in Graine* (London, 1640), sig. H2^v.
[2] *The Fable of Ovid Treting of Narcissus*, trans. T. H. (London, 1560). It is unclear whether T. H. is the publisher and bookseller Thomas Hacket; an alternative author is the sonneteer Thomas Howell. A version (but not a sustained attempt at translation) of Ovid's Midas was published by 1552, also written by a T. H.: Thomas Hedley, *Judgement of Midas* (London, *c*.1552).

and occasionally, as above, for no more than the sake of a crude joke.[3]
While it is known that Ovid is not the myth's original author, his version
in the *Metamorphoses* provides the definitive source for its early modern
appropriation.

> Then wee beginne, & let none hope to kisse us.
> The play wee play is Ovid's owne Narcissus.[4]

And this *is* appropriation: the anonymous playwright's promise of
'Ovid's owne Narcissus', an early modern precursor to Hollywood's
familiar insistence upon Shakespearean authenticity, cannot distract
from the variety of Narcissus myths that the Renaissance will offer.
Ovid's 'owne' Narcissus is quickly lost amongst the crowd of other
Narcissuses, appearing at various ages, dressed as huntsmen or wearing
dresses, pestered by variously vocal or mute Echoes, and dying a variety
of deaths, drowning, bleeding, bruising, melting, and metamorphosing.
This chapter considers the part Narcissus plays in early modern literature, first examining his representation in the original Latin source and
its Renaissance translations, before showing how the figure becomes
part of the moralizing *speculum* or Mirror tradition, embodying pride in
what becomes an overtly cautionary tale.[5] Ovidian poetic traits, first
rendered in translation, then become standard stylistic characteristics of
the period's literary treatment of introspective self-absorption.

In the epyllion tradition, exemplified by *Venus and Adonis* and *Hero
and Leander*, the narcissistic gaze can complicate a poetic tradition that
relies so heavily upon the motif of the loving and mutual gaze. Commonly, Narcissus is a representative figure of pride and vanity, but
Shakespeare presents the Ovidian youth as an embodiment of introspective and potentially subversive individualistic subjectivity, an introspection facilitated by Adonis' association with a relatively new model of
intromissive vision. We should not forget that there are at least two
stages of narcissistic development delineated in Ovid's tale: there is the
disdainful youth, who refuses the absolute reciprocations of Echo, and

---

[3] Paul Hammond, 'Marvell's Sexuality', *Seventeenth Century*, 11 (1996), 87–123 at
102.
[4] Anon., *Narcissus: A Twelfe Night Merriment Played by Youths of the Parish at the
College of S. John the Baptist in Oxford, A.D. 1602* (London, 1893), 6.
[5] See T. H., *A Looking-Glasse for Women* (London, 1644).

turns his back on loving response; and then there is the chastened gazer, whose previous refusal of participation is turned with sharp irony back upon a now isolated and lonely lover. Ovid provides both the narcissism of vanity and self-absorption, where the boy refuses erotic participation, and a more complex narcissism where, inducted into the state of desire by the arrow of a vengeful Cupid, he seeks total response from an identical beloved. First he denies echo (aural response); then he craves reflection (visual response). In short, we have within a single figure the potential condemnation of opting out and a caution against excessively opting in: Narcissus can therefore be appropriated both by those who wish to warn against pride and encourage selfless interaction, and by those who see the potential for selfish gratification even within the dynamic of erotic response.

1. THE RHETORIC OF REFLECTION: TRANSLATING OVID'S NARCISSUS

> For as he dranke, he chaunst to spie the Image of his face,
> The which he did immediately with fervent love embrace.
> He feedes a hope without cause why. For like a foolish noddie
> He thinkes the shadow that he sees, to be a lively boddie.
> Astraughted like an ymage made of Marble stone he lyes,
> There gazing on his shadow still with fixed staring eyes.
> Stretcht all along upon the ground, it doth him good to see
> His ardent eyes which like two starres full bright and shyning bee.[6]

Arthur Golding's translation of the *Metamorphoses*, first appearing in 1565 and therefore the text to which Shakespeare is apparently indebted for many of his frequent allusions to and appropriations of Ovidian myth, provides us with what could be the seminal early modern depiction of Narcissus. Drinking, chancing to spy his image, and embracing it with fervent love, the youth lies astounded, feeding his hopeless hope, gazing with ardent eyes: he is, says Golding, a 'foolish noddie'.

---

[6] *Shakespeare's Ovid; being Arthur Golding's Translation of the Metamorphoses*, ed. W. H. D. Rouse (London, 1904), iii. 519–26.

Any work of translation, by necessity, is an act of mediation; accordingly, from lost source to original Latin, in many cases via an encounter with the sixteenth-century reader's schoolroom exercise-book, and finally ventriloquized through its translator, Golding's *Metamorphoses* is ultimately a work of many authorial voices. It is a rare moment that any one of these voices can distinguish itself and be heard alone. 'Foolish noddie' is one such moment. This colloquialism is Golding, as far as is possible, all on his own. If 'all translations are provisional, essays at the original rather than reproductions of it', I am interested in what decisions Renaissance authors are making in their reproductions of, and appropriations from, Ovid's first-century tale of Narcissus.[7]

A foolish noddie: this potentially ungainly example of how the translator has 'English'd' his Ovid has often been remarked upon, cited as indicative of the translator's eagerness to incorporate the Latin poet into an English vernacular tradition.[8] For a moment, the Roman boy, beloved of nymphs and Aonian ladies, suffers additional metamorphosis into a country bumpkin. As Raphael Lyne describes, this is by no means an isolated instance of Golding's re-nationalizing tendencies. As part of the adoption and indeed sanitization of the classical text (remembering that Marlowe's translation of the *Amores* was burnt by Whitgift's censors in 1599), the dangerously pantheistic Latinate original is frequently translated to resemble something more akin to a quaintly pagan English pastoral; Golding's work is readable as both a linguistic and cultural act of translation. So, 'foolish noddie' is an example of the translator's addition to the original and a typical imposition of a potentially anachronistic sixteenth-century rustic idiom. But this addition to the Ovid, introducing tonal discrepancy, obscures a more significant omission. Rhetorical figures of repetition act as the building blocks of Ovid's passage, a characteristic with which Golding only partly engages but which repays close examination.

---

[7] Lee T. Pearcy, *The Mediated Muse: English Translations of Ovid, 1560–1700* (Hamden, Conn., 1984), p. xiii. On Renaissance translations of Ovid, see Raphael Lyne, *Ovid's Changing Worlds: English Metamorphoses, 1567–1632* (Oxford, 2001); Heather James, 'Ovid and the Question of Politics in Early Modern England', in Yvonne Bruce (ed.), *Images of Matter: Essays on British Literature of the Middle Ages and Renaissance* (Newark, Del., 2005), 92–122; Liz Oakley-Brown, *Ovid and the Cultural Politics of Translation in Early Modern England* (Aldershot, 2006).

[8] See Lyne, *Ovid's Changing Worlds*, 78.

Ovid's original text, from the moment that the youth first bends to drink from the limpid and undisturbed pool, runs as follows:

> dumque bibit, visae conreptus imagine formae
> spem sine corpore amat, corpus putat esse, quod unda est.
> adstupet ipse sibi vultuque inmotus eodem
> haeret ut e Pario formatum marmore signum.[9]

D. E. Hill, deciding against maintaining the immediacy of Ovid's present tense, offers this translation:

> While he drank, he saw a beautiful reflection and was captivated, he loved a hope without a body, and what he thought was body was but water. He was overwhelmed by himself and, unmoving and holding the same expression, he was fixed there like a statue moulded out of Parian marble.[10]

From the outset, the depiction of Narcissus' all-encompassing self-absorption is characterized by rhetorical strategies of reflection, fashioning lines increasingly structured around verbal mirroring, echoes, and the entwine of repetition. Quite clearly, Ovid intends the thematic importance of self-mirroring to be emphasized by the predominance of verbal echoes and rhetorical repetition in this episode.

What will prove to be an extended sequence of some rhetorical complexity is initiated with the grammatically dense construction *adstupet ipse sibi*. Here, Ovid deliberately overplays the pronoun: *adstupet* gives the third-person singular sense of 'he is stunned by'; *ipse* provides the nominative, intensive 'himself'; and the sequence is completed by the dative reflexive pronoun *sibi*. Unavoidably, the condensed grammatical economy of Latin would force a translator to expand the line to something like 'He himself is stunned by himself'. Simply, each word in the phrase *adstupet ipse sibi* contains a pronoun referent: 'he himself himself stunned'. Significantly, these multiple pronouns are representative of the formal qualities of the entire passage, part of the rhetorical challenge Ovid sets himself. Accordingly, to remain true to the intentions of the original, where

---

[9] Ovid, *Metamorphoses: 1–5*, ed. with commentary William S. Anderson (London, 1989), 3. 415–19.

[10] Ovid, *Metamorphoses I–IV*, ed. and trans. D. E. Hill (Warminster, 1985), 3. 416–19.

the reflections of pronoun upon pronoun encapsulate the larger theme of excessive self-absorption, their presence is integral too to our challenge as translators.

So with typical economy, Ovid prefigures the tale of Narcissus with a tight bind of self-reflexive pronouns, quite literally figuring the isolated introspection and intersubjective overinvolvement of the narcissist. Hill's 'he was overwhelmed by himself', faithful to the sense of the line, captures only part of that grammatical density, as does Melville's translation to '[s]pellbound he saw himself'.[11] Both modern translators attempt to stay true to the peculiarity of the Ovidian line, where a pronoun occupies both subject and object positions (intensive and reflexive respectively), forming a line of grammatical exclusivity, or narcissine self-involvement; as Anderson points out, the 'repetition, the apparent distinction between object and subject, makes the mirror effect and the paradoxical experience of Narcissus graphic'.[12] Indeed, Ovid employs the active verbs *adstupet*, and later *haeret*, but allows their status as active to be complicated by the passivity of their grammatical context ('he himself is stunned by himself', in effect); essentially, an active verb is made to incorporate a secondary passive sense. Ovid's formal ingenuity provides a model for depictions of Narcissus, heavy on the pronouns, with the single subject caught in simultaneously active and passive context.

So to Golding's omission: Hill and Melville give us two pronouns in the place of Ovid's implicit three, but Golding removes them altogether. After the distracting addition of 'foolish noddie', Golding's translation does not engage with *adstupet ipse sibi*:

> For like a foolish noddie
> He thinkes the shadow that he sees, to be a lively boddie.
> Astraughted like an ymage made of Marble stone he lyes,
> There gazing on his shadow still with fixed staring eyes.

While providing most of the elements of Ovid's lines, Golding, avoiding the grammatical issue completely, effaces this *abstupet ipse sibi* sense of the self-referential action. Perhaps the sense of *stupet* is picked up in 'Astraughted', but otherwise Golding jumps from Ovid's line 417 to line 419.

---

[11] Ovid, *Metamorphoses*, trans. A. D. Melville (Oxford, 1986), 63.
[12] *Metamorphoses*, ed. Anderson, 381.

Without making this an issue of evaluating the success or failure of respective translations, it is arguable that Golding's exclusion misses an opportunity others welcome. Even T. H., whose 'The Fable of Ovid Treting of Narcissus' is the earliest known Renaissance translation of the tale, tackles the construction; his eventual solution is to straighten out the grammatical knot in his line: 'he rapt, fell straight in love, with shadowe of his face | And museth at him selfe . . . astonished'.[13] The significance of Golding's omission only becomes apparent when we consider William Shakespeare's aside to Ovid's boy from *Venus and Adonis*:

> Narcissus so himself himself forsook,
> Who died to kiss his shadow in the brook. (ll. 161–2)

Requiring quick encapsulation of the thematically apposite tale of Narcissus and Echo, Shakespeare employs Ovid's rhetorical device of self-reflection. Far from relying on his copy of Golding, who as we have seen has opted to ignore the line in question, Shakespeare takes his cue from the source text itself. The gemination of 'himself himself' replicates Ovid's foreshortened pronoun construction, neatly mimicking the reflection of the youth in the surface of his pool and providing the Renaissance poet with a suggestively condensed rhetorical figure: it confuses subject and object, blurs the distinction between active and passive, and works through self-enclosed reflection. In short, the figure has come to encapsulate Narcissus and its grammatical thrift signals the erotic economy of his self-directed desire.[14]

This telescopic grammatical figure is itself subject to moral opprobrium, as the medieval commentator Alain de Lille, in his *Complaint of Nature*, equates grammatical and sexuality impropriety; according to its

---

[13] T. H., *Narcissus*, ll. 87–92.

[14] Leonard Barkan makes a comparable argument in relation to Ovid's employment of paradox: 'Narcissus and his reflection make up a complete and theoretically satisfying system . . . yet in its completeness there is no real satisfaction, since Narcissus cannot unite, cannot have sexual relations, and cannot produce offspring with his love object. The language of paradox is similarly complete and yet unsatisfying: it seems to affirm all things at once, but it affirms nothing. When a linguistic action meets an equal and opposite linguistic action, no effective statement is made.' 'The result of all these paradoxes about form and the self', Barkan concludes, 'is the loss of form and the destruction of the self.' Leonard Barkan, *The Gods Made Flesh: Metamorphosis and the Pursuit of Paganism* (London, 1986), 51.

construction, 'he is both predicate and subject, he becomes likewise of two declensions...push[ing] the laws of grammar too far'.[15] The effeminizing practice of sodomy—where 'the sex of the active genus [i.e. the masculine] trembles shamefully at the way it degenerates into passivity [as man] is made woman'—has, for Alain, blackened 'the honour of his sex' as 'the craft of magic Venus hermaphrodites him' (just as the allure of the watery reflection awakens homosexual desire in Narcissus).

The popularity of Shakespeare's text is evinced by how often this rhetorical device is appreciated and in turn appropriated by his immediate successors; in 1640, Alexander Hart juggles with Shakespeare's lines in warning how Narcissus 'in a brooke, | To kisse himselfe, | himselfe there hath forsooke', and Thomas Beedome's 1641 'The Jealous Lover' repeats Shakespeare's lines word for word.[16] Fond of analogies with Narcissus, Richard Brathwaite offers his less verbally compressed version when he explains that '*Narcissus*, selfe-conceited Elfe, | Did love himselfe by looking on himselfe.'[17] Shakespeare, turning back to his Ovid rather than to Golding in this instance, provides an example others appear to follow. George Sandys, whose translation of *Metamorphoses* was first published in 1632 and at times appears to be 'a synthesis of earlier interpretations', offers economic renderings of Ovidian verse and appreciates the applicability of this figure of instant and preposterous repetition.[18] That Sandys employs the figure as his solution to the *adstupet ipse sibi* challenge suggests that he, like Beedome, is familiar with Shakespeare's lines, or that both Shakespeare and Sandys respond to the Ovidian phrase with the same ingenious solution:

---

[15] Alanus de Insulis, *De planctu naturae*, trans. D. M. Moffat as *The Complaint of Alain de Lille* (New York, 1908), 3. See Lisa Jardine, *Still Harping on Daughters: Women and Drama in the Age of Shakespeare*, 2nd edn. (New York, 1983), 16; Elizabeth Pittenger, 'Explicit Ink', in Patricia Parker and Carla Freccero (eds.), *Premodern Sexualities* (London, 1996), 223–42.

[16] Alexander Hart, *Alexto and Angelica* (London, 1640), sig. G4^r; Thomas Beedome, 'The Jealous Lover', in *Poems, Divine and Humane* (London, 1640), sig. C1^r.

[17] Richard Brathwaite, 'The Ape of Fancy', in *The Honest Ghost* (London, 1634), ll. 5–6. See also Richard Brathwaite, 'An Elegie Entituled Narcissus Change', in *The Golden Fleece* (London, 1611), sig. D4^r–D7^v.

[18] Jonathan Bate, *Shakespeare and Ovid* (Oxford, 1993), 27.

Quenching his thirst, another thirst doth rise;
Rays'd by the forme which in that glasse he spyes.
The hope of nothing doth his powers invade:
And for a body he mistakes a shade.
Himselfe, himselfe distracts: who pores thereon
So fixedly, as if of Parian stone.[19]

Shakespeare has initiated a trend. Or perhaps it is more likely that both men, looking at the same three words, come to the same translation independently. After all, this himself-himself construction is such a suitable figure partly because its employment prefigures examples of repetition in subsequent lines; Ovid's 'cunctaque miratur, quibus est mirabilis ipse' is given by Sandys as 'Admireth all; for which, to be admir'd: | And unconsiderately himselfe desir'd', where the chiasmus demonstrates Sandys's willingness to match the rhetorical flourishes of the original.[20]

But while the geminative construction is suggested by the text, and comes as a neat resolution to a textual intricacy, the figure operates on a further level than even the Latin text could allow. Not only does 'himselfe, himselfe' signal that impossible distinction between subject and object (so we feel the incongruity of a single subject so divided), but the visual mirroring of word against itself, pronoun against pronoun— impossible in the inflections of the Latin source—simultaneously insists on that single state. A single word is given twice; within the assertion of singularity, that singularity is lost. It creates a Narcissus graphic. Indeed, this is a divided self, but defiantly an insistent agent, inescapably passive in its self-defeat, but actively assertive, resounding the subject. The rhetoric of gemination that Shakespeare finds in Ovid—that Sandys admired in Shakespeare, that Shakespeare then uses and reuses throughout his narrative poems, and that will resonate throughout this study in plays, poems, and prose, in suicide notes and suicidal oratory, from pulpits and pamphlets—in each instance emphasizes the triumph and failure of a subject defined only in relation to itself. Arthur Golding was a foolish noddie not to use it.

---

[19] *Ovids Metamorphosis English'd, Mythologiz'd, And Represented in Figures*, trans. George Sandys (London, 1640), 50–1.
[20] *Metamorphoses*, ed. Anderson, 425–6; *Ovids Metamorphosis*, trans. Sandys, 51.

2. RENAISSANCE VERSIONS OF NARCISSUS

Shakespeare plays on the aesthetic potential of the inherent paradoxes of self-love. Narcissism, boasting both complete self-reliance and yet ultimately acknowledging the untenable nature of an ultimately self-defeating isolationism, provides an ontological model of triumphant failure, of feted but deferred subjectivity. This paradox of self-assertion and negation presides over the early modern depiction of Narcissus.

But now to the morall.[21]

As we shall see, the majority of early modern references to Narcissus are uncomplicated in their condemnation, yet the most straightforwardly moral text will still enjoy the rhetorical influence of its Ovidian source. George Turberville, as a writer of epitaphs and epigrams, directs his readership that 'this be a Glasse & Myrror for them to gaze upon', explaining how '*Narcissus* may example bee | and myrrour to the prowde'.[22] But, due perhaps to his experience as a translator of Ovid's *Heroides*,[23] he also demonstrates an aesthetically inventive approach to the presentation of his lesson, playing, for example, the by-now familiar game of multiplying pronouns:

> He had that he so fondly looued:
> and yet it was not so:
> And from himselfe he was remooude
> that thence did neuer go.
> He was the Boy that tooke the vewe,
> he was the Boy espide,
> And being both he neither knewe,
> such was the ende of pride.[24]

Turberville provides a selective roll-call of Ovidian techniques. Familiarly, the repetition of pronouns causes an almost comic confusion of referent, demonstrating the preposterous nature of Narcissus' desire,

---

[21] *Ovids Metamorphosis*, trans. Sandys, 60.

[22] George Turberville, 'A Myrrour of the Fall of Pride', in *Epitaphes, Epigrams, Songs and Sonnets* (London, 1567), prefatory matter; fo. 87ᵛ.

[23] Ovid, *The Heroicall Epistles*, trans. George Turberville (London, 1567).

[24] Turberville, 'A Myrrour', fo. 88ʳ.

and thereby enforcing a complete but impossible distinction between the 'he' and 'that [other] he'. Perhaps, moreover, there is something in the difficulty of reading, or the abstruseness of this epitaph, that seeks to correlate some deliberate impropriety of poetic construction with the impropriety of Narcissus' self-love. Word jars against word, and the proximity of pronouns in 'from himselfe he was remooude' belies the line's expressed sense of division (he is removed from himself, but the 'he' and 'himself' remain tightly together on the page); the poem, constructed around a scheme of contradictory enjambement, is a work of intentional self-contradiction, clearly participating inventively in Ovidian tactics to bring Turberville to an ingeniously revealed moral: 'And being both he neither knewe, | such was the ende of pride.' His single state separated into a multiplicity of subject positions, Narcissus is no longer able to identify with any; by being both 'he' and 'he', he now knows neither. Turberville's epitaph, by engaging with the rhetorical strategies of narcissism, unpacks with an illogical logic or computes an impossible equation that, through multiple multiplication, only subtracts.

Narcissus is frequently alluded to as a negative exemplum of self-sufficiency. Wishing that heaven had endowed him with the beauty of his beloved, William Cartwright's Misander explains that then '[t]o love her would | Be a superfluous thing, my self sufficing | My self, as once *Narcissus* did *Narcissus*'.[25] Those tonally Ovidian keynote repetitions come together to form enclosed pockets of lexical self-relation, enforcing Cartwright's sense that anything beyond the parameters of 'my self [and] My self', 'Narcissus [and] Narcissus', would be superfluous to the self-contained self-lover. But other authors, like Matthew Prior in his *Dialogues of the Dead*, emphasize the pathos of Narcissus' self-sufficiency:

> O happy Youth what can destroy
> The long Excesses of thy Joy
> For nothing in the whole Creation
> Will prove a Rival to thy Passion.[26]

---

[25] William Cartwright, *The Siedge*, in *Comedies, Tragi-comedies, with other Poems* (London, 1651), III. vii. 77–9.

[26] Matthew Prior, 'Narcissus', in *Dialogues of the Dead*, ed. A. R. Waller (Cambridge, 1907), 334.

Prior, like Cartwright's Misander, describes narcissistic desire as un-
rivalled in its passionate intensity, yet undercuts the happiness of his
youth, calling his joy excessive, while implicitly suggesting that the
consequence of this total isolation will be a resultant flatness of all
other experience; the whole creation, we are told, appears dull by
comparison. More explicitly, Samuel Sheppard's epigram is typical in
suggesting the self-destructive potential of self-adoration: 'While with
Narcissus on our selves we doate', he explains, 'we lose our selves, and
act we know not what.'[27] It is the excess and success of narcissism's
introversion, Prior and Sheppard suggest, that causes its concomitant
failure; too much self-regard proves self-destructive as narcissism and
suicide are revealed as interrelated: 'His selfe-loue', explains William
Warner, 'wrought his selfe-losse, & his beauty prou'd his bain.'[28]

While Warner refers to narcissism's suicidal quality, his use of the
Narcissus myth is actually more typical for the moral implications he
finds in Ovid's story. Jonathan Bate is right to identify an increasing
willingness to complicate reductively moral approaches to Ovid's tales,
identifying a 'radical transformation, as a newly unapologetic delight in
the poetic and erotic qualities of the *Metamorphoses* came to compete
with the predominant medieval practice of moralizing and even
Christianizing them'.[29] However, as Bate acknowledges, 'a millenni-
um-long tradition of reading Ovid's poems as if they were allegorical
and as if their sentiments were morally elevated rather than erotically
charged' continues to influence Renaissance treatments. For a large
number of Renaissance writers, Narcissus' tale still has a straight didactic
purpose. Having translated Ovid's words, these early modern poets and
playwrights attempt to translate his meaning, repackaging the morally
ambiguous pantheistic and unashamedly libidinous text for a monotheistic

---

[27] S[amuel] Sheppard, 'Epigram 24; The Transformation of Narcissus', in *Epigrams
Theological, Philosophical, and Romantick*, 6 books (London, 1651), iii. 52.
[28] William Warner, *Albions England* (London, 1612), 215.
[29] Bate, *Shakespeare and Ovid*, 25. Citing Chaucer, Bate concedes that moral readings
were not the only medieval approach to Ovid. See Bate on development of the moral
tradition in Ovidian texts, from the anonymous *Ovide moralisé*, via the work of Pierre
Bersuire, Natalis Comes, and Vincenzo Cartari, to Stephen Batman's *Golden Booke of the
Leaden Goddes* (1577). See also Douglas Bush, *Mythology and the Renaissance Tradition in
English Poetry* (New York, 1963).

audience, or a prurient sixteenth-century censor.[30] Again the Ovidian text, with its potentially dangerous lack of authorial moral guidance, receives a sanitizing treatment, with each translator offering either marginalia or supporting commentary indicating the lesson of what become explicitly cautionary tales. So, Warner explains that Narcissus' tale provides 'example of how like pride may cause like plague to vs', and the majority of early modern authors who cite the Ovidian youth do so with a similarly didactic purpose.[31]

Since that first translation of T. H. in 1560, Narcissus' tale is accompanied by the advice that through its careful consideration we 'maye be learned how to perceuer | synne to abhore [and] vertue to vse'.[32] T. H. explains, in his 'Moralization of the Fable', how 'I meane to shewe, accordyng to my wytte | That Ouyd by this tale no follye mente | But soughte to shewe, the doynges far vnfytte | Of soundrye folke' (ll. 15–21); his conclusion is simply that Ovid 'by Narcissus warnith vs to be ware | Of the mishap, that pride doth still repare' (ll. 174–5). Any potentially ambivalent message, any sense that a Narcissus narrative may in fact be charged by an admittedly precarious and ultimately subsumed self-celebratory individualism, is masked by unconditional warnings for the reader 'who dothe couet him selfe of wyser skole' and 'doth [therefore] prove him selfe a fole' (ll. 572–4). The Narcissus of these texts' semi-apologetic authorial commentaries is 'rash and ignorant', 'infected with that poison', 'transported with self-love', 'intoxicated with self admiration', and, for Golding, 'of scornfulnesse and pryde a mirror cleere'.[33]

Concocting a social critique from the episode, Sandys explains how those who 'sequester themselves from publique converse and civill affaires' and surround themselves only with those who 'applaud and admire them, assenting to what they say, like as many Ecchoes', become

---

[30] See James on the tradition of moral treatments, initiated by the mythographer Pierre Bersuire (*Ovidius Moralizatus*, 1340), that demand that readers 'resist Ovid's passionate verse and reconcile themselves, no matter how extravagant the tale, to the lowest common denominator among moral lessons', imposing 'interpretive stability and piety [upon] Ovid's dangerously fluid poem' ('Ovid and the Question of Politics in Early Modern England', 96; 97).

[31] Warner, *Albions England*, 215.

[32] 'The prenter to the Booke', in T. H., *Narcissus*, ll. 3–4.

[33] *Ovids Metamorphosis*, trans. Sandys, 60; Golding, 'The Epistle', *Shakespeare's Ovid*, l. 105.

'depraved, puft up with uncessant flattery'.[34] Here, Sandys is echoing
Francis Bacon's description of Narcissus, almost word for word; both
Bacon and Sandys even allegorize the moment of metamorphosis,
suggesting that the self-admirer contracts 'a wonderfull sloth, as stupifies
their sences, and deprives them of all their vigour and alacritie', until
'Narcissus is therefore converted to a flower of his name, which signifies
stupid'.[35] 'Neither is it impertinent that this Flower is said to be
consecrated to the infernal Deities', concludes Bacon, adding, in the
vein of Shakespeare's early sonnets: 'because Men of this disposition
become unprofitable to all humane things: For whatsoever produceth
no Fruit of it self, but passeth, and vanisheth as if it had never been, (like
the way of a Ship in the Sea,) that the Ancients were wont to dedicate to
the Ghosts, and Powers below.'[36] While these social allegories certainly
fit the Ovidian narrative, Bacon and Sandys have converted a tale that
in its original form acknowledged the guilty thrill of a proffered individualism to something merely prohibitive; the alluring quality of Ovid's
undisturbed, virginal pool and the comforting fiction of potential self-
affirmation are absent from Sandys's commentary as moral arbitrator:
'which signifies stupid'. It is never more clear than in in Sandys's social
allegory that translators had to approach the *Metamorphoses* with one
eye on a potentially censorial reception: '*Eccho* and *Narcissus*', explains
Warner, 'haunt, and hurt, each Sex and State.'[37]

Anti-social behaviour is condemned, and loose ends are tied up:

> Narcissus is of scornfulnesse and pryde a myrror cleere,
> Where beawties fading vanitie most playnly may appeere.
> And Echo in the selfsame tale dooth kyndly represent
> The lewd behaviour of a bawd, and his due punishment.[38]

As Golding's epistle of 1567 makes apparent, all is to be rendered clear,
made plain to see, until each of Ovid's characters kindly and straight-
forwardly represents some specific lewd behaviour whose transgressions
can be accordingly met with due punishment. By the time we reach his

---

[34] *Ovids Metamorphosis*, trans. Sandys, 60.
[35] Ibid., 60.
[36] Francis Bacon, *The Wisedome of the Ancients*, trans. Arthur Gorges (London,
1619), missing page supplied from edition of 1696 (p. 22).
[37] Warner, *Albions England*, 217.
[38] Arthur Golding, 'The Epistle', ll. 105–8.

preface, Golding has tidied the tale so effectively that via each Ovidian character, '[e]che vice and vertue seemes too speake and argue to our face' (l. 153), and the reader is ready to '[s]ee if corrupted nature hane [*sic*] the like within thee wrought' (l. 158). Henry Reynolds provides a refreshing voice amongst these standardized readings, speaking up for the multivalence of myth against the 'myriads of hot headed wranglers, & ignorant writers and teachers' who, 'out of the bare priuilege of [being a] puny graduate in some Vniuersity, will vent[ure] vpon all, euen the most remoued and most abstruse knowledges'.[39] He regrets how, at the hands of the moralists, these myths are 'deflowred and broke open, or broke in pieces . . . to vnlocke them' (l. 3), and argues that 'their meanings were of more high nature, and more difficult to be found out, then any booke of Manners wee shall readily meete withall affoordes; else they had not writ them so obscurely' (l. 45).

Whether Reynolds approves or not, Narcissus' crystal pool has been superseded by a new mirror:

The yoong, the old: the good, the bad: the warriour strong and stout:
The wyse, the foole: the countrie cloyne: the lerned and the lout:
And every other living wight shall in this mirrour see
His whole estate, thoughtes, woordes and deedes expresly shewd too bee.[40]

Revisioned as advice book, the *Metamorphoses* becomes part of the *speculum* text tradition, readable as a sequence of emblems or exemplary mirrors. Geffrey Whitney's *Choice of Emblemes* includes verses that, displaying their debt to the translators' additions, demonstrate how Ovid's text becomes something akin to a source book for morality figures, a vice figure lexicon: Whitney is quoting Golding when he describes how '[t]he riche, the pore, the learned, and the sotte' all '[o]ffende therein: and yet they see it not'.[41] Again, the latent moral of the Ovidian tale is clarified and systematized for its Renaissance audience, just as the 'secret sore' of self-love that 'lies hidden from our eyes' within the individual is revealed until 'plainlie see[n]' and safely visible.[42] Finally, by the mid-sixteenth century, Narcissus becomes

[39] Henry Reynolds, *Mythomystes* (London, 1632), 3.
[40] Golding, 'The Preface', 193–6.
[41] Geffrey Whitney, *A Choice of Emblemes* (Leiden, 1586), 149.
[42] Ibid.

almost exclusively a cautionary figure, employed as a warning for vain courtiers and those susceptible to flattery, or as chastisement to those unsusceptible to the charms of the courting poet. Narcissus, accordingly, often appears in brief verses dedicated 'To a Lady wearing a Looking-glass at her girdle' or 'To his Mistresse... being at her Looking-glasse'.[43] The paradox—and Narcissus is a figure for whom paradox is peculiarly apposite—is complete; warning the reader against looking in the mirror, these texts demand we read them as mirrors. A mirror condemns a mirror:

> I would haue them to behold themselues in this glasse; not doubting, but that as *Narcissus*, viewing himselfe in that pure cleare Fountaine, wherein he saw his own most beautifull Image, dyed ouercome with... selfe-love; so these men will either die, or their vices in them, through... hate of themselues.[44]

As the period progresses and the poetic vogue moves away from the epyllion tradition with its playful appropriation of classical sources, references to Ovid's self-absorbed youth become increasingly incidental, used predominantly as a moral example, a glass in which to behold oneself beholding oneself.

Narcissus therefore acts as cautionary metonym for the broader *speculum* tradition as categorized by Herbert Grabes, enlisted to make clear otherwise worryingly blurred distinctions between the Socratic mirror of self-knowledge and the vain mirror of self-idolatry.[45] Discussing the Delphic injunction carved into the stone of Apollo's temple ('know thyself'), Socrates explains to Alcibiades that it should be understood as 'see thyself'; 'the eye [should] be looking at something in which it could see itself', he continues, suggesting either a mirror or the reflective surface of the beloved's eye ('then will an eye see itself if it observes an eye'):

Come now, how might the self itself [*auto to auto*] be discovered?[46]

---

[43] Robert Heath, 'To a Lady wearing a Looking-glass at her girdle', in *Clarastella* (London, 1650); Thomas Jordan, 'To his Mistresse Philonella, being at her Looking-glasse', in *Love's Dialect* (London, 1661).

[44] Don Diego Puede-ser, 'To My Worthy and Much Esteemed Friend, Sir Thomas Richardson, Knight', in Fernando de Rojas, *The Spanish Bawd* (London, 1631), prefatory matter.

[45] Herbert Grabes, *The Mutable Glass: Mirror-Imagery in Titles and Texts of the Middle Ages and English Renaissance*, trans. Gordon Collier (Cambridge, 1982).

[46] Plato, *Alcibiades I*, in *Complete Works*, ed, John M. Cooper, trans. D. S. Hutchinson (Cambridge, 1997), 129 B; 130 C–D.

Both Bartsch—citing Christopher Gill's preferred translation 'the itself itself'—and Charles Taylor emphasize that the focus of Socratic speculation looks beyond the private 'self' (itself a classical anachronism) towards the soul and consequently to the divine, locating the Good externally. So, the soul itself should know itself; as John Davies explains, 'the *Soule workes by her selfe alone* is 'indiuisible, vncorruptible still' and 'onely one'.[47] Reading Plato, '[w]e are left with a definition of self-knowledge that cannot be pushed further than the soul's recognition that it is divine', Bartsch concludes: this is not 'internalization' in Taylor's terms.[48] Yet, as Gill's qualification of the translation suggests, it requires a precise eye to distinguish between Narcissus' autolatry and Socrates' theolatry: they both seem to be looking in mirrors.

Any distinction between vanity and self-scrutiny is, therefore, potentially unstable; even Socrates, beside the 'pure and clear' rivulets in which young girls wash and reflect themselves, is prophetically aware of the 'summery shrillness [of] the cicada's song' that 'echoes' around his pastoral idyll.[49] While knowing thyself becomes the objective of the Platonist philosopher or Stoic wise man, the latent threat of narcissism always disturbs their introspection. Davies worries that 'the Diuill mockes our curious braine, | When *know thy selfe* his oracle commands', and he wrestles to equilibrate the conflicting implications of self-scrutiny:

> . . . now beyond my selfe I list not go;
> My selfe am *Center* of my circling thought,
> Onely *my selfe* I studie, learne, and know.
> . . .
> . . . I know my selfe a *Man*,
> Which is a *proud* and yet a *wretched* thing.[50]

His verse becomes the site of conflict, offering these surprising correlations:

> Look in thy *Soule*, and thou shalt *beauties* find,
> Like those which drownd *Narcissus* in the floud,
> *Honor*, and *Pleasure* both are in thy mind,
> And all that in the world is counted *good.* (p. 100)

[47] John Davies, *Nosce teipsum* (London, 1599), 22; 39; 40.
[48] Bartsch, *The Mirror of the Self*, 52; Taylor, *Sources of the Self*, 124.
[49] Plato, *Phaedrus*, trans. Christopher Rowe (London, 2005), 229 b5–230 c1.
[50] Davies, *Nosce teipsum*, 4; 8.

Here, Narcissus' corporeal attractions are, just about, superseded by the spiritual beauties of the mind (however, to be invoked is to be present; to be denied is to be an anxiety). But elsewhere, his presence is more invidious:

> And while the face of outward things we find,
>   Pleasing, and faire, agreable, and sweete;
>   These things transport, and carrie out the mind,
>   That with her selfe her selfe can neuer meete. (p. 6)

It is, Davies cautions, hard to resist the transports offered by the image (*adstupet ipse sibi* being such a transport) when the mind 'her selfe her selfe' can never meet; the mind cannot easily enact the same self-gratifying and self-regarding turn available to the narcissist.

In its entirety, *Nosce teipsum* demands a sharp distinction between involvement in the body and scrutiny of the soul—'*Sense* outsides knowes, the *Soule* through all things sees, | . . . *Sense* sees the barke, but she the life of trees' (p. 19)—and therefore draws a line between narcissine involvement with the exterior and spiritual 'knowledge of my self' (p. 9). As such, Davies's poem operates with similar tactics to one of Grabes's categories of mirror-text, with an Augustinian division between the 'propinquity of . . . the sensuous image and the inward image of the soul'.[51] Here, the mirror's shadow is offered as self-confessed image; the flat representation explicitly acknowledges its pictorial artificiality and therefore gestures beyond the shade, to the spiritual content beyond (the Platonic resonances are clear). Seneca, while doing away with the Platonic emphasis on spiritual transcendence that would see the self-speculator move from corporeal reflection to specular interaction with the soul, equally stresses the artificiality of the reflected image and the need to penetrate the representational surface: 'the mirror doth nothing', he says, 'but onely represent the obiect'.[52] The reflections are like clouds with 'no proper substance or body . . . but a fiction and resemblance without the thing' (not a camel or a weasel or a whale, Hamlet would add: just an empty sign, like a word or a word or a word); 'there is not', the Stoic concludes, 'any thing but fallacious in

---

[51] Grabes, *The Mutable Glass*, 85.
[52] Seneca, 'His Seven Bookes of Naturall Questions', in *The Workes of Lucius Annaeus Seneca, both Morall and Naturall*, trans. Thomas Lodge (London, 1614), 764.

mirrors, which doe but represent a body subsisting without them; . . .
[t]hey are Images and vaine representations of true bodies'.[53] Narcissus,
absorbed in private interaction with the image, is what Jaś Elsner
describes as 'the ideal viewer, whom all artists would wish for', open to
unguarded interaction and, like Pygmalion, filled with 'the desire to
possess as if it were real what is no more than pigment, to embrace
what is no more than a reflection writ on water'.[54] Leonard de Marandé
provides an apposite image: '[o]ur thoughts runne after obiects to embrace them, but in vaine, for they can ouertake nothing but shaddowes'
and grasp at nothing but 'a handfull of water'.[55]

Accordingly, we can see why Alberti calls Narcissus the first painter,
and why Philostratus, a Greek Sophist of the Roman imperial period,
describes how 'the pool paints Narcissus', providing what becomes a
familiar correlation between the precision of reflection and the craft of
Zeuxis; Philostratus is describing a Pompeian wall-painting of Narcissus, in layers of *ecphrasis* that threaten to muddy distinctions between
the artificial and the real: 'The painting has such a regard for realism
that it even shows . . . a bee settling on the flowers—whether a real bee
has been deceived by the painted flowers or whether we are to be
deceived into thinking that a painted bee is real, I do not know.'[56]
Philostratus provides an extraordinarily exact description of the painting's extraordinarily exact depiction of the pool's extraordinarily exact
reflection of Narcissus, until the reader almost fails to notice that they
have become as involuted in these deceptions as Narcissus (rolled into
the entwining fictions in preposterous cycles), almost tricked into
accepting Philostratus' unblinking act of Pygmalion animation:
'Whether the panting of his breast remains from the hunting or is
already the panting of love I do not know.'[57] The picture pants: we
are asked to forget it is paint and canvas not flesh and blood, to forget
like Narcissus. Callistratus, deliberately echoing Philostratus in the

---

[53] Ibid., 767; 773–4.
[54] Jaś Elsner, *Roman Eyes: Visuality and Subjectivity in Art and Text* (Princeton, 2007),
133.
[55] Leonard de Marandé, *The Judgment of Humane Actions*, trans. John Reynolds
(London, 1629), 42.
[56] Philostratus, *Imagines and Callistratus*, trans. Arthur Fairbanks (London, 1931),
89.
[57] Ibid., 91.

description of a statue of Narcissus positioned by a real brook, raises the bar: 'the spring [struggles] to match the skilful efforts of art in the marble'; the water then 'envelop[s] the reflection which came from the statue with the substance of water as though it were the substance of flesh' (it seems likely that Callistratus is recalling versions of the tale where Narcissus eventually drowns, and is foreshadowing his immersion); and finally, alongside disingenuous disavowals of the writer's craft, we learn how 'words cannot describe how the marble softened into suppleness and provided a body at variance with its own essence' as the hard marble metamorphoses into a yielding, sensational, softness.[58] Ovid's boy is deeply implicated in these deceptions, trapped in the fallacious reflection, barred from truth by his vanity, and incapable of accessing matter (a Shakespearean keyword) lest he ripple his glassy portrait. Bartsch, in relation to the Senecan passages, quotes Gérard Simon: 'the entire study of mirrors and refracting surfaces is thought of as a *science of the false*'.[59] The influential Ovidian scholar Leonard Barkan draws an equally fine line between productive self-scrutiny and destructive over-investment in the image: while 'metamorphosis becomes a means of creating self-consciousness because it establishes a tension between identity and form' compelling the individual 'to look in the mirror', excessive involvement in that 'mirror world' causes it to lose its 'profound meaning' and become 'a place of confusion, mistaken identity, and self-absorption without self-understanding'.[60] Such absorption, he concludes, 'denies the substantiality of real life without affirming any transcendent realities', leaving the 'hopelessly impercipient' Narcissus 'caught in the traps of shadow and substance that the world lays'.[61]

Therefore as a model of facilitated ipseity, as Seneca makes clear, self-reflection remains duplicitous: 'mirrors have been invented to the end that a man might know himselfe', the Stoic explains; 'the faire ought to learne herein how to auoide infamie [and] the foule, to redeeme by their vertuous behauior, the imperfection of their countenance'.[62] So far, so

---

[58] Callistratus, *Descriptions*, trans. Arthur Fairbanks (London, 1931), 393.
[59] Gérard Simon, 'Behind the Mirror', *Graduate Faculty Philosophy Journal*, 12 (1987), 311–50 at 320, cit. Bartsch, *The Mirror of the Self*, 39.
[60] Barkan, *The Gods Made Flesh*, 46; 48.
[61] Ibid., 48; 50.
[62] Seneca, 'His Seven Bookes', 775. See Bartsch, *The Mirror of the Self*, 10–11.

Delphic, but his explanation that 'nature [has] ministred vs the meanes to see our selves [in, for example, a] cleare fountaine' admits in unwelcome mythic connotations.[63] While, 'at the first' men chanced upon their reflections in fountains and flat stones, 'afterwards, when as self-loue had insinuated it selfe amongst mortall men', they turn to their crafted mirrors, and find their gratification in self-speculation.[64] Gazing in a brook with Socratic self-awareness or Stoic self-control is very different (or troublingly similar) to the rapt attention of a Narcissus, or, much worse, a Hostius, whose story repulses and fascinates Seneca: 'In this place I will tell thee a storie, to the end thou mayest vnderstand that lust forgetteth not any instrument to prouoke his desire, but is diligent and ingenuous to excite his own furie.'[65] We already sense the presence of the Ovidian youth, burning in his self-substantial fuel, feeling the 'furie' of his lust.[66] Next, we graphically encounter the homoeroticism that was always latent in his desire (although clumsily effaced by a number of translators):[67]

[Hostius] made certain mirrors . . . that shewed the images of men far greater than they were, wherein one finger exceeded the arme in measure, length, and thicknesse. . . . [W]hen he endured the company of men, he sawe in the mirrour all the execrable motions of him he had admitted, enioying by this meanes a false greatnesse of their members, as if it had beene true. . . . [He] delighted he his insatiable lusts with fained appearances also. Goe now and say that Looking-glasses were inuented for vncleannesse sake.[68]

[63] Seneca, 'His Seven Bookes', 776.

[64] Ibid., 776.

[65] Ibid., 774.

[66] Golding, *Shakespeare's Ovid*, 583.

[67] For example, Clement Robinson, presumably trying to keep his *Handefull of Pleasant Delites* as free from what he perceives as Roman unpleasantness as possible, denies the tale's homoerotic content, with the unexpected result of providing a rare example of a cross-dressing Narcissus: 'Himself forsooth he did array I In womans attire of a new devise, I And over a bridge as he did go. Ladie, ladie. I In the water he sawe his own shadow, My.' This convoluted addition allows Robinson to steer a now overtly heterosexual hero to this version of the reflection episode: 'A Ladie faire he saith it seemeth: I Forgat himself that it was he.' Clement Robinson, *A Handful of Pleasant Delights (1584)*, ed. Hyder E. Rollins (Cambridge, 1924), 30.

[68] Seneca, 'His Seven Bookes', 774.

We feel the narcissine involvement with the mere image, the commitment to the artificial, to the surface of deceptive display. We realize the pleasure of visibility and performance (Hostius seems less concerned with sexual fulfilment than the deferring erotics of spectatorship, repositioning his mirror to view his refracted anatomy) as the *speculum* tradition braces itself for inevitable corruption:

> It is shamefull to be spoken what this monster (worthy to be torn with his owne teeth) both spake and did; when as on every side mirrors were opposed against him, to the end he might be a beholder of his owne hainous villainies. . . . Undoubtedly haynous sinnes are afraid to behold themselves . . . but this man . . . hath made them come before his sight, and was not onely contented to see the greatnesse of his sinne, but thought good to plant about himselfe his mirrors, whereby he divided, and disposed his villainies. (ibid.)

We feel Hostius threatening to evade the punishment of the autoerotic Narcissus, refusing to be 'torn with his owne teeth' or to beat his 'pale cold fists upon his naked breast'.[69] We witness him revelling in being a beholder of himself, delighting in the self-division that Narcissus comfortingly comes to regret: 'he represented his monstrous action to himselfe by resemblances: . . . diuiding himselfe betwixt a man and a woman . . . [he] durst shew himselfe those monsterous embracements, and approue them vnto himselfe'.[70] Hostius is a defiant Narcissus: he approves himself; he dares show himself to himself. 'I will feede myselfe with the similitude', he declares (Seneca, transported by opprobrium, slips into the first person); 'my villanie shall see more than it can conceiue, and shall admire at his owne patience'.[71] The nadir of dangerous speculation has been reached, Hostius not only refusing to submit to social standards of decorum but also triumphing in his self-sustaining gratification. While Ovid ventrilocutes any moral unease through Narcissus' self-censure and self-destructive grief, and Ovid's translators exacerbate that condemnation in their commentaries, it is left to Seneca merely to express his relief that this dangerously self-made man meets an apposite end. While suicide would have been most apt,

---

[69] Ovid, *Metamorphoses*, trans. Melville, 483.
[70] Seneca, 'His Seven Bookes', 774–5.
[71] Ibid., 775.

most reassuring, most 'deserving', Hostius' end, 'massacred before his mirror' by his own servants, finally completes the circuit of self-absorption:

O detestable wickednesse.[72]

It is immediately after Hostius has blackened the mirror's image that Seneca conforms to Delphic type—'mirrors have been invented to the end that a man might know himselfe'—but have his sentiments been comprehensively undercut?[73]

It is understandable that Seneca, his Stoic ethics demanding 'the jettisoning of the body as so much annoying baggage', requires what Bartsch describes as 'the elimination of any erotic potential from the philosophical gaze', needing from the outset to distance himself from the lascivious vocabulary of a Platonic specular model.[74] Accordingly, just as Seneca feels the need to massacre Hostius before endorsing the autodidactic capabilities of his sanitized mirror, each Renaissance translator, commentator, or moralist must invoke-to-revoke Narcissus. By adding Tiresias' prophetic caution that Narcissus' long life depends on the youth not knowing himself, Ovid sets up his myth as counterbalance or even contradiction to the *nosce teipsum* injunction; the Socratic implication that knowing oneself necessarily implicated knowledge of a higher Good has been overwritten by the Ovidian suspicion that the libidinal body is susceptible to distraction, and that the formerly easy incorporation of eroticism into the specular model (so apparent in the *Phaedrus*, as shall be discussed) is now complicated by a less soulful physicality. Staring into the eyes of an Ovidian beloved rarely results in soul-searching.

Narcissus has, at least for a sixteenth-century poet like John Davies, come close to spoiling his Delphic auto-analysis; the 'Diuill mockes' as the poet tears his sight away, above, and beyond the body; 'the best

---

[72] Ibid.

[73] Hostius' tale is often repeated in the context of visual theory or experimental optics: see John Baptista Porta's *Natural Magick* (London, 1658), 361. Here, Hostius is evoked alongside the vanity of feminine cosmetics: 'so women pull hairs off their eyebrows for they will shew as great as fingers'.

[74] Bartsch, *The Mirror of the Self*, 12.

Soule, with her reflecting thought, | Sees not her selfe, without some light divine' until 'to iudge herself, she must her selfe transcend'.[75] And while this transcension attempts to discard corporeal restrictions—

> who so makes a mirror of his mind,
> And doth with patience view himselfe therein,
> His *Soules* eternitie shall clearly find,
> Though th'other beauties be defac't with sinne. (p. 55)

—Davies cannot quite deny that even as his soul turns 'to view the beames of thine owne face divine', he knows 'that thou canst know nothing perfectly, | While thou art Clouded with this flesh of mine' (p. 101). Narcissus, a representative of frustrating corporeality—incapable of piercing through his image and therefore caught on the level of image and mere matter—suffers a similar distress: 'O would to God I for a while might from my bodie part.'[76]

The commentators provide an expected exegesis: Narcissus, '[v]iewing his outward face in watery glasse', 'the inward nought attends', giving excessive attention to his physical rather than spiritual condition.[77] So 'being amorous | Of his shade in the water (which denotes | Beautie in bodies . . .)', and remaining ignorant of anything more than his 'vile bod[y]', Narcissus neglects one-half of his natural condition.[78] The narcissine rhetorical dynamic, so well equipped to talk of self-division and ready with its multiple subject positions to signal subjective plurality, easily incorporates this disjunction of form and spirit, '*bodily beauty* [and] *the shadow of the soule*:'[79]

> [Narcissus d]espisd himselfe, his soule, and so let fade
> His substance for a neuer-purchast shade.[80]

By inserting 'his soule' into the usual 'himself himself' geminative construction, George Chapman, translating Petrarch, incorporates this theologically inflected sense of spiritual and physical division into the

---

[75] Davies, *Nosce teipsum*, 4; 9; 12.

[76] Golding, *Shakespeare's Ovid*, 489.

[77] Henry More, 'A Platonic Song of the Soul', in *Divine Hymns* (London, 1706), 4.

[78] George Chapman, 'A Hyme to our Saviour on the Crosse', in *Petrarchs Seven Penitentiall Psalmes* (London, 1612), 43.

[79] *Ovids Metamorphosis*, trans. Sandys, 60.

[80] Chapman, 'A Hyme', 43.

verbal structures of narcissistic duality. Marsilio Ficino, Plato's first Latin translator and founder of the Florentine Academy that did so much to popularize Socratic thought in the Renaissance Italy, similarly resituates Narcissus into a Christian context, understanding narcissine self-involvement with an undue fascination with the corporeal: Narcissus' adoration of his reflection correlates with the soul's admiration for the body, 'which is unstable and in flux, like water, a beauty which is the shadow of the soul itself'.[81] So 'seduced, like Narcissus', the soul, in pursuing the body, 'neglects itself, but finds no gratification in its use of the body'; the Christian conclusion is that 'in loving bodies we shall really be loving the shadow of God'.[82]

Consequently, writers like Thomas Churchyard easily explicate the Narcissus myth in a Christian context, demonstrating how we 'are in loue, with fond *Narcissus* face [and drown] our selves, in that whereon wée stare, | And feede the flesh'.[83] The self-destructive quality of self-adoration receives the exegesis that '*the soule so alienated from itself, and doting on the body, is tortured with miserable perturbations*', so the suicidal drowning of Narcissus (suicide not being an Ovidian feature but one found in his contemporary Conon and reintroduced by early modern authors) comes to represent how 'the minde is drowned with [the body's] desyre'.[84] Narcissism's construction of a powerfully independent subject complete with self-scrutinizing gaze is construed as sinful, indeed so sinful as to be effectively suicidal, and ultimately as idolatrous:

> It is the shadow of my selfe, I see,
> And I am curst to be enamoured.
> Where did I lose my soule? or where am I?
> What god shall pardon me this sin, if here,
> I must become my owne Idolater?[85]

[81] Ficino, *Commentary on Plato's* Symposium *on Love*, 140.

[82] Ibid., 141; 144.

[83] Thomas Churchyard, 'Sir Simon Burleis Tragedie', in *Churchyard's Challenge* (London, 1593), 25–44 at 28.

[84] *Ovids Metamorphosis*, trans. Sandys, 60; T. H., *A Looking-Glasse for Women*, 764. Conon's telling has Narcissus killing himself with the sword of a previously suicidal scorned lover. For the text of Conon, see Felix Jacoby, *Die Fragmente der Griechischen Historiker*, vol. 1 (Leiden, 1957), 193–9, no. 24.

[85] James Shirley, *Narcissus; or, The Selfe-Lover* (London, 1646), 26.

These lines from James Shirley rigorously challenge the status of the subject, countering any suggestion of active agency on the part of the 'I' with warnings against sinful wilfulness: so 'I see', and as a consequence, 'I am curst'; self is acknowledged as mere shadow; 'I' loses its soul and consequently itself; and, following the established pattern of Protestant despair and redemption, the arrival of a pardoning God is dependent upon the realization that the 'I' is synonymous with idolatry (the upper case of 'Idolater' graphically insists on the association of subjectivity and idolatry, the I becoming Idol). Narcissism, the worshipful gaze upon the self, demonstrates how individualism sinfully displaces proper faith in God.

This correlation between self-assertion with suicidal and idolatrous introspection will be further discussed in relation to Renaissance attitudes to self-slaughter, but the association is already becoming apparent:

> Narcissus drownde himselfe, for his selfes shew,
> Striuing to heale himselfe, did himselfe harme,
> These drownde them selues on earth, with their selues woe,
> Hee in a water-brooke by furies charme.[86]

Thomas Middleton's adoption of the repeated pronoun in this attack on idolaters is in no way a positive assertion of subjectivity, but rather a concerted assault on those subject-positions. No sooner is the self shown than drowned, healed than harmed, and this is the lesson for all selves on earth. Self-assertion is narcissistic, is therefore idolatrous, is therefore woeful, is therefore suicidal. The Narcissus myth has become the site for a sustained attack on the overconfident subject: 'Disjoin me from my self, I ask no more.'[87]

---

[86] Thomas Middleton, *The Wisedome of Solomon Paraphrased* (London, 1597), sig. Q3ʳ.

[87] John Hopkins, *The Metamorphosis of Love*, in *Amasia; or, The Works of the Muses*, 3 vols. (London, 1700), iii. 65.

2

Narcissistic Vision

A Spring there was, whose silver Water
As Smooth as any mirror, nor lesse cleare.[1]

[P]ut a *Looking-Glasse* into a *Basen* of *Water*, I suppose you shall not see the
Image in a *Right Line*, or at equall *Angles*, but aside. I know not, whether this
Experiment may not be extended so, as you might see the *Image*, and not the
Glasse, Which for *Beauty* and *Strangenesse*, were a fine Proofe: For then you
should see the *Image* like a *Spirit* in the *Aire*.[2]

Put a looking-glass into a basin of water: Francis Bacon's disarmingly
conjectural foray into the intricacies of optic theory, uncharacteristically
hampered by the scientist's reluctance to put his own experiments into
practice and consequently undermined by his own admissions of uncertainty, nonetheless provides an apposite image with which to begin a
discussion of the narcissistic gaze. In this commonplace watery experiment and its mirror-enhanced reflections (this optical illusion is frequently described in discussions of visual deception and the fallibility of
the eye), we see an oblique reconfiguration of the Ovidian youth and the
'fatall Looking-glasse' of his pool; the period's seminal poeticized image
of self-absorption is inadvertently mimicked by the hypothesizing
Bacon and his reflexive liquid looking-glass.[3] But the Renaissance
scientist with his basin of water and his submerged mirror does more
than simply unwittingly replay the Ovidian scene; Bacon's experimental
enthusiasm, so influential to sixteenth- and early seventeenth-century
scientific endeavour, discloses a characteristic integration of the scientific and the mythic, the seemingly empirical with the poetic, the fictive,

---

[1] *Ovids Metamorphosis*, trans. Sandys, 50.
[2] Francis Bacon, *Sylva Sylvarum; or, A Naturall Historie* (London, 1628), 191.
[3] Shirley, *Narcissus*, 26.

and the fanciful. The conflation of mythic Narcissus and scientific *perspectiva*, although not in this instance deliberate, is a crucial correlation for an accurate understanding of early modern depictions of self-reflecting narcissism, and is integral to appreciating how poetic descriptions of vision are informed by discovery in the fields of optics and anatomy. In what follows, we examine the presence of Narcissus or the narcissine impulse as they appear in the erotic epyllion tradition and, more specifically, in Shakespeare's contribution to the genre, *Venus and Adonis*. Reading narcissism in the context of contemporary optics demonstrates how visual theory impacts upon conceptions of interiority and provides an introspective model for an increasingly introverted ipseic model.

1. EYE TO EYE REFLECTED: VISION IN THE EPYLLION

By the late sixteenth century, there were a number of 'radically different ways' of understanding the workings of the eye, leading to what Marcus Nordlund has described as a 'confused and muddled state of affairs, as a modern conception of sight was gradually doing away with traditional theories'.[4] Advances in anatomical study were forcing received wisdom that vision occurred due to the emission of eyebeams into obsolescence. Long-held faith in the active nature of the speculative gaze, popularized by the Neoplatonist Galen, was gradually superseded by proof of the eye's receptivity. While Platonic or Galenic eyebeam theory was effectively and conclusively discredited within the scientific community by Kepler's publication of his work on optics in 1604, clearly there is slippage either side of the turn of the century, where old and new conceptions of vision compete, coexist, or become confused; indeed, Aristotelians had been repudiating Platonic notions of emission since

---

[4] Marcus Nordlund, *The Dark Lantern: A Historical Study of Sight in Shakespeare, Webster, and Middleton* (Goteburg, 1999), p. viii. For a history of optic theory, see Teresa Brennan and Martin Jay (eds.), *Vision in Context: Historical and Contemporary Perspectives on Sight* (London, 1996); Stuart Clark, *Vanities of the Eye: Vision in Early Modern European Culture* (Oxford, 2007); David C. Lindberg, *Theories of Vision from Al-Kindi to Kepler* (Chicago, 1976); Willem Van Hoorn, *As Images Unwind: Ancient and Modern Theories of Visual Perception* (Amsterdam, 1972).

their inception.[5] One such slippage, where the supposedly discredited theory remains in circulation, can be observed in poetry's treatment of the eye.

We can see a tangible reluctance, notably within the epyllion and in the sonnet tradition, to abandon the now apparently fanciful yet enduring aesthetically pleasing theories of eyebeam emission. When John Weever announces that his lover's eyes 'were such, my Muse yet hardly can | Emblazon forth the beutie of [the] man', he executes a neat play on 'emblazon': the eye blazing forth becomes a much worked image, an integral emblazoning blazon for the erotic narrative tradition.[6] It is worth considering the continued commitment of Shakespeare and his fellow neo-Ovidians to this feature of a discredited ocular theory, for in doing so it becomes clear how notions of reflection and mutuality—the definitive features of extramission—are integral to an amatory poetic compelled towards erotic coupling. The narcissist is an unnerving presence in these tales precisely because of the parallels that emerge between his censured self-reflection and the sought-after reciprocation of the genre's lascivious youths.

Mirrored in his pool, lost in self-reflection, Narcissus offers his alternative to, and surrogate version of, the gaze of lovers, each looking upon the other with 'imitating eye[s]' described as the 'looking glasse of lovers'.[7] Feeding himself with self-substantial fuel, the self-lover subverts eroticism's governing dynamic where the male lover may 'liue by [his beloved's] faire eyes reflect'.[8] Eyebeams directed only against himself, the solitary narcissist is both dangerously incongruous and yet apposite, constantly denied yet a constant presence in the erotic narrative tradition. Within the pastoral environment—a landscape presided over by a Platonic drive of attraction-and-response and the impulses of natural kindness—Narcissus' reflexive erotic model may simply exaggerate or indeed epitomize the governing dynamic of mutuality. But

[5] Johannes Kepler, *Optics: Paralipomena to Witelo and Optical Part of Astronomy*, trans. William H. Donahue (Santa Fe, 2000).
[6] John Weever, *Faunus and Melliflora* (London, 1600), ll. 45–6.
[7] Christopher Marlowe and George Chapman, *Hero and Leander* (London, 1598), III. 319; Michael Drayton, *Endimion and Phoebe*, in *The Poems*, ed. John Buxton, 2 vols. (London, 1953), i. 480.
[8] Richard Lynche, *Diella* (London, 1596), repr. in *Seven Minor Epics of the English Renaissance (1596–1624)*, ed. and intro. Paul W. Miller (New York, 1977), 70.

could the narcissist also come to stand as an ambassador for the new model of post-Keplerian vision, challenging the reciprocal beams of emission theory with the introspection of intromission?

Empedocles provides the following description of the eye:

As when a man who intends to make a journey prepares a light for himself, a flame of fire burning through a wintry night; he fits linen screens against all the winds which break the blast of the winds as they blow, but the light that is more diffuse leaps through, and shines across the threshold with unfailing beams. In the same way the elemental fire, wrapped in membranes and delicate tissues, was then concealed in the round pupil—these kept back the surrounding deep water, but let through the more diffuse light.[9]

Extramission is a speculative sight, one radically different from the receptivity of the post-Keplerian eye or that belonging to the post-Cartesian subject. Vision, which since Kepler has been conceived of as intromissive, occurring internally behind the eye, was originally perceived as extramissive, external. According to Plato's description in his *Timaeus*, the eye emits an ocular beam, a ray of 'fire as had the property not of burning, but of providing a gentle light'.[10] As in the Empedocles quotation above, the elemental fire, from which the body is 'fashioned', from 'within us... flow[s] through the eyes in a fine stream'.[11] Galen does much to popularize the Platonic theory for his scientifically educated early modern audience, talking of a 'sense instrument of vision' both 'bright and radiant' and properly supplied with 'a great deal of pneuma' to keep it 'radiant [and] gleaming' in its 'visual stream'; 'it is shewed by Galen, that these senews be hollowe as a reede... that the visible spirit might passe freely'.[12] There is, to my knowledge, not a single poem from the erotic narrative tradition that fails to utilize the 'transpiercing eye[beams]' of extramissive theory; it would appear that

---

[9] Empedocles, *The Extant Fragments*, ed. M. R. Wright (London, 1995), 240. A contentious passage: see A. A. Long, 'Thinking and Sense-Perception in Empedocles: Mysticism or Materialism?', *Classical Quarterly*, 16 (1966), 256–76.

[10] Plato, *Timaeus and Critias*, trans. A. E. Taylor (London, 1929), 45 B.

[11] Ibid.

[12] Galen, *On the Usefulness of the Parts of the Body*, trans. Margaret Tallmadge May, 2 vols. (Ithaca, NY, 1968), i. 465; ii. 56; Galen, *On the Doctrines of Hippocrates and Plato*, trans. Phillip de Lacy (Berlin, 1984), 7. 6. 8; Thomas Vicary, *The Anatomie of The Bodie of Man*, ed. F. J. Furnivall and Percy Furnivall (London, 1888), 37.

not one poet in this tradition can resist the 'furious dart[s]' of eyebeams, and that '[n]o armour might be found that could defend [their lovers from the] I Transpearcing rayes of Christall poynted eyes'.[13]

In these epyllion descriptions, with their lovers for ever '[d]arting these rayes from th[eir] transpiercing ey[es]',[14] Platonic and Galenic theory has been amalgamated with the mythic convention of Cupid's amorous dart, and extramission is kept alive as a poetic figure, as here in Marston's 1598 description:

> He thinks he see'th the brightnes of the beames
> Which shoote from out the fairenes of her eye:
> At which he stands as in an extasie.[15]

These shooting beams are recognizably the speculative corpuscular rays, the Platonic 'pure fire', the 'visual fire from out the eye', that shares the quality of love, 'a spirit all compact of fire' (*Ven.*, l. 149).[16] The fiery particles in the optic beam consequently have the power to inspire or incense a 'deepe desiring':

> To spie a Nimph of such a radiant glancing,
> As when I lookt, a beame of subtill firing
> From eye to heart incenst a deepe desiring.[17]

Radiating out the 'beame[s] of subtill firing', a glance kindles the 'amorous fire' of love with its 'fired gaze'.[18] This extramissive 'visual stream' is made of, variously in different texts and scientific incarnations, fiery particles, atoms, *simulacra* (i.e. likenesses or films), or the Stoic's *pneuma*.[19] But the visual fire is not enough to bring about the act of vision by itself since sight requires the coalescence of this ocular ray with a corresponding stream of fiery particles from the viewed object.

---

[13] Anonymous, *A Pleasant and Delightfull Poeme of Two Lovers: Philos and Licia* (London, 1624), repr. in *Seven Minor Epics*, ed. Miller, 33; Thomas Lodge, *Glaucus and Silla*, in *Scillaes Metamorphosis* (London, 1589), l. 541; Samuel Daniel, *Delia and Rosamund* (London, 1592), sig. F2ʳ.

[14] Drayton, *The Poems*, 372.

[15] John Marston, *The Metamorphosis of Pigmalions Image*, in *The Poems*, ed. Arnold Davenport (Liverpool, 1961), ll. 28–30.

[16] Plato, *Timaeus*, 45 B.

[17] Lodge, *Glaucus and Silla*, ll. 274–6.

[18] William Barksted, *Hiren*, in *Seven Minor Epics*, ed. Miller, 50.

[19] Plato, *Timeaus*, 43 C.

Chapman, in his *Phillis and Flora*, employs terms almost identical to a description from Theophrastus of these corpuscular sparks: 'For as when steele and flint together smit, | With violent action spitt forth sparkes of fire, | And make the tender tynder burne with it.'[20]

In other words, in this 'eye-emitted ray paradigm', both the eye and the object viewed are emitting tangible physical beams or visual currents, one at the other, which meet and merge in the coalescence (*sunancheia*) of sight.[21] This participational conception of vision, predicated upon give and take, has real amorous potential when the object viewed is the beloved's eye. Beams, both projected at and received from the beloved, construct a material connection between them; we recall how, in Donne's 'The Ecstasy', his lovers' 'eye-beams twisted, and did thread | Our eyes, upon one double string'.[22] The individual subject has little primacy in this act of vision, sight being an exercise in mutuality: perfect, therefore, for a poetic where the drive is towards coupling, but potentially problematic for that isolated figure of intense privacy, Narcissus. To conceive of vision in this manner is to conceive of 'an active, participational, specular, and homogeneous . . . relationship between perceiver and perceived', where 'observer and observed are welded together through the act of seeing' along the lines of the eyebeam: or twisted, threaded, strung together on a 'sympathetic chain'.[23]

Unsurprisingly, it is this reciprocation which makes extramission so appealing to the epyllion poet whose poems' narratives typically culminate in the coming together of a loving couple, a culmination prefigured in the reciprocation of eyebeams: 'And (looking on his eies) him she entrates.'[24] This line from Thomas Edwards's 1595 *Cephalus and Procris* initiates a movement where loving union is predicated upon ocular union which one-half of the couple entreats from the other, sending out the eyebeam and begging the beloved to 'lend them foorth againe' (l. 344). The proximity of gendered pronouns—'him she

---

[20] George Chapman, *Ovid's Banquet of Sence* (London, 1595), sig. B4ᵛ. See Lindberg, *Theories of Vision*, 10.

[21] Van Hoorn, *As Images Unwind*, 43.

[22] John Donne, 'The Ecstasy', in *The Complete English Poems*, ed. Smith, ll. 7–8.

[23] Nordlund, *The Dark Lantern*, p. ix; 51; Francis M. Cornford, *Plato's Cosmology* (London, 1935), 153.

[24] Thomas Edwards, *Cephalus and Procris; and, Narcissus (1595)*, ed. W. E. Buckley (London, 1882), l. 212.

entrates'—plays a heterosexual variation of the rhetorical game I have been tracing in the 'himself himself' construction, predicting the coming together of the couple. Elsewhere, verbal near-reflections within a line become indicative of hermaphroditic union. The conclusion of Beaumont's 1602 epyllion works towards the final metamorphosis of Salmacis and Hermaphroditus, a physical merging which, as so often, is made mimetically manifest in the verse: 'Nor man nor mayd now could they be esteem'd: | Neither, and either, might they well be deem'd.'[25] Using the same mimetic concurrence of loving entwine and poetic structure, Philip Sidney's protégé Abraham Fraunce, recounting Salmacis and Hermaphroditus' union in his *Aminta's Dale*, describes the couple as 'either, yet neither of either'; both lovers and words 'all intangled lie... all intermingled about'.[26] If Shakespeare's 'The Phoenix and the Turtle' works with a logically illogical amatory arithmetic—where number is slain as division grows together, uniting two in one and celebrating one containing two—it equally operates with the grammatical compression of this erotic rhetoric: 'Reason in itself confounded, | Saw division grow together, | To themselves yet either neither, | Simple were so well compounded' (ll. 41–4).

Because reciprocation is built into the dynamics of extramission, a mode of vision becomes an ideal emblem of sympathetic coupling where the invariably female lover is required to 'reflect her beauty on another', who begs that 'with a sweet kisse [she may] cast [her] beames on mee, | And Ile reflect them backe againe on thee'.[27] All these extramissive statements are characterized by carefully constructed rhetorical strategies, frequently chiastic, implicating each lover in a network of pronouns, embedding 'she' amongst an embrace of masculine signifiers:

> For still on faire *Gyneura* were his eyes,
> And shee reciprocally on his replies.[28]

---

[25] Francis Beaumont, *Salmacis and Hermaphroditus* (London, 1602), sig. E4[r].

[26] Abraham Fraunce, *The Third Part of the Countesse of Pembrokes Yvychurch: Entituled Amintas Dale* (London, 1592), 49.

[27] Beaumont, *Salmacis and Hermaphroditus*, sig. C4[v].

[28] Lynche, *Diella*, 66.

Richard Lynche's use of 'reciprocally' demonstrates how the vocabulary
of extramissive science is incorporated into the poetic lexicon. Plato has
described the lovers who 'watch over each other, and want to please each
other' as craving the 'reciprocation of love', and scientific descriptions of
emission, as can be seen in the following from Theaetetus, lend themselves easily to the erotic genre:

[Engendering] the visible world by its projection of spiritual substance, the
'pneuma' that flows out through the hollow optic nerve, excit[es] the surrounding air ... translating it into a receptive body made 'sympathetic ... with the
change effected by the outflow of the pneuma into it'.[29]

There is an exciting, engendering sexiness, where vision forges a kind of
mutual accord between viewer and viewed, who both, through eye
contact, participate in the emission and merging in an act of 'sympathetic' ocular coupling, an 'intercourse of ... bright Messengers'.[30]
There is already an inherent emotive poeticism to these theories, Plato's
translators describing the beams or 'motions' as the 'kindred fire', the
phrase playing on the range of connotations for 'kind'.[31] These beams
engender sight, having the fertile potential of coupling because sight is
kindred to, and offspring of, coalescence. Equally, these beams are kind
in their sympathy; they are 'akin'.[32] The mirroring and kind reciprocation of one to one, of fiery beam to beam, has led, the poets suggest, to
the 'kinde increase' of coupling.[33]
    A 'flame ... streams off from bodies of every sort', Plato explains,
'and has its particles so proportioned to the visual ray as to yield
sensation', again emphasizing the likeness, the proportionality, of subject and object beams: Galen quotes Plato, saying 'like to like [is] firmly
united'.[34] Even without the element of the eyebeam, early models of
vision all emphasize the importance of likeness. Empedocles argues, in
the words of John Beare, that '[e]manations from what we may call the

[29] Ficino, *Commentary on Plato's* Symposium *on Love*, trans. Jayne, 42; Sergei
Lobanov-Rostovsky, 'Taming the Basilisk', in David Hillman and Carla Mazzio (eds.),
The Body in Parts (London, 1997), 194–217, cf. at 198.
[30] Lynche, *Diella*, 67.
[31] Plato, *Timaeus*, 45 D; see Lindberg, *Theories of Vision*, 6.
[32] Plato, *Timaeus*, 45 B.
[33] Lodge, *Glaucus and Silla*, l. 493.
[34] Plato, *Timaeus*, 45 B–D; Galen, *Doctrines*, 7. 6. 6.

percipiendum, or object, enter into the pores of the *percipiens,* or percipi-
ent organ'.[35] 'These emanations', he continues, 'to result in perception,
must be "symmetrical" with the pores: if they are either too small or too
large for these, no perception takes place.'[36] It is most pronounced in
the extramissive context, Plato explaining that

> the visual stream . . . issues forth, like to like, coalesces [with daylight] and forms
> a single uniform body with the light in the direction of the line of vision in
> which the ray emitted strikes upon the external object it encounters. So the
> whole, in virtue of its uniformity, is affected uniformly when it has contact with
> another thing or another thing with it, transmits the motions of that thing
> through all the body to the soul, and causes the sensation we call seeing.[37]

Crucially, for Plato, and for a neo-Platonist like Ficino, who makes
Plato so readily available to an early modern readership in his commentary upon the *Symposium,* vision offers access to the divine. Through a
correlation of the beautiful with the celestial, Plato can describe specular
attraction as a drive towards the transcendent: 'Beauty is a certain grace
which most often originates above all in a harmony.'[38] Corporeal
attraction, therefore, is a recognition of a higher beauty, for the lover
'does not desire this or that body, but he admires, desires, and is amazed
by the splendour of the celestial majesty shining through bodies'.[39]
Love, for a Platonist, shares the quality of this beauty, and once again
we see how similitude underpins a simultaneously erotic and spiritual
yearning; 'this divine beauty has generated love', which is 'a desire for
itself, in all things'.[40] 'Likeness generates love.'[41]

Thus, loving vision, indeed all vision, requires the suspension of
difference; the same could be said of the epyllion's conception of desire,
one indebted to Ficino and Plato. Much of the work of these poems is to
efface the distinctive nature of an individual, readying each lover for
incorporation into a new coupled identity; as George Chapman in his

---

[35] John I. Beare, *Greek Theories of Elementary Cognition: From Alcmaeon to Aristotle*
(Oxford, 1906), 14.
[36] Ibid.
[37] Plato, *Timaeus,* 45 c–d.
[38] Ficino, *Commentary on Plato's* Symposium *on Love,* 40.
[39] Ibid., 52.
[40] Ibid., 46.
[41] Ibid., 57.

continuation of Marlowe's well-known contribution to the epyllion genre demonstrates with a typically compressed phrase, '*Hero Leander is, Leander Hero*'.[42] A handy excuse for eager youth: 'if then *Leander* did my maidenhead get, | *Leander* being myself I still retain it'.[43] 'It repeatedly happens', Platonists have suggested, 'that someone wishes to transfer himself into the person of the beloved': 'Those who have been trapped by love alternatively sigh and rejoice. They sigh because they are losing themselves, because they are destroying themselves, because they are ruining themselves. They rejoice because they are transferring themselves into something better.'[44] 'Anyone who loves', Ficino summarizes, 'dies'; love is suicidal.[45] Accordingly, a concomitant and requisite sense of self-abandonment is already becoming clear and we see how a model of vision that insists on likeness might lend itself to an ontological model of desire that seeks to suppress the integrity of the individual for the sake of a sexual, mutual identity. The self-slaughter of desire hopes to deny the self-absorption of the narcissist, and our rhetorical knot is simply unpicked, separated out, and resolved: 'the lover removes himself from himself and gives himself to the beloved'.[46]

The erotic narrative tradition acknowledges this loss, while sweetening the pill; the 'force' of love, John Weever explains, is that its 'excellence | Is to transforme the verie soule and essence | Of the louer, into the thing beloued'.[47] The language of optic sympathy reinforces the positive sense of dependency between lover and beloved, self and other, subject and object: 'lovers [feed] on glaunces of their eyes, | 'Tis heavenly food when both do sympathise'.[48] Lynche's feeding lovers display the potential of the sympathetic radiant glance, a sympathy which overwhelms the single identity of the lover, making each dependent upon the other, even, as Beaumont explains, for their lives:

> Fayrer than fayrest (thus began his speech)
> Would but your radiant eye please to inrich

    [42] Chapman, *Hero*, III. 369.
    [43] Ibid., III. 371–2.
    [44] Ficino, *Commentary on Plato's* Symposium *on Love*, 52.
    [45] Ibid., 55.
    [46] Ibid., 57.
    [47] Weever, *Faunus and Melliflora*, ll. 553–5.
    [48] Lynche, *Diella*, 67.

My eye with looking, or one glaunce to giue,
Whereby my other parts might feede and liue,
Or with one sight my sences to inspire,
Far liuelier then the stole *Promethean* fire;
Then might I liue, then by the sunny light
That should proceed from thy thrise-radiant sight.[49]

The loving glance is sustenance to those whose identity entirely depends upon union. This particular example is the apotheosis of the Platonic conception of sympathetic optics and an ontology predicated upon union. Accepting the fine line between subject and objective reality, we can see how on a simple level a 'radiant eye [gives] lustre to the hew | Of all the dames'.[50]

Taken further, this sympathetic dealing of lustre and the provision of sustaining visual food can occur on an even larger scale:

Loue-blest *Leander* was with loue so filled,
That loue to all that toucht him he instilled.
And as the colours of all things we see,
To our sights powers communicated bee:
So to all obiects that in compasse came
Of any sence he had; his sences flame
Flowd from his parts, with force so virtuall,
It fir'd with sence things meere insensuall.[51]

Chapman's Leander becomes a complete correspondent, instilling, infusing, and firing a world of total receptivity. Again, this harmonic receptivity is an integral quality of the extramissive universe. Plato is particularly concerned with emphasizing the role of daylight in the coalescent process, and it becomes clear that the surrounding world is incorporated into these ocular relations, air becoming the medium for the mingling beams, sunlight playing an equal third-party part. Stoic writers also emphasize the importance of the air as sentient medium participating in the process of *alloiosis* or structural change, which occurs when the beams of pneuma encounter each other: 'the air itself',

[49] Beaumont, *Salmacis and Hermaphroditus*, sig. C4^r.
[50] William Barksted, *Mirrha the Mother of Adonis* (London, 1607), ll. 115–16.
[51] Chapman, *Hero*, III. 95–102.

says Cicero, 'sees together with us'.[52] So when Chapman describes, in the fourth sestiad of *Hero and Leander*, the 'streames of fire' that are driven through the 'rarefied air . . . I In flashing streames' (ll. 259–61), his use of 'rarified air' is informed by and true to extramissive theory. As Nordlund explains, this is 'an active and participational extension of the self which bound the observer to the surrounding world'; unlike the 'strictly passive and neutral reception of preordained images into the eye', which Kepler and the anatomists were beginning to posit at the turn of the century, this mode of vision militates against the isolation of the seeing subject, instead incorporating, physically, tangibly, the viewing eye/I into its receptive surrounds, the air seeing with us.[53]

But while the poets maintain the literary currency of extramissive vision, the scientific community of 'Most Exquisite *Anatomists*' and the '*Great Masters* of the *Knife*' is moving on: 'Both Eye-Lids being removed, first, with your Fore-Finger feel gently for the *Trochlea* . . . with the Assistance of a small Hook and Scissars extract the Fat and Membranes. . . . [T]he whole Eye dislodg'd; Disingage its Muscles, and display them, whereby you may observe.'[54] The visual organ goes under the dissecting knife of a Vesalius, or a Witelo, Jessenius, Platter, or Kepler—the new wave of early modern anatomists—who, seeking to replace the once predominant ocular theories of eyebeam emission, come to a new conception of intromissive, receptive sight.[55] The visual metaphor is rewritten: the visual lantern is replaced by the camera obscura.

Take, for example, Willem van Hoorn's description of Cartesian, essentially modern, ocular theory:

[52] Cicero, *De natura deorum*, trans. H. Rackham (London, 1951), 2. 83; see Lindberg, *Theories of Vision*, 9, and S. Sambursky, *Physics of the Stoics* (London, 1959), 28.

[53] Nordlund, *The Dark Lantern*, pp. vii–viii.

[54] John Browne, *Myographia Nova; or, a Graphical Description Of All The Muscles in the Humane Body, As Arise In Dissection* (London, 1698), p. iv; William Cowper, *Myotomia Reformata; or, A New Administration of all the Muscles of the Humane Bodies* (London, 1694), 46.

[55] Andreas Vesalius, *On the Fabric of the Human Body*, trans. William Frank Richardson, 2 vols. (San Francisco, 1999); Witelo, *Witelonis Perspectivae*, trans. A. Mark Smith (Wrocław, 1983); Joannes Jessenius, *Præs; Universalis humani corporis contemplatio* (Wittenberg, 1598); Felix Platter, *Observationum, in hominis affectibus plerisque, corpori et animo* (Basle, 1641).

Constellations of material particles in motion impinge upon the visual organ and there an inverted *image* of the outside object is projected on the retina. By means of the immediate traction of the nervous fibre in the hollow optic nerve, this *image* is transferred to the interior surface of the brain where a second *image* is formed. This second *image* serves as a *sign* for the mind to experience the corresponding perception.[56]

Notice, first, the direction of the passage's activity: the particles 'impinge upon' the eye, from where an image is 'projected on[to]' the retina, before being 'transferred to the interior'. This is a sequential movement towards a corporeal inside where each element of the eye and brain becomes receptive, impinged upon, projected onto. Secondly, however, this is not simply a physical interior: van Hoorn's Cartesian-inspired description of modern visuality draws a firm distinction between the 'material' exterior, the 'outside object', and the 'interior' 'image'. Post-Cartesian optic theory is predicated upon the separation of the exterior object from its subjective, imaged reception. While the mediated quality of vision has always been acknowledged—Nicolaus de Cusa looks at 'snow through a red glass' and attributes 'the redness not to the snow, but to the glass'—this subjective model of vision is emphatically predicated on dislocation; the seeing subject internalizes mere images which are 'perce[ived]' and 'experience[d]' within as '*sign*[s]' to be defined by the individual mind.[57] This is an intromissive vision, and this is a subjective vision: subjective in that it implicates only the single subject, and subjective in that the received image is open to interior translation, subjective reading.

We have moved from an understanding of vision that sought to locate the individual seeing subject in a network of correspondence and relationship, to a scientifically updated understanding that champions the isolation of the viewer.

But the eye vvhich is vvont vvith curious inspection to prye into all other thinges, and to finde out the nature and order of them, hath been vnable to vnfold his ovvne vvonderfull constitution, and hath bene alvvay blind in iudging of it self.[58]

[56] Van Hoorn, *As Images Unwind*, 4.
[57] Cit. Barbara Freedman, *Staging the Gaze: Postmodernism, Psychoanalysis, and Shakespearean Comedy* (Ithaca, NY, 1991), 17.
[58] Philip Barrough, *The Method of Phisick* (London, 1583), 38.

These lines from Philip Barrough's early anatomical text, *The Method of Phisick*, signal this change in the fortunes of his 'litle round subiect', the eye.[59] Once, it would seem, the eye was a privileged, curious inspector, prying into and finding out the natural order of 'all other thinges'. Now, however, Barrough announces, the eye is to have its own mystery, its own 'vvonderfull constitution', unfolded and judged. The eye is to be inspected, pried into, made subject to its own gaze. Barrough's text displays an almost duplicitous eye, paradoxically made 'blind' by the power of its own intrusive observation. Accordingly, Sergei Lobanov-Rostovsky describes the anatomist, during the latter years of the sixteenth century, looking with increasing detail at the eye's construction, which, its secrets revealed, becomes 'not a window for the soul but a frail organ, a proper object of anatomy', a tamed basilisk.[60] The epyllion poets' refusal to abandon their apposite metaphor allows the eyebeam to become just that—metaphoric. A new scientific realism replaces the emotive fictions of extramission, superseding Cupid's bow and arrow with curiously unromantic literalism:

> Betwixt mine Eye and obiect, certayne lynes,
> Moue in the figure of a Pyramis,
> Whose chapter in mine eyes gray apple shines,
> The base within my sacred obiect is.[61]

2. HERSELF HERSELF BEHELD: *VENUS AND ADONIS*

> Thy eyes' shrewd tutor, that hard heart of thine,
> Hath taught them scornful tricks, and such disdain,
> That they have murd'red this poor heart of mine;
> And these mine eyes, true leaders to their queen,
> But for thy piteous lips no more had seen. (ll. 500–4)

---

[59] Barrough, *The Method of Phisick*, 38.
[60] Lobanov-Rostovsky, 'Taming the Basilisk', 196.
[61] Chapman, *Phillis*, sig. D1ᵛ.

Shakespeare, in his 1595 contribution to the epyllion tradition, complicates the extramissive motif, playing new variations on what Samuel Daniel described as the 'silent rethorique of perswading eyes'.[62] In what is essentially a poem of amorous persuasion, the eye has particular importance as the site for an eroticized encounter, for a 'war of looks' (l. 355). Venus, Shakespeare's heroine and the poem's prominent voice, understands the dynamics of love poetry, her advances utilizing the romantic potential of the extramissive ocular embrace as a lover's tool; the eyebeam is, she understands, a motif to motivate love, working with 'powre [to] moue the blood, l More then the words', to 'rauish sence'.[63] Explicitly describing her eyes with the imagery of speculation, associating her with Plato's loving eyebeam, Shakespeare describes Venus' 'fiery eyes [that] blaze forth' (l. 219), becoming, in the above quotation, 'true leaders to their queen'. She is both tempted *by* the sight of Adonis, and is therefore led on by her vision, but also, more literally, she is led onwards, led *outwards*, her agency extended into the world on the material beam. Venus, requiring the reciprocal flame from Adonis, wishes that the reluctant youth would 'dart . . . forth the fire' to burn her (l. 196). As Nordlund has described, the poem presents opposing visual regimes, characterized by Venus' desire to participate and Adonis' 'hard heart[ed]' ocular 'disdain', demonstrating the 'shrewd' and 'scornful tricks' he employs in avoidance of Love's beams. Here we are shown both the loving and the 'murd[erous]' capacity of extramissive vision.

This for Venus is a loving vision, sharing the quality of love which is 'a spirit all compact of fire' (l. 149), and one which participates in love's harmonious union. Venus' conception of vision, and her sense of the fertile and reproductive world around her, is akin to those virtuoso passages of the *Phaedrus* where Socrates expounds his vision of desire and the growth of 'love's light wings' (*Rom.*, II. ii. 66):

as a breath of wind or an echo rebounds from smooth hard surfaces and returns to the source from which it issued, so the stream of beauty passes back into its possessor through his eyes, which is its natural route to the soul; arriving there and setting him all of a flutter, it waters the passages of the feathers and causes the wings to grow, and fills the soul of the loved one in his turn with love. So he is in love.[64]

---

[62] Daniel, *Delia and Rosamund*, sig. E8^v.
[63] Ibid.
[64] Plato, *Phaedrus*, 255 c1–d5.

But, no, he is not: this is the mode of perception that Venus is eager to inspire in the unwilling Adonis: a vision that would bind the two together, but which he repeatedly avoids. He will not be 'the man who has caught eye-disease' (255 D5); indeed, Adonis, with his 'downward eye' (l. 1106) and 'low'ring brows' (l. 183), becomes associated with a notably lifeless model of vision, a vision which owes far more to the dead-eyed introspection of the anatomist's intromissive gaze, objectifying the youth as '[w]ell-painted idol, image cold and dead, | Statue contenting but the eye alone:' the eye alone, an isolated eye, a lonely member for the solitary Adonis with his 'heavy, dark, disliking eye' (l. 182), precisely dis-liking, unlike, refusing to conform to the optical principles of likeness employed by Venus.

With his heroine advocating the mutual and participatory quality of the 'kindred fire', Shakespeare realizes the range of extramissive connotations of being 'kind'. Adonis participates in a tradition of unwilling and unkind lovers, a typical example being Lodge's Scilla, who being 'vnkind rewarded [Glaucus] with mockes' (l. 340). Shakespeare perhaps noted the recurrence in Lodge of a motif of ocular kindness: 'Oh kisse no more kind Nimph he likes no kindnes, | Love sléepes in him, to flame within thy brest, | Cléer'd are his eies' (ll. 613–15). Venus' persistent complaint of Adonis' 'unkindness' (*Ven.*, l. 478) emphasizes both his cruelty and his unwillingness to participate in the meeting of kindred fire: 'Look in mine eye-balls', she demands, 'there thy beauty lies: | Then why not lips on lips, since eyes in eyes?' (ll. 119–20). Perhaps these lines owe something to Fraunce's *Aminta's Dale* of 1592—'*Adonis* lipps with her owne lipps kindely she kisseth'—which again uses the repetition of 'lipps' in correlation to the notion of being kind: a verbal echo among kind and akin words.[65]

To illustrate the benefits of kind coupling, Venus turns to the love-struck horses, and urges Adonis to follow their natural example ('natural' of course being another meaning of 'kind'). As the unwilling Adonis and Venus lie, contemplating this equine erotica, they reprise a Socratic scene. In the following, the lover is divided into three parts, comprised of the charioteer (who acts like the presiding consciousness), the 'bad

---

[65] Fraunce, *The Third Part of the Countesse of Pembrokes Yvychurch*, 44.

horse' (an ugly and untameable nag, champing on its bit, representing the passions), and the 'good horse' (a handsome proud courser, its passions carefully controlled and ruled by 'reason and opinion' and deference to the divine): 'So as they lie together, the lover's licentious horse has something to say to the charioteer and claims the right to a little enjoyment as recompense for many labours endured.'[66] Most simply, Venus can stand in for the intemperate horse, and Adonis the nobler beast 'constrained then as always by shame', so it is with some relish that Shakespeare allows Socrates' 'high-necked' stallion off the rein in his refashioning of the scene: Adonis' 'strong-necked steed' turns 'trampling courser' to leap, snort, and whinny, to bite his bit (see *Phaedrus*, 254 D5), and break it asunder.[67] The metaphor of the temperate horse is elided in its new Shakespearean setting with Socrates' preceding description of the lover's sprouting wings; in mockery of Adonis' restraint, his formerly reined steed now jumps at 'the stirring of a feather' (l. 302) and, as he runs free, the hairs in his tail 'wave like feathered wings' (l. 306).[68] To Venus' delight, the shamefaced horse has, metaphorically, taken flight. As Socrates acknowledges, even the 'good' horse can be tempted, especially when caught in the emitted beams of beauty 'flashing like lightning' from the beloved's face.[69]

It is this mutual gaze that Venus promotes: 'He sees his love', she points out, noting the courser's eye, which, seeking to 'captivate the eye | Of the fair breeder' (ll. 281–2), suitably 'glisters like fire' (l. 275), 'and nothing else he sees, | For nothing else with his proud sight agrees' (ll. 287–8); nothing else agrees, nothing else is kind. This interlude is characterized by terms of reciprocation, of responsive passions, of answering neighs, and looks: 'He looks upon his love and neighs unto her, | She answers him as if she knew his mind', and although the jennet 'puts on outward strangeness, seems unkind' (ll. 307–8; 310) she only *seems* to do so and soon grows 'kinder, and his fury [is] assuaged'

---

[66] Ficino, *Commentary on Plato's* Symposium *on Love*, 171; Plato, *Phaedrus*, 253 D1–256 A5.

[67] Ibid., 254 A; 253 D5; 261–5. Shakespeare employs a particularly ingenious construction as the 'iron bit he crusheth 'tween his teeth' (l. 269), where aural punning on 'bit . . . 'tween' positions the 'crush[ed]' bit, 'be-tween' the components of a single broken word (a typically well-ordered piece of disorder).

[68] Plato, *Phaedrus*, 251 B1.

[69] Ibid., 254 B5.

(l. 318). The mutual look, the neigh, the answering neigh, and the meeting of minds, all fuse in an image of kindness initially predicated upon a participatory extramissive gaze, an ideal of reciprocation that Venus is denied and yet craves, lures with, and offers to Adonis: 'the kiss', she says, 'shall be thine own as well as mine' (l. 117), offering a fusion of 'thine' with 'mine' within the single but mutually 'own[ed]' kiss.

However, Adonis, in his refusal to fulfil his role in the traditional poetic model and in his frequently referenced immaturity, can be seen to figure as part of a new generation, 'young and so unkind' (l. 187), like the upcoming generation of scientists, rejecting the kindred flame.

> O what a war of looks was then between them,
> Her eyes petitioners to his eyes suing!
> His eyes saw her eyes as they had not seen them;
> Her eyes wooed still, his eyes disdained the wooing. (ll. 355–8)

His disdain disturbs the loving poetics from within, negating the visual rhetoric of love by emptying the image out with his blank and lifeless stare: 'His eyes saw her eyes' fits the lyric trope, but 'as they had not seen them' rejects its logic in a quick chiastic reversal along the line. Notice how each repetition of the gendered pronouns, 'his' and 'her', enforces the discreteness of both parties; rather than entering into an optic system which promotes amalgamation into a couple—one which delineates a self-identity dependent upon the viewed reciprocating other—Adonis exhibits visual characteristics typical of intromission, drawing those firm lines of distinction between self and other, subject and object, his and her, 'they' and 'them', insisting upon an identity which is emphatically 'his'. What Shakespeare describes is therefore precisely a 'war of looks', of two contrary modes of perception, of opposing ocular theories, as Adonis refuses to enter into the extramissive give and take, its movement of to and fro, but rather introspects and withdraws.

The benefit, for Shakespeare, of playing with a received ocular motif is that the two modes of vision run concurrent with two seemingly oppositional modes of selfhood: the extramissive reciprocating couple and the intromissive, introspective individual. The extramissive vision is one of mutuality, and is used heavily in erotic and romantic poetry because it is an ideal motif for an aesthetic that believes that perfect identity is achieved through coupling (think, for example, of Spenser's Scudamour and Amoret, who find hermaphroditic union in 'sweet countervaile').[70] As opposed to this, the intromissive gaze is receptive, and vision becomes an individual translation of sensory stimulus, occurring behind the eye, in the brain, and is therefore suitable for an introspective solitary viewing subject; 'when we turn to the gaze', as Elsner has argued, 'we move from the material and the objective into the world of subjectivities'.[71] Teresa Brennan explains, with Lacanian inflection:

It can seem that this turn is a move away from subject-centeredness, that it is an abdication of the subject's power if it no longer imposes its view but rather humbly receives it. However, this passive move makes the subject the center of the world: however passively it sees, it does so from its own standpoint, which also happens to be the world's center. . . . If the way we see one another is no longer a way of touching, it makes us truly independent and alone.[72]

Even within the word 'speculation' we can see how one mode of vision/being gives way to the other: 'speculation' first connotes an emission, a speculative progression outwards to speculate upon the external object; later, 'speculation' becomes more akin to 'contemplation', an interior, self-studying, inward glance, a private thought, a subjective specu-lation.[73] We can see, in a text like George Hakewill's *The Vanitie of the Eye*, how the loss of visual emission occasions the transference of

---

[70] Edmund Spenser, *The Faerie Queene*, ed. A. C. Hamilton (London, 1977), III. xii. 47.1.

[71] Elsner, *Roman Eyes*, p. xi. Elsner is employing a contemporary sense of 'the gaze' here, connoting a subjecting vision.

[72] Teresa Brennan, '"The Contexts of Vision" from a Specific Standpoint', in Brennan and Jay, 217–30 at 224–5. Brennan's emphasis on 'passivity' potentially underemphasizes period anxiety about the deceptive potential of vision; Stuart Clark's *Vanities of the Eye* is a compelling corrective to what seems a common peculiarity in a number of mutually influenced and theoretically motivated critics, including, most notably, Jonathan Cracy, *The Techniques of the Observer: On Vision and Modernity in the Nineteenth Century* (Cambridge, Mass., 1992).

[73] This is a movement towards the interior, from *OED*, s.v. 'Speculation' I. 2 (the exercise of the faculty of sight), via II. 4 (the contemplation of some subject), to 5 (an act of speculating or a conclusion reached by abstract or hypothetical reasoning), and 6 (contemplation of a profound, far-reaching, or subtle character).

extraspective models of reciprocity to the interior, thereby encouraging
an introspective reflectivity ('reflection' undergoing a similar semiotic
shift to 'speculation'):

The soul being shut vppe, and kept in from peeping out, and as it were gazing
through the casements of the body, shee must by constraint reflect her beames
vpon the contemplation of her selfe, and such thinges as shee hath before
apprehended.[74]

Unsurprisingly, these contemplative structures are precariously close
to narcissine absorption and those of a philosophical bent are cautioned
against letting 'the *Mind* turn . . . in upon *it self*' to only 'convers[e]
with its own *Idaeas*'.[75]

These structures of ipseity, their delineation facilitated by advances in
specular theory, build upon well-established binaries of erotic identity.
Neoplatonic thought would suggest that '[t]here are two kinds of love'
where 'one is simple, the other reciprocal'.[76] 'Simple love is where the
beloved does not love the lover' or where the isolated subject refuses
participation in reciprocal individualism (indivisibility).[77] Whereas this
unconnected subject may increasingly become the ipseitic norm in a
regime of specular introspection, Plato would consider this lover
'completely dead. For he neither lives in himself, nor does he live in
the beloved.'[78] Narcissus is brutally initiated into this state: the exchange of eyebeams is an illusion; love is not reciprocated; he is first
unwittingly and then unwillingly self-reliant. '[H]e who loves another,
but is not loved by the other, lives nowhere'; the fragility of this
Neoplatonic dogmatism will eventually be revealed by an introspective
subject who loves himself and locates *everywhere* within.[79] Unapologetic
self-speculation, unashamed self-reliance, unconditional self-approval
and affirmation (all fragile and ultimately untenable in themselves)
will aggressively short-circuit these Platonic constructions:

[74] George Hakewill, *The Vanitie of the Eye* (Oxford, 1615), 109–10.
[75] Joseph Glanvill, *Plus Ultra; or, The Progress and Advancement of Knowledge Since
the Days of Aristotle* (London, 1668), 52.
[76] Ficino, *Commentary on Plato's* Symposium *on Love*, 55. For an early modern
reader, 'simple' has real resonance, suggesting, via medical usage, an unmuddied,
uncombined state of pristine singularity.
[77] Ibid.   [78] Ibid.   [79] Ibid.

Wherever two men embrace each other in mutual affection, this one lives in that; that one, in this. Such men exchange themselves with each other; and each gives himself to the other in order to receive the other. . . . Each has himself and has the other. Certainly this one has himself, but *in* that one. That one also possesses himself, but in this one. Certainly while I love you loving me, I find myself in you thinking about me, and I recover myself, lost by myself through my own negligence, in you, preserving me. You do the same in me. . . . After I have lost myself, if I recover myself through you, I have myself through you; if I have myself through you, I have you before and more than I have myself, and I am closer to you than to myself, since I approach myself in no way other than through you as an intermediary.[80]

The Platonic compulsion to avoid narcissism is torturous. Whereas the narcissist and the introspective self-scrutinizer appropriate and condense this preposterous interdependence and owe responsibility (the duty of response) only to themselves, Ficino's entire paragraph can be succinctly encapsulated within the geminative 'myself myself'.

If Shakespeare's poem acts as a battleground for hostile conceptions of vision, desire, and subjectivity, it may be possible to discern a few of the philosophical antagonists behind its competing poetics. While Venus appropriates the kindred fire and responsive passions of Plato, Adonis appears to pay more attention to the type of cautious pragmatism endorsed by Lucretius:

> 'tis better to prevent
> Than flatter the disease, and late repent;
> Because to shun th'allurement is not hard
> To minds resolved, forewarned, and well prepared:
> But wondrous difficult, when once beset,
> To struggle through the straits, and break th'involving net.[81]

Resolutely shunning the goddess's allurement, Adonis has been seemingly forewarned, coming well prepared to struggle, to break the circling snares of Venus' entwining arms, and to evade becoming 'tangled in the nets of love' (see *Ven.*, l. 67).[82] Could the Roman philosopher have provided Shakespeare's youth with an alternative to the Grecian

---

[80] Ibid., 55–6.
[81] Lucretius, 'The Fourth Book Concerning the Nature of Love', trans. John Dryden, in *The Poems*, ed. Paul Hammond, 5 vols. (London, 1995), ii. 332–44, ll. 128–33.
[82] Ibid., 81.

eroticism that assails him? Could the Lucretian renunciation of a mythicized world view provide Shakespeare with a philosophical spokesperson for the non-responsive isolationism that will be shown to trouble him at the conclusion of the poem?[83]

Critical consensus finds no evidence of Shakespeare having directly studied Lucretius. The atheistic Epicurean atomist had been suppressed by the condemnation of St Augustine, and even when *De rerum natura* did receive English translation, by John Evelyn and later by Lucy Hutchinson, it was with significant caveats:

I abhorre all the Atheismes and impieties in it, and translated it only out of youthfull curiositie. . . . I found I never understood him till I learnt to abhorre him, and dread a wanton dalliance with impious bookes. Then I reapd some profitt by it for it shewed me that sencelesse superstitions drive carnall reason into Atheisme. . . . Let none, that aspire to eternall happiness, gaze too long, or too fixedly on that Monster . . . lest he draw infection in att his eies, and be himselfe either metamorphosed into the most ugly shape, or stupefied and hardned against all better impressions.[84]

Lucretius, it seems, is an Epicurean Medusa, as infectious as the evil eye.

But, as both philosopher and playwright would attest, 'out of nothing, nothing ever came'.[85] Shakespearean texts do display awareness of Epicurean philosophy, to the extent that it proves

---

[83] It is worth noting the suggestive detail that Ficino, *the* translator of Plato, sees fit to burn his explication of Lucretius.

[84] Lucy Hutchinson, *Translations of Lucretius: De rerum natura*, ed. Hugh de Quehen (London, 1996), 23, 26–7. There may be a trace of Ovid's narcissine *adstupet* in Hutchinson's stupefaction.

[85] Lucretius, *An Essay on the First Book of T. Lucretius Carus*, De Rerum Natura, trans. John Evelyn (London, 1656), 23. Lucretian Epicureanism was certainly available to an early modern reader: in the classroom, Roger Ascham's *Scholemaster* would admit the atheistic philosopher-poet into the second tier of Latin writers alongside Catullus, Horace, and Virgil; in the hospital, John Banister in 1578 is citing him while expounding anatomist wisdom, and William Bullein incorporates Lucretian wisdom as he seeks his *Defence Against all Sicknesse*; in the pulpit, Calvin knows 'the blasphemous sayings of the filthy dogge' well (*The Institution of Christian Religion* (London, 1561), 8); Montaigne's study walls are inscribed with Lucretian quotation; Francis Bacon revives his atomism; Burton's *Anatomy* is well versed; Spenser incorporates *De rerum natura*'s introductory 'Hymn to Venus' in Book IV of his *Faerie Queene* and his influence is felt throughout the allegorical epic, particularly during his telling of the Venus and Adonis story (which features Narcissus) in Book III. This third book contains descriptions indebted to Ovid, and in his turn Ovid was influenced by the explicitly anti-Platonist writing of the Epicureans.

productive to consider the refracted influence of Lucretius on his work. For example, while extricating the dedicatory epigraph for *Venus and Adonis* from Ovid's *Amores* 1. 15, ll. 38–9 ('let boors like dross; to me may Phoebus bring | His goblets filled from the Castalian spring'), Shakespeare would not have missed lines 26–7, where Ovid acknowledges his debt to Lucretius: 'Sublime Lucretius' verses shall not die | Till one day ends the world in tragedy'.[86] Undeniably, Shakespeare knows of Lucretius, and if he did not read him in Latin, he encountered him frequently in many of his more habitual sources; Jonathan Gil Harris charts influence via Montaigne to conclude that 'Lucretian philosophy resonates with a noteworthy materialist strand in his plays.'[87] Ovid's Lucretian inflections can be found at a further remove, operating in the Shakespearean text.[88]

Offering her translation as an inoculating 'antidote against the poyson' of Lucretius' libidinal depravity, Lucy Hutchinson anticipates the Epicurean's own vaccinatory tactics: he administers a substantial dose of explicit description to frighten his audience from excessive sexual indulgence.[89] In the same terms, a later translator such as John Dryden offers a more empathetic appreciation of Lucretius' depictions of passionate desire; 'I am not yet so secure from that passion, but that I want [lack] my Authors Antidotes against it' (i.e. 'I am not secure enough to be able to do without the antidote'), Dryden admits, adding: 'He has given the truest and most Philosophical account both of the Disease and Remedy, which I ever found in any Author: For which reasons I translated

---

[86] Ovid, *Amores*, in *The Love Poems*, trans. A. D. Melville (Oxford, 1990).

[87] Jonathan Gil Harris, 'Atomic Shakespeare', *SS*, 30 (2002), 47–51 at 48. For extended discussion of Lucretius, see Jacques Lezra, *Unspeakable Subjects: The Genealogy of the Event in Early Modern Europe* (Stanford, 1997).

[88] L. C. Martin sees any Lucretian influence occurring later in Shakespeare's career, arguing that 'it begins to seem admissible that Lucretius, at first or second or tenth hand, may have been among the influences which affected Shakespeare during his mainly tragic period'. 'Shakespeare, Lucretius, and the Commonplaces', *Review of English Studies*, 21 (1945), 174–82 at 178. George Depue Hadzsits concludes that, by the time Burton writes his *Anatomy of Melancholy* (pub. 1621), 'Lucretius' text was a familiar one to all educated readers'; *Lucretius and his Influence* (London, 1935), 306. A. B. Taylor traces a connection from Lucretius, via Shakespeare's familiarity with Fraunce's *Amintas Dale* in 'Two Notes on Shakespeare and the Translators', *Review of English Studies*, 38 (1987), 523–6.

[89] Hutchinson, *Translations of Lucretius*, 27.

him.'[90] Dryden's response to the erotically charged Book IV of
De rerum natura understands its graphic indulgences as self-consciously
excessive; they are written 'that surfeiting, | The appetite may sicken and
so die' (*TN*, I. i. 2–3).

Dryden is not alone in responding to the emotional honesty of
Lucretius' often uncomfortable combination of titillation and disgust.
As Lambinus explains, in the preface to his 1570 edition, Lucretius' lack
of discreet sensibility is more valuable than reductively anti-heretical
condemnations may allow. There is a sustained demythologizing intent
to Lucretian verse, allowing less impeded access to natural causality and
carnal impulse:

> Lucretius, without these fables and obscure wrappings, speaks of the origins and
> causes of things . . . not always accurately, indeed, or piously, but with simpli-
> city and clarity; and . . . shall we not hear him? If in many places he dissents
> from Plato, and says much which is contrary to our religion, we should not
> therefore reject that which is consonant with those principles. How wonderfully
> he writes about the compulsion of desire, about calming the turbulence of the
> spirit, about attaining quiet of mind![91]

This appraisal is productive: it draws attention to Lucretius' aggressive
rebuttal of myth; it positions him as Plato's antagonist; it stresses the
compulsive quality of desire. In each of these three areas, Lucretius will
be shown to offer compassionate support to the aggrieved Adonis, who
finds himself deeply affronted by the mythic personification of Platonic
libido and as horrified as Lucretius at the sweaty, unconfined, annihi-
lative arousal of his desperate wooer.

Venus discourses on her visual allure, keen not to be thought 'hard-
favoured, foul, or wrinkled-old' (l. 133); Lucretius debunks depicted
beauty, showing the 'dowdies' and 'deformity' behind the 'extenuating
name'.[92] Throughout his representation of Love, Shakespeare employs
deliberately discordant or distasteful vocabulary, allowing her rapacious appetite to undermine her self-presentation. So, nervous Adonis
blushes 'red for shame' (l. 36) and, recalling the alarmed 'good' horse

[90] John Dryden, *Sylvæ; or, the Second Part of Poetical Miscellanies*, in *The Works of John Dryden*, ed. Earl Miner, 20 vols. (Berkeley, 1969), iii. 2–90 at 12.
[91] Lambinus, 'Preface', in *De rerum natura* (Paris, 1570), sigs. B2^{r-v}, trans. Paul Hammond, 'The Integrity of Dryden's Lucretius', *MLR*, 78 (1983), 1–23 at 6.
[92] Lucretius, in Hammond, ibid. ll. 142–4.

of the *Phaedrus* who is 'drenche[d] . . . with sweat from shame', has a 'sweating palm' (l. 25) that denotes his resistance and disturbance.[93] Venus, meanwhile, exhibits the 'sweat' and 'high fever' of a Platonic lover as Shakespeare's 'love-sick queen [begins] to sweat' (l. 175).[94] But the moisture Shakespeare's goddess exudes—described by Adonis as merely 'sweating lust' (l. 794)—feels more akin to the lusty perspiration of Lucretius' copulating couple: 'the blue coat, that with embroidery shines | Is drunk with sweat of their o'er-laboured loins'.[95] Locked in their embrace, the 'panting youth[s] their pliant limbs they move, | And cling, and heave, and moisten every kiss'; these descriptions deliberately evoke a cloying 'sweet[ness]', an integral desperation, and a tactile sloppiness that allows a peculiarly Lucretian combination of fascination and repulsion.[96] Panting, moisture, consumption:

> Panting he lies and breatheth in her face.
> She feedeth on the steam as on a prey,
> And calls it heavenly moisture, air of grace. (ll. 62–4)

Whispering a 'thousand honey secrets' (l. 16), Venus similarly arouses both desire and disgust as she 'smother[s]' Adonis with kisses (l. 18). Desire, as Lucretius cautions and as Venus repeatedly illustrates, is 'but a restless wandering joy', prone to 'wild excess' where 'hands or eyes' struggle to 'possess'; it 'strains at all, and fastening where [it] strains', it 'closely presses with . . . frantic pains'.[97] Rarely in control of her yearning, Venus (beset by the cravings she herself embodies) sees only increase in love's endless capacity; like Cleopatra, she will not 'cloy [Adonis'] lips with loathed satiety, | But rather famish them amid their plenty' (ll. 19–20), exemplifying the Lucretian warning that 'full possession does but fan the fire; | The more we still enjoy, the more we still desire'.[98] Incapable of finding the 'repletion' that is 'to love denied', Venus' 'glutton-like' (l. 548) Lucretian 'endless appetite'

---

[93] Plato, *Phaedrus*, 254 c5.
[94] Ibid., 251 b1.
[95] Lucretius, in Hammond, 'The Integrity of Dryden's Lucretius', ll. 103–4.
[96] Ibid., ll. 190–1; 189.
[97] Ibid., ll. 36; 37–8; 39–40.
[98] Ibid., ll. 51–2.

'devour[s] all in haste' (l. 57).[99] The cannibalistic passion of Shake-speare's heroine—who 'murders with a kiss' (l. 54)—is all too remin-iscent of the 'biting kisses' of the imperfect Lucretian lover, who, 'stung with inward rage', inadvertently destroys the beloved as he subconsciously 'strives t'avenge the smart on that which gave the wound'.[100]

No wonder that Adonis, with his 'leaden appetite' (l. 34), complains about his over-wrung hand (l. 421); Lucretius' lovers, in hermaphroditic frenzy, seek to enact the loving logic of interdependence, turning kind incorporation into frustrated self-annihilating intercourse:

> Our hands pull nothing from the parts they strain,
> But wander o'er the lovely limbs in vain:
> Nor when the youthful pair more closely join,
> When hands in hands they lock, and thighs in thighs they twine,
> Just in the raging foam of full desire,
> When both press on, both murmur, both expire,
> They gripe, they squeeze, their humid tongues they dart,
> As each would force their way to t'other's heart—
> In vain; they only cruise about the coast,
> For bodies cannot pierce, nor be in bodies lost:
> As sure they strive to be, when both engage
> In that tumultuous momentary rage.[101]

The raging foam of full desire is simultaneously vital, quick (*OED*, s.v. 5b), and suicidal: 'thou didst kill me, kill me once again!' (l. 499). Shakespeare's descriptions will achieve this Lucretian syn-thesis of enthralling eroticism, thralled dependency, terrific energy, and terrifying effacement: 'her face doth reek and smoke, her blood doth boil' as 'careless lust stirs up a desperate courage, | Planting oblivion, beating reason back' (ll. 554–7). As Lucretius' lovers squeeze together, attempting total union, so too do Venus and the momentarily overwhelmed Adonis as their 'lips together glue' (l. 546); 'incorporate they seem, face grows to face' (l. 540) just as hands lock to hands and thighs to thighs entwine in Dryden's mimetic rhetorical translation. This is the union we have seen

---

[99] Ibid., ll. 56; 58.
[100] Ibid., ll. 43–4.
[101] Ibid., ll. 69–80.

otherwise denied by Adonis—'why not lips on lips, since eyes in eyes?' (l. 120)—but which elsewhere in the epyllion tradition arrives as the culmination of the 'kind encounter': '[h]e askt, she gaue, and nothing was denied, | Both to each other quickly were affied. | Looke how their hands, so were their heart vnited, | And what he did, she willingly requited.'[102] While Christopher Marlowe uses the uniting of hands and hearts to gesture to more fertile pursuits (in 'quickly'), it is the more explicitly 'wanton Muse[s]' of Thomas Nashe and John Marston who demonstrate the full erotic potential of these rhetorical patterns of verbal and physical affinity; Marston revels in Lucretian proto-pornography—

> His eyes, her eyes, kindly encountered,
> His breast, her breast, oft joined close unto,
> His armes embracements oft she suffered,
> Hands, armes, eyes, tongue, lips, and all did woe.
> His thigh, with hers, his knee playd with her knee,
> A happy consort when all parts agree.[103]

—while Nashe takes the dynamic of asking and giving, to-ing and fro-ing, to its natural extreme:

> He rub'd, and prickt, and pierst hir to the bones,
>> Digging as farre [as in earth] he might for stones.
> Now high, now lowe, now striking short and thick;
>> Now diving deepe he toucht hir to the quick.
> . . .
> [She] give's, and take's as blithe and free as Maye,
>> And ere-more meete's him in the middle waye.
> On him hir eyes continually were fixt,
>> With hir eye-beames his melting looke's were mixt,
> Which like the Sunne, that twixt two glasses plaies
>> From one to th'other cast's rebounding rayes. (ll. 145–8; 153–8)

---

[102] Marlowe, *Hero and Leander*, II. 25–8.
[103] Thomas Nashe, 'The Choise of Valentines', in *The Works of Thomas Nashe*, ed. Ronald B. McKerrow, 5 vols. (Oxford, 1966), iii. 397–416, prefatory matter; John Marston, *The Metamorphosis of Pigmalions Image*, in *The Poems*, ed. Davenport, ll. 97–102.

The response of visual beams mimics the give and take of copulation; the fixing of eye in eye, figured in the bind of 'him hir', enacts the proximity of their bodies. Nashe's extended description of the eye's workings, some twenty or thirty lines long and often thought of as a teasing or coy aside from the increasingly steamy action, is in fact an overt description of sexual activity, each element of extramissive mingling paralleling the development of their lovemaking.[104] By the time Nashe returns us to the most explicit section of his narrative—'And to and fro'—all has been prefigured in what Lynche has called the 'intercourse of those bright messengers'.[105] Even the climactic 'dissolve . . . as-though our dayes were donne' has been anticipated in a 'melting look'.[106]

Crucially, Shakespeare, Marston, Marlowe, and Nashe are all responding to the sexual tenor of extramissive sight. To avoid the 'pangs' of 'disastrous passions', Lucretius promotes not just the affectation of 'disdain' (see *Ven.*, l. 33) but also the total avoidance of love's 'fiery dart' (see l. 195).[107] Fearful that the 'wingèd arrow' will 'transfix' him, Adonis appears to have taken Lucretius to heart.[108]

Shakespeare can merely tantalize his reader with the possibility of visual union:

> And as the bright sun glorifies the sky,
> So is her face illumined with her eye,
>
> Whose beams upon his hairless face are fixed,
> As if from thence they borrowed all their shine.
> Were never four such lamps together mixed,

---

[104] See Achilles Tatius, *Clitophon and Leucippe* (cit. Bartsch, *The Mirror of the Self*, 57): '[d]oing this is more pleasureable than actual consummation. For the eyes, mutually reflecting each other, receive simulacra of the body as in mirrors. This outward emanation of beauty, which flows through the eyes into the soul, is a kind of copulation between separated bodies, and it is not far from physical sex' (1. 9. 4–5).

[105] Lynche, *Diella*, l. 67.

[106] Nashe, 'The Choise of Valentines', l. 210. Plato's stream of 'desire' that 'brims over' (*Phaedrus*, 255 c1) is refigured in the Lucretian moment of climactic resolution (resolving into ejaculation): 'Till man dissolves in that excess of joy. | Then, when the gathered bag has burst its way, | And ebbing tides the slackened nerves betray'; *De rerum natura*, 4. 82–4. The inversions in gender roles in Shakespeare's text dictate that it is Venus who is typically associated with these images of overflowing and liquorous eruption (ll. 71–2).

[107] Lucretius, in Hammond, 'The Integrity of Dryden's Lucretius', 123–4.

[108] Ibid., 2–5.

Had not his clouded with his brows' repine;
But hers, which through the crystal tears gave light,
Shone like the moon in water seen by night. (ll. 485–92)

Again, Adonis avoids active participatory vision, refusing to enter into the extramissive dynamic of lend and borrow, refusing to mix together and, therefore, disturbing the to-and-fro lateral movement of beam to beam with his trademark repining brow and downward glance. Adonis, by avoiding the beams, is refusing to be defined merely as one-half of a couple, where identity is 'borrowed' from the other (like the sky which needs to be glorified by the sun). Rejecting an optic system that insists that both vision and identity are only achieved through participation, Adonis seeks to avoid the subjection of erotic verse. He is turning away from a tradition of lovers who seek, in Marston's words, to 'equalize affection, | And have a mutuall love', and it is here in *De rerum natura* that he could learn to shun the enforced kindness of an identity-effacing gaze:

> If absent, her idea still appears,
> And her sweet name is chiming in your ears;
> But strive those pleasing phantoms to remove,
> And shun th'aerial images of love
> That feed the flame.[109]

Here is the narcissistic paradox: on the one hand, to shun the 'idea' and to close the ears against the chiming of her name is to be blind to the narcissine image and deaf to the echo; on the other, to renege on the responsibility of response is to remain narcissistically isolated. Refusing to echo Venus' desire, Adonis risks affiliation with Narcissus.

3. HIMSELF HIMSELF FORSOOK: NARCISSISM IN *VENUS AND ADONIS*

When Venus demands erotic specular response—'Then why not lips on lips, since eyes in eyes' (l. 120)—she employs a familiar form of the Platonic optic conceit. As the philosopher suggests, the beloved's eye is a

---

[109] Marston, *The Metamorphosis of Pigmalions Image*, ll. 141–2; Lucretius, in Hammond, 'The Integrity of Dryden's Lucretius', 15–19.

mirror in which the lover beholds himself, 'unaware that he is seeing himself in his lover as if in a mirror'.[110] The beloved, it seems, is effectively effaced from the pattern, written out of what has, supposedly inadvertently, become self-absorbed and self-praising. This image, used by John Donne, and also John Davies in his *Elegies of Love* where '[w]ithin thine eyes...I Mine eies behold themselues', is the poet's economic acknowledgement of an affinity between the erotic and autoerotic: a subtle acceptance of a discordant narcissism underlying erotic exchange.[111] Traces of disconcerting narcissism suggest themselves throughout the poetic tradition's depictions of coupled love. Look closely enough, and a line which Venus (and I) originally presented as the ideal description of loving sight—'and nothing else [the courser] sees, I For nothing else with his proud sight agrees'—can echo a Spenserian description of Narcissus: '[y]et are mine eyes so filled with the store I of that faire sight, that nothing else they brooke, I but lothe the things which they did like before, I and can no more endure on them to looke'.[112] Suddenly, the—in this case, equine—lover's insistence on visual agreement demands near-narcissine structures of similitude, voicing the congruity of self-love and extramissive vision. The extramissive sight, binding through a form of reflection the perceiver with the perceived, mutualized through the lend and borrow of subject-to-object and object-to-subject beams, finds a dangerous apotheosis in the self-to-self reflection of narcissism; 'a theory predicated', agrees Nordlund, 'on visual homogeneity, sameness, and the joining of kind with kind obviously admits little room for *difference*'.[113] Obeying the extramissive and mutual rules of reciprocal identity, but simply positing himself in both subject and object positions, Narcissus becomes not extrinsic but meaningfully integral to the epyllion conception of desire.

Narcissus' cautionary value is not to stand as antithesis but to figure as an excessive yet exemplary representative of a kindly erotica. The anonymous poet of *Philos and Licia*, for example, first describes how lovers 'haue glassd themselues within [the] eies' of the beloved, then

---

[110] Plato, *Phaedrus*, 255 D5.

[111] John Davies, 'Sonnet VII', in *Wittes Pilgrimage* (London, 1605), sig. B3^r.

[112] Edmund Spenser, 'Sonnet XXXV', in *Amoretti and Epithalamion* (London, 1595), sig. C3^r.

[113] Nordlund, *The Dark Lantern*, 67.

makes the true object of attention more explicit, explaining that she is '[g]lassing herselfe within his matchlesse eyes, I Where little *Cupids* conquering forces lies' (ll. 12; 26). The status of 'matchlesse' is called into question as Licia exactly matches herself within Philos' eyes. Later, when the 'coloured flowers' growing around a 'faire fountaine [whose] loving banks like armes seeme to embrace it' are said to 'glasse themselues within that siluer brooke' (l. 29), we are alert to the Ovidian reference and the similarity of this fountain to Narcissus' pool. The comic potential of Hermaphroditus' confused enquiry, 'How should I loue thee, when I doe espie I A farre more beauteous Nymph hid in thy eye?' should not distract us from understanding that Beaumont is offering a serious critique of erotic love's affinity to self-love.[114] 'For the lover to believe fully in his or her subjective image of the beloved', as Elsner argues, 'the lover must suppress fully the worrying possibility that the subjective image may always be a self-image—a narcissistic self-love sublimated as the desire for another, a Narcissus-like self-objectification posing as love'.[115]

Consequently, Narcissus' role in *Venus and Adonis* is complex: persuasively, Venus understands the self-reliance of the unkind youth as narcissistic self-absorption; but equally compelling is the latent suggestion that Venus herself embodies a model of desire predicated upon kind and like reciprocation, characterized by specular narcissism. She is advocate for an erotic founded upon an ideal of perfect mutuality that would be exemplified in Narcissus' self-regarding visual exchange. Adonis, it could be maintained, is narcissistic in his refusal of kindness; Venus, it could be countered, is narcissistic in her insistence upon it. Adonis, the huntsman who will not be hunted, is a young Narcissus, who 'stande[s] betweene the state of man and Lad', whom the 'hearts of divers trim yong men his beautie... mov[d], / And many a Ladie' desired, but in whose mind 'pride did raigne': both youths are unkind.[116] Meanwhile, Venus, the lover who strives to kiss her beloved, is a smitten Narcissus who would likewise complain, 'why dost thou mee thy lover thus delude? I...I I wis I neyther am so fowle nor yet so growne in yeares, I That in this wise thou shouldst me shoon': both

[114] Beaumont, *Salmacis and Hermaphroditus*, sig. D4ᵛ.
[115] Elsner, *Roman Eyes*, 137.
[116] Golding, *Shakespeare's Ovid*, III. 338–41.

lovers crave kindness.[117] Adonis retreats within the geminative self-embrace—'in thyself thyself art made away' (l. 763)—whereas Venus looks to his eyes for affirmative reflection in these '[t]wo glasses where herself herself beheld' (l. 1129). Locating reciprocation within, the introspective youth gazes upon an internal mirror (and this conception of interior reflection will increasingly come to delineate early modern constructions of selfhood), while, locating reciprocation externally, the extramissive lover depends upon the reflective response of a kind nature. In short, there are intromissive and extramissive narcissists, and both variants can be seen to correspond to period conceptions of subjectivity.

Shakespeare's eponymous figures bandy accusations of narcissism, each conceiving the other as representative of self-absorption or gratification respectively.

> Is thine own heart to thine own face affected?
> Can thy right hand seize upon thy left?
> Then woo thyself, be of thyself rejected;
> Steal thine own freedom, and complain on theft.
> Narcissus so himself himself forsook,
> And died to kiss his shadow in the brook. (ll. 157–62)

Crucially, Venus' description of Adonis' self-absorption makes clear that rather than abandoning the rhetorical structures of gemination and reciprocation, the narcissistic self-speculator simply concentrates these structures' field; the exchange of beams no longer requires an extramissive projection beyond the confines of the subject, but rather relocates the mirror within. The narcissist is not alone: he is simply all-one with himself. He is thief and victim, lover and beloved; the cyclic movement here is of tight entwine, of involution, with heart affected to face, and right hand locked up within the left in an image of encircling isolation. Again we see a narcissistic configuration in the poetic form, initiated in the reflective replication of 'thyself' in 'woo thyself, be of thyself rejected', and epitomized in this study's keynote construction,

---

[117] Ibid., ll. 570–3. Maggie Kilgour makes this distinction between the disdainful and abject stages of Narcissus, exploring the appropriation of these respective types in Narcissus' literary history, in '"Thy Perfect Image Viewing": Poetic Creation and Ovid's Narcissus in *Paradise Lost*', *Studies in Philology*, 102 (2005), 307–39. See Louise Vinge, *The Narcissus Theme in Western European Literature up to the Early Nineteenth Century* (Lund, 1967).

'himself himself forsook'. The familiar reflection of 'himself' against
'himself' neatly figures what Linda Gregerson describes as the 'enclosed
embrace of narcissism' and is the closest we may get to what Barbara
Freedman has called the naive 'fantasy of completed vision', the 'dream
of seeing oneself seeing oneself'.[118] This naive fantasy is, however, fast
becoming a foundational fantasy, a cornerstone of the new optics, and a
precursor to developing ipseic models of self-affirming consciousness
(*cogito ergo sum*). This introspective self-speculation appropriates the
rhetorical strategies of the extramissive specular subject but frustrates
any demand for alterity, difference, or extrinsic reciprocation in its
insistence upon introversion. Venus reads this self-reliance as narcissism, perhaps rightly so, but it is a self-absorption that will increasingly
characterize the early modern and modern specular subject; as an
exponent of extramissive vision, she is fighting a lost cause.

She feels this loss in his selfish arithmetic. The doublet construction,
ultimately self-defeating, operates as an extreme compression of love
poetry's figures. To clarify, the construction is an exacerbated form of
the design Mariann Sanders Regan describes as a 'matrix sentence': the
'paradoxes [of] the language of fusion' are at 'the root' of love poetry
where love teaches 'how to make one twain' (Son. 39, l. 13).[119] So if, as
Regan suggests, these matrices represent the ideal logic of love poetry
and erotic coupling, they are, I would add, all dangerously close to
disclosing the narcissine fantasy of myself–myself adoration. The self-
defeating 'himself himself' construction simply vocalizes the insidious
subsumed impulse at the heart of erotic 'kind love' (*TGV*, II. vii. 2),
replaying in a new key that ''Tis thee (my self) that for myself I praise'
(Son. 62, l. 13).

---

[118] Freedman, *Staging the Gaze*, 26; Linda Gregerson, *The Reformation of the Subject:
Spenser, Milton, and the English Protestant Epic* (Cambridge, 1995). Shakespeare is not
the first to associate Adonis with Narcissus, and neither is Adonis the only epyllion youth
with that association. In 1589, Thomas Lodge describes Adonis' death—'The Ecchoes
ringing from the rockes his fall, | The trees with tears reporting of his thrall' (ll. 125–6)—
recalling the Narcissus and Echo story in relation to Venus and Adonis. In Edwards's
1595 *Narcissus*, the two youths 'meete each other' (l. 169) as 'haplesse boies together'
(l. 171) who bemoan the destructiveness of their beauties which 'bringeth on despaire'
(l. 173).

[119] Mariann Sanders Regan, *Love Words: The Self and the Text in Medieval and
Renaissance Poetry* (Ithaca, NY, 1982), 223–4.

Shakespeare's poem has this tendency to convolute its rhetorical tactics almost to a standstill; by this I mean that the preposterous logic of its habitual phrasing frustrates progression. Take, for example, the following phrases. In the first, a cyclic dynamic of reciprocation calculates an addition:

> Give me one kiss, I'll give it thee again,
> And one for int'rest. (ll. 209–10)

This is Venus' keynote rhetoric of 'increase' (l. 169), of 'turn and return' (l. 704), as befits her role as representative of a reproductive nature (these are revolutions, or, to use early modern mathematical vocabulary, 'resolutions'). But this call-and-response cycle is undermined or infected by Adonis' sterile self-multiplications which refuse addition (these are involutions) and which consequently Venus describes as a kind of substitution (or 'dissolution'):[120]

> Fair flowers...
> Rot and consume themselves in little time. (ll. 131–2)

But Adonis regards Venus' speculation and accumulation as preposterous subtraction (threatening his Euclidian 'prime'):[121]

> Who plucks the bud before one leaf put forth?
> If springing things be any jot diminished,
> They wither in their prime, prove nothing worth. (ll. 416–18)

Her eager additions only devalue his worth, he maintains.

This logic taints the poem: a natural cyclic structure of turn and return—where fleeing horses 'outstrip...crows that strive to overfly them' (l. 324)—is replaced by deadly preposterous implexion: 'his meaning struck her ere his words begun' (l. 462). Adonis' reductive arithmetic, which detracts via multiplication ('my love to love is love but to disgrace it' (l. 412)), poisons her generative cycles with callously ironic clusters of gemination: 'She's love, she loves, and yet she is not loved' (l. 610). These repetitions had been the reciprocating proof of

---

[120] David Abercromby, *Academia Scientiarum* (London, 1687), 4.

[121] Prime numbers are only divisible by themselves and one; they refuse to be divided by another: 'prime numbers, which also are called first numbers, and numbers vncomposed, have no part to measure them, but onely vnitie'. Euclid, *The Elements of Geometrie*, trans. Henry Billingsley (London, 1570), 186.

verbal kindness, of a fertile and productive language of love, but are now cruelly reinvested with the narcissine values that threaten Love's very identity:

> Poor queen of love, in thine own law forlorn,
> To love a cheek that smiles at thee in scorn. (ll. 251–2)

Shakespeare has borrowed Adonis' internally entwining dynamic from Ovid. A. D. Nuttall draws the comparison: 'Steal thine own freedom', Nuttall suggests, 'shows the young poet throwing off, in joyous rivalry, a Shakespearean answer to the Ovidian paradox *inopem me copia fecit* . . . , wealth made me poor [or "my riches beggar me"]', a paradox articulated at the moment of Narcissus' revelation in Golding's translation:

> It is myself I well perceyve, it is mine Image sure,
> That in this sort deluding me, this furie doth procure.
> I am inamored of my selfe, I doe both set on fire,
> And am the same that swelteth too, through impotent desire.
> What shall I doe? be woode or wo? whome shall I wo therefore?
> The thing I seeke is in my selfe, my plentie makes me poore.[122]

These self-defeating revolutions—these inverted cycles in which riches beggar themselves—characterize the Ovidian tale and as we have seen provide the model for Shakespeare's narcissistic dynamic: 'He is the partie whome he wooes, and suter that doth wooe, | He is the flame that settes on fire, and thing that burneth tooe'(ll. 535–6). The kindliness of words has become a dangerous property, reflection a constraint.[123]

Reworking this Ovidian motif in the first of his sonnet sequence, Shakespeare correlates this preposterous linguistic circumscription with the kindly reciprocation of extramission: 'But thou, contracted to thine own bright eyes, | Feed'st thy light's flame with self-substantial fuel, | Making a famine where abundance lies' (Son. 1, ll. 5–7). The extra-

---

[122] Golding, *Shakespeare's Ovid*, 582–7; A. D. Nuttall, 'Ovid's Narcissus and Shakespeare's Richard II: The Reflected Self', in Charles Martindale (ed.), *Ovid Renewed* (Cambridge, 1988), 137–50 at 139.
[123] Garth Tissol notes the etymological wordplay of Ovid's 'inopem me copia fecit' whereby the opposite states of riches (*copia*) and poverty (*inopia*) come from a kind derivation in *co-opia*: 'little more than the negative *in-* separated these terms in the first place'. *The Face of Nature: Wit, Narrative, and Cosmic Origins in Ovid's* Metamorphoses (Princeton, 1997), 13.

missive reciprocating flaming vision, taken to a negative extreme in the form of narcissistic self-to-self reflection, becomes an encompassing trap in which the youth is 'contracted'.

To this point, it seems that Shakespeare is comfortable with the simple association of Adonis' disdain with Narcissus' preposterous self-sufficiency. However, Adonis himself seems alert to the accusation; this dynamic, where the line turns back upon itself with the chronological inversion of the *hysteron proteron*, is one which Adonis himself is refuting in the recently quoted example: 'Who wears a garment shapeless and unfinished? | Who plucks the bud before one leaf put forth?' (ll. 415–16). Adonis is himself aware of the dangers of short-circuiting a natural progression, of partici- pating in this temporal cyclic reversal: 'Before I know myself, seek not to know me', he pleads, '[t]he mellow plum doth fall, the green sticks fast, | Or being early plucked, is sour to taste' (ll. 525, 527–8). Adonis is refusing to conform to the narcissistic prophecy. Tiresias' caution against self- knowledge is in fact heeded by Adonis, who acknowledges his youth and immature ripeness. Perhaps Shakespeare intends us to question the valid- ity of Venus' accusation; or perhaps we should understand that Venus, incapable of comprehending a world without kindness, imposes a model of extreme specular reciprocation on the unkind youth, glossing his introspection as merely a misguided compulsion towards loving response; or, I think most convincingly, Shakespeare's youth remains in that uniquely Ovidian moment of prerecognition.

Introducing stages in Narcissus' development into his rendition of the myth, Ovid provides Narcissus in triplicate: the proud youth; the besotted lover of another (unrecognized as himself); and the self-aware self-lover, alive to his error but committed to it. Shakespeare's Adonis, still a budding narcissist and hardly a capable spokesperson for nascent ipseitic sophistication, has not yet learnt to love, to self-scrutinize, to predicate his sense of self upon his self-cognizance: Adonis is not Descartes, he just *looks* like him.

4. WOE, WOE: ECHO'S COUNTERFEITING WAYS

The Platonic landscape is infused with responsive beauty: 'Venus trans- fers sparks of [her] splendour into the matter of the world' and 'because of the presence of these sparks, all of the bodies of the world seem

beautiful according to the receptivity of their nature'.[124] Adonis' unkindness (and here the sense of 'unkind' as 'unnatural' is paramount)
perverts Venus' description of generative cyclic repetition: 'Seeds spring
from seeds, and beauty breedeth beauty', she reasons, '[t]hou wast
begot, to get it is thy duty' (ll. 167–8). Like the youth of Shakespeare's
sonnet sequence, Adonis reneges upon the innate kindness of creation:

[God's] desire for propagating one's own perfection, which is innate in everything, explains the latent and implicit fecundity of everything, while it makes
seeds develop into an embryo, and draws out the powers of each thing from its
heart, and conceives offspring.... On this account all parts of the world,
because they are the works of one artist, parts of the same machine, and like
each other in being and life, are bound to each other by a certain reciprocal
love.[125]

We should understand Platonic optic emission (connotatively fertile
and engendering) as integral to this conception of naturally propagating
perfection; in rejecting the kindred fire, Adonis rejects the Neoplatonic
Weltanschauung of which Venus is ambassador and embodiment: deny
Venus; deny her world. So, 'things growing to themselves', she argues,
'are growth's abuse' (l. 166), but, as she later concedes, to 'grow unto
himself was [Adonis'] desire' (l. 1180).[126]

However, it is easy to see why Adonis is unresponsive to these
invocations of natural kindness. Considering depictions of his parent-
age, we come across similar 'natural' justifications for coupling: his
mother Myrha explains, in the words of H. A., that 'of one nature we
participate' and turns to 'the Kid, the Heifer, and the birds' to justify her
'natural' love.[127] Unfortunately, her advocation of generative kindness
seeks to justify a kindness too far; these animals, she claims, '[a]ffect [i.e.
desire] the same of whom they gotten be', and Myrha, the 'lustfull
Lady', is in love with her father, Cinyras:

[124] Ficino, *Commentary on Plato's* Symposium *on Love*, 54.
[125] Ibid., 67–8.
[126] Henry Reynolds, so disdainful of moralistic readings of myth, understands each
aspect of the tale as a piece of natural metonymy, concluding that the plants named
narcissi 'do powerfully extinguish the ability and desire of carnall copulation, by over-
cooling of the Animall seed' (*Mythomystes*, 107).
[127] H. A., *The Scourge of Venus; or, The Wanton Lady. With the Rare Birth of
Adonis* (London, 1613), sig. A6ᵛ; A5ᵛ.

> The cursed father then his bowels takes
> Into his bed, ô filthy blob and staine
>
> . . .
>
> And of his owne he doth his owne beget.[128]

'Yield[ing] . . . kindly in the night' to her father, the incestuous love of
Myrha for one she likes and is 'like' is too close to kin and much too
'kind'.[129] Consequently, Venus' fear that Adonis wishes to 'grow unto
himself' is astute: he is the child of self-begetting nature, and an
abomination of her fertile creed.

> Repugnant to the Law that nature set;
> May ones owne seed to procreation moue?
> No sure, vnlesse it doth a monster proue.[130]

Disastrously, the goddess of kindness has fallen for a monstrous perversion of her law; as R. A. Shoaf explains, incest is 'the ultimate degred-
ation of creation' as 'creation is differentiation'.[131] Shoaf, writing on the
incestuous birth of Milton's Sin, argues that 'incest is the ultimacy of
narcissism; . . . in incest, the self would produce itself without the alienation of *re*production'.[132] I would invert Shoaf's construction: narcissism (complete self-sufficiency) is the ultimacy of incest (still requiring
external response), but either of these two involutive urges adequately
undermines any confidence in the comforting kindness of nature and
desire. Adonis, outstripping even the incestuous love of his mother, is,
in (almost) every way, kind to himself.

Both Shakespeare and Ovid are alert to these discordant affinities
between kind likeness, which is to be promoted, and liking kindness,
which pushes us too far. Venus seems far less aware in the following
unpersuasive piece of courtship:

> O, had thy mother borne so hard a mind,
> She had not brought forth thee, but died unkind. (ll. 203–4)

---

[128] Ibid., sig. A5^V; A8^V; C2^r–3^r.

[129] Ibid., sig. B7^r; B1^r; B6^V.

[130] Ibid., sig. C3^r.

[131] R. A. Shoaf, *Milton: Poet of Duality. A Study of Semiosis in the Poetry and the Prose*
(London, 1985), 86.

[132] Ibid.

This is a tactless tactic. Adonis' mother certainly did not die 'unkind'— far from it: the kindness of which Venus unthinkingly approves has been Myrha's undoing. Ovid makes quite clear that Adonis' refusal of Love is an act of revenge, punishing the goddess for promoting the incestuous desire that engendered him; but Venus has no idea of Adonis' vendetta against her, and no sense that he is the pharmacal virus at the heart of her lovesickness (he is poisonous and remedial: simultaneously the nadir and epitome of her erotic model).[133] There is pathos in the realization that the narcissine progeny of an incestuous bed has adopted, adapted, and assaulted the motif of extraspective loving reciprocation simply by turning his gaze within, introjecting his kindness. Venus, representing kind love, finds herself attracted to impulses she would rather deny: she loves the narcissistic Adonis; who is born of the incestuous Myrha; who sleeps with Cinyras, son of that onanistic self-gratifying artist, Pygmalion (who is, like Narcissus, in love with his own image). J. Hillis Miller, tracing the genealogy of these kind kindred, reads Adonis as Venus' punishment for the animation of Pygmalion's Galatea that initiated this lineage of autoeroticists: 'the ancients told tales of how no wicked human deed was left unavenged', explains Natale Conti, 'for although God may defer vengeance for a while, it is only to exact it later on even more rigorously', concluding 'such is the moral of the Narcissus fable'.[134] It says much of L/love that it/she is attracted to these suppressed fantasies of self-eroticism. If anyone is the mother of Galatea it is Venus, who gives life to her; in this murky light, Venus seems very kind to Adonis.

It should be no surprise, therefore, that both the eagerly responsive Venus and the introspective Adonis exhibit aspects of narcissism and are significantly akin. But while both figures rely on kind response (from the crystalline humour of the beloved's eye, and the crystal surface of the pool respectively), we can clearly distinguish between these narcissine types. The extramissive speculator condemns introspection for locating its confirmation within, while the introspective contemplator scorns the extraspective viewer's search for its own reflection everywhere (Richard Lanham describes the 'glacial narcissism' and 'monstrous Platonic

---

[133] Golding, *Shakespeare's Ovid,* X. 521.
[134] J. Hillis Miller, *Versions of Pygmalion* (Cambridge, Mass., 1990), 10–11; Natale Conti, *Mythologies,* trans. Anthony DiMatteo (London, 1994), 388.

egotism' of this kind of vision).[135] There is no difference to the relational prerequisite of extramissive and introspective subjectivity: simply, one looks out, projecting; the other looks in, introjecting. The extramissive narcissist, who stares into his pool and craves response, loves being loved, and finds himself in the interaction; the intromissive narcissist, who will not share the glance, contemplates himself contemplating, and thinks himself into being. One contemplates, while the other contemplates; one speculates, while the other speculates; one considers, while the other considers (each of these words harbours connotative interplay of vision and thought). The meaningful distinction between these competing models, which are both specular and ipseic, is between extra- and intro-. Now we will see how a Lucretian demythologizing perspective will radically undermine a visual and ontological model that relies upon external reciprocation. In claiming that the world does not answer the gaze of the individual, Lucretius undermines the extramissive subject, and contradicts the pastoral echo. To deny the echo is a Narcissistic and Adonian tactic.

As we have seen, when Socrates associates the aural response of echo with the visual reply of the eyebeam, he initiates a rhapsodic description of an ultimately spiritual experience where the mutual participation in reflected beauty permits a glimpse of divine love and refracted perfection: the Platonic echo resonates.[136] Lucretius, starting from an identical description, hears an empty echo: '[Sounds] are flung at hard surfaces and bounce back, reflecting the sound and sometimes deluding us with the copy of a word.'[137] We are deluded by the echo, tricked by a mere auditory event into believing in a communicative world. We hear dialogue in mere repetition: this is the myth of Echo.[138] George Turberville's translation of an epigram by Ausonius captures the paradoxical potential of the nymph: 'I recite the latter word afreshe', she proudly announces, 'in mocking sort and counterfaiting wies'; but her

---

[135] Richard Lanham, *Motives of Eloquence: Literary Rhetoric in the Renaissance* (New Haven and London, 1976), 46–7.

[136] Plato, *Phaedrus*, 255 C1–D5.

[137] Lucretius, *De rerum natura IV*, ed. and trans. John Godwin (Warminster, 1992), ll. 570–2.

[138] See John Hollander, *The Figure of Echo: A Mode of Allusion in Milton and After* (Berkeley, 1981).

autonomy is circumscribed by her reception 'within your eares'.[139] Her agency is dependent upon our perception. The echo exists only in response to the speaker, and in the ears of the listener (she is in many ways like a word, existing in between mouth and ear, with her sense residing only in the intention of the speaker and the reception of the listener; this explains why gossips are described as babbling echoes, and why missive-carrying nurses, as we shall see, are bounced about like reverberations).

Consider the following example:

> ANTONIO. . . . you'll find it impossible
>   To fly your fate.
> ECHO.   *O, fly your fate!*
> DELIO. Hark! The dead stones seem to have pity on you
>   And give you good counsel.[140]

Platonism gives hope to an abandoned lover like John Webster's Antonio, who hears his dead wife's voice in the ruins of an ancient abbey, and the playwright teases both husband and audience alike with the dream of the echo's agency; if this *is* the Duchess, and if each response has *meaning*, we are not alone and there will be an echoing afterlife 'beyond death' (the play's final line, craving echoing applause).[141] But Lucretius confirms the malcontented Bosola for whom 'we are only like dead walls, or vaulted graves, | That, ruined, yields no echo'.[142] For both Bosola and Lucretius, the echo has no redemptive currency but simply resounds an atheistic emptiness; reading these demystifying explications of the echo, it is clear why Philip Hardie describes Lucretius as 'the great poet of the void':

When you see this clearly, you could explain to yourself and to others how in lonely regions rocks reflect the exact shapes of words in the correct sequence, when we are searching among the lightless mountains for our straying companions scattered afar, calling them at the top of our voices. Local people

---

[139] Ausonius, 'Epigram XXXII', in Turberville, *Epitaphs, Epigrams*, sig. O2ᵛ–3ʳ. See Joseph Lowenstein, *Responsive Readings: Versions of Echo in Pastoral, Epic, and the Jonsonian Masque* (New Haven, 1984).

[140] John Webster, *The Duchess of Malfi*, ed. John Russell Brown (Manchester, 1997), V. ɪᴠ. 34–7.

[141] Ibid., V. v. 121.

[142] Ibid., V. v. 97–8.

imagine that goat-footed satyrs and nymphs haunt these places, and say that
there are fawns, by whose night-roaming noise and playful pranks they commonly claim the speechless silences are broken as the sounds of stringed
instruments arise, and the sweet sad music which the pipe pours out when it
is struck by the players' fingers; farming folk, they say, become aware of Pan
from miles away, as he tosses the pine coverings of his half-bestial head.[143]

Lucretius provides his reader, in this case Ovid and Shakespeare at his
Ovidian remove, with a pragmatic pastoral landscape, resounding with
meaningless echoes and populated by credulous peasantry.

In the echoed hunting-call is an echo of the Narcissus myth:

> By chaunce the stripling being strayed from all his companie,
> Sayde: is there any bodie nigh? straight *Echo* answered: I.[144]

Ovid knows both Plato and Lucretius, sees the allure of the philosopher's meaningful echo and affirmative response, and yet knows how
the Epicurean poet he much admires would mock his myths; Hardie
describes how Ovid finds 'rich comedy in the Lucretian emptiness of the
misadventures of Narcissus and Echo, but also plays on the sophisti-
cated reader's nostalgia for a dream landscape where nature answers
human desires'.[145] By evoking Lucretius' dismissal of (E)cho's agency,
Ovid associates Narcissus' disdain for her responsive charms with
Lucretius' depiction of a deconsecrated nature, and provides a precursor
for Shakespeare's Adonis and his dismissal of Love; each figure of scorn
will deny Echo her voice. These stories become opportunities for
deriding the gullible and playing on their hope.

Consequently, pastoral is a genre that contains its own demystification; it is a genre that trades in nostalgia and therefore incorporates
awareness of its own outmoding. These pastoral, often Ovidian, land-
scapes are preposterously conscious of their own foundational obsolescence; this quiet admission is what instils their golden world fragility
with pathos and ephemeral idealism (these woods become increasingly
populated by holidaying city folk, who really do know better). When
Ovid incorporates Echo it is with full awareness of Lucretius' rebuttal,

---

[143] Philip Hardie, *Ovid's Poetics of Illusion* (Cambridge, 2002), 150; Lucretius,
De rerum natura IV, ed. Goswin, ll. 573–89.
[144] Golding, *Shakespeare's Ovid*, III. 473–4.
[145] Hardie, *Ovid's Poetics of Illusion*, 150.

and the poet must surely correlate her rejection with the demystification of a landscape that he, with ironic wit, repopulates with fictions of metamorphosis. The rejection of Echo is just part of his movement 'from the Worlds first fabrick to these times',[146] a narrative which is both driven by a sense of progressive futurity and lost origins (it is both allegoric prophecy and mythologized history).

As a residue of remote beginnings and lost origins (nostalgia meaning a return to home), and as a resounding of a finished sound, the echo is like a dream or spectral trace of faith; Lucretius, an atheist debunker of Platonic values, and an explicator of the science of (wet) dreams, is concerned with discovery of new meaning, not recovery of unempirical assumptions and distracting mythology. Pastoralists are well aware of Lucretian fact, as it legitimizes the idealistic faith in their Platonic fiction; just as the epyllion poets adopt the dead metaphor of the eyebeam, the pastoralist adopts Echo.[147] Her hollow sound resounds with meaning for the faithful; the very absence of empirical content permits emotive resonance, validates the ideals of pastoral nostalgia, and gives real pathos to the fallacy of response. Her presence offers affirmation to a world view in which nobody need ever feel alone; although 'I vnto my self alone will sing, | The woods shall to me answer and my Eccho ring.'[148] This Spenserian epistrophe echoes throughout his *Epithalamion*, and throughout pastoral poetics. Virgil's Tityrus, denied the response of the beloved and therefore craving substitute reciprocation, teaches the 'hollow woods, loud to proclaime, | And eccho, with the sound of *Amaryllis* name'; Corydon, in the second Eclogue, inhabits a world alive with responsive shared grief where '[t]he very shrubbs make mourne'.[149] Each lover finds 'answer' in a world of kindness that Shakespeare's Venus overtly aspires to and whose imagery she continually evokes:

> Is the ramme then to th'ewe an enimy,
> The bull to th'hayfer, is the turtle too,
> An enemy to his mate that loues him so?
> . . .

---

[146] *Ovids Metamorphosis*, trans. Sandys, 1.
[147] See Lowenstein, *Responsive Readings*, 5.
[148] Edmund Spenser, *Epithalamion*, in *Amoretti and Epithalamion*, sig. E4^r.
[149] Virgil, 'First Eclogue', in *Eclogues*, trans. W. L. Gent (London, 1628), 2; 28.

> And see'st thou not that e'ury thing that is,
> Breathes now a souereign ayre of loue, and sweetnesse,
> Pleasure, and health? behold that Turtle there
> With what a wooing murmur he sighes loue
> To his belou'de.[150]

This persuasive gesture towards a kind (hence 'natural') nature is mimicked by Venus' advocation of the horses' natural kindness—'O learn to love' (l. 407)—but forcibly repudiated by Lucretian cynical distaste:

> Stirred with the same impetuous desire,
> Birds, beasts, and herds, and mares, their males require;
> Because the throbbing nature in their veins
> Provokes them to assuage their kindly pains.
> The lusty leap the expecting female stands,
> By mutual heat compelled to mutual bands.
> Thus dogs with lolling tongues by love are tied,
> Nor shouting boys nor blows their union can divide.[151]

Where Venus sees a world of kindness, Lucretius sees dogs, copulating at street corners (this graphically reductive vision of nature's carnal appetite informs the tenor of Venus' depiction as a variety of rapacious animals).

The final movements of this poem chart a brutal devaluation of the echo's value. If we were to listen to Venus we would hear the 'clamorous cry' of hunting dogs resound as 'echo . . . replies, | As if another chase were in the skies' (ll. 693–6). We would see a personified world trip Adonis to rob him of a kiss (l. 723), and see flowers 'droop with grief and hang their head' (l. 666). But as he leaves, followed by the final 'dart' (l. 817) of her unreciprocated beams, Venus is left as lonely as the unanswered Echo:

> And now she beats her heart, whereat it groans,
> That all the neighbour caves, as seeming troubled,
> Make verbal repetition of her moans;
> Passion on passion deeply is redoubled:
>   'Ay me', she cries, and twenty times, 'Woe, woe',
>   And twenty echoes twenty times cry so. (ll. 829–34)

---

[150] Torquato Tasso, *Aminta English't*, trans. Henry Reynolds (London, 1628), sig. B4^r; B2^r.

[151] Lucretius, *De rerum natura IV*, ed. Godwin, ll. 193–200.

Echoing Echo, Venus articulates the despair of an isolated elegiac lover. Hardie suggests that 'Narcissus is the ultimate example of a solipsistic character trapped by delusive presences in a pastoral landscape', and the same could be said of Echo, whose identity depends upon what the world provides to give her responsive life: '[i]f Narcissus fails in his dream of a perfect pastoral amœbaic responsion, this is because he is trapped from the outset in an elegiac world', Hardie continues.[152] My only caveat is that the pastoral presupposes the elegiac, and that Echo equally feels how precarious that pastoral perfection may be. She is the grief counsellor of the pastoral landscape who redoubles 'passion on passion' and responds kindly to the isolated Venus when all other interaction has departed: 'Her heavy anthem still concludes in woe, | And still the choir of echoes answer so' (ll. 829–40). Echo offers external validation to an identity predicated upon response; to silence her, or to ignore her claims, is to assume her surplus to self-validating requirements (a narcissine and in many ways atheistic presumption).

The tone now changes to reveal Venus' self-delusion. Her demands for sympathetic response become 'tedious' and the poet acknowledges the self-serving quality of this self-indulgent grief; lovers, he explains, 'if pleased themselves, others they think delight' but their 'copious stories, oftentimes begun, | End without audience, and are never done' (ll. 841–51). Shakespeare is writing himself out of a world of response, emptying the natural auditorium. Is it with regret that Shakespeare cedes the following Lucretian reality?

> For who hath she to spend the night withal
> But idle sounds resembling parasites,
> Like shrill-tongued tapsters answering every call.
> . . .
> She says, ''Tis so', they answer all, ''Tis so',
> And would say after her if she said 'No'. (ll. 841–52)

We can choose between a parasitic echo, feeding with hostile intent upon the credulous host, or a Lucretian dead sonic reflection, bouncing back sounds we spoke. I feel Lucretian hostility here. It seems cruel to make Venus 'haste[n] to a *myrtle* grove' (l. 865, emphasis added), thereby reminding us of the vengeance narrative she is unwittingly

---

[152] Hardie, *Ovid's Poetics of Illusion*, 22.

victim of; it seems vindictive to offer us contrapuntal glimpses of hope
and despair as 'bushes . . . catch her by the neck, some kiss[ing] her face, I
Some twin[ing] about her thigh to make her stay' (ll. 871–3). Does
nature love her? try to kiss and embrace her? or is she just tangled in an
unresponsive bush?

   With 'the dismal cry' of Adonis' hounds 'ring[ing] sadly in her ears'
(l. 889), Venus' progression towards the gored and dying huntsman is
interrupted by a tableau of frustratingly indeterminate significance:
simply, she cannot decide if Adonis has been killed; more importantly,
she cannot read the auguries of nature. When an exhausted dog 'to
whom she speaks' merely 'replies with howling', it is unclear if he
provides a responsive pitiful echo, or is just kin to one of Lucretius'
dumb dogs, having a bark, making some noise:

> When he hath ceased his ill-resounding noise,
> Another flap-mouthed mourner, black and grim,
> Against the welkin volleys out his voice;
> Another, and another, answer him. (ll. 918–22)

The landscape erupts with echo. And while Venus, the eyes and ears
through which the reader sees and hears, prompts us to perceive a world
in 'mourn[ing]', Shakespeare's poetic voice offers his most Lucretian
caution of all:

> Look at how the world's poor people are amazed
> At apparitions, signs, and prodigies,
> Whereon with fearful eyes they long have gazed,
> Infusing them with dreadful prophecies. (ll. 925–8)

These may be the 'poor' (pitiable) people who crave meaning in the fall
of a sparrow, but Shakespeare sounds like Lucretius, denying augury,
and mocking the poor (poverty stricken) rustics who infuse the world
with unwarranted significance.

   Arriving at the corpse of Adonis, Venus' ontological and optical
certainties struggle to counter the death of response: 'Why hast thou
cast into eternal sleeping I Those eyes that taught all other eyes to see?'
(ll. 951–2), she demands. But this specular regime cannot survive the
death of the beloved. The 'solemn sympathy' of the grass, drinking
the spilt blood, is described as theft, and the poet is careful to ascribe
even this comparatively unsympathetic piece of pathetic fallacy to the

perception of 'poor Venus' (ll. 1055–7). Deprived of alterity, Venus resorts to the closed circuits of narcissine self-speculation—'O how her eyes and tears did lend and borrow, I Her eye seen in the tears, tears in her eye, I Both crystals, where they viewed each other's sorrow' (ll. 961–3)—as her generous extramission is superseded by an introverted ocular withdrawal:

> Which seen, her eyes, as murd'red with the view,
> Like stars ashamed of day, themselves withdrew;
> Or as the snail, whose tender horns being hit,
> Shrinks backward in his shelly cave with pain,
> . . .
> So at his bloody view her eyes are fled
> Into the deep-dark cabins of her head,
> Where they resign their office and their light
> To the disposing of her troubled brain. (ll. 1031–40)

Her eyesight has been murdered; the extramissive 'light' and the active eye 'resign their office' and cede responsibility to the 'troubled' interior.

As if to prove the vagaries of this new subjective perspective—presupposing the dead receptivity of the sensory eye but the activity of the internal senses (notice how 'sense' has to come to accommodate meanings of internal activity until 'good sense' is no longer the preserve of the senses)—Venus' disturbed interior state dictates the appearance of the world around her:

> Upon his hurt she looks so steadfastly
> That her sight dazzling makes the wound seem three,
> And then she reprehends her mangling eye
> That makes more gashes where no breach should be:
> His face seems twain, each several limb is doubled,
> For oft the eye mistakes, the brain being troubled. (ll. 1063–8)

Where pathetic fallacy had offered the hope of a responsive environment, the fallibility of the Keplerian eye actually permits the aggressive agency of the viewer, the unavoidable subjectivity of sight. We do not participate with a responsive object, or hope the world echoes our concerns; rather, we make the world within, projecting our vision with more force than the eyebeam could ever muster (this is the projection of an interior world onto the exterior that is facilitated by introjection and introspection). Any fallacy involved in this subjugation of the exterior has little pathos, but concerns the egotism essential to the privileging of private perception; Shakespeare and Venus acknowledge the regime of 'the gaze'. Attacking the body on which she had pinned her hopes of response, this subjective mangling eye distorts and ruptures, as her psychic troubles project diffracted doubles, enacting a violent parody of reciprocal participation.

This subjective projection and the concomitant superimposition of self is informed by a narcissistic fantasy of a self-circumscribed world; knowing that the received image is translated in the mental interior, we acknowledge the inaccessibility of objective truth and the unavoidability of subjective perception, abandoning any attempt to connect with the world. Simultaneously, the viewed object is approached only through a subjective lens, coloured by the viewer: 'the *representations* may be much varied according to the *nature* and *quality* of the *recipient*: . . . the same Object appears *red*, when we look at it through a Glass of *that* Colour, but *green* when we behold it through one of *such* a Tincture'.[153] Joseph Glanvill will call this 'deception' the '*translation of our own passions to the things without us*'.[154] Elsner correlates this mediated vision with the Narcissus myth, which raises 'the issue of how much viewing is in the beholder's eye—of how much the beholder imposes onto the autonomy of the viewed'.[155] The individual, behind the dead eye, is isolated (your sweet lips appear to move in speech, though to my ears your answer cannot reach . . .), withdrawn (why retreat beyond my reach? . . .), nonparticipational (I surely could touch him . . .), and therefore dominant (Oh, I am he!). It is myself I see, and now I know for sure that the image is my own: 'The image is handed over to the imagination, which can deal with it in complete detachment from the actual presence of the

---

[153] Joseph Glanvill, *Essays on Several Important Subjects in Philosophy and Religion* (London, 1676), 19.

[154] Ibid., 21. Like Montaigne, to whom he is often compared, Leonard de Marandé bases his scepticism on the subjective quality of vision: 'as much difference and distance, as there is betweene the thing, and the image and resemblance thereof: so much difference there is betweene the true reality of the thing, and that wee imagine wee know. . . . The more these figures or Images are borne to the common sense . . . the more they estrange themselves from the object which they represent, and consequently from his true being' (pp. 39–42). We are strangers in this world. Marandé, *The Judgment of Humane Actions*, trans. Reynolds.

[155] Elsner, *Roman Eyes*, 136.

original object. . . . In imagination the image can be varied at will.'[156]
The modern mode of perception, as described here by Hans Jonas, will
be welcomed by Iago (who plays upon the indeterminacy of ocular
proof and the power of the imagination), obsessed over by Leontes
(whose subjective vision overrules inaccessible empirical truths), and
regretted by Venus and all the epyllion lovers over whom she rules:[157]
'In seeing I am not yet engaged by the seen object. I may choose to enter
into intercourse with it, but it can appear without the fact of its
appearance already involving intercourse.'[158] Jonas's analysis of his
own seeing subjectivity would be anathema to the epyllion, where
engagement is immediate, and submission to the dynamics of reciprocation is fundamental to the entwine of eyebeam, bodies, and pronouns:
'He giues, she takes, and nothing is denide, | She his, he her loue's force
and valor tride.'[159] Weever, in his *Faunus and Melliflora*, offers a defiant
repost to Shakespeare's nostalgic regret, and refuses to cede as easily as
his precursor, fashioning increasingly convoluted pronoun combin-
ations to bind his lovers inextricably together until 'she from him, nor
he from hir could goe' (l. 308).

But Weever cannot deny the modern spectator:

Neither I nor the object has so far done anything to determine the mutual
situation. It lets me be as I let it be. . . . Neither invades the sphere of the other:
they let each other be what they are and as they are, and thus emerge the self-
contained object and the self-contained subject.[160]

---

[156] Hans Jonas, *The Phenomenon of Life: Toward a Philosophical Biography* (New York, 1966), 147.

[157] Jonas's conception of vision, while useful in its articulation of a position we may think of as the logical conclusion of introspective optic philosophy, does not represent contemporary opinion. Contemporary conceptions of vision, predicated upon the writing of Merleau-Ponty, Freud, and Lacan, have moved back towards participational vision, and an almost extramissive sense that the viewed object (a sardine can being the most familiar Lacanian example) acts back upon the viewer, subjecting the observer in its act of observation. It is this ahistorical proximity of Lacanian models of vision to Neoplatonic optics that would muddy the waters of my discussion, introducing com-parisons that would efface intrinsic historical difference through correlation of ideologi-cally unaligned conceptions. See Stephen Melville, 'Division of the Gaze, or, Remarks on the Color and Tenor of Contemporary "Theory"', in Brennan and Jay (eds.), *Vision in Context*, 101–16.

[158] Jonas, *The Phenomenon of Life*, 145.

[159] Weever, *Faunus and Melliflora*, ll. 1001–2.

[160] Jonas, *The Phenomenon of Life*, 145; 148.

The self-sufficiency of Jonas's subject is impossible in the nostalgic
poetic pastoral, where the 'force' of love '[i]s to transforme the verie
soule and essence I Of the louer, into the thing beloued', and where
identity is bestowed by interactivity; 'For mine or any other excellence, I
Were all imparted to me by your presence.'[161] Yet it is nostalgia, and
this natural respond is only available in recollection:

> When he beheld his shadow in the brook,
> The fishes spread on it their golden gills;
> When he was by, the birds such pleasure took
> That some would sing, some other in their bills
>   Would bring him mulberries and ripe-red cherries:
>   He fed them with his sight, they him with berries. (ll. 1099–104)

Here, Venus attempts to omit Narcissus, rewriting Adonis' moment of
self-speculation in her own kind terms; the lively fish animate the dull
dead image, offering sympathetic participation in the place of self-
absorption. The narcissist, feeding his own fire, has become a correspondent, feeding the world with his sight and receiving its sustenance.

But, as with all pastoral, the representation of the idyllic only presupposes its loss, and its displacement by an accurate but seemingly
unpoetic reality:

> I see without doing and without the object's doing anything. . . . It is the
> complete absence of such a dynamical situation, of any intrusion of causality
> into the relation, which distinguishes sight. I am not affected.[162]

'Shun not such kindnesse', Weever can retort: 'Give, or take, or both,
relent, be kind.'[163] Lining up the epyllion poets and their sympathetic
lovers to counter Jonas, we see how Thisbe kisses Pyramus' 'lips, I And
he from her, sweet *Nectar* drops out sips' in Dunstan Gale's contribution to the genre.[164] His lovers, unlike Jonas, clearly are affected:
'spying Thisbe, Thisbe made him start, I And he her blush, so tender
was her heart'.[165] The proximity of word and word may well carry the
taint of narcissine gemination, but the introspective reflective construc-

---

[161] Weever, *Faunus and Melliflora*, ll. 553–5; 901–2.
[162] Jonas, *The Phenomenon of Life*, 146.
[163] Weever, *Faunus and Melliflora*, ll. 493; 497.
[164] Dunstan Gale, *Pyramus and Thisbe* (London, 1617), sig. A4ʳ.
[165] Ibid., sig. A3ᵛ.

tion is simply picked apart by the actions of these lovers—'Her former kisses kisses gainde such plentie, I That she receiu'de for one kisse more than twentie'—so that the imitative increase of word on word redeems Narcissus' famished poverty or Adonis' miserly unresponsivity in re-sounding, redoubling increments of linguistic plenty.[166]

> [The object] is apprehended in its self-containment from out of my own self-containment, it is present to me without drawing me into its presence. . . . This complete neutralization of dynamic contact in the visual object, the expurgation of all traces of causal activity from its presentation, is one of the major accomplishments of what we call the image-function of sight.[167]

'Why [should you] desire to be alone?' the epyllion poet asks.[168] Or rather, why unkindly appropriate the rhetoric of indivisible individuality and forget that 'with their kisses' these extramissive lovers 'make two bodies one I And so their hearts with kisses liue alone'?[169] 'We are all one', Robert Chester asserts, and the all-oneness of the individuate identity knows no loneliness: '*Faunus* alone, with her alone required, I Alone with him, which she alone desired'.[170] In contrast, the narcissine Adonis 'takes value from himself alone' (l. 786) aspiring to the 'onto-logical pattern of subjectivity which vision has first created'.[171] 'Thus the mind has gone where vision pointed', Jonas continues; Adonis hears in the responsive world only a 'deceiving harmony' that he will not let 'run I Into the quiet closure of my breast' to disturb his heart that 'soundly sleeps while now it sleeps alone' (ll. 781–5).[172] Having facilitated this 'fateful freedom', the subjective, objectifying gaze will 'eventually turn back, with the burden of mediacy, upon the subject itself and make *it* in turn the object', revealing, as I have described, 'the new dimension of reflection . . . where the subject of all objectification appears *as such* to itself', becoming 'objectified for a new and ever more self-mediating kind

---

[166] Weever, *Faunus and Melliflora*, ll. 797–8.
[167] Jonas, *The Phenomenon of Life*, 146–7.
[168] Beaumont, *Salmacis and Hermaphroditus*, sig. C4^r.
[169] Weever, *Faunus and Melliflora*, ll. 827–8.
[170] Robert Chester, *Loves Martyr; or, Rosalins Complaint*, ed. Alexander B. Grosart (London, 1878), sig. S^v; Weever, *Faunus and Melliflora*, ll. 989–90.
[171] Jonas, *The Phenomenon of Life*, 149.
[172] Ibid., 152.

of relation'.[173] Jonas's conception of vision is no longer current, but the tenor of description not only catches the interplay of gain and loss that is so pertinent to the early modern debate, but also resonates with self-conscious concern about the proximity of what he describes to narcissistic involution:

> In reflection upon self the subject-object split . . . reaches its extreme form. It has extended into the center of feeling life, which is now divided against itself. Only over the immeasurable distance of being his own object can man 'have' himself. . . . The enjoyment of selfness in the meeting with otherness, has here by a daring detour found its true and, in a way, original object.
> . . .
> The loss: . . . No force-experience, no character of impulse and transitive causality enters into the nature of the image, and thus any edifice of concepts built on that evidence alone must show the gap in the interconnection of objects.[174]

Jonas is delineating the dislocation that Steven Connor describes as the characteristic of modern vision when he argues that 'the control which modernity exercises over nature depends upon that experience of the world as separate from myself'.[175] That gap is the distance in which subjectivity is enabled, locating 'self-definition in the act of separation, which vision seems to promote'.[176]

This gap, created by the isolation of subject from object, is made manifest in the *paraclausithyron* (an obstruction, typically a door, that divides two lovers).[177] Jonas explains that 'the object, staying in its bounds, faces the subject across the gap' that optic division has opened up; Pyramus, obstructed by the wall, is divided from Thisbe, and Leander, on one side of the Hellespont, can only stare across the watery gap at Hero's tower.[178] The epyllion tradition attempts to retangle the threads of eyebeam, reconnect a divided vision, to cross the gap, un-divide the indivisible individual, swim the Hellespont:

---

[173] Ibid., 185.

[174] Ibid., 186; 147.

[175] Stephen Connor, 'The Modern Auditory I', in Porter (ed.), *Rewriting the Self*, 203–23 at 204.

[176] Ibid., 204.

[177] Hardie (*Ovid's Poetics of Allusion*, 144–5) and Don Fowler discuss the *paraclau-sithyron* in relation to language, describing the word as obstruction to presence. Don Fowler, *Roman Constructions: Readings in Postmodern Latin* (Oxford, 2000), 157.

[178] Jonas, *The Phenomenon of Life*, 148.

> Off went his silken robe, and in he leapt;
> Whom the kinde waues so licorously cleapt,
> Thickning for haste one in another so,
> To kisse his skin, that he might almost go
> To *Heros* Towre, had that kind minuit lasted.[179]

The 'kind minute' has not lasted, and 'we consciously stand back and create distance in order to look at the world'.[180] In the new optic regime the *paraclausithyron* cannot be breached, the Hellespont cannot be swum as the kindness of the world becomes self-destructive effacement:

> And forth they brake, the Seas mixt with the skie,
> And tost distrest *Leander*, being in hell,
> As high as heauen; Bliss not in height doth dwell.
> The Destinies sate dancing on the waues,
> To see the glorious windes with mutuall braues
> Consume each other.[181]

Charged with matching the set-piece bravura of Leander's first attempt at the Hellespont after Marlowe's unkind premature death, Chapman replays what was for Marlowe the language of loving consummation and shows its perils. The 'mutual rays'[182] of lovers become the 'mutual braves' of the battling winds, and although the waves' kisses initially, and for a 'kind minute', aid Leander, it is eventually precisely the kindness of the waves that 'so licorously cleapt' to him in erotic tenderness that causes his drowning. Kindness and mutuality become, in the meeting of wave with wave and wind with wind, a destructive impulse, too kind. The logic of loving addition, when taken to its furthest extreme, threatens a violent mixture, a loss of definition, here between sea and sky, heaven and hell. The dependence, one upon the other, of lover to lover, is revealed to have life-threatening potential; the separate identity is defeated as these winds

---

[179] Chapman, *Hero*, VI. 187–91.
[180] Jonas, *The Phenomenon of Life*, 150.
[181] Chapman, *Hero*, VI. 196–201.
[182] 'So cast these virgins beauties mutuall raies, I One lights another, face the face displaies; I Lips by reflexion kist, and hands hands shooke, I Euen by the whitenes each of other tooke.' Marlowe, *Hero*, V. 211–14.

with mutual braves consume each other. Preferable, Jonas would suggest, that 'the self becomes engulfed in the distinctness in which all things are kept by man'.[183]

Venus is 'striv[ing] against the stream' (l. 772) of visual science. There is nothing that she has proven 'that [Adonis] cannot reprove' (l. 787) with his introspective model of love. Her generosity is now foreign to him; he 'does not hate love but your device in love, | That lends embracements unto every stranger' (ll. 789–90). But Shakespeare, as Nordlund maintains, was 'more committed to a nostalgic (though disillusioned) view of the traditional assumptions of speculative participation, mirroring, and likeness', so Venus, like Shakespeare, as the kind and poetic theories of extramission are rejected, is left in a world which disappoints her need to find reciprocation; it is a 'wonder of [their] time' '[t]hat thou being dead the day should yet be light' (ll. 1133–4).[184] His eyes, the glasses in which 'herself herself beheld / A thousand times, . . . now no more reflect' (ll. 1129–30). Shakespeare, in a world of intromissive science, of anatomy and *camera obscura*, and Venus, in a 'poor world' without the answering fiery beams of love, are both nostalgic for their extramissive ideals, both ultimately admitting that these 'true [and] beaut[iful]' ideas have 'lived and died':

> 'Alas, poor world, what treasure hast thou lost?
> What face remains alive that's worth the viewing?
> Whose tongue is music now? What canst thou boast
> Of things long since, or anything ensuing?
>   The flowers are sweet, their colours fresh and trim,
>   But true sweet beauty lived and died with him.'
> . . .
> [Venus], mounted, through the empty skies,
> In her light chariot quickly is conveyed,
>   Holding their course to Paphos, where their queen
>   Means to immure herself, and not be seen. (ll. 1075–80; 1191–4)

[183] Jonas, *The Phenomenon of Life*, 185.
[184] Nordlund, *The Dark Lantern*, 184.

As the poem's final image, Venus' retreat from sight could not be more apt or more poignant. But the specular subject who has displaced her has only borrowed her rhetorical and ipseic strategies and will himself find himself under threat from himself, as my study continues.

It is in the gulf opened by this confrontation of oneself with oneself, and in the exercise of the relation which in some way or other has to span the gulf, that the highest elations and deepest dejections of human experience hold their place.

. . .

Suicide, this unique privilege of man, shows the ultimate manner in which man can become the object of himself.[185]

[185] Jonas, *The Phenomenon of Life*, 187; 186–7.

3

Narcissism to Suicide:
Romeo and Juliet

Let me alone, me alone lament and mourne my beloued.[1]

Me alone, me alone. Deprived of the response of the beloved, Amintas
seeks sympathy elsewhere; just as Shakespeare's Venus was left dependent upon increasingly introspective reflections as she 'herself herself'
beheld, Thomas Watson's Amintas is forced to find reciprocation alone.
He sits, his 'eyes cast down upon the waters', and finds comfort in the
narcissine self-absorption of lament.[2] Again, we see how the concentrated involutions of narcissistic self-relation supply substitute sympathy
in an unkind environment. The geminative rhetorical structures integral
to a dynamic of amatory response—where lovers locked eyes to eyes and
themselves themselves reflected—are, in the elegiac world of lost lovers,
resounded in introspective grief. Abraham Fraunce's translation of
Watson's Latin verse resonates with the echo of 'resound', 'rebound',
and 'repeat', as the formerly indivisible lover, now left in divided
isolation, searches for the dialectic response that would affirm his fragile
and unsubjected identity (subjectivity requiring subjection; to be alone
is to be nothing).[3]

Echo, echo. But the gratifications of grief ultimately prove as hollow
as an echo: 'O what meane you gods, to prolong this life of *Amintas*? I ô
what meane you gods, with an hollow sound he repeated.'[4] 'Adding

---

[1] [Thomas Watson], *The Lamentations of Amintas for the Death of Phillis*, trans.
Abraham Fraunce (London, 1588), sig. A3^r.
[2] Ibid., sig. B^v.   [3] Ibid., sigs. A^r; A^r; E1^v.   [4] Ibid., sig. E1^v.

teares to [his] teares, and sorrows vnto [his] sorrows', Amintas' lament is an empty surrogate, turning a verbal plenty into an ipseic poverty: these are the elegiac echoes at the heart of the pastoral nostalgic idyll where reliance on response corresponds with a commitment to lost ideals and a failure to move with the intromissive times. The death of the beloved betrays the futility in an increasingly untenable allegiance to extrinsic validation. The pastoral predisposition to pathetic fallacy and the concomitant predication of identity upon response is revealed as empty egotism, deserving correlation with the narcissist who, like the grieving Amintas, '[b]ears this fire in his hart, and stil [his] fire is a feeding':[5]

> *Phillis* thy sweet banks and beds did water at eu'ning,
> *Phillis* amidst thy flowres alwaies was wont to be walking.[6]

The pastoral exists in the past tense, recalling (like an echo) a bygone world of bucolic sympathy.

> But now no walking, but now no water at eu'ning,
> Now best flowre is dead, now *Phillis* gone fro the garden.[7]

Now, now we are insistently in the present, reflecting on a lost world governed by what felt like innocent responsivity but which, through fallen eyes, we now, now see as narcissistic self-involvement:

> And you Christal springs with streames of siluer abounding,
> Where faire *Phillis* saw faire *Phillis* face to be shyning,
> Powre forth fluds of teares from those your watery fountains,
> From those your fountains with greene mos al to be smeared:
> *Phillis* wil no more see *Phillis* sitt by the fountains,
> *Phillis* wil no more her lips apply to the fountains,
> Lips to be ioin'd to the lips of *Ioue* that ruleth *Olympus*.[8]

This narcissistic tableau is a relic, smeared in moss, of an inaccessible ideal (further undermined by the recollection that Phillis died from a broken heart, having been used and then refused by Amintas). The culpable Amintas does not deserve the sympathy of the natural world,

---

[5] Ibid., sig. D2ᵛ: recalls Golding, *Shakespeare's Ovid*, III. 584–5.
[6] Ibid., sig. C3ʳ.   [7] Ibid.   [8] Ibid.

which refuses to allow him the self-reflection he desires: 'If that I come
to the banks and cast mine eyes to the waters. . . . Then these foule
mouth'd frogs with iarring tunes do molest me.'[9] Narcissine harmony
is jarred, and the echoes that 'reboundeth' his lament—'*Phillis, Phillis*—
signal only loss: 'com[ing] back with an echo, | Eccho returns *Phillis* fiue
times fro the rocks, fro the mountains'.[10]

Death, death. All that could redeem this unresponsive, unloving
world would be to find some form of reciprocation that would
reinvolve the unsympathetic Amintas. He finds this reflexive potential in suicide.

> What shal I do, shal I dye? shal *Amintas* murder *Amintas?*
> . . .
> Must then *Amintas* thus but a stripling murder *Amintas?*
> . . .
> Dye then *Amintas*, dye, let *Amintas* murther *Amintas.*[11]

His 'delight is death; death only desireth *Amintas*', and he looks to
reinstate himself via the reflexive action of self-slaughter into the network
of response that his desiring-therefore-narcissistic nature requires.[12]
Desire, as I evidenced by Jeremy Collier's assertion that '[d]esire is a
conscious Emptines, an unsatisfied Capacity', is predicated on a lack in
the subject that demands completion via the pragmatic incorporation of
a necessary object (the beloved): 'It implies Want in the very Notion,
and supposes the Absence of the Thing desired.'[13]

Myselfe myselfe. As my study makes a transition from the involuted
gaze of the narcissist to the involuted response of the self-slaughterer, we
see how both of these geminative self-subjects respond to the loss of
external validation (the loss of extramissive reassurance: the loss of the
sympathetic beloved) with a reflexive retraction towards self-owned
action. But before arriving at Stoic self-murderers and their claims for

⁹ [Watson], *The Lamentations*, sig. D2ᵛ: recalls Golding, *Shakespeare's Ovid*,
III. 584–5.
    ¹⁰ Ibid.
    ¹¹ Ibid., sigs. B1ᵛ; E1ʳ; D2ʳ.
    ¹² Ibid., sig. D4ʳ.
    ¹³ Jeremy Collier, *Miscellanies Upon Moral Subjects* (London, 1695), 41. See
Catherine Belsey, *Desire: Love Stories in Western Culture* (Oxford, 1994), 38–9.

self-sufficiency, we should consider the sympathetic suicide, the loving response, the suicide of a lover like Amintas who hopes to 'bring me my selfe to my selfe, and bring me to *Phillis*'.[14] Suicide becomes part of what Donne describes as the loving 'dialogue of one', punctuating their sympathetic union with a death that 'sustain[s] this myth of symmetry and synchronicity'.[15] In Shakespeare's *Romeo and Juliet* we see a couple comparable to Watson's death-marked lovers, who find companionable comfort in the reciprocation of suicide:

> One loue, one liking, one sence, one soule for a great while,
> Therefore one deaths wound, one graue, one funeral onelie
> Should . . . ioyn . . . in one both loue and louer.[16]

1. SYMPATHETIC RESPONSE

> Every being seized by an enormous passion, be it joy or grief, or fear sunk to despair, loses the character of its own individual expression, and is absorbed by the power of the feature that attracts it. Niobe . . . Clytia, Biblis, Salmacis, Narcissus, tell only the resistless power of sympathetic attraction.[17]

Echo, whose individual expression is effaced by the demands of sympathetic reciprocation, exemplifies the compulsive responsiveness that Henry Fuseli identified in Ovid. This irresistible power of sympathetic attraction is integral to Shakespeare's conception of tragic desire. In *Romeo and Juliet*, the proliferation of rhetorical and textual echoes, or 'woeful symmetr[ies]' (III. III. 84), attests to what Heather Dubrow describes as the play's 'compulsion to repeat', where a word ('civil blood') calls up its repetition—'civil hands' (Prologue, 4); where each repetition incites further response—'say "better"' (I. I. 50); or where

---

[14] Watson, *The Lamentations*, sig. D4ᵛ.

[15] John Donne, 'The Ecstasy', in *The Complete English Poems*, ed. Smith, l. 74; Robert N. Watson, *The Rest is Silence: Death as Annihilation in the English Renaissance* (Berkeley, 1994), 183.

[16] Watson, *The Lamentations*, sig. C4ʳ.

[17] Henry Fuseli, *Lectures on Painting: Delivered at the Royal Academy* (London, 1830), 65.

every image provokes its oxymoronic counter.[18] This verbal friction, sparking either erotic heat or violent combustion, initiates a seemingly irresistible and inescapable escalation of loving and violent retortion. Robert O. Evans identifies how 'Shakespeare does not let up on us' with his 'rhetorical display [of oxymoron which is] a bit too prominent to be sheer fireworks', but he need not have limited his remarks to oxymoron; it is Shakespeare's extensive display of the rhetorical devices of chiastic reciprocation, *geminatio,* pun, oxymoron, ploce, that 'does not let up'.[19] Harry Levin identifies 'well over a hundred such lines'.[20] In *Romeo and Juliet,* there is something woeful in symmetry and something inexorable in its propagation.

Brief consideration of Shakespeare's comedic Echo can contextualize the compulsive reiterations of this tragedy, as comedy too is driven by the demands of sympathetic attraction. Shakespearean comedies—whose '[j]ourneys end in lovers meeting' (*TN,* II. III. 37)—work towards the exchange of love and, synonymously, the successful reciprocation of a trustworthy word (with some form of 'I love you', an 'I do', or an 'I am' as their performative culmination). The semiotic union of word with confirmatory deed—or signifier with referent—is actualized in the coming together of lover and lover, typically making good on the exchange of dangerously insubstantial words with a reliably tangible kiss. Comedy asserts the responsibility of response and therefore 're-' is *the* comedy prefix: the 'recompense' (I. v. 240) of love for love must be 'returned' (II. II. 12) from lover to lover, 're[-]member[ing]' (II. IV. 14) and 're[-]collect[ing]' (l. 5) that which had been divided. Between lover and lover, word and referent, there exists an interim that comedy must bridge.

In *Twelfth Night,* with two twins and two singletons in separate spaces, the play's action demands the crossing and recrossing of a divide. In this structurally responsive play, each character is impelled by the

---

[18] Heather Dubrow, *Echoes of Desire: English Petrarchism and its Counterdiscourses* (Ithaca, NY, 1995), 264. E. Pearlman's analysis of quarto texts demonstrates that Shakespeare's revisions of the play emphasize figures of oxymoron and reflection: '[t]he intricate rhetorical patterning that is the hallmark of *Romeo and Juliet* was not effortlessly achieved'. E. Pearlman, 'Shakespeare at Work', *ELR,* 24 (1994), 315–42 at 321.

[19] Robert O. Evans, *The Osier Cage: Rhetorical Devices in* Romeo and Juliet (Lexington, Ky., 1966), 21.

[20] Harry Levin, 'Form and Formality in *Romeo and Juliet',* in John F. Andrews (ed.), Romeo and Juliet: *Critical Essays* (London, 1993), 41–53 at 48.

responsibility to reply: letters are words in physical form and are sent in-between; rings are exchanged as voluble declarations; coins act as material words or symbols of exchange that function as manifest interaction comparable to that of Pandarus, the infamous bawd who likewise embodies the interim, corporealizing the space of exchange between divided lovers (III. I. 43–4); and martial blows are offered and 'answer[ed]' (III. II. 47) like verbal interaction physicalized in 'give... [and] take' (III. IV. 204).[21] Most importantly, Viola/Cesario embodies the exchanged word, acting as love letter in human form, sent to and fro; repeating the words of another and bouncing back and forth across the interim, she is the echoing word, speaking only on another's behalf (III. I. 91):

> [I would h]allow your name to the reverberate hills,
> And make the babbling gossip of the air
> Cry out 'Olivia!' O you should not rest
> Between the elements of air and earth
> But you should pity me! (I. v. 227–31)

Viola's task, as echo, is to break the narcissine introspection of the unpitying Olivia, who is currently at 'rest' in-between solid and immaterial elements, therefore momentarily caught in water like Ophelia, who bent too close to the brook, paused in this transitional element as was Narcissus' image.

It is fitting that Olivia hovers in-between as Narcissus and Echo are both inhabitants of the liminal space, caught on the surface of the pool or trapped in the air between things. If Olivia figures as the unresponsive Narcissus, Orsino is her desperate narcissine counterpart, full of self-gratifying desire in the second stage of Narcissus' Ovidian development. It is crucial not only that Viola breaks up these dangerously self-speculating dynamics, but also that she breaks out of her own place in the interim, learning not just to ventriloquize but to speak, not just to fill others' words with the merest trace of her own agency but to make them her own. If she stays caught somewhere between the houses, between genders, 'between boy and man', she will remain caught 'in standing water' (l. 132), a mere reflection of the two narcissists who speak through her (Orlando, the early Narcissus) or see

---

[21] This is also to 'catechise' (I. v. 51), the Renaissance catechism typically taking the form of call and response, question and answer. Iago, locking Othello into responsive reliance, utilizes catechistic tactics (see *Oth.*, III. IV. 13).

themselves in her (Olivia, the later). As an echo, or as Narcissus' reflection, she must admit that 'I am not what I am' (III. i. 126) but she has not learnt the potential power of being an echoing word—'by heaven, he echoes me' (*Oth.*, III. iii. 107)—which will be realized only by Iago, who knows well that to embody the word is to command its deceptive manipulative power and therefore asserts as his triumph, 'I am not what I am' (I. i. 66). '[S]ick of self-love' (*TN*, I. v. 73), Malvolio may remain stuck in his own 'singularity' (II. v. 125), 'practising behaviour to his own shadow' (ll. 14–15), but Viola has to convert introspection into reciprocation, turning 'one face, one voice, one habit, [into] two persons' (V. i. 200). 'How have you made division of yourself?' (l. 206): in a tragedy, such self-division will entail suicide, but here we are let off the narcissine hook by a mirror-image twin (III. iv. 33–5) who revitalizes the reflected image and turns it to responsive life (the image made flesh in positive Pygmalionism). The 'solemn combination' (V. i. 360) of lovers is sealed by performative verbal and physical 'contract' in the 'mutual joinder of . . . hands', the 'holy close of lips', the 'interchangement of . . . rings', and 'sealed . . . by . . . testimony' (ll. 145–50): lovers contract together; semiotic division heals, and 'each circumstance, | Of place, time, fortune, do cohere and jump' to permit that characteristic redemptive utterance of unified identity, 'I am Viola' (ll. 235–7). Now 'that's all one, our play is done' (l. 386).

From the outset of *Romeo and Juliet*, we are conscious that the play is equally concerned with a divided single state, which needs, perhaps via the pull of sympathetic attraction, to be made individuate and indivisible. Consider the prologue, here divided into its constituent parts. First, William Painter's translation of Pierre Boaistuau's French version of Matteo Bandello's original of 1554:

there were *two families* in the Citie, of farre greater fame than the rest, *aswell* for riches as Nobilitie: . . . but *like* as most commonly there is discord amongs them which be of *semblable* degrée in honor, euen so there hapned a certaine enimitie between *them.*[22]

Secondly, Arthur Brooke's 1562 freer verse translation:

[22] William Painter, *Rhomeo and Julietta*, in *The Second Tome of the Palace of Pleasure* (London, 1567), 218–47 at 219–20, emphasis added.

There were *two auncient stockes*, which Fortune high dyd place
Above the rest, indewd with welth, and nobler of *their* race,
Loued of the common sort, loued of the prince *alike*,
And *like* vnhappy were they *both*, when Fortune list to strike;
Whose prayse, with *equall* blast, Fame in her trumpet blew;
The one was cliped Capelet, and thother Montagew.[23]

Finally, Shakespeare's rendition:

Two households, both alike in dignity,
In fair Verona (where we lay our scene),
From ancient grudge break to new mutiny,
Where civil blood makes civil hands unclean.
From forth the fatal loins of these *two foes*
A *pair* of star-crossed lovers take their life. (Prologue 1–6, emphasis added)

Shakespeare inherits the vocabulary of comparison, then compresses his rhetorical structure. Taking his predecessors' emphasis on relational likeness, Shakespeare concentrates expression until the pressure of tight verbal comparison activates the antagonism inherent in comparability: Bandello's suggestion that 'there is discord' in resemblance is economically captured in Shakespearean fractious linguistic friction. 'Equality of two domestic powers' breeds 'scrupulous faction' (*Ant.*, I. III. 47–8), and Shakespeare pushes this adopted reciprocal scheme to new extremes in 'both alike', and forces discord to 'break' out 'from forth' the constrictions of a 'crossed' system of duality and repetition. Repetition is aggression; civil citizens are made uncivilized in civil war. Shakespeare's compression is such that the several meanings of an individual word—'civil'—divide and suicidally self-antagonize. Repetition delineates a constraint out of which squeeze propulsive fricatives, in a passage that binds the star-crossed lovers even into temporal constraints: ancient grudge to present scene to new mutiny. Into a tight interim their complete spans are incorporated, caught from birth to death within a phrase—'take their life'—that connotes both their conception and suicide.[24]

---

[23] Arthur Brooke, *The Tragicall Historye of Romeus and Iuliet* (London, 1562), sig. A1ᵛ, emphasis added.
[24] See Lloyd Davis, ' "Death-Marked Love": Desire and Presence in *Romeo and Juliet*', *SS*, 49 (1996), 57–67.

These tactics are learnt from source:

> As of a little spark oft ryseth mighty fyre,
> So of a kyndled sparke of grudge, in flames flashe out theyr yre.
> And then theyr deadly foode, first hatchd of trifling stryfe:
> Did bathe in bloud of smarting woundes, it reued breth and lyfe.
> ...
> [The Prince hoped] that when he had the wasting flame supprest,
> In time he should quyte quench the sparks that boornd within their brest.
> Now ... these kyndreds do remayn in this estate,
> And eche with outward frendly shew dooth hyde his inward hate.[25]

The opposing factions, 'these kyndreds', are like lovers with their own deadly version of the erotic kindred fire in the 'kyndled sparke of grudge' and the flashing flames of ire enacted in the fire of fricative friction and alliterative antagonism. Within the idiom of erotic extramission, likeness and kindness, Brooke fuses the opposed kindred, adapting a tradition of mutuality and revealing the tension it can potentially engender: 'The woords that Tybalt vsd to styrre his folke to yre, | Haue, in the brestes of Montegews, kindled a furious fyre.'[26] In the world of *Romeus and Iuliet*, linguistic repetitions and reflections signify both the bonds of love and the binds of a repressive social environment internally divided by civil war. Accordingly, Jonathan Sawday describes civil war as 'a nation caught up in a kind of mass suicide, intent on self-destruction'.[27] All these kind words make kindness too kind, kindling kindred unkindness:

> Thus foote by foote long while, and shield to shield set fast:
> One foe doth make another faynt but makes him not agast.[28]

So close to the lips-on-lips, hand-in-hand patterns of erotic exchange, the foot-by-foot and shield-to-shield figures provide a key linguistic model for Brooke, utilized repeatedly to signal a latent similitude between martial and erotic encounters, a suppressed violence within desire.

---

[25] Brooke, *The Tragicall Historye*, sig. A2^r.

[26] Ibid., sig. D4^r.

[27] Jonathan Sawday, ' "Mysteriously Divided": Civil War, Madness, and the Divided Self', in Thomas Healy and Jonathan Sawday (eds.), *Literature and the English Civil War* (Cambridge, 1990), 127–43 at 127.

[28] Brooke, *The Tragicall Historye*, sig. D4^v.

'And if civil intestine wars are worse then forreign', as texts of the 1640s insist, 'then the most dangerous of all is that which we make to our selves.'[29] Similarly, Shakespeare's Histories dictate that the 'intestine shock . . . of civil butchery' (*1H4*, I. i. 12–13) and the self-defeating act of warfare are inextricably linked to the intrasubjective division of self-doubt or madness: 'in thyself rebellion to thyself' (*Jn.*, III. i. 289). Furthermore, these environments dictate inevitable suicidal conclusions (see Constance's powerful suicide oration, graphic and visceral, in Act III of *King John*). Juliet's macabre 'O happy dagger . . . This is thy sheath' (*Rom.*, V. iii. 170) will be recalled when the weary Henry IV compares civil war to 'an ill-sheathèd knife [that] cut[s] his master' (*1H4*, I. i. 17–18). Shakespeare has already associated the patterns of ploce with suicidal civil war, describing in *Richard III* how 'themselves, the conquerors, | Make war upon themselves, brother to brother, | Blood to blood, self against self. O preposterous | And frantic outrage' (II. iv. 61–4). Again, we see how Shakespeare understands rhetorical reflection as a kind of preposterous involution or as a mimetic structure which fashions a moment of lexical revenge. 'Here have we war for war and blood for blood, | Controlment for control' (I. i. 19–20), he writes in *King John* (perhaps contemporaneous with *Romeo and Juliet*). The clash of 'alike' powers here is not one of civil conflict—although the play frequently announces the self-contradiction inherent in oath-breaking to be 'like a civil war' which 'sett'st oath to oath, | Thy tongue against thy tongue' (III. i. 263–5)—but the alliterative and reiterative rhetoric is again indicative of the compulsive repercussions of military response: 'Blood hath bought blood, and blows have answered blows; | Strength matched with strength, and power confronted power' (II. i. 329–31). The inexorable drive towards a climax captures the escalation of self-perpetuating and self-destructive violence: no wonder that Puttenham calls climax the 'marching figure', as the combatants are pulled 'face to face and bloody point to point' (l. 390).[30] These rhetorical repetitions, Shakespeare prompts us to realize, are echoes that bind these plays to the violent logic of reiterative 'reverberat[ing]' response:

[29] Various, *A General Collection of Discourses*, trans. G. Havers (London, 1664), 520.
[30] Puttenham, *The Arte of English Poesie*, 217.

start
An echo with the clamour of thy drum.

. . .

Sound but another, and another shall,
As loud as thine, rattle the welkin's ear. (*King John*, V. ii. 167–72)

2. BANDYING BLOWS

[Echo is] a *Tossing* of the *Voice*, as a Ball, to and fro; Like to *Reflexions* in *Looking-glasses.*[31]

'A *Reflexion Iterant*, which we call *Eccho*' is thought to 'bandy' back and forth, rebounding like the to and fro of a tennis ball.[32] Shakespeare uses the image to denote the kind of reciprocation enacted by the coming and going of Viola, the repeated voyages of Pericles across the intervening ocean (*Per.*, II. i. 60), or the witty flyting of 'mock for mock' (V. ii. 140) in the courtship of *Love's Labour's Lost*: 'Well bandied both, a set of wit well played' (l. 29). This is how Shakespeare makes 'comedy a sport' (l. 858); literally, comedy is tennis. Throughout his canon, Shakespeare uses 'bandy' in association with varieties of ploce, denoting the ability of one speaker to reply in kind and match her witty opponent: 'To bandy word for word and frown for frown' (*Shr.*, V. ii. 173). But even within a comedy, Shakespeare signals the thin line between erotic and martial engagement. So in the comic 'sport' (II. iii. 134) of *Much Ado*, Beatrice 'speaks poniards, and every word stabs' (II. i. 187) as the lovers retort like 'tennis balls' (III. ii. 35). The metaphor loses its humour, most notably when Henry V turns the Dauphin's mocking gift of tennis balls to gun-stones, bandying back with added violence on the 'courts of France' (see *H5*, I. ii. 258–96).[33] To bandy may be to exchange the eyebeam (see *Lr.*, I. iv. 72; II. iv. 168) or trade blows; 'in bastinado, or in steel! I will bandy with thee . . . I will kill thee a hundred and

[31] Bacon, *Sylva sylvarum*, 67.

[32] Ibid., 65; *OED*, s.v. 'Bandy', v. I.1.

[33] John Webster provides the desperate nadir, in Bosola's 'We are merely the stars' tennis balls, struck and band[i]ed I Which way please them': a line that comes closely followed by his denunciation of Echo. *The Duchess of Malfi*, ed. Russell Brown, V. v. 54–5.

fifty ways' (*AYL*, V. i. 47–9). The multivalent application of the bandying dynamic is fully realized in *Romeo and Juliet*, where the figure
is employed to correlate the sympathetic aggression at the heart of both
love and violence, and to disclose the self-destruction entailed in responsibility.

> Had she affections and warm youthful blood,
> She would be as swift in motion as a ball;
> My words would bandy her to my sweet love,
> And his to me. (II. v. 12–15)

Nurses, in Renaissance literature, are invariably panders. The elderly
female confidante is a staple of early modern erotica, as 'prattling' (*Cor.*,
II. i. 204) and verbally profligate in her dotage as she was physically
liberal in her youth. Narcissus' mother, Myrha, is aided and abetted in
her incestuous deception by an experienced nurse, and Echo herself,
babbling like a gossiping housewife or a loose-tongued madam, plays
her bawdy role in the liaisons of Jove with his harem of nymphs. Both
Emilia, in *Othello*, and the nurse of *Romeo and Juliet* are worldly women
with uncheckable tongues, who would only confirm the nurse-killing
Aaron (in this and many ways akin to Iago) in his suspicion of 'long-
tongued, babbling gossip[s]' (*Tit.*, IV. ii. 153). The stock type of the
babbling nurse is clearly correlated with 'babbling [E]cho' (II. ii. 17),
that 'babbling gossip of the air' (*TN*, I. v. 277) derived from Ovid's
'babling Nymph'.[34] Juliet's nurse is a frustratingly embellishing and
gossiping Echo: constantly in rebound as she 'leave[s]' and 'come[s]'
back' (I. iii. 8–9); resoundingly repetitious; by her own estimation not
a 'flirt-gill' (II. iv. 127) but correctly identified as 'a bawd, a
bawd, a bawd!' (l. 107) even before she tries to pimp Paris. She is a
ponderous panderous go-between, receiving payment (again a sign of
exchange), and bandying the words of others.[35] Although more efficient

---

[34] Golding, *Shakespeare's Ovid*, 443.
[35] The extramissive eyebeam is emitted into the interim and is a motif of exchange,
whereas the ponderous nature of the intromissive eye is in its very receptivity: '[the eyes]
are panders, and brokers, or rather traiterous porters, for the inletting of these enemies
vpon the soule, but also as false reporters in naturall, & artificall things'. Hakewill, *The
Vanitie of the Eye*, 49.

in bridging the interim than Friar John, this echoed nurse is the tragically inept counterpart to the comedic Cesario, as the play struggles to find erotic and semiotic union.

At the crucial moment, Juliet's nurse fails to supply the comfort of counsel, but advocates semiotic dishonesty and the breakage of solemn vows. 'Speak'st thou from thy heart?' (III. v. 226): Juliet learns with amazement that the babbling Echo can 'dispraise my lord with that same tongue | Which she hath praised him with' (ll. 237–8). The semiotic uncertainty associated with Echo comes from the distinction her incorporeal volubility attests to between airy word and tangible form. Her unchosen words either resound in harmony with her intent, suggesting the innate aptness of signification, or, disassociated from her body (or referent), Echo can exemplify the unattached signifier. An echo can be an affirmation of verbal plenitude through confirmatory repetition, or evidence of the word's hollow lack of essential content: 'O woe! O woeful, woeful day!' the nurse is left to wail, 'O day, O day, O day, O hateful day!... O woeful day, O woeful day!' (IV. v. 49–54).[36] Here, in a play of constant resound and pun (where again the semiotic structure is prised apart to reveal unexpected echoes), Juliet finds herself supported only by a duplicitous echo, a confidante in whose verbal integrity she can no longer have confidence: 'Go, councillor, | Thou and my bosom henceforth shall be twain.... If all else fail, myself have power to die' (III. v. 239–42). Echoes will struggle in a play of structural, social, psychic, and erotic division; with only the ultimately unfaithful nurse to echo her, Juliet is denied the comfort of affirmation and reciprocation:

> Bondage is hoarse, and may not speak aloud,
> Else would I tear the cave where Echo lies,
> And make her airy tongue more hoarse than mine
> With repetition of my Romeo's name. (II. ii. 160–3)

---

[36] So, theological texts insist that the echo is a faithful imitation of the original, insofar as all images should derive from and represent divine source with perfect 'correspondency'; 'the dead letter, so far as not depraved from its *primitive purity*, doth as truly answer and hold proportion with the *light*, and *living word*, as the *shadow* doth with the *substance*, the life-less *picture* with the *living person* it represents, and as the voice, which is *Imago verbi* the *Image of the Word*, with the *Word* it is the *Image* of, or the *Eccho*, which is the *Image of the voice*, doth with the *voice* it answers to'. Samuel Fisher, *The Rustick's Alarm to the Rabbies* (London, 1660), 66.

Juliet, although she craves response, has no echo. Nonetheless, bandying takes on a life of its own.

Where civil blood makes civil hands unclean.

Civil, civil. Shakespeare takes an individual word and divides it. In Verona, the single state divides, as two seemingly selfsame groups turn against each other (effectively against themselves); the play's action and expression fractures along these fault-lines. Civil war in the state is reflected in or driven by linguistic civil war, social and poetic fracture becoming encapsulated in a word. As the hands of civilians are made uncivilized by the shedding of civil blood, 'civil' turns back upon itself, making itself unclean via *paregmenon*, enacting violence upon itself, committing linguistic suicide in self-denial. The bandying begins here. This is a small-scale encapsulation of the potential of kind words, disclosing the dangers of reciprocation where exchange of word for word can be loving, kind, or civil, but may well be aggressive, uncivil, suicidal, and violent: 'I will not bandy with thee word for word | But buckler with thee blows twice two for one' (*3H6*, I. iv. 49–50). Shakespeare structures the encounters between Capulet and Montague according to the give-and-take reciprocation of 'bandying': 'beat down their weapons . . . the Prince expressly hath | Forbid this bandying in Verona streets' (III. i. 78–81). Their civil war is propelled by a verbal bandying logic, these 'civil brawls [having been] bred of an airy word' (I. i. 80). If the conclusion of comedy found semiotic healing in performative utterance or simply in performed action, here we see how the formerly redemptive progression from manipulable and insubstantial lexis to enacted and substantiating praxis is less a triumph than a tragedy. The word breeds and becomes action; action finds rhetorical structure. Verona's ancient citizens 'wield old partisans, in hands as old, | Cankered with peace, to part your cankered hate' (ll. 85–6), the gemination of each word demonstrating the potential for faction in a formerly unified state. As Levin notes, Shakespeare's word choice of 'partisans' (halberds) evokes 'the embattled atmosphere of partisanship', suggesting the zealous civil factionalism verbalized in long sequences of aggressive reciprocation:[37]

[37] Levin, 'Form and Formality', 47.

I will *bite my thumb* at them, which is a disgrace to them if they bear it.
Do you *bite your thumb* at us, *sir*?
I do *bite my thumb, sir.*
Do you *bite your thumb* at us, *sir*?
. . .
No, *sir*, I do not *bite my thumb* at you, *sir*, but I *bite my thumb, sir.*
Do you *quarrel, sir*?
Quarrel, sir? No, *sir.*
. . . I serve as good a man as you.
No *better.*
Well, *sir.*
. . .
Say '*better*', here comes one of my master's kinsmen.
Yes, *better, sir.*
You lie.
Draw, if you be men. (I. i. 35–54; emphases added and speakers omitted)

   Quarrel, quarrel. This antagonism closely follows the witty bandying
of Sampson and Gregory who play words back and forth, turning coals
to colliers, choler to collar, allowing the sense of each word to 'move'
(l. 7) till it 'runn'st away' (l. 9) into whatever 'sense thou wilt' (l. 23); the
fertility of a quick word quickly handled alerts the audience to the
explosive potential of deconstructive wordplay. The subsequent exchange of antipathy, built up of repetitions, of words sent to and fro,
makes it clear that violent action demands these initiatory exchanges:
the offer is sent (the bitten thumb) and must be answered (it would be
disgrace to bear it, to keep it); a word is offered up ('better') and must be
ritually returned ('Say "better" . . . Yes, better'); the requisite slight ('you
lie') instigates violence ('draw'). Escalating from word to deed, each
response demands reply in a verbal acceleration both systematically
figured and yet out of control. This scene, still on a small scale and
kept between those of low rank, develops the dangerous potential
glimpsed in the repetition of 'civil'. According to Susan Snyder, Shakespeare effaces 'individual temperament or initiative' in the 'exaggerated
symmetry of the whole sequence' and therefore enforces what Göran
Therbon describes as an 'assigned form of subjectivity'.[38]

---

[38] Susan Snyder, 'Ideology and the Feud in *Romeo and Juliet*', *SS*, 49 (1996), 87–96
at 89; Göran Therbon, *The Ideology of Power and the Power of Ideology* (London, 1980),
15–28.

While we were *interchanging* thrusts and blows,
Came *more* and *more*, and fought on *part* on *part*,
Till the Prince came, who *parted* either *part*. (I. i. 104–6, emphases added)

The scene has also brought the bandying dynamic to full view, into the streets.

More and more. Arguably, reflective configurations of combat are informed by the period's fencing manuals (vogue texts from the Continent).

In Giacomo DiGrassi's *True Arte of Defence*, each figure is characterized by the mirror-image symmetry of its combatants, mapping reflections of fighter facing fighter, head to head, tip to tip, even eye to eye.[39] The description of Tybalt as 'the courageous captain of compliments' (II. iv. 18–19) with a fencing style learnt from the 'book of arithmetic' (III. i. 93) recalls Caranza's *coda duello* that emphasizes the fencing figures of 'complement', depicting the symmetrical movement of the fencers' feet in foot-diagrams.[40] As Vincentio Saviolo instructs:

[let] the ward of his hand, be directlye against his right knee: and let the teacher also put him selfe in the same ward, and holde his Rapier against the middest of his schollers Rapier, so that the pointe be directlye against the face of his scholler, and likewise his schollers against his, and let their feete be right one against another.[41]

These manuals are made up of responsive construction, mapped both linguistically and pictorially according to 'like measure', governed by the rhythm of 'selfsame time', 'counter-time', and 'requital'.[42]

> Away to heaven, respective lenity,
> And fire-eyed fury be my conduct now!
> Now, Tybalt, take the 'villain' back again
> That late thou gavest me. (III. i. 114–17)

---

[39] Giacomo DiGrassi, *His True Arte of Defence* (London, 1594).

[40] See Joan Ozark Holmer, "'Draw, if You be Men'": Saviolo's Significance for *Romeo and Juliet*', *SQ*, 45 (1994), 163–89 at 188; Horace S. Craig, *The Duelling Scenes in Shakespeare* (Berkeley, 1940), 21–4.

[41] Vincentio Saviolo, *His Practice* (London, 1595), 8.

[42] Ibid., 8; William Segar, [extracts from] *Honour Military and Civill (1602)*, in *Miscellaneous Antiquities*, ed. Horace Walpole (London, 1772), 4.

These are Shakespeare's most overtly informed fight sequences, and as Jill Levenson suggests, the 'protocols of fighting inform the narrative'.[43]

Point to point. Romeo's renunciation of 'respective lenity' is more than a simple rejection of effeminate softness but a repudiation of passive correspondence or yielding respectiveness (*OED*, s.v. a5). Romeo will answer 'villain': he will give it back; make the exchange; bandy that word in the streets; return what Tybalt gave him. This aggressive bandying is 'conduct[ed]' by the movement of the visual beam, not burning with the gentle heat of love but with the 'fire-eyed fury' of the revenger. Reciprocating with violent words, Romeo refashions figures of love into an expression of hostility, which, as Colleen Kelly illustrates, fits into the prescribed patterns and elaborate architectural reciprocating figures of the *coda duello*. Kelly strips out all but the active instruction from lines 112–17, revealing an underlying kinetic structure, a Shakespearean foot-pattern for the combatants' interaction:

	back again.
Again	
Away	
	now!
Now,	back again
. . .	

They fight; Tybalt falls.[44]

The fight sequences, in their retelling by Benvolio, are constructed from these figures, both rhetorically and physically architectural, as the fighters turn 'deadly point to point', while 'one hand beats | Cold death aside, and with the other sends | It back to Tybalt, whose dexterity | Retorts it' (III. i. 151–5). Given, beaten aside, sent back, retorted, the blows enact the patterns of bandied reciprocation.

---

[43] Jill Levenson, ' "Alla Stoccado Carries it Away": Codes of Violence in *Romeo and Juliet*, in Jay L. Halio (ed.), *Shakespeare's* Romeo and Juliet: *Texts, Contexts, and Interpretation* (Newark, Del., 1995), 83–96.

[44] Colleen Kelly, 'Figuring the Fight: Recovering Shakespeare's Theatrical Sword-play', in John W. Frick (ed.), *Theatre and Violence* (Tuscaloosa, Ala., 1999), 96–108 at 98.

Love for love. Among the geminative verbal violence, the interim bridging desire of Romeo and Juliet seeks to reaffirm the kind quality of like response. Accepting a sustained correlation of bandied violence and erotic exchange, and employing a similar approach to Kelly's, finds, in Romeo's 'Now Romeo is beloved, and loves again' (I. v. 148), a floor-plan pleasingly reminiscent of the *coda duello* patterning above:

Now   again.

Offering kind compliments, receiving them, allowing the bandy back again, Romeo and Juliet invest the retortive dynamic with new intima-cy, enacting response not on the streets but privily, between themselves, standing 'palm to palm' (I. v. 99), 'let[ting] lips do what palms do' (l. 103), kissing and counter-kissing: 'Give me my sin again' (l. 109). Examples of ploce multiply, insistently constructing the conditions of erotic mutuality and generous bandying: 'Her I love now I Doth grace for grace and love for love allow' (II. III. 85–6). As the lovers verbally lock themselves together amongst the kind reciprocation of loving words—the 'exchange of thy love's faithful vow for mine' (II. II. 127)—his heart becomes set 'on hers, [and] so hers is set on mine, I And all combined' (II. III. 59–60). Shakespeare reminds us of the affinity these 'exchange[s] of vow' (l. 62) have with the exchanges of amorous vision:

> Now Romeo is beloved, and loves again,
> Alike bewitchèd by the charm of looks. (I. v. 148–9)

Shakespeare, says Kiernan Ryan, 'employs symmetrically balanced syn-tax and diction to express the perfect equivalence of attraction and power that distinguishes their relationship'.[45] These patterns of equiva-lence—of loving and being loved in return, of loving alike, of being beloved, bewitched, happily entangled in these soft echoes—are familiar and quietly reminiscent of the passage of the kindred beams.

Wounded, wounded. But perhaps '[a]like' cannot be ignored. The subtle recollection of the opening lines—the families 'alike' in their dangerous dignities—jars, establishing a tragic likeness between the

---

[45] Kiernan Ryan, *Shakespeare* (Basingstoke, 1989), 80.

lover's close kindness and the claustrophobic doublings of civil unrest. And the vocabulary of these two discourses collides: 'on a sudden one hath wounded me | That's by me wounded' (II. iii. 50–1).

Blood for blood. Now 'violent delights have violent ends' (II. vi. 9), and Lady Capulet asserts the logic of legal equivalence and respective justice: 'For blood of ours, shed blood of Montague' (III. i. 140); as 'Romeo slew Tybalt, Romeo must not live' (l. 172). Here these constructions have proverbial provenance ('blood will have blood'), but the phrasing is wilfully ambiguous: the biblical inflection is evident, recalling the Old Testament God's threat, 'Whoso sheddeth man's blood, by man shall his blood be shed', and the *lex talionis* model of retributive justice in 'an eye for an eye'; conversely, these phrases recall the temporal retribution of vengeance, and a generation of neo-Senecan avengers' demands that 'Blood cries for blood, and murder murder craves'.[46] The conflict of Christian and classical codes—recalling Kyd's Hieronimo, caught between passive acceptance of divine vengeance and active adoption of Senecan violence—displays an eroded distinction between social forms of legal response and the uncivilized private reprisals of Veronese vigilantism.[47]

Joint by joint. The give and take of word becomes destructive—'I will tear thee joint by joint' (V. iii. 35)—and repetition breeds a kind of hollowness through excess. See how Juliet, in her grief, unpacks and empties the sense from the bare vowel 'I':

> JULIET. Hath Romeo slain himself? Say thou but 'ay',
> And that bare vowel 'I' shall poison more
> Than the death-darting eye of cockatrice.
> I am not I, if there be such an 'ay',
> Or those eyes shut, that makes thee answer 'ay'.

---

[46] Robert W. Dent, *Shakespeare's Proverbial Language: An Index* (Berkeley, 1981), B458; Genesis 9: 6 (see Ezekiel 35: 6); Exodus 21: 23–7 and Matthew 5: 38–9 (these are contested passages, by no means as clear cut in their condemnation of violent retribution as is commonly assumed); John Marston, *Antonio's Revenge*, ed. G. K. Hunter (London, 1966), III. i. 215. See V. iii. 113; 'Blood asketh blood, & death must death requite' (Thomas Sackville and Thomas Norton, *The Tragedie of Gorboduc* (London, 1565), IV. ii. 283); 'for vengeance asketh vengeance, & bloud bloud, and they that sowe slaughter, shal bee sure to reape ruine and destruction' (George Pettie, *A Petite Pallace of Pettie: His Pleasure* (London, 1576), 22).

[47] Thomas Kyd, *The Spanish Tragedy*, ed. J. R. Mulryne (London, 1989), III. xiii.

If he be slain, say 'ay', or if not, 'no':
Brief sounds determine my weal or woe.
NURSE. I saw the wound, I saw it with mine eyes. (III. II. 45–52)

The figures of reciprocation have lost their respective lenity. This passage contains each exchange motif: Romeo's suicidal reciprocation; the retorted word 'I/ay'; and the lend and borrow of the eyebeam. Self-destruction is revealed as latent in each example of reciprocation. So the eroticized orgasmic death of Romeo from line 21 of this scene now becomes his suicide. So the bandying logic of 'palm to palm' and 'love for love' is carried to an apotheosis where reciprocation has incurred nothing but loss. So the kind to and fro of eyebeams is now given deadly association with the cockatrice, darting death. And so eyes must now be shut, or else see nothing but wounds: not loving wounds, given and taken, but '[a]ll in gore blood' (l. 56), 'bedaubed in blood' (l. 55). The bandied exchanges of 'villain' have permeated Juliet's vocabulary, where she applies and reapplies the term, giving it to both Romeo and Tybalt in turn, bandying it about: 'But wherefore, villain, didst thou kill my cousin? | That villain cousin would have kill'd my husband' (ll. 100–1). Each model of reciprocation is displayed in self-defeating extremis, each textual echo affirming that disaster depends from the bandying dynamic of love.

Romeo, Romeo. The text begins to echo. Lines are revisited in new conditions of confusion—'O Romeo, Romeo, wherefore art thou Romeo?' (II. II. 33), becomes 'O Romeo, Romeo! | Who ever would have thought it? Romeo!' (III. II. 41–2)—and repeated in new states of woe:

My bounty is as boundless as the sea,
My love as deep; the more I give to thee
The more I have, for both are infinite. (II. II. 133–5)

resounds as:

There is no end, no limit, measure, bound,
In that word's death, no words can that woe sound. (III. II. 125–6)

The endlessness of love becomes the infinite expanse of death; in breaking the bounds, the loving couple seem to have initiated an inexorable progression towards their ends. The fertile rolling additions

of 'more' upon 'more'—the more I give, the more I have—are supplanted by deep loss signalling an unplumbable linguistic deficiency
rather than an accumulation of worth; 'more [and] more' is infinite in
its promise, boundless in its generosity, whereas 'no . . . no . . . no . . .
woe' and 'word's death; no words' are delineations of absence, of
negation, and of linguistic failure. Eventually even 'more [and] more'
becomes a repetition revisited, reapplied as explicitly tragic, echoed in
an abundance of negative ploce: 'More light and light, more dark and
dark our woes!' (III. v. 36). The text is shot through with these tragic
repetitions, so in Romeo's grief, falling to his knees and weeping, the
Nurse recognizes Juliet's condition: 'O he is even in my mistress' case, |
Just in her case' (III. III. 84–5). Together the couple enact the 'woeful
sympathy', as 'even so lies she, | Blubb'ring and weeping, weeping
and blubbering' (ll. 85–7). Verbal rendition, in this instance *anti-
metabole*, appears to have generated or to have been submerged within
exhausting proliferation where iterative rhetoric insists on an inextricable bind between the lovers and their environment, limiting them to a
'death-marked love'. The play is made hoarse with repetition, echoing
with empty iteration.

I am not I. Initially welcoming Fuseli's irresistible power of sympathetic attraction, the lovers, losing the character of their individual
speech, are indeed absorbed by the features of each other's expression.
Throughout, as Snow suggests, language has operated 'like a medium'
where 'their relationship takes form' as well as being 'an instrument for
bringing it about'.[48] Snow, describing lovers with 'two imaginations
working in the same idiom . . . tuned to the same imaginative frequency',
notes the 'subliminal correspondences' between their speeches: Romeo
talks of the 'night's cloak' (II. II. 75), and Juliet of 'the mask of night'
(l. 85); he of the chiaroscuro of 'a snowy dove trooping with crows'
(I. v. 47), and she of 'l[ying] upon the wings of night, | Whiter than new
snow' (III. II. 18–19); he declares 'It is the east, and Juliet is the sun'
(II. II. 3), while she describes him as 'thou day in night' (III. II. 17).[49]
These subtle correlations disclose their movement towards what Davis
describes as 'intersubjective union' where the 'lovers re-characterize

---

[48] Edward Snow, 'Language and Sexual Difference in *Romeo and Juliet*', in Andrews
(ed.), 371–401 at 372.
[49] Ibid., 372.

each other as much as themselves', a movement initiated in Juliet's entreaty 'Romeo, doff thy name, I And for thy name, which is no part of thee, I Take all myself' (II. II. 87–9), and epitomized in 'I am not I'.[50] While Juliet's rejection of the name—doff thy name—figures as what Ryan describes as the shrugging off of 'the weight of words, [and] the discursive gravity that pins individuals to involuntary lives', the later denial of identity—I am not I—represents a more fundamental rejection of Juliet's sense of single-self or personal agency for the sake of the loving 'double-self', the 'freshly powerful joint identity' that mutuality yields.[51]

3. SYMPATHETIC SELF-SLAUGHTER

The generosity of love, necessitating the payment of privacy for the purchase of indivisible identity, is understood as an act of self-renunciation prefigured by the renunciation of one's name and perfected in the renunciation of one's life: 'Call me but love, and I'll be new baptised; I Henceforth I never will be Romeo' (II. II. 50–1). The lovers, struggling to articulate a loving *parole* within a determining *langue* and looking to liberate themselves from the social language that appears to predetermine their ends, explicitly renounce their social identities as denoted by their titles:

> I know not how to tell thee who I am,
> My name, dear saint, is hateful to myself,
> Because it is an enemy to thee;
> Had I it written, I would tear the word. (II. II. 54–7)

This rejection of public nomenclature takes the form of violence against the word and, for now, the word alone, but provides a precursor both to the lovers' later rejection of individuate identity and to their eventual suicides. Subjective gemination—that familiar division of individualism that allows the subject to do violence upon itself—is made manifest in

---

[50] Davis, '"Death-Marked Love"', 65.

[51] Ryan, *Shakespeare*, 59; Gordon Braden, 'Beyond Frustration: Petrarchan Laurels in the Seventeenth Century', *Studies in English Literature, 1500–1900*, 26 (1986), 5–23 at 15.

the repudiation of a linguistic identity and the refusal of verbal signs of subjection: the given name; the word; the act of telling or writing; all these modes of expression, not of being. Liberation from linguistic constraint will entail not kissing 'by the book' (I. v. 109). The mannered Petrarchanism of Romeo's unrequited, unanswered adoration for Rosaline (where he was the solitary sonneteer) cedes to the dialogic and interactive loving kindness of Juliet (where the sonnet is shared), charting a progression from the self-gratification of a narcissine absorption in unshared desire to the self-sacrifice implicated in a shared identity. This critical commonplace can become potentially reductive in its elision of Petrarch with English popular Petrarchism, as even within the *Rime sparse* Petrarch provides loving vocabulary predicated upon self-renunciation that expressly attempts to avoid the charge of narcissism. Yet we see Amintas, Romeo, and Petrarch walk in contemplative isolation as they 'utter forth the smart [they] bide within'; and although we hear from each how 'that by love my selfe I stroy' and how 'I love another, and thus I hate my selfe', we also see how he 'fede[s] ... in sorrow', perpetuating his introspective dolour as he '[drinks] all mine owne disease'; we see how in seemingly selfless grief, even self-denial echoes narcissine gemination in the claim that 'I my self, my selfe always to hate | Till dreadfull death do ease my dolefull state'; ultimately, we are unsurprised by the admission that 'I am one of them, whom plaint doth well content ... For, there is nothing els, that toucheth me so within.'[52] While the rhetoric of lament may claim 'I am not mine, I am not mine', Petrarchan verse self-consciously concedes, '[f]rom without, my desire | Has no Food to its Fire, | But it burns and consumes me within'. This echo of Narcissus is fully realized in the *Rime sparse*, where Petrarch is 'content to weary out my pain, | To be Narcissus so she were a spring, | To drown in her'.[53]

[52] Francesco Petrarca, 'The waueryng lover wylleth, end dreadeth, to move his desire', trans. Thomas Wyatt, 3; 13; 'Description of the contrarious passions in a louer', trans. Wyatt, 11–12; 'Charging of his loue as vnpiteous and louing other', trans. Wyatt, 13; 'The louer here telleth of his diuers ioyes ...', trans. anon., 115; 'The louer lamentes the death of his loue', trans. Wyatt, 13–14; 'Complaint of the absence of his loue', trans. Wyatt, 56–63. *Petrarch in English*, ed. Thomas P. Roche (London, 2005).

[53] 'The louer here telleth of his diuers ioyes', trans. anon., 154; John Dryden, 'Song, In Two Parts', 13–15; 'I wage the combat with two mighty foes ...', trans. Thomas Lodge, 9–11, in *Petrarch in English*, ed. Roche.

Only the reciprocation of Juliet, who unlike Petrarch's Laura will 'render love for love', aids the abandonment of masculine introspection, allowing an identity now entirely reliant upon interaction; 'Let me be tane, let me be put to death', he explains, 'I am content, so thou wilt have it so' (III. v. 17–18).[54] Only the requital of love redeems all assertions of selfless mortification, invalidating introspection through rewarding generous self-sacrifice. Dying for unrequited love unavoidably attests to self-concern, whereas dying for love is just what requited lovers do, giving themselves up and away.

> JULIET. Art thou not Romeo, and a Montague?
> ROMEO. Neither, fair maid, if either thee dislike. (II. ii. 60–1)

Only in name are the couple dislike, unlike, distinct each from the other. Accordingly, Friar Lawrence identifies the interdependence of one lover's identity upon the other: 'If e'er thou wast thyself, and these woes thine, I Thou and these woes were all for Rosaline. I And art thou changed?' (II. iii. 77–9). Romeo's exchange of one beloved for another has unsettled his own identity—'if e'er thou wast thyself'—and occasioned an exchange, a change, in himself—'And art thou changed?' This is more than violence against a word or a name. Rather, Romeo's sense of being ineluctably and unchangeably himself is threatened by his dependence upon the beloved.

As the focus of violence shifts from the word to 'me . . . me', Romeo's 'I am' is revealed as dependent solely on what 'thou wilt', just as Juliet's proliferation of 'ay . . . I . . . I am not I' attested to her commitment to an 'intersubjective privacy that weaves its boundaries around them'.[55] This is the lovers' intersubjective union, identified by Sawday as double-self, verbally constructed by Snow's 'antiphonal response[s]', by the extramissive tenor of give and take, by the loving kindness of word for word, the perfect equivalence of grace for grace, love for love, palm to palm.[56] These are the compulsive sequences of reciprocation and mutuality that lock the lovers into a coupled identity, a union predicated upon

---

[54] 'The louer sendeth his complaints and teares to sue for grace', trans. Wyatt, ibid., 31.
[55] Snow, 'Language and Sexual Difference', 371.
[56] Sawday, '"Mysteriously Divided"', 137.

self-dissolution of self and the 'incorporat[ion of] two in one' (II. VI. 37). The lovers have come a long way from single-voiced Petrarchism and its love-model that 'flourishes in the absence of mutuality'.[57]

Ryan and others locate the 'real tragedy' of *Romeo and Juliet* in the 'culture which precludes the survival of such an emancipated love'; yet in addition, theirs is a love incapable of emancipating itself from the prescribed structures of retributive justice, the constriction of civil violence, and the stricture of rhetorical bandying.[58] Social and rhetorical prescriptions become imperatives to act violently and suicidally back upon the self. Equally, this love locks lovers into systems of reciprocation that occlude dividualism, require sacrifice, and therefore find apt culmination in mutual self-slaughter as the ultimate responsive act of a mutually dependent identity. The perfect equivalence, the complete mutuality of their love becomes a compelling and dangerous bind. As Dympna Callaghan suggests, the 'mutuality of mirrored passion fosters the notion that one's authentic identity is revealed in romantic love'.[59] The play additionally allows that this identity first requires the generosity of self-abandonment and is finally authenticated by the symbolic act of sympathetic suicide. Brooke shows that the inexorable development of image groups dictate this progression: nutritional extramissive exchange ('[she] onely seeketh by her sight to feede his houngry eyes'); becomes a hazardous consumption (through his eyes 'he swalloweth downe loues sweet impoysonde baite'); which occasions painful self-renunciation ('the poyson [i.e. love] spred throughout his bones and vaines, I That in a while (alas the while) it hasteth deadly paines'); finding apotheosis as Romeus 'gredely deuowr[s]' the 'poyson that he brought'.[60]

The final irresistible pull of sympathetic attraction is towards the 'incorporat[ion]' of two in one' (II. VI. 37). Playing on the double sense of incorporate ('to combine' and 'incorporeal'), Shakespeare presages passage beyond the body. Vision, which once played its part in binding

---

[57] Marianne L. Novy, '"And You Smile Not, He's Gagged": Mutuality in Shakespearean Comedy', *Philological Quarterly*, 55 (1976), 178–94 at 182.

[58] Ryan, *Shakespeare*, 81.

[59] Dympna C. Callaghan, 'The Ideology of Romantic Love: The Case of *Romeo and Juliet*', in ead., Lorraine Helms, and Jyotsna Singh (eds.), *The Weyward Sisters: Shakespeare and Feminist Politics* (Oxford, 1994), 59–101 at 81.

[60] Brooke, *The Tragicall Historye*, sigs. A7r; B2r.

the lovers together—the charm of looks bewitching both lovers alike—
has become intrusive: they are talked about; they are seen. Desperate to
escape the gaze of those around them, to become 'untalked of and
unseen' (III. ii. 7), Juliet declares that 'Lovers can see to do their
amorous rites | By their own beauties' (ll. 8–9); their 'mode of "seeing"
is tactile, sensational . . . [in this] pure sensation [they are] sightless,
speechless organisms in conjunction, flesh on flesh'.[61] As Juliet, her
cheeks flushed, contemplates bodily consummation in the beloved's
arms, she invokes his white body in the sexually charged *epanalepsis* of
'Come, Night, come, Romeo, come' (l. 17). In envisaging his physical
'mansion of a love', their loss of 'a pair of stainless maidenhoods', her
own orgasmic death, and Romeo's starry explosion (see ll. 1–31), she
depicts this as the purely tactile love of sightless organisms. Eyes now
wink, and love is blind (ll. 6; 9). The flesh on flesh of amorous rites
replaces its ocular precursor, eye to eye. And it is in their deaths that the
lovers finally leap unseen into their final act of loving mutuality; it is in
their ends that they finally find an apotheosis of reciprocation beyond
that of the extramissive bandying. The ocular motif is abandoned in
favour of the ultimate model of amorous sympathy and intersubjective
union: loving-suicide.

> Eyes, look your last! (V. iii. 112)

Romeo, left alone, understands the dialogic quality of suicidal action,
allowing his body to 'remain | With worms' (ll. 108–9), while his
liberated soul is guided 'to my love' (l. 119):

> Come, bitter conduct, come, unsavoury guide!
> Thou desperate pilot, now at once to run on
> The dashing rocks thy seasick weary bark!
> Here's to my love! [*Drinks.*] (V. iii. 116–19)

Their 'reciprocal death[s]' represent the symbiotic union of an individuate couple, coming together across all interims in a performative declaration of erotic self-sacrifice.[62]

---

[61] Catherine Belsey, 'The Name of the Rose in *Romeo and Juliet*', in R. S. White (ed.),
Romeo and Juliet: Contemporary Critical Essays (Basingstoke, 2001), 47–67 at 52.
[62] Davis, '"Death-Marked Love"', 58.

Brooke's depiction of this 'mutuell and . . . piteous sacrifice' emphasizes the physicality of their deaths: the entwined 'embrace' of their
dying bodies as she lies 'panting on his face'; the 'thousand times she kist
his mouth . . . | And it vnkist again', which recalls the 'thousand times
she kist him, and him vnkist agayne' during their first passionate
encounter.[63] Clearly Brooke sees the suicides of his couple as the
symbolic culmination of the 'piteous pangs' of love that had made
them 'both at once to liue and eke to dye'.[64] The deadly potential of
the erotic embrace is more than merely a portent of what is to come: it
gestures towards an inextricable connection between loving and dying.
This, as they consummate their sexual relationship in eroticized suicides
('She grones, she stretcheth out her limmes, she shuttes her eyes, | And
from her corps the sprite doth flye; what should I say: she dyes'), is not
simply the traditional correlation of *petite mort*, but rather an assertion
of the self-destructive nature of loving reciprocation, 'love . . . as a form
of suicide', a suggestion that love of the other precipitates the death of
the self, and that mutual loving suicide therefore represents an apotheosis of the dynamic of erotic exchange.[65]

'Well, Juliet, I will lie with thee tonight' (V. i. 34): finally, Shakespeare, in depicting these loving self-slaughterings as moments of
reciprocation, as 'friendly' (V. iii. 163), has united the figures of violent
bandying—myself against myself, death answering death—with the
figures of amorous bandying. The logic of bandy, martial and erotic,
has run this course, reached its suicidal culmination:

> Do thou but call my resolution wise,
> And with this knife I'll help it presently.
> God joined my heart and Romeo's, thou our hands,
> And ere this hand, by thee to Romeo's sealed,
> Shall be the label to another deed,
> Or my true heart with treacherous revolt
> Turn to another, this will slay them both. (IV. i. 53–9)

---

[63] Brooke, *The Tragicall Historye*, sigs. K3ᵛ; K4ᵛ; C7ᵛ.
[64] Ibid., sig. C7ᵛ.
[65] Ibid., sig. K7ᵛ; Margaret Higonnet, 'Speaking Silences: Women's Suicide', in
Susan Rubin Suleiman (ed.), *The Female Body in Western Culture* (Cambridge, Mass.,
1986), 68–83 at 73.

Juliet's suicidal resolution is explicitly described as resulting from a succession of reciprocation: a hand that was sealed to a hand will slay a heart that was joined to a heart. The fusion of amatory and martial feeling comes to its suicidal culmination. The irresistible pull of sympathetic attraction towards the fusion of double-self, with its concomitant effacement of each individual's subjectivity, has brought the lovers to this conclusion: '[*Falls on Romeo's body and dies*]'.

'What ho, apothecary!' (V. I. 57): the pharmaceutical logic of coexistent binaries—the *pharmaco*-etymon connoting both 'cordial [and] poison' (l. 85)—is the acme of paradoxical rhetoric, and is the keynote of the couple's suicides. They 'die with a restorative' (V. III. 166) and on the tip of a 'happy dagger' (l. 169), reunified by a 'friendly drop' (l. 163) and a killing kiss. The compressed logic of the prologue's 'take their life', where birth and death coexisted in a single phrase, reappears as the 'dram of poison . . . disperse[s] itself through all the veins' until the body is 'discharged of breath | As violently as hasty powder fired | Doth hurry from the fatal cannon's womb' (V. I. 60–5). The woeful symmetries of this text come to kind conclusions where textual echoes speak of coherence and redemption. This desperate resolution always entails dissolution (as does 'resolve', connoting both 'firm intent' and 'to melt'). But, as Friar Lawrence made explicit in a cautionary prophecy that Romeo's military metaphor now echoes, some 'violent delights have violent ends', yet it is their fitting 'triumph' that they 'die like fire and powder, | Which as they kiss consume' (II. VI. 9–11). Encapsulating the violence of loving reciprocation in familiar verbal bandying, the Friar captures the integral paradox in the act of sympathetic suicide. In sympathetic suicide, the lovers invert the typical sequential connection of sex-as-death, to achieve an eroticized conclusion; they literalize Plato's correlation of generous love with its requisite self-abandonment—'O wondrous contract in which he who gives himself up for another has the other, and does not cease to have himself!'—in a suicidal act of 'inestimable gain', so that 'two become one' in a climactic 'happy death!'[66] Theirs is a consummation devoutly wished.

---

[66] Ficino, *Commentary on Plato's* Symposium *on Love*, 56.

PART II
SUICIDE

4

Romana mors in *Julius Caesar*

[W]e are not so much concerned at him, who ends his life in a . . . natural course, and in an even pace walks off to the Chambers of the Dead; for why, 'tis a common Road of Mankind; but for a man to break up the door of Nature, and with rude hands to thrust himself out of the world; for a man to hurry himself on all the unknown hazards of Self-violence, [we] will say this is a very quaint undertaking. . . . Now, what account can be given of an Adventure so preposterous?[1]

As the 'subject is ripening apace for some desperate design', we turn from the reciprocal suicides of indivisible lovers to the 'unkind' and unnatural act of intrasubjective self-slaughter.[2] It seems that not 'every Being [is] kind and courteous to it self'.[3] Rather, 'banished from his own essence [and] disjointed from humanity it self', the isolated self-slaughterer renounces his kindred affiliations and the responsibility of extrinsic relation, preferring an act of 'self expedition' and 'self-dispatch'.[4] Whereas, as Ezra Pierce's seventeenth-century anti-suicide polemic insists, 'a Being essentially depend[s] on another, [and therefore] must certainly [be] responsible to it', the self-slaughterer responds only to himself, finding a dialogic dependency within the introspective but antagonistic reflection of himself to himself.[5] While Pierce may voice standard Renaissance theological disgust at the 'dangerous Usurpation' of divine authority—'Fie! Melancholy to such a degree! 'tis

---

[1] E[zra] P[ierce], *A Discourse of Self-Murder, Lately Written, and now Published as a Disswasive from so Horrid a Thing* (London, 1692), sig. A3[r].

[2] Ibid., sig. A3[v]; p. 10.

[3] Ibid., 3.   [4] Ibid., 4; 7.   [5] Ibid., 4.

beneath the scorn of men'—he seems nonplussed by this 'quaint under-taking' (i.e. cunning), which, in its 'inver[sion]' of the natural order, is a 'preposterous' involution, and a sad revolution:[6] 'For a man to be a Suicide, for that Royal Creature to be the Regicide of himself, and to fall a Sacrifice to the flames of his own revenge, this is a sad revolution indeed.'[7] Caught in cycles of response, as the insistent re- prefix sug-gests, the suicidal subject enacts revolutionary rebellion and revolves back upon himself as he 'separate[s] himself so preposterously'.[8] To appropriate Richard Huloet's description of the preposterous rhetorical figure, the self-murderer is 'out of order', 'overthwarth' (i.e. contrary and perverse) to natural law, and, in his self-cancelling act of self-assertion, he 'transvert[s]' any easy relationship of subject to object.[9]

Pierce is quite clear where he lays the blame for this anti-social illness: the revolutionaries who would lead a Renaissance subject to consider suicide a pharmaceutical deadly 'Remedy', who would talk in terms of breaking down the doors of life, and who would deny dependency upon both social and divine authorities, could only be the classical Stoic philosophers.[10] Suicide, understood as a 'Stoical Paradox', acts as an antagonistic crux, a contested intersection of classical and Christian ideology, a stumbling block for an incorporation of Graeco-Roman philosophy into early modern life:[11]

Strange are the Effects of Despair, running Men headlong into Destruction many times, not only of the Body, but of the better part, by prompting them . . . to lay violent Hands upon themselves, and hazard thereby their own Eternal Welfare, as in many sad Examples, in past Ages, have appeared.[12]

The uneasy conflation of Christian teaching—here, it is Satan who promotes despair and prompts the violent hand—with classical bad

---

[6] Ibid., sig. 9; sig. A3^v–A4^r; p. 6.

[7] Ibid., sig. A4^r.

[8] Ibid., 30.

[9] Huloet, *Abecedarium Anglicolatinum*, s.v. 'Preposterouse, out of order, ouerthwarth, transuerted, or last done which should haue ben first.'

[10] Pierce, *A Discourse*, 7.

[11] Ibid., 13.

[12] Anon., *A Sad and Dreadful Account of the Self-Murther of Robert Long, alias Baker* (London, 1685), 1.

example makes suicide such a characteristically Renaissance concern, and an innately preposterous subject.

Turning to classical texts, the Renaissance reader comes in potentially corrupting contact with an extraordinary number of suicidal deaths, to the extent, as Miriam Griffin suggests, that it seems we are 'dealing with a fashion'.[13] Advocation of self-slaughter comes with such frequency that even a resolute Stoic like Epictetus concludes with bleak wit that 'whenever someone has the feeling that it's reasonable, he goes off and hangs himself!'[14] We are therefore unsurprised when Cicero reports with admiration that Cato was 'delighted to have a reason for dying'.[15] But other classical authors regret that the exemplary nobility of this *Romana mors* has set a dangerous precedent. Martial is shocked by hoards of self-slaughterers 'rushing bare-breasted upon drawn swords', and rebukes these emulative 'heroes': 'I am not for the hero who buys fame with easy blood, I am for him who can win glory without dying.'[16] While Renaissance poets and dramatists inherit the blood thirst of their classical predecessors, a Renaissance philosopher like Pierre Charron is both fascinated and unnerved by this predilection, concluding that 'the *Stoicks* do not stand upon so much Ceremony, but give Men leave to dislodge and pack off, whenever they are disposed to it'.[17]

1. *AUTO TO AUTO*: CLASSICAL SUBJECTIVITY

But O yee *Stoickes*, what will be your felicity in torments![18]

Leonard de Marandé—secretary to Cardinal Richelieu, Stoic sympathizer, and a Sceptic considered by his translator John Reynolds to be 'a

[13] Miriam Griffin, 'Philosophy, Cato, and Roman Suicide', *Greece and Rome*, 33 (1986), 64–77 and 192–202 at 64.

[14] Epictetus, *A Stoic and Socratic Guide to Life*, trans. A. A. Long (Oxford, 2002), 1. 2.

[15] Cicero, *Tusculan Disputations I*, ed. and trans. A. E. Douglas (Warminster, 1985), 74.

[16] Martial, *Epigrams*, ed. and trans. D. R. Shackleton Bailey (Cambridge, Mass., 1993), 1. 8.

[17] Pierre Charron, *Of Wisdom*, trans. George Stanhope, 3 vols. (London, 1707), II. xi. 18.

[18] Marandé, *The Judgment*, 305.

second Montaigne'—is frustrated by his inability to integrate the competing claims of his intellectual Classical inheritance and his contemporary Christian ideological context. This characteristic period complaint is localized in a discussion of self-slaughter. Negotiating hard-line Classical tenets with the more pragmatic concerns of self-preservation, Marandé seeks to 'palliat and sweeten' the 'sharpe, and bitter' remedies of a Senecan wise-man or Socratic philosopher; 'for [they take] the Axe to the rootes', whereas he merely 'loppe[s] and prune[s] off the twigges and smaller branches'.[19] Marandé protests that it cannot be an action 'either iust or commendable . . . [t]hat a wise man should foresee the blowe which threatens him' and, like Socrates, suicidally 'rush out of our selues'. Nonetheless he remains ashamed by historical comparison:

> it belongs to none but to *Socrates*, or spirits which haue raised themselues to the height and sublimity of the same flight, to select and make choyse of vigorous and masculine reasons, in comparison of those which wee commonly vse and employ for our consolation, which are as weake, lame, and feeble, as our courage. It some times falls out, that the same reasons issu[e] from our mouth or pen, as from theirs, but not from our hearts, [or] from the very bottome of our breasts.[20]

The Renaissance philosophers and dramatists may emulate their Classical predecessors and depict their suicidal passions 'all rawe', but Marandé concedes that 'we onely prefere these words without knowing their price or value':

> Our too rawe and indigested stomack cannot consume this meat, and draw its nutriment thence. Wee discourse in the same manner, language, and tearmes as they doe, but yet we thinke differently: Our words are but as the rinds and barkes of our conceptions.[21]

This is the paradox of neoclassicism, where a dramatic rhetoric is admired, but the actual action is unpalatable.

Marandé, feeling the pressure of his predecessors, could empathize with Shakespeare's Brutus. Both character and philosopher know that man 'nourisheth a discord, and a perpetuall ciuill warre within him', where the dictates of introspection—as the look is turned in upon

---

[19] Marandé, *The Judgment of Humane Actions*, 255.
[20] Ibid., 255; 251; 256.   [21] Ibid., 256–7.

himself—determine that 'hee cannot take himselfe from himselfe' and 'escape' the 'sensible blowes and assaults' of self-induced doubt and division:[22]

> If I have veiled my look
> I turn the trouble of my countenance
> Merely upon myself. Vexèd I am
> Of late with passions of some difference,
> Conceptions only proper to myself,
> Which give some soil, perhaps, to my behaviours.
> But let not therefore my good friends be grieved
> (Among which number, Cassius, be you one)
> Nor construe any further my neglect
> Than that poor Brutus, with himself at war,
> Forgets the shows of love to other men. (*JC*, I. ii. 37–47)

Brutus' catoptric solipsism, articulated with familiar pronoun-heavy rhetorical involution, discovers only a divided mind. Crucially, his speech emphasizes 'difference', and thoughts 'only proper to myself', unshared with his 'good friends', unshown to 'other men'; opting out of specular structures of interaction and ipseic models of mutual indivisibility, he consequently underappreciates the value of friendship dynamics integral to both Socratic/Aristotelian and related Senecan conceptions of identity. Cassius' chastisement—'can you see your face?'—and Brutus' admission that 'the eye sees not itself | But by reflection [in] other things' (ll. 51–3) successfully reintegrate Brutus into networks of participatory subjection as championed in Socratic and Hellenistic thought:

> it is very much lamented, Brutus,
> That you have no such mirrors as will turn
> Your hidden worthiness into your eye
> That you might see your shadow. (I. ii. 55–8)

In *Alcibiades I*, we read how Platonism champions extrinsic reflection 'when a man looks into an eye [and] his face appears in it, like in a mirror'.[23] 'Then an eye will see itself if it observes an eye and looks at

---

[22] Ibid., 301; 315.
[23] Plato, *Alcibiades I*, 133 A.

the best part of it', he continues, promoting the characteristic transcendence facilitated in all Platonic descriptions of vision: the 'best part' correlates to divine nature, the trace of an ideal shadowed in shadows.

Cassius, leading Brutus from private contemplation to public rebellion, enlists this sense of transcendence only insofar as it brings Brutus beyond the confines of self-speculation and into the eyes of others: 'in seeing your face in the mirror you know yourself as others know you, face-to-face, in an exchange of glances', explains Jean-Pierre Vernant in a vocabulary indebted to Socratic formulations, concluding that 'access to the self is gained through an external projection of that self, through being objectified, as if one were an other'.[24] As Christopher Gill has cautioned, we should resist the temptation to dehistoricize this 'self' and rather allow for a model of introspection that does not seek to locate an asocial locus of private subjectivity, but rather promotes the introjection of ideological values into the subjected interior. As Seneca suggests:

> Mirrors were invented in order that man may know himself, destined to attain many benefits from this: first, knowledge of himself; next, in certain directions, wisdom. The handsome man, to avoid infamy. The homely man, to understand that what he lacks in physical appearance must be compensated for by virtue. . . . This is why nature has given us the opportunity of seeing ourselves. A clear fountain or a polished stone returns to each man his image.[25]

Both 'disgrace' and 'virtue' are societal qualities and this self-scrutiny is circumscribed—for now—by Seneca's simple correlation of external appearance with internal value. The self-reflection required of Brutus— 'you would have me seek into myself | For that which is not in me?' (I. ii. 64–5)—explicitly seeks to bring the interior man into line with his social reception, correlating and effacing distinctions between private state and state persona. Gill describes this extra-dividual as an 'objective-participant' in order to suppress any tenor of 'subjective-individualism' he may detect in any discussion of this 'intersubjective discourse of self-formation'.[26]

---

[24] Jean-Pierre Vernant, *Mortals and Immortals: Collected Essays*, ed. Froma I. Zeitlin (Princeton, 1991), 142.

[25] Seneca, *Naturales Quaestiones*, trans. Thomas H. Corcoran, 2 vols. (London, 1972), 2. 1. 17. 4–5.

[26] Christopher Gill, *Personality in Greek Epic, Tragedy, and Philosophy: The Self in Dialogue* (Oxford, 1996); Laurie Shannon, *Sovereign Amity: Figures of Friendship in Shakespearean Contexts* (Chicago, 2002), 194.

'Perhaps it is not preposterous, to see first *what* kind of thing this *Friendship* is?'[27] Explaining that 'since you cannot see yourself | So well as by reflection, I, your glass, | Will modestly discover to yourself | That of yourself which you yet know not of' (I. ii. 67–70), Cassius appropriates Seneca's equally politic request to his tyrannical former pupil that 'I have undertaken to write on mercy, Nero Caesar, in order to act as a kind of mirror, showing you to yourself.'[28] In both instances, friendly reflection is synonymous with the application of delicate influence, refashioning the 'honourable metal' of the subject which 'may be wrought | From that [to which] it is disposed' (I. ii. 298–9). In the negotiation of this subjected participatory individualism Jacques Derrida detects 'the silent unfolding of that strange violence that since forever insinuated itself into the origin of the most innocent experiences of friendship'.[29] The befriended is responsible for a response:

We are already caught, surprised . . . in a certain responsibility . . . at the moment we begin to signify something. . . . And we see it coming from the Other. It is assigned to us by the Other, from the Other, before any hope of reappropriation permits us to assume this responsibility in the space of what could be called *autonomy.*[30]

The demands of correspondence, or the call for reciprocation inherent in this model of dialogic identity, preserves, in Derrida's formulation, 'the sense of the asymmetrical "anteriority" even within the seemingly most inward and solitary autonomy of reserve . . . one's heart of hearts'.[31] This is vital to an understanding of early modern friendship and the dialogic or preposterous subjectivity it enables; interiority cannot be disassociated from this seemingly anterior reciprocating relationship. The reciprocity of friendship shows the formative potential of anterior response (friend to friend, second-self to self), and in so doing delineates a map for an imitative interiority (self to self) built upon the rhetoric of response and reciprocation. Accordingly, Ullrich Langer describes 'the rarefied

[27] George Wither, *Friendship* (London, 1654), 2–3.
[28] Seneca, 'On Mercy', in *Moral and Political Essays*, ed. and trans. John M. Cooper and J. F. Procopé (Cambridge, 1995), 1. 1. 1, 117–64.
[29] Jacques Derrida, 'The Politics of Friendship', *Journal of Philosophy*, 85 (1988), 632–44 at 634.
[30] Ibid., 634.
[31] Ibid., 639.

yet intimate, nearly redundant style through which perfect friendship is often evoked' in 'elaborate yet semantically simple formulation[s]' that provide a 'hyperbolically inward "subjective" feeling'.[32]

A friend, in Aristotle's much repeated formulation, should be 'a kind of second self', and we see again how intersubjectivity is considered a prerequisite for any state of individuality, allowing a low-level narcissine self-scrutiny via the mediation of an interlocutor:

> We are not able to see what we are from ourselves [so] when we wish to see our own face, we do so by looking into the mirror, in the same way when we wish to know ourselves we can obtain that knowledge by looking at our friend. For the friend is, as we assert, a second self. If . . . it is not possible to know this without having someone else for a friend, the self-sufficing man will require friendship in order to know himself.[33]

Michel de Montaigne acknowledges his classical debt when he marvels that 'it is a great and strange wonder for a man to double himself'.[34] While in Narcissus this solipsistic involvement was considered selfish, the generosity of friendship permits the 'transportation of two hearts into one body: and therefore a friend is called *alter idem*, another moity, or another selfe'.[35] 'The question arises', throughout Classical and Renaissance friendship texts, 'whether a person should love himself most or someone else' and the narcissine impulse is repeatedly suppressed.[36] So while it would be wrong, as Francis Bacon counsels, for Narcissus to 'think himself All in All', it is a commonplace imperative to find a 'faithfull friend . . . as a mans owne selfe', to 'knit . . . in coniunction' until 'two seuerall bodies shall meete in one minde, and bee, as it were, maried and ioyned in one maner of disposition, . . . fast locked in a league of loue'.[37]

---

[32] Ullrich Langer, *Perfect Friendship: Studies in Literature and Moral Philosophy from Boccaccio to Corneille* (Geneva, 1994), 16; 18.

[33] Aristotle, *Magna Moralia*, in *Metaphysics X–XIV*, ed. and trans. G. Cyril Armstrong (Cambridge, Mass., 1947), 1213^{a}10–26.

[34] Michel de Montaigne, *Essais*, trans. Florio, 94.

[35] M. B., *The Triall of True Friendship; or Perfit Mirror, wherby to Discerne a Trustie Friend from a Flattering Parasite* (London, 1594), B2.

[36] Aristotle, *Nicomachean Ethics*, 1168^{a}28–9, in St Thomas Aquinas, *Commentary*, trans. C. I. Litzinger (Notre Dame, Indiana, 1964).

[37] Francis Bacon, 'Of Friendship', in *Essayes and Counsels: Civil and Moral* (London, 1664), 156; Walter Dorke, *A Tipe or Figure of Friendship* (London, 1589), sig. A4^v; Thomas Churchyard, *A Sparke of Frendship and Warme Goodwill* (London, 1588), sig. C^r.

These early modern commonplaces provide rhetorical and narrative structure to a number of Shakespearean dramas from *The Two Gentlemen of Verona* to *The Merchant of Venice*; the classically informed depiction of friendship is inflected with Aristotelian discussions of *homonomia* and Stoic affirmations of the inextricability of 'free and friendly conference' (*JC*, IV. II. 17) and participatory identity formation.[38] This is what Cicero calls the 'goodly rule' or 'naturall order' of self-speculation and understanding.[39]

'Alike in their excellence', and 'mutually know[ing] . . . that well-wishing of this kind is reciprocated', each friend finds in each other a comforting affirmation of identity, and an identical receptacle 'into whom he may transport his affections, repose his secrets, and commit his enterprises'.[40] Friendship is an extension of the private space, a 'faithfull and inward friend' acting as a repose or 'secret bosome' for personal thoughts, offering the 'excellent, comfortable, yea, heavenly' comfort of a 'sweet sympathetic' correspondency: 'He is as good a man as I, and we are bound each to other, so that his wants must be my wants, his sorrowes my sorrowes, his sickness my sickness, and his welfare my welfare, for I am as he is.'[41] This material is saturated by the figures of repetition, simple and overt games of verbal familiarity and friendly vocabulary, bringing word and word together, and forging internal connections between kind words that 'jointly join' like the 'mutuall offices and kindnesses that passe from friend to friend' in returning 'love for love'.[42]

Classical friendship literature provides an ipseic structure of participational identity, and it seems a simple step to correlate this reflexive model with one of introspective reflection, where self-speculation supersedes extraspection and finds the recipient and participant within. Simply, when Brutus turns his gaze upon himself, has he not acted as

---

[38] Aristotle, in Aquinas, *Commentary*, 1166^{a}30–3.

[39] Cicero, *The Booke of Freendship*, trans. John Harrington (n.p., 1550), sig. A6^r.

[40] Aristotle, in Aquinas, 1156^{a}3–7; M. B., *The Triall*, B^v.

[41] Thomas Breme, *The Mirror of Friendship* (London, 1584), sig. A3^r; Dorke, *A Tipe*, fo. 3^r; Robert Cushman, *A Sermon Preached at Plimmith in New-England* (London, 1622), 13.

[42] Dorke, *A Tipe*, sig. A3^r; Aristotle, in Aquinas, 1157^{a}629–31; Plutarch, *The Philosophie*, trans. Philemon Holland (London, 1603), 91.

his own interlocutor and stood as mirror to himself? Perhaps in early modern contributions to the friendship literature subgenre such as the essays of Montaigne and Bacon, this causal progression is less controversial; Cartesian models of what Charles Taylor calls radical reflexivity clearly develop from catoptric and ipseic models of self-speculation prefigured in, for example, the narcissistic negative exemplum, the introspective seeing subject, the dialogue with one's conscience, and the responsivity of early modern amity. Losing Étienne de La Boétie—the death of his friend—initiates and necessitates Montaigne's self-scrutinizing project and the substitute construction of his textual mirror. Throughout this study, the reflex reaction to the loss of a reflecting other *is* reflexive reflection (self-speculation surrogating for the loss of reciprocation elsewhere). Each configuration of indivisibility will ultimately be co-opted as a formative structure for (post-) Cartesian subjective individualism, until the formerly indispensable ipseic structures of indivisibility are subsumed within a celebration of isolationism and the radical self-speculation of an avowedly dividuate subject. Only the rhetorical structures and vocabulary of reciprocation will remain as lexical archaeological evidence of the former primacy of interaction; our modern rhetoric of subjectivity remains demonstrably indebted to reflective rhetoric and relational terminology and yet arguably has only comparatively recently returned to objective-participant discourse. The status of self-speculation in the late sixteenth and early seventeenth century is in contestation: the very prevalence of the Narcissus myth—here, as a cautionary extreme amongst advocation of kind response—betrays how permeable the distinction is between these approved models of socialized self-scrutiny and the antisocial self-involvement of an often demonized autonomy (literally, in the case of Milton's Satan). Likewise, Stoic structures of politicized self-ownership and aggressive individualism are only uncomfortably incorporated into their new ideological context where they are continually evoked to be revoked. Suicide is the Stoic assertion of autonomous ownership and consequently the least easily incorporated aspect of Classical doctrines.

Gill is resistant to critics—late Foucault, Amélie Rorty, and A. A. Long, for example—who seek to introduce a similar narrative of development into Classical philosophy. Long's work locates 'a new focus on consciousness, on the individuality of the perceiving subject, as the fundamental feature of the mental'; in contrast, Gill is 'highly sceptical', suggesting that the conception of personality found in *Alcia-biades I*, then in Seneca or Cicero, remains 'objective-participant rather than subjective (or subjective-individualist)', and arguing that 'the fact that the dialogue centres on self-knowledge, and on exploring the nature of the self which is human, does not mean that its project is subjective in a post-Cartesian sense'.[43] Gill's analysis is persuasive yet it is not to contradict his position to suggest that the Renaissance reception of, in particular, Senecan texts may fasten upon the ipseic structures formulated and find them apposite, ripe for Cartesian appropriative realignment. Although an advocate of Gill's work, Shadi Bartsch does see innovative emphasis on 'the self-observant self' in Seneca: 'I will observe myself continually and . . . I will review my day. It is this that makes us bad—that no one turns his gaze on his life.'[44] Describing the 'doubled self' as 'the self that provides its own watcher, its own interlocutor', Bartsch sees in Seneca a 'new' emphasis on the duplicity involved in public self-presentation—a concern about the falsity of persona that distinguishes Seneca from Cicero—which consequently provokes a conception of private and troubled subjectivity:

> Constant observation of oneself is torturous, and one fears to be caught out of one's usual role. Nor can we ever relax, when we think we're being assessed every time we're looked at. . . . It's not a pleasant life, nor one free from anxiety, to live constantly wearing a mask.[45]

Seneca's precarious position as a tyrant's confidant would, Bartsch argues, have isolated him in the imperial court, dislocated him from participation in the formative exchanges of friendly interaction, and necessitated the introjection of an 'internalized other' by 'a conscious product of the will of the Stoic individual. One *must set up* a Cato or Epicurus in one's mind and pretend he is watching.'[46] This is much closer to Cartesian radical reflexivity, where, in Harry Frankfurt's terms, there is a sense of second-order awareness (reflecting upon the act of

[43] A. A. Long, *Stoic Studies* (Cambridge, 1996), 266; Christopher Gill, *The Structured Self in Hellenistic and Roman Thought* (Oxford, 2006), 326; 359.

[44] Bartsch, *The Mirror of the Self*, 203; Seneca, *Letters from a Stoic: Epistulae Morales ad Lucilium*, trans. Robin Campbell (Harmondsworth, 1969), 83. 1–2.

[45] Bartsch, *The Mirror*, 207; Seneca, *De Tranquillitate Animi*, in *Four Dialogues*, ed. C. D. N. Costa (Warminster, 1994), 17. 1.

[46] Bartsch, *The Mirror*, 244.

reflecting, thinking about thinking, desiring to desire).[47] So, 'we might say that the "objectivity" is there—supplied by the tenets of Stoic philosophy—but the "participant" aspect of the individual in his community is etiolated'.[48] Or, to rephrase slightly, the 'participant' requirement is self-fulfilled. I find this compelling, although Gill would not.

For my purposes, even if Bartsch does provide a misreading it seems comparable to an early modern misreading and provides two productive points of contact with this study. First: 'the level of linguistic reflexivity in Seneca represents an innovation in literary Latin'.[49] The reflexive constructions Bartsch catalogues become the characteristic features of Shakespearean self-speaking.[50] Equally, whether we agree with Gill that the much-discussed phrase *auto to auto* in Plato's *Alcibiades I* should be translated as 'the self itself' or, as Gill suggests in order to circumnavigate the ahistorical connotations of 'self', 'the itself itself', it remains the case that such reflective models are made available for Renaissance adoption and reinvention. Jean-François Pradeau's explanation of how *auto to auto* allows a metamorphosis of reflexive pronoun (*soi*) into a noun or substantive (*le soi*) shows how the phrase prefigures early modern 'myself my self must kill' constructions, allowing 'myself' both to be subject of the sentence and subject to the subject's action, ergo radically subjected.[51] To represent Gill fairly, who refutes the implications of Pradeau's *soi* to *le soi* movement,

The English term, 'self' (even more, 'the self') is a rather peculiar usage, representing the conversion of a reflexive suffix (as in 'himself') into a noun.... One factor that has surely promoted this usage is the tendency, in post-Cartesian European thought, to give a privileged status to a certain kind of reflexivity, namely that involved in an 'I'-centred self-consciousness. In general, this linguistic phenomenon did not take place in Greek or Latin.... Similarly,... we do not find in ancient thought the post-Cartesian shift towards a notion of personality centred on subjective reflexivity (self-consciousness).[52]

---

[47] Harry G. Frankfurt, 'Freedom of the Will and the Concept of a Person', *Journal of Philosophy*, 68 (1971), 5–20.

[48] Bartsch, *The Mirror*, 254.

[49] Ibid., 246.

[50] Richard Hillman, *Self-Speaking in Medieval and Early Modern English Drama: Subjectivity, Discourse and the Stage* (Basingstoke, 1997).

[51] Plato, *Alcibiade*, trans. Chantal Marboeuf and Jean-François Pradeau (Paris, 1999).

[52] Gill, *The Structured Self*, 347.

Gill, Pradeau, Long, Bartsch, and Gail Fine contest these Classical cases, but the sheer weight of early modern examples running throughout my study attests that we do find this linguistic phenomenon in pre-Cartesian texts, initially in order to fulfil mimetically the demands of objective-participant identity or extramissive catoptics, but ultimately as appropriated by pre- and post-Cartesian writers who are learning to articulate a radical reflexivity born of participational origins.

Secondly:

> Seneca's writing . . . generates a model of selfhood that, in splitting the I into (potentially errant) agent and (morally superior) witness, lets the identification of the self be as much with the *errant* as with the ethically sanctioned of the two selves.[53]

The ability to identify with the errant will be hotly contested in Renaissance suicide debate, and this sense of aggressive self-subjection is fundamental to the act of self-slaughter. The suppression of the ethical agent by the errant is precisely what anti-suicide polemic will be shown to militate against in its insistence upon moral and theological values that seek to bolster the defence of the ethical agent in its resistance of the errant Stoic agent. Marandé, as a Stoically inclined Renaissance Sceptic employed by a Cardinal, suffers the internal conflict of the Christian ethical agent and the consequently errant Stoic, correlating his very contemporary conflict with the contesting claim of soul and body; he sees 'how violently and maliciously [the senses] . . . conspire to corrupt our bodies, and to betray our soules to sinne, and voluptuousnesse', and sees how the soul 'can no longer retaine her selfe, and that forgetting her selfe, she suffers her selfe to be led and carried away by the violent streame of her passions, which after, by little and little estrangeth her from her selfe'.[54] Forced into identification with the errant body, Marandé's 'will is weake towards good or euill, and cannot absolutely beare it selfe towards the one and the other' just as he is pulled between his philosophical and contemporary moral positions: his mind still on Socrates' suicide, Marandé regrets that 'we can difficultly agree with our selfe, and none with a firme and an assured heart can suggest any wicked act; but that his conscience repines and murmures

---

[53] Ibid., 245.
[54] Reynolds, 'The Epistle Dedicatorie', in Marandé, *The Judgment*, sig. A5[V]; Marandé, ibid., 118.

within him'.[55] Thus, conscience will make a coward of any Renaissance gentleman, divided by a university education (in Wittenberg, say) that would include both Hellenistic philosophy and (Lutheran) doctrine. 'One of these two opinions, is necessarily false; if they are not both false', the Sceptic Marandé can conclude, although to be or not to be would be the more stringent question.[56]

Aspiring to Stoic self-sufficiency but incapable of being equanimous to external events or internal conflict, Marandé comes to doubt the humanity of Stoic resolve, denying the efficacy of political suicide—'a Captiue who spets iniuries in her Masters face, is yet no lesse his Slaue'—and implying that Stoic self-slaughter may be the action not of the autonomous individual but of the desperate, divided, and damned:

> But O yee *Stoickes*, what will be your felicity in torments! If your reason forsake you, and play false company with you; what will then become of this Vertue, which no longer knowes her selfe: is this it which she hast promised you? Whiles the Enemie sackes you, and Fortune teares and dragges you by the haire, shee will abandon you at neede, and dares not shewe her selfe.[57]

2. CASSIUS FROM BONDAGE WILL DELIVER CASSIUS: CLASSICAL SUICIDE

> Whether or throat is strangled by a knot, or water stops the breathing, or the hard ground crushes in the skull of one falling headlong to its surface, or flame inhaled cuts off the course of respiration—be it what it may, the end is swift. Do you not blush for shame? You dread so long what comes so quickly![58]

Caligula kept a notebook entitled *pugio* (dagger) in which he recorded the names of every man he had ordered to commit suicide.[59] Then, in

---

[55] Ibid., 14.

[56] Ibid., 54.

[57] Ibid., 308; 305.

[58] Seneca, *De Providentia*, in *Moral Essays*, trans. John W. Basore, 3 vols. (London, 1928), i. 47.

[59] Paul Plass, *The Game of Death in Ancient Rome: Arena Sport and Political Suicide* (Madison, 1995), 93.

1674, Thomas Philipot provides 'a Copious Register of some Elder and Braver Romans, who embelzeld their Lives'.[60] What follows is my *pugio*, my register, situating Shakespeare's *Julius Caesar* amongst a catalogue of Classical self-slaughterers:

> How I approve of Theremenes! What a lofty spirit he has!... That fine man jested with his last breath when he had already absorbed and was grasping death in the depths of his being.[61]

Cicero, descendant of the exemplary self-murderer Cato, sees heroism in Theremenes' act of suicidal rebellion. Thrown into prison on the instructions of the thirty tyrants, Theremenes displays the 'calmness in a great soul at the point of death' that Cicero admires, and, particularly in his jesting, subverts the connotations of his punishment, reclaiming his death by refusing to cede authority to his captors.[62] While displaying the contempt for one's body that Seneca describes as 'absolute freedom', Theremenes' cheerful end illustrates the Epicurean tenet that the wise man 'neither begs off from living nor dreads not living.... As in the case of food he prefers the most savory dish to merely the larger portion, so in the case of time he garners to himself the most agreeable moments rather than the longest span'.[63] As Cicero suggests, 'it is the appropriate action for a wise man to abandon life while enjoying the greatest happiness if he can make a suitable exit'.[64]

'To the same prison and to the same cup a few years later came Socrates.'[65] The *Phaedo*, Plato's account of the suicide of Socrates, is the *locus classicus* of suicide discussion. Both in the *Phaedo* and in his *Laws*, Plato offers only a conditional advocation of self-slaughter, rehearsing the common view that suicide is an act of injustice to the state, a view

---

[60] T[homas] P[hilipot], *Self-Homicide-Murder; or, Some Antidotes and Arguments... Against that Horrid and Reigning Sin of Self-Murther* (London, 1674), 23.

[61] Cicero, *Tusculan Disputations*, 99.

[62] Ibid., 97.

[63] Seneca, *Letters*, 65. 21; Epicurus, 'Letter to Menoeceus', in *The Philosophy of Epicurus: Letters, Doctrines, and Parallel Passages from Lucretius*, trans. George K. Strodach (Easton, 1963), 1. 126.

[64] Cicero, *De Finibus Bonorum*, in *On Stoic Good and Evil: 'De Finibus Bonorum et Malorum Liber III' and 'Paradoxa Stoicorum '*, trans. M. R. Wright (Warminster, 1991), 19. 61.

[65] Cicero, *Tusculan Disputations*, 97.

shared with Aristotle, who asserts 'we are legally forbidden' from 'doing injustice to the city'.[66] While in *Laws* (9. 873 c–d) Plato appears to consider shame a justification for self-murder, the *Phaedo* makes clear that only upon compulsion or after higher instruction (political or spiritual) could suicide be deemed defensible.[67] Cicero's record of his final words confirms that Socrates is eager to depict suicide not as an act of individual assertion but rather one that cedes authority to the divine: 'it is time', he says, 'to depart hence, for me to die, for you to live. Which is better the gods know: I think it is known by no human being.' These words, writes the awed Cicero, were 'best of all'.[68] Socrates' death, adopted as an iconic model, becomes the precursor to a sequence of self-killings which explicitly fashion themselves on his example: Cleombrotus of Ambracia, the first of a long line of emulative self-slaughterers, 'had suffered no misfortune but still threw himself off a wall into the sea after reading Plato's book'.[69]

Typically, late-Stoic and Senecan appropriation of Socrates' death underplays his transcendent emphasis:

> Imprisonment, exile, drinking poison, loss of wife, leaving orphaned children, these were the context of his game, but none the less he deftly played and handled the ball. So too we should deploy the ball-player's consummate skill, but also his indifference as to its object, a mere ball.[70]

Stoicism was the first 'true doctrine of emotional impassivity', and Epictetus celebrates indifference while displaying the admiration that characterizes all Stoic depictions of suicide.[71] Cassius' complaint that '[o]f your philosophy you make no use | If you give place to accidental evils', and Brutus' response, '[n]o man bears sorrows better' (IV. III. 145–7), are Stoic doctrinal commonplaces. Evolving from Cynicism, which permitted a rational exit from life, and adopted fully by the

---

[66] Plato, *Phaedo*, trans. David Gallop (Oxford, 1975); Plato, *Laws*, in, *Complete Works*, ed. Cooper, trans. Trevor J. Saunders; Aristotle, *Nicomachean Ethics*, trans. Terence Irwin (Indianapolis, Ind., 1985), 5. 11. 1138 A.

[67] Plato, *Phaedo*, 62 C.

[68] Cicero, *Tusculan Disputations*, 99.

[69] Ibid., 84.

[70] Epictetus, 2. 5.

[71] William V. Harris, *Restraining Rage: The Ideology of Anger Control in Classical Antiquity* (Cambridge, Mass., 2001), 86.

Romans from its Greek origins in the second century BC, Stoicism presents suicide as the ultimate expression of a philosophical outlook, asserting the rights of self-ownership and refusing to condemn a rationally chosen death when life is no longer 'in accordance with nature': the prime prerequisite of all Stoic existence.

When a man's condition is for the most part according to nature, the appropriate action is to stay alive, but the appropriate action for a man whose condition is for the most part contrary to nature or seems likely to be so is to leave life... for the Stoics maintain that the happy life is a question of suitability. So it is wisdom which bids the wise man leave her when the need arises.[72]

Cicero articulates what is a crucial convolution in all Stoic advocatory writing on self-slaughter; a philosophical school insistent on living 'in conformity with nature' should first obey the 'instinct for self-preservation' which is a 'primary instinct' that 'should be recognised as based on [a therefore entirely justifiable] self-love'.[73] But the 'question of suitability' that Cicero allows permits the wise man to leave a life that otherwise exists contrary to nature; the 'supremacy of reason', as Pliny reports in his description of the death of Corellius Rufus, allows that 'reasons for dying [can] outweigh... everything that life could give him'.[74] Sickness, therefore, or even a tell-tale weariness (*taedium vitae*), may indicate to the Stoic that to continue living would no longer reasonably be in accordance with nature, indeed would be to ignore her promptings: Zeno, the Stoic founder, stubbed his toe in the street, cried out 'I come, why do you call?' and killed himself.[75]

So we come to Cato in 46 BC, from whose 'bravest of wounds more glory flowed than blood'.[76] Cato reads twice through his *Phaedo* as 'he pursued his studies', and like Socrates carries out his overtly political,

---

[72] Cicero, *De Finibus Bonorum*, 19. 60–1.

[73] Cicero, *Letters to Atticus*, ed. and trans. D. R. Shackleton Bailey, 4 vols. (Cambridge, Mass., 1998), 5. 5; *De Finibus Bonorum*, 5. 16.

[74] Pliny the Younger, *Letters*, trans. William Melmoth and W. M. L. Hutchinson (London, 1915), 1. 12.

[75] J. M. Rist, *Stoic Philosophy* (Cambridge, 1969), 243.

[76] Valerius Maximus, *Memorable Doings and Sayings*, ed. and trans. D. R. Shackleton Bailey (Cambridge, Mass., 2000), 3. 3. 14.

theatrical suicide. The gods 'looked on with exceeding joy'; 'what nobler sight', asks Seneca, 'than the spectacle of Cato?'[77] Indeed, Seneca even suggests that Cato's initial bungling of his death is simply part of the noble performance: 'it was not enough for the immortal gods to look but once at Cato. His virtue was held in check and called back that it might display itself in a harder role. . . . Surely the gods looked on with pleasure upon their pupil as he made his escape by so glorious and memorable an end!'[78] In Cato's death we see how suicide is learnt or studied, representing the pursuit of philosophical study, providing a role, and offering a noble sight to be remembered and re-enacted. The theatricality of Stoic suicide is in this role-playing; so the dying Lucan in AD 65 recites verses 'about a wounded soldier who had died a similar death', playing the role of Socrates or Cato and acting out a part that carries an accumulation of inherited connotations of nobility and glory.[79] The recitation of verse simply makes the analogy clear: we are dealing with a staged death, an aesthetic event.

Similarly, in *Julius Caesar*, Portia's act of self-harm and her subsequent self-slaughter initiate Brutus into a suicidal pattern instigated by Cato, her father. Historically, Valerius Maximus explains that Portia's voluntary wound was delivered as a demonstration of her willingness to commit suicide should her husband's plot fail: 'I wanted to try out how coolly I could kill myself.'[80] And indeed, this is, as Shakespeare puts it, a 'strong proof of . . . constancy' that shows she can 'bear . . . with patience' (II. i. 299–301). In addition, she provides a model for Brutus, who asks, 'O ye gods, | Render me worthy of this noble wife!' (ll. 302–3).[81] Significantly, Shakespeare reverses the sequence of self-murder, making Portia provide precedence for Brutus' self-destruction. Martial informs us that Portia, on hearing of the death of Brutus, announces, ' "I had thought my father had taught that lesson by the manner of his dying." So saying, she eagerly imbibed glowing embers. What now, you tiresome servitors? Deny

[77] Seneca, *De Providentia*, 11.

[78] Ibid., 10.

[79] Tacitus, *The Annals of Imperial Rome*, trans. Michael Grant (London, 1996), 15. 67.

[80] Valerius Maximus, 3. 2. 15.

[81] Portia fits into a tradition of female didactic self-murderers, another much cited example being the death of Arria (see Pliny, *Letters*, 3. 16).

steel?'[82] Portia's suicide oratory insists on the sequential progression of these didactic suicides, and binds father, daughter, and husband into suicidal kinship and kindness. Sure enough, in Shakespeare, Brutus announces, 'farewell, Portia. We must die . . . | With meditating that she must die once, | I have the patience to endure it now' (IV. iii. 190–2). Brutus' suicide expressly asserts his sufficient agency, but it is also a response to his wife's suicidal demand. As discussed elsewhere in relation to Renaissance friendship, the once-vaunted male relationship must adjust to incorporate a cultural imperative to marry—a negotiation central to *The Two Gentlemen of Verona*—yet in *Julius Caesar* the all-male league of revolutionaries demand an aggressively intense amity that threatens to overwhelm heterosexual relationships. Cassius' reformative friendship has 'work[ed] so much upon [Brutus'] shape' (II. i. 253) that Portia hardly recognizes a man once 'incorporate' (l. 273) with her; he has been incorporated back into the body of a male alliance. Typically in Shakespearean comedy, male friendship is supplanted by the demands of matrimony, often with real regret, as in the case of the two Antonios of *Twelfth Night* and *The Merchant of Venice*, as one model of indivisible identity is superseded by another (arguably a Christian model mapped over a Classical). But in *Julius Caesar*, it is the wife who is left enquiring, 'am I your self?' (l. 282), forced into suicide by her separation from Brutus. Even the news of her death is drowned out by male interaction, lost among reaffirmation of the conspirators' increasingly fragile friendship; rather than being figured as one-half of a romantic, self-sacrificial couple, Portia becomes another of Shakespeare's suicidal women, dispatched offstage, and forgotten in the heat of masculine warfare and aggressive reciprocation: 'She should have died hereafter' (*Mac.*, V. v. 16).

Returning to the April of AD 65, Lucan's uncle, Seneca, under orders from his former pupil Nero, commits the act of *necessitas* (enforced suicide) that comes to exemplify the Stoic noble death in a 're-enactment of the death of Socrates for which Plato . . . had provided the script'.[83] Tacitus' account of Seneca's death shows how clearly this 'apostle of suicide' saw his death not just as a grand gesture to ensure his historical fame but also as part of a didactic narrative of self-slaughter.[84] The

---

[82] Martial, 1. 42.   [83] Griffin, 'Philosophy', 66.
[84] Miriam Griffin, *Seneca: A Philosopher in Politics* (Oxford, 1976), 384.

philosopher-politician announces 'I leave for you my one remaining possession, and my best: the pattern of my life', and these words, adds Tacitus, 'were evidently intended for public hearing'.[85] Seneca has demonstrated his theatrical sensibilities: 'As it is with a play, so it is with life—what matters is not how long the acting lasts, but how good it is', adding that one can leave life 'wherever you will—only make sure that you round it off with a good ending'.[86] Tacitus' account of Seneca's 'slow and lingering' death moves from an account of an apparently composed oration—'Surely nobody was unaware that Nero was cruel!'—to an increasingly grotesque catalogue of self-inflicted sufferings.[87] Ironically, after announcing that 'tranquillity can be purchased at the cost of a pin-prick', Seneca found that his aged body, 'lean from austere living', would not allow the blood to run free from his wrists, his ankles, or behind his knees, and yet that he had lost enough blood to inhibit the effects of the poison he then took.[88] Finally, 'he was placed in a bath of warm water [then] carried into a vapour-bath, where he suffocated'.[89] Clearly, Seneca was firm in his resolve to dictate the terms of his own death.

In his writing, which in general presents the more permissive face of the frequently dogmatic Stoicism and softens its harsher dictates, Seneca also significantly adapts traditional Stoic views on self-slaughter. We are not to wait passively for divine prompting; rather, we are invited actively to seek 'a tolerable pretext to die':

In whatever direction you may turn your eyes, there lies the means to end your woes. See you that precipice? Down that is the way to liberty. See you that sea, that river, that well? There sits liberty—at the bottom. . . . See that throat of yours, your gullet, your heart? They are ways of escape from servitude. . . . Do you ask what is the highway to liberty? Any vein in your body![90]

The world is full of suicidal possibility. Nature is no longer providing subtle signs but suddenly seems structurally designed to point towards 'the highway of liberty'. As Rist marvels, 'to allow suicide in certain situations is one thing, to exalt in it is quite another', and it becomes clear from

[85] Tacitus, 15. 58–62.
[86] Seneca, *Letters*, 72. 18.
[87] Tacitus, 15. 62.
[88] Seneca, *Letters*, 70. 16; Tacitus, 15. 62.
[89] Ibid., 15. 62.
[90] Rist, *Stoic Philosophy*, 249; Seneca, *De Ira*, in Basore, 295.

Senecan texts like *De Ira* or *De Providentia* that the Cynic intellectual inheritance which presented death and life as matters of extreme indifference has given way to Seneca's eager *promotion* of self-inflicted death.[91] Death is privileged:

> A person who has learnt how to die has unlearned how to be a slave. He is above, or at any rate beyond the reach of, all political powers. What are prisons, warders, bars to him? He has an open door. There is but one chain holding us in fetters, and that is our love of life.[92]

Life is no more than a fetter. Should you be ill, end the suffering; imprisoned, free yourself; troubled with a broken heart, commit suicide: 'Cast out your heart whatever torments it, and if it cannot be extracted, tear out your heart along with it.'[93]

> I know where I will wear this dagger then:
> Cassius from bondage will deliver Cassius.
> Therein, ye gods, you make the weak most strong;
> Therein, ye gods, you tyrants do defeat.
> Nor stony tower, nor walls of beaten brass,
> Nor airless dungeon, nor strong links of iron,
> Can be retentive to the strength of spirit. (I. iii. 89–95)

The close repetition of the proper noun allies Cassius to the Stoic approbation of independence—the wise man 'retires to his inner self, . . . his own company'—providing the dividual duplication that self-directed action requires, and asserting *autarkeia*, a self-sufficiency that 'make[s] the weak most strong' and 'tyrants do defeat'.[94] Previously, Cassius describes his 'single self' (I. ii. 94) in a construction indebted to dualistic rhetoric: 'I had as lief not be as live to be | In awe of such a thing as I myself' (ll. 95–6). Here, the 'strong links of iron', the 'airless dungeon', and 'worldly bars' that Cassius invokes are overtly Senecan: both Cassius and Seneca advocate a life lived with the suicidal 'power to dismiss itself'. 'That part of tyranny that I do bear', both men assert, 'I can shake off at pleasure' (I. iii. 99–100). Casca's agreement that '[s]o can I, | So every bondman in his own hand bears | The power to cancel his captivity'

---

[91] Rist, *Stoic Philosophy*, 248.
[92] Seneca, *Letters*, 26. 8.
[93] Ibid., 51. 13.
[94] Ibid., 9. 16.

(ll. 100–2) confirms that Cassius is not alone in his connotatively Stoic philosophy, and that Stoicism provides the prevailing philosophical and suicidal atmosphere of this play: 'I am armed, | And dangers are to me indifferent' (ll. 114–15); 'Men at some time are masters of their fates' (I. ii. 139).

The political implications of self-slaughter are clear, and the action is easily understood as one of rebellion that 'subverts . . . subjection'.[95] Imprisoned by Nero, who feared the aged philosopher had become the focal point of increasing dissent, Seneca commits an act of enforced suicide. Jon Davies suggests discordance between old Stoic and Senecan Stoic attitudes towards suicide when he concludes that Seneca's was a 'defeated suicide *from this life, not* a victorious death *into* another, better life with God'.[96] Seneca's death is explicitly worldly, grounded in politics, 'an act of defiance and self-liberation committed in the face of oppression and tyranny'.[97] Paul Plass's analysis of the 'moral-political logic of suicide' finds an 'unusual hybrid passive activism' in these *necessitas* suicides (although I hope that 'unusual' is challenged by this study, passive activism being a familiar theme). A death of *necessitas* is peculiarly susceptible to paradoxical interpretation—'no one', Lucan satirically remarks, 'is forced to die willingly'—as McGuire summarizes: 'Suicide, after all, as eloquent an act as it might be, is an act of self-destruction, and so, at the same time as it defines the absolute opposition to tyranny of the person who carries it out, it also terminates this opposition.'[98]

Necessitas is a punishment. While this type of death sentence allows the self-murderer the *dignitas* of taking his own life, making the good ending as he sees fit, it is still an enforced punishment; this is still a case of being allowed and therefore licensed, and as such cannot simply figure as an act of 'absolute opposition'. Consider first that Stoicism as a code proved so politically useful to the emperors, breeding a significant pacifism in the upper classes; Augustus, the first emperor, found that the potentially unruly wealthy plebeians were withdrawing from political

[95] P[hilipot], *Self-Homicide-Murder*, 8.
[96] Jon Davies, *Death, Burial and Rebirth in the Religions of Antiquity* (London, 1999), 207.
[97] Donald T. McGuire, *Acts of Silence: Civil War, Tyranny, and Suicide in the Flavian Epics* (Hildesheim, 1997), 185.
[98] Cit. Plass, *The Game of Death*, 102; McGuire, *Acts of Silence*, 186.

activism in favour of a retreat into private introspection, aspiring not to positions of power or privilege but rather to the role of the Stoic wise man, by definition uninvolved in the machinations of civil politics. In addition, Stoicism's liberal attitude towards self-slaughter is curiously useful to a ruler who can condemn his enemies to deaths of *necessitas*, allowing them what is seen as a noble way out, while getting them out of the way. Letting the philosophers glorify their deaths as *iactatio*, a ruler like Nero can hide the true face of *necessitas*. Whether this is *necessitas* or *iactatio*, whether the victim is 'pushed or jumped', Nero has developed an effective judicial tool, one facilitated by what is unwittingly an effective philosophical sanction.[99]

Plass's discussion convincingly employs game theory to trace the fluctuations of political and private power at play in an act of *necessitas*, opening out the symbolism of Seneca's evaluation of the suicide of Canus. Canus, interrupted in a game of draughts by Caligula's soldiers, who had come to pronounce the *necessitas* demand, tells his opponent that he should not dare claim the game ('You will be witness that I am leading by one piece'); Seneca remarks that Canus invests a game of draughts with more importance than the fatal game that Caligula wanted him to play.[100] What Plass locates in his discussion of Seneca's suicide is a politicized exchange of public and private moves (fluctuating between Nero's assertion of authority and Seneca's assertion of individual agency), which presents this death of *necessitas* as simultaneously an assertive self-slaughter and a passive, instructed suicide.[101] Self-slaughter becomes a gambit, an attempt to escape the rules of an oppressive authority; but suicide becomes a validation of the authority's powers of oppression. Self-slaughter shows disdain for the machinations of politics left behind; but suicide is political machination. These are the paradoxes of suicidal action, 'both vacuous and real'.[102] The final scenes of *Julius Caesar* and *Antony and Cleopatra* exhibit the tension of this interplay as self-slaughterers are re-socialized, state-sanctioned, edified as national icons where they themselves had offered dissidence and oppositional suicidal gestures. Shakespeare avoids resolution, providing neither a

---

[99] Plass, *The Game of Death*, 90.
[100] Seneca, *De Tranquillitate Animi*, in *Four Dialogues*, 14.
[101] See Plass, *The Game of Death*, 101–2.
[102] Ibid., 90.

triumph for individuate agency, nor a victory of Octavian oppression; rather, what we receive in these suicide narratives is something integrally paradoxical, founded in ambiguity. Suicide itself, as Elise Garrison concludes, 'is a paradox. The motivation, e.g., desire for good reputation, may be honorable, but the act itself is brutal and frightening.'[103]

So, to conclude the *pugio* sequence of self-murderers, we arrive at the death of Nero, himself the cause of so many similar deaths:

When he understood it implied thus much, that the man so condemned should be stripped all-naked, his head locked fast in a fork, and his body scourged with rods to death, he was so terrified therewith that he caught up two daggers.[104]

This is a suicide, as Suetonius describes it, which enacts 'a play in which his love for power and fear of losing it struggle against each other until the very end' but which finally encapsulates Garrison's paradox: Nero panics; he begins 'to lament, weep, and wail'; calls for *fides* (assisted suicide); begs for help.[105]

'I live shamefully'.... 'It becomes not Nero, it becomes him not. In such cases as these he had need to be wise and sober; go to man! Pluck up thy heart and rouse thyself!'... he yielded up his breath, with his eyes staring out and set in his head, to the great fear and horror of all that were present.[106]

Nero, needing to construct a 'good ending'—something memorable, something noble—comes only to this 'timorous' realization of the brutal and frightening reality of self-slaughter.[107]

Brutus similarly demands *fides* from his soldiers—'Hold thou my sword-hilts whilst I run on it' (V. v. 28)—requesting participational suicide as a loving act of friendship. Refusing responsibility, Clitus and Dardinius deny that this is 'an office for a friend' (l. 29), driving Brutus to introspection with the dereliction of their friendly duty:

---

[103] Elise P. Garrison, *Groaning Tears: Ethical and Dramatic Aspects of Suicide in Greek Tragedy* (Leiden, 1995), 174.

[104] Suetonius, 'Nero Claudius Caesar', in *History of Twelve Caesars*, trans. Philemon Holland (London, 1606), 49.

[105] Asko Timonen, *Cruelty and Death: Roman Historians' Scenes of Imperial Violence from Commodus to Philippus Arabs* (Turku, 2000), 238.

[106] Suetonius, 49.

[107] Ibid., 49.

BRUTUS. Sit thee down, Clitus. Slaying is the word,
    It is a deed in fashion. Hark thee, Clitus. [*Whispering*]
CLITUS. What, I, my lord? No, not for all the world.
BRUTUS. Peace then, no words.
CLITUS.   I'll rather kill myself.
BRUTUS. Hark thee, Dardanius. [*Whispers*]
DARDINIUS.   Shall I do such a deed?
  ...
CLITUS. What ill request did Brutus make to thee?
DARDINIUS. To kill him, Clitus. Look, he meditates. (V. v. 4–8; 11–12)

In reflection, Brutus becomes a 'noble vessel full of grief' (l. 13), his fullness speaking of complete and overflowing sufficiency. 'It is more worthy', he says, 'to leap in ourselves | Than tarry till they push us' (ll. 24–5), reclaiming both his active agency and his worthy reputation. It is 'Brutus' tongue' that shall have 'ended his life's history' (ll. 39–40) in an act of simultaneous self-authorship and self-destruction that encapsulates the double-edged Roman desire to write one's own heroic ending. 'I shall have glory by this losing day' (l. 36) he announces, his verbal expression now thoroughly bound up in the paradoxical inversions of the suicidal dynamic where losing is winning and winning figures loss.

Suicide, in *Julius Caesar*, emphatically accommodates the Senecan 'good ending', even the mistaken self-murder of Cassius on his birthday providing preposterous pattern and logic to an increasingly disordered battlefield of civil war: 'This day I breathèd first, time is come round | And where I did begin there shall I end' (V. iii. 23–4). In stabbing Cassius, Pindarus commits an act of *fides* that completes a long debt to his master (ll. 37–40), accepting the final twist of symmetry that suicide so often proffers: 'Caesar, thou art revenged | Even with the sword that killed thee. [*Dies*]' (ll. 45–6). The logic of suicide often runs like this, with small ironies, paradoxical traces, symbolic symmetries; depicting an act of perfection (to bring to an end) a sense of structural involution fashions integrity, building discrete lexical units, and moments of symbolic self-sufficiency.

And self-sufficiency is key:

[*Runs on his sword*]
              Caesar, now be still,
I killed not thee with half so good a will. [*Dies*] (V. v. 50–1)

By betraying friendship in the murder of Caesar, Brutus initiated civil war both within Rome and within himself; it was intended as a 'piece of work that will make sick men whole' (II. ii. 327) but occasioned only division. In his final suicidal action, Brutus has rediscovered his will. Where previously his language disclosed his self-estrangement, the wilful act of self-murder makes the half-man whole. The assertion of what Cassius called single self is achieved via the self-sufficiency of self-directed action, self on self, 'for Brutus only overcame himself, | And no man else hath honour by his death' (V. v. 56–7). No man else, but Brutus only: the suicidal self-reflections achieve the integral identity, discovering himself to himself in involuted kindness. Lucilius had predicted that Brutus would ultimately be found 'like Brutus, like himself' (V. iv. 25), and, in this deed, Lucilius can now confirm that '[s]o Brutus should be found. I thank thee, Brutus, | That thou hast proved Lucilius' saying true' (V. v. 58–9). Finally like himself, his self accurately reflects his self, the 'noblest Roman of them all' (l. 68).

Typically, as with all these moments of high selfhood, the play quickly subsumes the suicidal expression of individual agency back into the high order of solemnity. Antony, Odysseus-like, ennobles the 'Roman', re-packages his memory for the 'common good' (l. 72), already elevating Brutus to the level of Roman myth, legendary and therefore removed from the political, taken from the actual location of the present reality to be celebrated by 'all the world', and glorified at heroic distance: '"This was a man!"' (l. 75). The suicidal leader of an aggressive civil faction is taken with 'all respect of rites of burial' (l. 77), taken within the tent (l. 78) of his enemy, Octavian, and translated from dangerous murderer to an ideal of Roman masculinity, '[m]ost like a soldier' (l. 79): 'This is a Roman's part' (V. iii. 89).

Reason . . . advises us to die, if we may, according to our taste. . . . Farewell.[108]

---

[108] Seneca, *Letters*, 70. 28.

5

Romana mors in *Antony and Cleopatra*

> O you, our wretched Parents (thus severe
> To your owne bloud!) my last Petition heare:
> Whom constant love, whom death hath joyn'd, interre
> Without your envy in one Sepulcher.
> And thou, O Tree, whose branches shade the slaine;
> Of both our slaughters beare the lasting staine:
> In funerall habit: ever clothe your brood;
> A living monument of our mixt blood.[1]

Romeo and Juliet—whose parents' division was symbolically healed in their shared sepulchre, a monument to mixed blood—may not have been Shakespeare's first suicidal couple. During the period 1595–6, Shakespeare offers both his romantic tragedy and its parodic counterpart in his restaging of Ovid's tale of Pyramus and Thisbe. Thisbe's suicidal oration, above, is an evident source for all Romeo and Juliet narratives and consequently Ovid's suicidal scene is revisited in both generic contexts.

> Approach, ye Furies fell!
> O Fates, come, come,
> Cut thread and thrum,
> Quail, crush, conclude, and quell. (*MND*, V. i. 268–71)

Pyramus' exuberant death throes—'Now die, die, die, die, die. [*He dies*]' (l. 290)—find ample support in Ovid's gratuitously horrific episode; perhaps Bottom should accompany his oration with a twitching limb,

---

[1] *Ovids Metamorphosis*, trans. Sandys, 66–7.

his legs convulsing as he 'str[ikes] the stained earth'.[2] As the 'smoke' of spraying 'hissing' blood is 'up-spun' and 'through the aiery Region spout[s]' as if 'a Spring-conducting pipe is broke', Ovid's description recalls the projectile blood of Luctetius' wounded lover, springing from the body towards the beloved, desperate to merge and mingle in their body.

Yet Bottom, far too fond of the limelight, is too self-absorbed to make a kind Pyramus or a receptive Thisbe, both of whom, in every other telling of the story, are representatives of a generous, selfless sympathy:

> (Quoth he) I loue, for loue (quoth she) I die.[3]

Dunstan Gale, in his *Pyramus and Thisbe* of 1617, imagines self-slaughter as a romantic ideal: 'And for a signe of mutuall loue in either, I Their ill shed bloud congealed both together' (ll. 479–80). This mutual declaration of love is articulated with the radically compressed rhetorical efficiency that befits the intersubjective identity of lovers—'I him, he me, loue him and me hath slaine' (l. 466)—bringing pronouns together, congealing clotted constructions of inextricably convoluted reflection. First- and third-person pronouns frame and reframe each other, working the rhetoric of undividable individualism into the texture of a line, thereby presaging the moment of self-reflexive suicide:

> Then with resolue, loue her resolue did further:
> With that same blade, her selfe, her selfe did murther. (ll. 467–8)

We return to the 'herself herself', 'himself himself' construction via the doubly stressed 'resolue' of self-slaughter, and it is this resolute suicidal self that can claim that '[h]imself was author of his death' (l. 451).

> now behold Hieronimo,
> Author and actor in this tragedy,
> Bearing his latest fortune in his fist:
> And will as resolute conclude his part
> As any of the actors gone before.
> And, gentles, thus I end my play:
> Urge no more words: I have no more to say.[4]

---

[2] Ibid., 66.
[3] Gale, *Pyramus and Thisbe*, l. 94.
[4] Kyd, *The Spanish Tragedy*, IV. iv. 146–52.

Through suicide the lover lays claim to narrative agency, their resolution, 'as if a man were author of himself' (*Cor.*, V. III. 36).

However, 'resolve' contains pertinent paradoxical sense when employed to describe this most paradoxical of assertively destructive
actions. 'Resolve'd to die he sought the pointed blade': the claim,
found in almost all representations of suicide, that 'therefore am I
fully resolued' suggests the agency and self-mastery of the suicidal.[5]
But, the word discloses a secondary sense, that of 'dissolve': 'his olde
marrow to a cold iuyce quickly resolued'.[6] That 'resolue' can carry this
double weight of meaning—'myne eyes be resolud in watery fountains'
which will 'mollify . . . the flintstone'—suggests a crucial dichotomy: the
self-slaughterers have taken their own resolve, asserted their self-author-
ship, but have also dissolved, bled out, destroyed themselves.[7] As with
the narcissine identity, the potential for self-construction is undercut by
concurrent self-destruction.

Both of these simultaneously affirmative and negative models of
resolved/dissolved identity, the suicidal and narcissine selves, have affinity with an impulse described by Shakespeare in his second narrative
poem, *The Rape of Lucrece* (1594). Shakespeare's poem, once again
structured around a 'war of looks', this time between the 'greedy eye-
balls' (l. 368) of Tarquin and Lucrece's 'pity-pleading eyes' (l. 561),
describes the motivation of Tarquin's lust in the following terms:

> Save sometime too much wonder of his eye,
> Which having all, all could not satisfy;
>   But, poorly rich, so wanteth in his store,
>   That cloyed with much, he pineth still for more. (ll. 95–8)

The reflexive 'all, all' encapsulates the passage's reckoning: repetition of
'all' leads to its own surfeit, the second 'all' coming devalued and
worthless, unsatisfactory. So an increase and repetition leads to a de-
crease and loss, until the word itself—'all'—becomes 'cloyed' and
'poorly rich'. 'All' is in fact nothing, and 'so by hoping more they
have but less; | Or gaining more, the profit of excess | Is but to surfeit,

---

[5] Gale, *Pyramus and Thisbe*, l. 337; [Watson], *The Lamentations*, sig. E1[r].
[6] Watson, *The Lamentations*, sig. E1[v].
[7] Ibid., sig. A2[r].

and such griefs sustain, | That they prove bankrupt in this poor rich gain' (ll. 137–40). The logic of 'poorly rich' and 'poor rich gain' applies equally to affirmed yet denied suicidal and narcissine identities, transforming attainment into lack, achieving 'nothing' in an attempt for 'all': 'so then we do neglect | The thing we have; and, all for want of wit, | Make something nothing by augmenting it' (ll. 152–4). The preposterous turn, where a chronological involution allows cause to be pre-cursed (Hamlet's pun) by an effect that both pro- and pre-cedes it, characterizes suicidal rhetoric and structures the suicidal self-subject who 'himself himself confounds' (l. 160):

> Such hazard now must doting Tarquin make,
> Pawning his honour to obtain his lust;
> And for himself himself he must forsake. (ll. 155–7)

Appropriating the logic of 'poor rich gain', the 'all, all', 'something nothing', and now 'himself himself' constructions precisely 'confound' themselves, becoming definitions of self-loss. The tenor of affirmed agency—Tarquin forsakes himself '*for* himself'—is coupled with the reality of self-denial as he 'himself himself seek[s] every hour to kill' (ll. 997–8).

Shakespeare's geminative rhetoric, most pure and frequent in his narrative poetry where the young imitative poet showcases his Ovidian influence, figures a resolute subject, firm and fluid: 'For now against himself himself he sounds this doom, | That through the length of times he stands disgracèd' (ll. 717–18). Tarquin, 'hat[ing] himself for his offence' (l. 738), raving 'against himself' (l. 982), has revealed the threat to identity of 'himself himself' reflection. As the action of a self-hating man, suicide complements the self-scrutinizing, intradialogic quality we find in, for example, Robert Burton's description of melancholic introspection where men are 'beside themselves for the time'.[8] That sense of bifurcation that allows dialogic monologue, and is understood as correspondence with oneself, is commonplace in depictions of dejection: here, Lucrece insists that 'I alone, alone must sit and pine'

---

[8] Robert Burton, *The Anatomy of Melancholy*, ed. Thomas C. Faulkner, Nicolas K. Kiessling, and Rhonda L. Blair, 6 vols. (Oxford, 1989), i. 438.

(l. 795) after a sexual assault that 'hath made herself herself detest' (l. 1566). These repetitions of 'alone, alone' and 'herself herself' provide only hollow resounding and loneliness. But ultimately, it is Lucrece who correlates geminative pronominal construction with the resolution of suicide, potentially redeeming a word and the imaginative lexicon of reciprocation:

> Dear lord of that dear jewel I have lost,
> What legacy shall I bequeath to thee?
> My resolution, love, shall be thy boast,
> By whose example thou revenged mayst be. (ll. 1191–4)

Holding back womanish tears and the dissolving tenor of 'melt' (l. 1218), 'melting eye' (l. 1227), and 'swelling drops' (l. 1228) that threatens to soften her stiff resolve, Lucrece offers her suicidal resolution as exemplary prefiguration for masculine revenge: 'My resolution, husband, do thou take; | Mine honour be the knife's that makes my wound' (ll. 1200–1).

Lucrece's noble suicide presents a dilemma for early modern Christian commentators who warily absolve or reluctantly condemn her: as a victim, she is innocent; as a self-murderess, she is guilty.[9] Rhetorical gemination circumnavigates this debate, legitimizing a potentially uncomfortable correlation of the defiled body with moral pollution, allowing the innocent soulful second self to act not as self-murderer but judge, jury, and executioner of a sinfully complicit corporeality. The standard geminative structure of corporeal humoral subjectivity understands the soul as indivisible from its material constraint until its liberation in bodily death. There is an integral and typically fractious dialogue between body and soul, made irritable by their inseparability. This dialogic structure will be extended until riven by Cartesian dualism as it relocates the locus of selfhood beyond (or beneath) the confines of a non-humoral body. The geminative structures of subjectivity persist but are confined ever more narrowly within the mental perimeters of a radical self-relation; the interaction between body and soul will be less integral to the Cartesian subject than the intra-activity of second-order

---

[9] See Ian Donaldson, *The Rapes of Lucretia* (Oxford, 1982); Wymer, *Suicide and Despair*, 96–110.

consciousness, thinking on thinking. Acceptance of the absolute division between mind and body will facilitate re-evaluation of the merely material, and a refocusing of ipseic attention on the interactivity of the mind with itself. Lucrece's suicide takes advantage of body-soul gemination to permit self-repudiation and self-denial while simultaneously aggressively liberating an incorrupt iconic identity, subjecting its own body to its own revenge:

> How Tarquin must be used, read it in me:
>   Myself thy friend will kill myself thy foe,
>   And for my sake serve thou false Tarquin so. (ll. 1195–7)

Although Plotinus would warn Lucrece that 'you should not expel the soul from the body'—arguing that 'he who effects this separation, is not liberated from passion, but is under the influence of some molestation, or pain, or anger'—Lucrece's refraction into 'myself thy friend' and 'myself thy foe', murderer and murdered, is perfect explication of the dichotomy that a suicidal self-resolution allows.[10] She forces 'brief abridgement' between 'soul and body' (ll. 1998–9) to hold innocence and guilt, resolution and dissolution, richness and poorness, agency and effacement in a state of precarious simultaneity.

But in death, as Thomas Middleton's ghost of Lucrece attests, she finds only a pharmacal 'antidote'.[11] Fighting to wrestle back her narrative—'He writes himselfe the shamer, I the shame'; Lucrece feels the loss of agency—'The Actor hee, and I the tragedie'; feels how he has dictated her subjectivity—'The subiect I, and he the rauisher'; grasps for autonomy in self-slaughter—'He murdring me, made me my murderer'; but loses hold of her appropriated identity: '*Lucrece* I say how canst thou *Lucrece* bee?'[12] Only the merest trace of narrative authority resides in her suicidal conclusion:

> Bleede no more lines, (my heart,) this Knife, my pen,
> This bloude my incke, hath writ enough.[13]

---

[10] Plotinus, *Collected Writings*, trans. Thomas Taylor (Frome, 1994), 417.

[11] T[homas] M[iddleton], *The Ghost of Lucrece* (London, 1600), sig. A5^v.

[12] Ibid., sigs. B8^r; C5^v.

[13] Ibid., sig. C6^r.

1. I AM ALONE: ENOBARBUS' SUICIDE

I will tell you.
The barge she sat in, like a burnished throne
Burned on the water.

(*Ant.*, II. II. 200–2)

Enobarbus' much analysed speech, heavily indebted to Plutarch, finds all description 'beggar'd' (l. 208) by the rare Egyptian's 'own person' (l. 207). His report of Cleopatra's entrance circumnavigates the central figure, moving from the 'barge she sat in', to the pavilion '[o]'er-picturing' her, to 'each side of her', to the 'invisible perfume' on 'adjacent wharfs' (ll. 201–23). Short bursts of oxymoron—'Burned on the water' (l. 202), 'what they undid did' (l. 215)—fashion a self-defeating language that in doing undoes itself, beggaring its own description. 'Language itself', says Linda Charnes, 'generates a kind of haze in the air.'[14] It is a vivid and ornate description of adjacency where 'the sensual artifice of the whole scene radiates outward from her', but avoiding the 'deflected, oblique' invisible centre, outlining a lack every bit as tangible as the airless 'vacancy' around Antony in the market-place.[15] Catherine Belsey has described Cleopatra as the 'absent centre', 'consistently exploiting the lack that is the cause of desire'.[16] The 'gap in nature' (II. III. 228) equates to a gap in depiction, gazed upon but unseen; 'by drawing everything to herself', Belsey explains, 'she emblematically isolates Antony in an absence which precipitates desire'.[17] Charnes correlates the speech's 'abstracted language' with what Frank Whigham describes as a 'phenomenological notion of glamour [that] links mystery and value' or what Andrew Fichter calls the 'elusiveness which keeps desire alive'.[18] With her

[14] Linda Charnes, *Notorious Identity: Materializing the Subject in Shakespeare* (Cambridge, Mass., 1993), 124.
[15] Alexander Leggatt, *Shakespeare's Political Drama: The History Plays and the Roman Plays* (London, 1988), 164; Catherine Belsey, 'Cleopatra's Seduction', in Terence Hawkes (ed.), *Alternative Shakespeares*, vol. 2 (London, 1996), 38–62 at 45.
[16] Belsey, 'Cleopatra's Seduction', 45; 42.
[17] Ibid., 42.
[18] Frank Whigham, *Ambition and Privilege: The Social Tropes of Elizabethan Courtesy Theory* (Berkeley, 1984), 64; Andrew Fichter, '*Antony and Cleopatra*: "The Time of Universal Peace"', *SS*, 33 (1980), 99–111 at 105.

infinite variety refusing to settle, the Egyptian queen is partly 'hidden beyond description', partly effaced through the play's sheer weight of tangential depiction.[19] Amongst these critical voices, these further descriptions, is an embodiment of necessarily undepictable desire that makes hungry as it satisfies. Antony will be 'beguiled . . . to [this] the very heart of loss' (IV. xii. 28–9).

In Samuel Brandon's 1598 *The Virtuous Octavia*, Cleopatra's handmaiden warns against the correlation of desire and lack: a desire that 'doth spring, from what we wish, and want' (i.e. wont), she reasons, will 'loose himselfe in winning of his saint'.[20] Mary Herbert, in her translation of Robert Garnier's 1583 *Marc Antonie*, is equally guarded against the 'absence [that] besottes'.[21] Her Antony, however, is susceptible:

> ANTONY. So foolish I, I can not her forget.
> Though better were I banisht her my thought.
> Like to the sicke, whose throte the feauers fire
> Hath vehemently with thirstie drought enflam'd,
> Drinkes still, albee the drinke he still desires
> Be nothing else but fewell to his flame:
> He can not rule himself: his health's respect
> Yealdeth to his distempered stomacks heate.
> LUCILUS. Leaue of this love, that thus renewes your woe.[22]

The feverish or love-sick man—'I, I can not her forget'—is caught in the Ovidian preposterous narcissine dilemma, *inopem me copia fecit* or 'my plentie makes me poore'.[23] Second-order desire, so artfully aroused by depictions of lavish absence, has only itself to feed upon, only an absent presence to sustain it, only its own desire to admire. The alliterative abundance of drought, drinks, and desires, followed by a spate of fricatives, runs tight rhyming correspondences across Herbert's lines, linking word to word, imposing the reaction of one upon the other in suitably cyclic patterns of 'fire' to 'enflam'd' back to 'fewell' and back again to 'flame'. Each word feeds, calls up, generates its rhyming

[19] Charnes, *Notorious Identity*, 164.

[20] Samuel Brandon, *The Virtuous Octavia, 1598* (Oxford, 1909), V. i. 1967–9.

[21] Robert Garnier, *The Tragedie of Antonie*, trans. Mary Sidney Herbert (London, 1595), sig. A6^v.

[22] Ibid., sigs. D3^v–D4^r.

[23] Golding, *Shakespeare's Ovid*, III. 587.

partner, and is recalled in turn, neatly enacting the *inopem me copia fecit* dynamic, feeding its own fuel, verbally both renewing itself and yielding to its own replacement. The movement combines the double quality of narcissistic and suicidal action, both asserting and destroying itself, caught within the cyclic boundaries of self-absorption and self-to-self action. The escalation of perceived value (my plenty) is an actual loss (makes me poor), as Plutarch had warned in his depiction of the greedy yet devaluing queen: 'Cleopatra . . . did waken and stirre up many vices yet hidden in him, and . . . if any sparke of goodnesse or hope of rising were left in him, Cleopatra quenched it straight, and made it worse than before.'[24] Accordingly, Herbert's passage is driven by the overreaching of Antony's desire—'he still desires'—which strives for more while he becomes less: 'He can not rule himself.' An insatiable loving dynamic predicated upon an absent centre correlates narcissism (filling the absence with one's own desire) with the suicidal impulse (feeding a self-destructive fire), and, in 1607, Shakespeare borrows this association from Pembroke:

> Age cannot wither her, nor custom stale
> Her infinite variety. Other women cloy
> The appetites they feed, but she makes hungry
> Where most she satisfies. (II. ɪɪ. 245–8)

Cleopatra feeds but never abates the appetite, fulfilling to encourage further consumption, with what Jonathan Gil Harris describes as a 'hunger-inducing reflection'.[25] A more Roman reading than even Enobarbus could provide would point out the constant hungry lack, the refusal of consummation and fulfilment in self-perpetuating Egyptian neediness. Accordingly, Caesar's accusation that Antony fills his 'vacancy with his voluptuousness' and his suggestion that this full vacancy is both a kind of 'surfeit' (I. ɪv. 25–8) and yet also a moral vacuity is a standard Roman evaluation of the desire Egypt evokes. Voluptuousness and vacancy oscillate and exchange with what John Danby describes as

---

[24] Plutarch, *Lives of Noble Grecians and Romanes*, in Geoffrey Bullough (ed.), *Narrative and Dramatic Sources of Shakespeare*, trans. Thomas North, 8 vols. (London, 1964), v. 273.

[25] Gil Harris, ' "Narcissus in Thy Face" ', 412.

'the logic of a peculiarly Shakespearean dialectic' where opposites are 'juxtaposed, mingled, married', and which I would associate with his Ovidian influence.[26]

On the larger political scale, the fluctuations of the play's action, the ebb and flow of each combatant's fortunes in the sea battle, enact a similar oscillatory movement. Enobarbus can compare the 'full Caesar' with Antony's 'emptiness' (III. xiii. 35–6), and Thidias can describe Caesar as the 'fullest man' (l. 89). It is in Enobarbus' Act III description of Antony that we receive the clearest indication of the dialectic quality of the two terms, as the Roman soldier articulates his attitude towards the Egyptian excesses of his general. His description of the revelling Antony is characterized by terms of filling and increase; the revellers '[f]ill [their] bowls once more' (l. 188) until the 'wine peep[s] through their scars' (l. 194) in an image of satiated repletion that simultaneously signals a dangerous lack of Roman measure, and a more critical implication of Antony's diminishing moral sense. The full bowl, the satiate soldier, is merely a vacancy filled with voluptuousness. Egypt offers to the Roman observer only overflowing measures (I. i. 2), 'surfeits' (I. iv. 27), 'voluptuousness' (l. 26), and the 'lascivious wassails' of 'rioting in Alexandria' (II. ii. 78). This is a far remove from the Roman impulse to keep things 'square' (l. 195) and 'by th'rule' (II. iii. 6), to 'hold', to 'knit', to 'knot' (II. ii. 133–5), a far remove too from Caesar's insistence on containment, from the tight and literally all-encompassing political 'hoop [that] should hold us staunch, from edge to edge I O'th'world' (ll. 122–3). When an Egyptian thought strikes him, Antony can break this hoop, come out of compass, not keep his square (II. iii. 6), melt Rome in the Tiber, escaping the 'wide arch I Of the ranged empire' (I. i. 35–6). From an Egyptian perspective, this surfeiting beggars reckoning (I. i. 15), breaks the bourns, overflows like the 'swells' (II. vii. 19) of the Nile, and is full of promise and fertile harvest (ll. 20–2).

However, the poeticism with which Enobarbus associates plenitude and absence, absence and value, asks to be compared to an antithetical passage from Act I: Caesar's speech beginning 'Antony, I Leave thy lascivious wassails' (I. iv. 56–72). The gilded, presumably yellow

---

[26] John F. Danby, '*Antony and Cleopatra*: A Shakespearean Adjustment', in John Drakakis (ed.), Antony and Cleopatra: *New Casebooks* (Basingstoke, 1994), 33–55 at 51; 36.

piss-filled puddle of Caesar's speech is a far cry from the beaten gold of the Egyptian barge; the savages entirely antithetical figures to the pretty dimpled boys; the roughest berry and bark of trees diametrically opposed to Antony's 'Egyptian dish' (II. VI. 123); the strange flesh which some die to look on playing counterpart to Cleopatra, the 'morsel for a monarch' (I. v. 32) whom Antony eats with his eyes (II. II. 235–6). Rather than the ornate 'haze in the air' language of Enobarbus' description, Caesar's speech is both verbally and imaginatively tactile, physical in its tenor, rougher and ruder. Caesar speaks a 'virile' language, masculine in its semantic accuracy, whereas Enobarbus is lulled into effeminate superabundance, articulating ornate emptiness.[27] The absent centre is a semiotic rupture, inducing indulgence in verbal gratification to feed the craving of desirous description; early modern erotic depiction is predicated upon the wonting absence at the heart of signification—an unavoidable vacuum at the epicentre of all description, every word—that fuels desire but can never consummate. A word wonts its object. Consequently, Cleopatra's Egyptian entrance as the embodiment of desire—viewed through the haze of perfumed air—has a counterpart in the image of her captive entry into Rome, emerging in the 'posture of a whore' (V. II. 220) among another gawping populace who 'encloud' her with their 'thick breaths' (ll. 210–11).[28] Part of this play's tragedy is that Egyptian structures of desire are demystified and displayed as degraded: Cleopatra on her barge, the absent presence that evokes wonting desire; a whore displayed on a Roman stage, the absent object of all pornographic description. Language, as ever in Shakespeare, is a faith-based system, therefore either conceived as a perfumed haze, or a rank cloud, but always desiring to fill its intrinsic vacancy. Enobarbus revels in that desire-inducing vacancy, while Caesar aims at

---

[27] Patricia Parker, 'Virile Style', in Louise Fradenburg and Carla Freccero (eds.), *Premodern Sexualities* (London, 1996), 199–222.

[28] The *OED* has Shakespeare's 'posture' as the earliest citation for 'demeanour, attitude', but this seems to me to be an erotic posture as found in the pornographic engravings of Giulio Romano for the 'Sixteen Postures' of Pietro Aretino (perhaps known to Shakespeare, who may be playing on Romano's association with pornography by making him the sculptor of Hermione's reanimated statue that so insistently recalls that early modern pornographic standard, the statue of Pygmalion's Galatea).

immediacy that would make words wound (I. iv. 70). Both men delimit a vaunted lack: the vacuity integral to desire, wanting to be filled; the wont of a lean sufficiency, desiring no surplus.

In her analysis of Caesar's speech, Janet Adelman explains how Antony's male and pseudo-mythic identity is predicated upon his reaction to lack: 'Caesar and his Romans', she argues, 'have claimed . . . scarcity as their own, institutionalizing it and making it the basis of their male selfhood.'[29] The Roman Stoics are—perhaps with a certain hypocrisy considering the opulent lifestyle of some such as Seneca— advocates of austerity: 'For this we were born.'[30] Rather than 'bursting with unlimited and immoderate blessings' the wise man should see that 'they glitter and deceive', and while God may 'bedeck' you with 'gold, and silver, and ivory . . . within there is nothing good' (like the ornate word).[31] Seneca's language, sitting well alongside Shakespeare's imagery of excess and scarcity, graphically discloses the Roman abhorrence of excess and immoderation; 'death from starvation', he says, 'comes very gently, but from gorging men explode', with Shakespeare's wine peeping through their scars.[32] 'The hungry self', Adelman concludes, 'is the manly self', allowing total self-sufficiency, admitting no need for exterior sustenance.[33] There is a forceful isolationist tendency at work here, an 'economy of the self' central to Stoic subjection. Stoics from Zeno, and his emphasis on *autarkeia*, to Arius Didymus' discussion of self-sufficient *virtus* promote a retreat towards a frugal solipsistic interi- or.[34] As Seneca concludes, 'Retire into yourself as much as you can': 'the supreme ideal does not call on any external aids. It is home-grown, wholly self-developed', he argues, suggesting that the wise man 'retires to his inner self, is his own company'.[35]

---

[29] Janet Adelman, *Suffocating Mothers: Fantasies of Maternal Origins in Shakespeare's Plays* (London, 1992), 176.

[30] Seneca, *De Providentia*, in *Moral Essays*, trans. Basore, i. 43.

[31] Ibid., 31; 43.

[32] Ibid., 31.

[33] Adelman, *Suffocating Mothers*, 179. In Adelman's argument this includes an exclusion of the female.

[34] Ibid., 178; Arius Didymus, *Epitome of Stoic Ethics*, ed. Arthur J. Pomeroy (Atlanta, Ga., 1999), 11h 75.

[35] Seneca, *Letters from a Stoic*, 7. 10; 9. 16.

As evinced by his description of Cleopatra, Enobarbus displays a
Roman perspective while acknowledging his propensity for Egyptian
excess. Even more than his General, Enobarbus provides a Roman voice
in Egypt, his suicidal deliberations playing a staunch Roman ethos
against an underlying Egyptian emotive tenor. In his preposterously
constructed complaint against Antony that 'he'll outstare the lightning.
To be furious | Is to be frighted out of fear' (III. xiii. 199–200),
Enobarbus demonstrates a Roman propensity to find only frenzied
madness in—in this case verbal—profligacy. Fear acts upon itself: fear
fear has slain. Recognizably the suicidal rhetorical turn, this structural
involution demonstrates precisely how Egyptian excess can be revealed
as Roman loss; the preposterous roll maps out a movement where the
increase or the doubling of a single quality creates only a lack and a
diminution. Fear added to fear only results in meaningless empty fury,
'an irrational and unnatural movement of the soul' and 'an impulse
which is excessive', in the words of the Greek Stoic founder, Zeno.[36]
Antony comes to fit the Senecan model of the angry man as set down in
De Ira, refusing to be ruled, becoming unbalanced; 'anger', Seneca
concludes, 'is a swelling'.[37] So, with characteristic Roman insight,
Enobarbus has identified the key tenor of Antony's passion, identifying
the wanting desire's distinctive self-defeating quality, and sees its sus-
ceptibility to suicidal resolution, providing a Roman reading—in accordance with Caesar's perception that things are 'deared by being
lacked' (I. iv. 44)—of the lovers' wanting desire:

> I see still
> A diminution in our captain's brain
> Restores his heart. When valour preys on reason,
> It eats the sword it fights with. I will seek
> Some way to leave him. *Exit* (III. xiii. 201–5)

Restoration and diminution exist in dialogue, the binaries of fullness
and emptiness again interweaving to suggest ever more clearly how
Antony's Egyptian-influenced notion of increase and restoration can
simultaneously be Rome's notion of self-defeating diminution.

---

[36] *Stoicorum Veterum Fragmenta*, ed. Joannes Arnim, 4 vols. (Leipzig, 1905), i. 205.
[37] Seneca, *De Ira*, in *Moral Essays*, trans. Basore, 161.

Appreciating preposterous danger, Enobarbus leaves Antony, reject-
ing Egyptian influence: 'I see men's judgements are | A parcel of their
fortunes, and things outward | Do draw the inward quality after them |
To suffer all alike' (ll. 31–4). 'The rational mind [should be] unaffected
by external adversity' so once the 'supreme ideal . . . starts looking
outside itself for any part of itself it is on the way to being dominated
by fortune';[38] the brave man's spirit 'gives its own colour to everything
that happens; for it is mightier than all external things'.[39] Drawn by
fortune and 'things outward', Antony lacks Stoic constancy, 'depend
[ing] for stability on external things that may fail him at any time:
honour and love', which, by its nature, resists the stability of fulfilled
attainment.[40] 'The assaults of adversity do not weaken the spirit of a
brave man', says Seneca, as he always maintains his 'poise', but Antony,
in the eyes of a Stoic whose 'goods are directed inward', fails to be self-
sufficient, fails to take value from himself alone, fails in his dependence
on external influence, on infinite variety.[41] For Stoic Enobarbus, the
fear of an unacceptable intrusion of external fortune into private *autarkeia* dictates that to remain Roman he must depart.

   However, leaving Antony proves fatal to Enobarbus; 'self-sufficient
through he is, [the Senecan wise man] still desires a friend, a neighbour,
a companion', and Enobarbus' tragic conclusion depends upon this
concession.[42] Enobarbus' rejection of Antony equates with a rejection
of himself, initiating a catastrophic self-division resulting in the self-
accusatory realization that 'I have done ill, | Of which I do accuse myself
so sorely | That I will joy no more' (IV. vi. 18–20). An accusatory
inward turn involving a doubling of self signals the start of Enobarbus'
division and subjective proliferation: I see; I will seek; I have done; I do
accuse myself; I will joy no more. The self-assertive Roman, constant
and true to himself—whose departure declared 'I am none of thine'
(IV. v. 9)—finds that individuate identity was critically dependent
upon its affiliation with the dangerously inconstant and dissolute Antony. Where once he defined himself in terms of his reflexive quality—

---

[38] Geoffrey Miles, *Shakespeare and the Constant Romans* (Oxford, 1996), 183; Seneca,
Letters, 9. 16.
[39] Seneca, *De Providentia*, 7.
[40] Miles, *Shakespeare and the Constant Romans*, 183.
[41] Seneca, *De Providentia*, 7; 45.
[42] Seneca, *Letters*, 9. 2.

'your considerate stone' (II. ii. 117)—Enobarbus' tragic end is emphatically solitary, isolated, and lonely: the tragedy of a self-willed man who underestimated his reliance upon the beloved other.

> I am alone the villain of the earth,
> And feel I am so most. O Antony,
> Thou mine of bounty. (IV. vi. 31–3)

The largesse of Antony's Egyptian 'bounty' counters the loneliness of the isolated Roman; no longer do bounty and excess denote emptiness and lack; rather, it is Roman self-assertion that leads to isolation, to absolute lack. All your goods, it now appears, are not directed inwards: the lack of his companion is the loss of a mine of bounty (semantic play on 'mine' being a familiar feature of Shakespearean love lyricism). The self has not proved sufficient. 'Thou mine of bounty' juxtaposes the 'thou' and 'mine', the self and other, bisecting individuate amity; Enobarbus' split from Antony enacts self-slaughter, as articulated in his despairing question, 'I fight against thee? No' (l. 38); to fight Antony would be to fight himself, his mine of bounty.

> This blows my heart.
> If swift thought break it not, a swifter mean
> Shall outstrike thought; but thought will do't, I feel. (IV. vi. 35–7)

Again, a preposterous turn provides linguistic impetus towards death: suicidal action—the swiftest means to break the heart—is outstruck by the devastating guilty thought. This is, pronominal frequency suggests, the death of a solitary 'I', a man left only with his 'I', who feels that 'I am alone', 'I am', 'I feel', 'I fight', until 'I will go seek | Some ditch wherein to die' (ll. 37–9). His death stands alone in the play as an unambiguously tragic example of a painfully divided double self—'Throw my heart | Against the flint and hardness of my fault' (ll. 15–16)—where bipartite individualism allows his 'life' to be 'a very rebel to my will' (IV. ix. 15), and his guilt delineates a separate identity self-defined as that of a 'master-leaver and a fugitive' (l. 22). There is a dialectic reaction within the self: my heart against my fault. Enobarbus, as his final words attest, has broken a relationship of loving reciprocation or reflexive considerateness and consequently has found his 'I' to be 'alone', a 'poor Enobarbus' (l. 9), divided from Antony, divided from himself. His suicide oratory cannot speak of lovers' union, but of the isolation of lover from the distanced beloved: 'O Antony! O Antony! [*He dies*]' (l. 23). The words of the watching sentry provide Enobarbus with his postscript: 'The hand of death hath raught him' (l. 29). 'Raught' here carries its etymological association with 'ratch', to pull or tear asunder.[43] It is not death that has raught Enobarbus: it is Enobarbus who has raught himself from the moment that the soldier condemned the preposterous dynamics of his general's desire, announcing '*I* will seek I Some way to leave *him*' (emphasis added).

Reading only lack and loss into bounty and excess, renouncing loving largesse and mutuality in favour of a Roman form of willed individualism, Enobarbus has tragically endorsed an *autarkeia* that raughts 'I' from 'him', but neglected the friendly violence of interdependence integral to participatory-subjectivity. I am, I shall, I fight: this total self-sufficiency entails genuine loss, complete lack, and ultimately results in an act of lonely, self-responsive but non-reciprocal, non-loving suicide: a kind of worthless semi-Stoic suicide where self-assertion is a poor substitute for mutual love. As Leonard de Marandé warned aspirant Stoics, the 'poyson of paine and griefe' affects even the rational mind 'and infects it with its contagion': 'there is no point of wisedome so pure, which can hinder this trouble, or secure it selfe from it'.[44]

2. OURSELVES TO END OURSELVES: THE SUICIDES OF ANTONY AND CLEOPATRA

> Why do I, not my self occasion finde
> To breake the bounds wherein my selfe am stayd?[45]

Solitary suicide, in Samuel Daniel's *Tragedie of Cleopatra*, represents an attempt to escape the conflict of an antagonistic subjective dialogue, to break the bounds of the self, and disprove the Chorus's insistence that a man 'from himselfe can finde: I No way to start aside I Out of the hell of minde. I But [is] in himselfe confin'd'.[46] Alternatively, the introspective

---

[43] *OED*, s.v. 'Raught'.
[44] Marandé, *The Judgment of Humane Actions*, 308; 304.
[45] Samuel Daniel, *The Tragedie of Cleopatra* (1594), in *The Whole Workes of Samuel Daniel* (London, 1623), 462.
[46] Ibid., 435.

bounds of the solitary individual can be broken through an act of sympathetic suicide. The 'like distresse' of Antony and Cleopatra 'doth simpathize', presaging a conclusion where 'both wrought a like destruction unto either'.[47]

In his initial suicidal attempt, Antony aspires to an act of self-will, self-assertion, and annihilation, resembling Enobarbus' solitary suicidal grief more than it would Cleopatra's loving suicide. Like Hamlet and like Lucretius, Antony stares at the clouds:

> That which is now a horse, even with a thought
> The rack dislimns and makes it indistinct
> As water is in water . . .
> > . . . now thy captain is
> Even such a body. Here I am Antony,
> Yet cannot hold this visible shape, my knave.
> I made these wars for Egypt, and the queen,
> Whose heart I thought I had, for she had mine—
> Which whilst it was mine had annexed unto't
> A million more, now lost . . .
> . . .
> Nay, weep not, gentle Eros, there is left us
> Ourselves to end ourselves. (IV. xiv. 9–22)

Renouncing Cleopatra, Antony expresses his Roman intent to subdue 'my worthiest self' (IV. xii. 47) with the club of Hercules, to turn ourselves against ourselves in self-slaughter. Via the exchange of heart for heart, of 'mine' for hers, the Queen had offered Antony a glimpse of the escalating arithmetic of Egyptian excess where one and one equals a million more. She had presented him not the famine and lack crucial to Roman identity, but rather the quantity of her heart, not as loss but as addition. But out of love with Egypt, Antony rejects the mutuality and possessive bounty of love that he believes to have misled his better Roman nature. It is, he implies, the fluidity of Egypt that has unfixed him, preventing him from holding his identity as 'Antony' (whereas no one 'ever saw a change in Cato [even] in death itself').[48] Unsquared and dislimned, Antony becomes mixed; the 'man of steel' (IV. iv. 33) melts, and the 'firm Roman' (I. v. 45) softens. Against dangerous Egyptian

---

[47] Ibid., 433.
[48] Seneca, *Letters*, 104. 32.

liquidity, permeability, and the fluid obscurity of 'water in water'—
where repetition is subsumption—Antony must now assert the high-
Roman ideal of 'ourselves to end ourselves', and 'embrace, at last, Stoic
constancy'.[49] This violent bandying has a rhetorical precursor in
Antony's challenge to Octavian to meet 'sword against sword, | Our-
selves alone' (III. xiii. 27–8). There is a reflexive duality in depictions of
man-to-man combat that is carried over into descriptions of self-to-self
violence: sword against sword refashioned as ourselves against ourselves,
or self against opponent replayed as self against self, suggesting that
suicidal brutality internalizes the patterns of martial encounter.

Jonathan Dollimore describes this phrase—'ourselves to end ourselves'—as an 'assertion of a negative, inverted autonomy' but at
this moment this is all that is left to an increasingly evanescent
Antony, and does at least offer some form of the stabilizing autonomy he desperately seeks.[50] Within the speech, Shakespeare employs paradoxical examples of ploce: initially to denote the
dangerous fluidity of language, where water simply loses its own
identity within itself; subsequently, to fix or bolster the self in a
solid block of epanalepsis, fashioning a line of linguistic stability
both beginning and ending in 'ourselves'. Indeed, suicide, and its
rhetorical trope, becomes a final attempt, both actual and linguistic,
to reinstate this fixity of identity, to hold this visible shape of
Antony. Suicidal gemination represents the apotheosis of a
Roman ethos that understands self-identity to be predicated on
the loss and the absence of all else. Dollimore sees this self-
sufficiency as the keynote of Roman identity construction, a *virtù*
akin to the Greek tenet expressed by Agamemnon that 'what hath
mass or matter by itself | Lies rich in virtue and unmingled' (*Tro.*,
I. iii. 29–30). Antony, as 'man of men' (*Ant.*, I. v. 75), is occasionally credited with this independence, figured in these 'Lord of
lords' (IV. viii. 16) phrase constructions.

But Cleopatra has circumvented his suicidal attempt:

---

[49] Miles, *Shakespeare and the Constant Romans*, 184.
[50] Jonathan Dollimore, *Radical Tragedy: Religion, Ideology and Power in the Drama of Shakespeare and his Contemporaries* (Brighton, 1984), 211.

ANTONY.   O, thy vile lady!
    She has robbed me of my sword.
MARDIAN.   No, Antony,
    My mistress loved thee, and her fortunes mingled
    With thine entirely. (IV. XIV. 22–5)

Literally robbed by Egypt of his sword, Antony cannot keep his Stoic resolution, while figuratively too, Egypt has robbed him of his Roman resolve and refuses to allow his individuate ending. Mardian's words— the emasculated Egyptian eunuch an apt messenger to the feminized swordless Roman—tie Antony back into the 'thee' and 'thine' patterns of mutuality, linguistically binding him back into the characteristic idiom of loving reciprocation, of mingling entirely. Mingling, which both Agamemnon and Caesar describe as a threat to the single suffi- ciency of virtue, is of course central to the loving identity: 'O heavenly mingle!' (I. v. 62). Such 'admixture, compounding, combination, mor- tising, [or] complexity' is anathema to the Stoic Cicero, who must be 'free from all'.[51] But while Ciceronian impassivity insists that 'the soul cannot be separated off nor split up nor taken apart nor torn asunder', the early modern dramatist would be attuned to philosophical emphasis on mutability—via the likes of Montaigne, Charron, or Marandé—and would feel contestation between competing visions of Stoic simplicity and Cynical compounding: 'among the compounded, there is none more multiplied then man'.[52] While the example of Cato, 'endowed by nature with an austerity beyond belief... unswerving consistency... true to his purpose and fixed resolve', is alluring to the fluctuating Antony, his resolve repeatedly fails to be fixed, and his purpose remains troublingly unclear.[53]

In this exchange we witness the final and irreversible turn from Roman self-sufficiency back to Egyptian admixture, and, in place of Antony's threatened act of solitary self-slaughter, Shakespeare sets up an alternative suicidal model in Cleopatra's feigned suicide: her Egyptian revision of the Roman death.

---

[51] Cicero, *Tusculan Disputations I*, 71.
[52] Ibid., 71; Marandé, *The Judgment of Humane Actions*, 301.
[53] Cicero, *De Officiis*, trans. Walter Miller (London, 1913), 1. 31.

> The last she spake
> Was 'Antony, most noble Antony!'
> Then in the midst a tearing groan did break
> The name of Antony; it was divided
> Between her heart and lips. (IV. xIV. 29–33)

This is emphatically the death of a lover, split in two, torn by the beloved's absence. Her verbal breakage enacting the division of the loving double self, Cleopatra allies herself to a literary tradition of lovelorn lovers, rewriting suicide as an act not of Roman individualism but of Egyptian love, and contesting the symbolic meaning of suicide.

Antony's subsequent desertion of the heroic identity—'the sevenfold shield of Ajax' cannot help him now (l. 38)—is figured in the removal of his armour, the renunciation of his martial role, and his acceptance of overflowing, bourn-breaking emotion, distinctively Egyptian in tenor; containment becomes restriction, and Antony wills his sides to 'cleave' as his heart expands beyond its measure to 'crack [its] frail case' (l. 41). In his suicide oration, Antony has recourse to the preposterous turn, the rhetorical self-slaughtering revolution that insistently recalls the *inopem me copia fecit* dynamic, as 'all labour I Mars what it does' and 'force entangles I Itself with strength'.

> I will o'ertake thee, Cleopatra, and
> Weep for my pardon. So it must be, for now
> All length is torture; since the torch is out,
> Lie down and stray no farther. Now all labour
> Mars what it does; yea, very force entangles
> Itself with strength. Seal then, and all is done.
> Eros!—I come, my queen.—Eros!—Stay for me.
> Where souls do couch on flowers, we'll hand in hand,
> And with our sprightly port make all the ghosts gaze.
> Dido and her Aeneas shall want troops,
> And all the haunt be ours.—Come, Eros, Eros! (IV. xIV. 44–54)

Terence Eagleton describes this 'self-defeating action' as 'continually involving its own breakdown', noting the appropriateness of this figure to the suicide oration context: 'the ultimate self-defeating action possible to a man, suicide'.[54]

---

[54] Terence Eagleton, *Shakespeare and Society* (London, 1970), 124.

But Antony is rejecting worldly narcissism, and in a final wonderfully paradoxical twist he turns away from entwining self-directed action associated with a degraded existence in the 'now . . . Now'. Invoked in its place is a triumphantly mutual and reciprocal ideal of lovers hand in hand. It is worth recalling the final lines of Brandon's 1598 *The Virtuous Octavia*, where the eponymous heroine, in pious condemnation of her Egyptian rival, watched as 'hand in hand the stormes of mischief goe', commenting that '[g]riefe is enchain'd with griefe, and woe with woe'.[55] While the earlier text correlates the rhetorical structures of repetition with a love that binds both parties to mutual and general destruction, Shakespeare associates the ploce motif not with the 'stormes of mischief' but with a vision of near-mythic love. The disjunction between the two playwrights' application of the same phrase is indicative of their divergent approaches to this destructive and death-marked love: Brandon, championing the virtuous Octavia, sees mischief in mutuality; Shakespeare, feeling the allure of Antony and Cleopatra, appreciates their mythic potential. This is an insistently vital mythic vision as the quiet pun on 'sprightly' suggests; their ghosts are indeed dead spirits and therefore have a 'sprightly port' but despite their deathliness they maintain a certain sprightliness, lively and animated even beyond life. There is, it would seem, potential to slip the enchaining grief and the bind of woe upon woe and find something animated, something spirited beyond.

Hand in hand, these lovers outdo the suicidal precedent of Dido, who is here seemingly reunited with Aeneas (a couple who notably failed to find reconciliation in their deaths).[56] As the Virgilian couple 'want' (lack) their ghostly troops who have gone to 'gaze' upon Antony and Cleopatra, Shakespeare revisits the imagery and language of Enobarbus' speech, now providing not an unfulfilling absence but an Egyptian vision of mutual possession ('all the haunt be ours'). Suicide is no longer an enforcement of the individual's delineated single self, his private fixed, firm, and squared identity, but an act of hand-in-hand loving reciprocation, run to as to a lover's bed (IV. xiv. 100–1).

[55] Brandon, *The Virtuous Octavia*, V. iii. 2274–7.

[56] Shakespeare's 'hand in hand' acts as redemptive revision of Dido's final verbally reflexive curse on Aeneas: 'Shore to shore, sea to sea, weapon to weapon opposed—I I call down a feud between them and us'. Virgil, *The Aeneid*, trans. C. Day Lewis (Oxford, 1986), 4. 628–9.

Amatory suicide redeems the pharmaceutical oxymoron, 'for with a wound I must be cured' (l. 77), and finds assertion in an act of self-negation: by her death Cleopatra tells Caesar that '"I am conqueror of myself"' (l. 62).

After death, in his absence, Antony begins to live, his material loss occasioning an opportunity for mythic revisionism. Alexander Leggatt demonstrates how Antony, as he dies and after his demise, is written back into the narrative, reconstructed as heroic by the mourning Cleopatra: 'for Antony, loss is a final step to transformation... as the physical Antony fades, he is replaced by the heroic Antony for whom Cleopatra is the spokesman'.[57] Antony's departure, leaving an 'absence | No better than a sty' (IV. xv. 63–4), effectively leaves him open for reinterpretation as '[n]oblest of men' (l. 61), ultimately not to be read in terms of 'loss' (V. ii. 100) as the Roman Dolabella does, but in terms of excess, 'past the size of dreaming' (l. 96). In fact, it is Antony who reveals the poverty of nature by comparison: 'Nature wants stuff' (l. 96). Into this space of lack, this valueless, meaningless lacuna at the heart of the Egyptian queen's world, comes a revisioned Antony, a mythic hero whose legs bestride oceans (l. 81) and whose arms encompass worlds (l. 82): the stuff of Cleopatra's dreams (ll. 75–93). As Adelman suggests, Antony's posthumous construction is symptomatic of his 'heroic grandeur' that has always been 'constructed retrospectively, in his—and its—absence' so that even when he is on stage 'his presence is suffused with a sense of absence or loss'.[58] In retrospective depictions—from Caesar, Enobarbus, Cleopatra, and occasionally himself—we receive the full, complete 'Antony', a character of legend and far removed from the drunken wassailer we see before us. The very absence of depiction's semiotic structure, the removal of the corporeal Antony, facilitates a fictive construct of heroism, writing him into a distinctly Roman death, fitting him into a Roman model of suicide whose language owes a significant debt to Plutarch's final evaluation: 'now he was overcome not cowardly, but valiantly, a Roman by another Roman'.[59]

---

[57] Leggatt, *Shakespeare's Political Drama*, 181.

[58] Adelman, *Suffocating Mothers*, 177.

[59] 'The Life of Marcus Antonius', in *Shakespeare's Plutarch: The Lives of Julius Caesar, Brutus, Marcus Antonius, and Coriolanus in the Translation of Sir Thomas North*, ed. T. J. B. Spencer (Harmondsworth, 1968), 120–1.

> Not Caesar's valour hath o'erthrown Antony,
> But Antony's hath triumphed on itself. (IV. xv. 15–16)

As previously in 'ourselves to end ourselves' and now in 'Antony, | But Antony', Shakespeare borrows a Roman language of suicide, an identity of valiant double self so emphatic in the Plutarch source that Antony the Roman became 'another Roman', a literal second self acting upon itself. Later Antony will explicitly paraphrase the Plutarch passage in his lines 'and do now not basely die, | Not cowardly put off my helmet to | My countryman—a Roman by a Roman | Valiantly vanquished' (ll. 59–60).

The play perpetuates a distinction between a Roman suicidal double self, where identity is deliberately split in order for action to be entirely self-sufficient, himself acting only upon himself with his 'self-hand' (V. i. 21), and a (perhaps 'Egyptian') mutual loving suicidal self, where duplication and doubling simply speak of coupled reciprocation and renounces the paucity of solitude. This is made explicit as this exchange continues:

> CLEOPATRA. So it should be, that none but Antony
>   Should conquer Antony, but woe 'tis so!
> ANTONY. I am dying, Egypt, dying; only
>   I here importune death awhile, until
>   Of many thousand kisses the poor last
>   I lay upon thy lips. (IV. xv. 17–22)

It is, Cleopatra must acknowledge, appropriate that Antony should conquer Antony; it is fit that he should fit this Roman model. The line construction is a complex piece of antitheton (proof constructed from contradiction): the epanaleptic '*So* it should be . . . but woe 'tis *so!*' combines with internally overlapping paregmenon of '*should . . . Antony should . . . Antony*'. It *should* be that Antony the Roman *should* conquer Antony but that it *should* is woeful. *So*, this fits, squares up with the perfect balance and symmetry of a re-established order that re-limns the previously unholdable shape of Antony: but woe 'tis *so*. Using the very rhetorical figure that establishes this Roman linguistic order, Cleopatra appears to undercut its structural logic; her framing repetition rebukes the Roman logic it contains. The exchange is caught between triumphalist assertions of self-conquering and these more woeful strains of regret that ally the pair to the literary tradition of star-crossed lovers. The 'many thousand kisses' Antony lays upon Cleopatra's lips invoke the dying kisses of the lovers in *Romeo and Juliet* narratives from Brooke, through Painter, to Shakespeare, and sound a familiar chord from these narratives of amatory suicide. The speeches throughout this scene seemingly fluctuate from the aggressively political to the gently tender, from overthrowing, triumphing, and conquering to kissing lips, and loving 'sport indeed' (l. 33).

Here, the fluctuations from political to private, from Egyptian to Roman, from solitary self-slaughter to loving suicide, finally find some form of resolution. Shakespeare brings a play structured around contrapuntal action and the vicissitudes of vacillation to its terminus figured in the acts of self-slaughter:

> My resolution and my hands I'll trust. (IV. xv. 51)

Adopting high-Stoic vocabulary of resolute suicide, Cleopatra successfully unifies the Roman and Egyptian, bringing both models together in a single act. Clearly, Shakespeare inherits a figure with a contradictory aesthetic pre-history, condemned as an icon of feminine immoderation, immortalized as the epitome of beauty and generous love. Yet, almost without exception in her various literary manifestations, her suicide redeems nobility, redeeming her via association with what are connotatively Roman virtues—'Nobly she to death resigned'—and masculine values—'Not with woman's shrinking mind'—that are simultaneously martial yet erotic—'Gazed upon the deadly knife':

> Firm of purpose, calm she stood,
> Holding with unflinching grasp
> To her breast applied the asp
> Sternly resolute she dies.[60]

In her death, as described here by Horace, Cleopatra adopts the qualities of firmness, stability, and marble constancy that are so central to the Roman ideal of fixed resolve, firm masculine resolution. Crucially, Horace's description applies *the* specific Roman designation of idealized planned death (*deliberata morte ferocior*). For Cleopatra to be accredited with *deliberata morte ferocior* is for her to achieve Roman heroic status, to become iconic, a model self-slaughterer, another Lucrece.

---

[60] Horace, *The Odes of Horace in English Verse*, trans. various (London, 1929), 1. 37.

Accordingly, in Shakespeare, her act is 'what's brave, what's noble' and is done 'after the high Roman fashion' (IV. xv. 92). Her end will 'make death proud to take us', insistently demanding to be read, to be viewed, as both public spectacle and private action: 'Come, we have no friend I But resolution and the briefest end' (ll. 91–6). 'We have no friend' says Cleopatra, just as Antony, on the brink of Roman self-slaughter, announced 'we are left us I Ourselves'. Cleopatra, dying for love, dying to avoid political shame, achieves an incorporation of Rome and Egypt in an act of loving resolution. She is indeed 'the noblest Roman of them all' (*JC*, V. v. 68).[61] In her suicide Cleopatra plays the Stoic, in an action that is both emphatically private and yet proudly presents itself on the political stage as an act of self-presentation and political potency: 'This mortal house I'll ruin, I Do Caesar what he can' (V. ii. 50–1). This is not, as Proculeius protests, the 'undoing of yourself' (l. 43), but rather, in an act of Stoic self-presentation and Egyptian reciprocation, her way of being 'noble to myself' (l. 191), of fulfilling her immortal longings (l. 275), and answering the call of her departed lover: it is an act of loving reciprocation ('I hear Antony call . . . '), even of erotic reciprocation ('I see him rouse himself . . . '); and it is an act of presentation ('to praise . . . '); of Stoic nobility and theatricality ('my *noble act*') (ll. 277–9).

Suicide is both an ultimate act of finality, and a gesture beyond the end to a projected future either in reunification with the beloved, or in the creation of a posthumous mythic identity. Cleopatra's death, on so many levels a death that unifies dual perspectives, typically welcomes this paradox and in doing so insists on the simultaneity of contradictory elements:

> And it is great
> To do that thing that ends all other deeds,
> Which shackles accidents and bolts up change,
> Which sleeps, and never palates more the dung,
> The beggar's nurse and Caesar's. (V. ii. 4–8)

---

[61] Leggatt, *Shakespeare's Political Drama*, 183. See Miles, *Shakespeare and the Constant Romans*, 185, and Charles and Michelle Martindale, *Shakespeare and the Uses of Antiquity: An Introductory Essay* (London, 1990), 181.

In defiant paradox, suicide draws no distinction between Caesar and a beggar, and yet makes Cleopatra 'great'; it is both the end of worldly deeds and the ultimate act. Enforcing and effacing distinction, her suicidal action simultaneously attests both to Cleopatra's enduring fame and greatness, and to the finality of her death:

> My resolution's placed, and I have nothing
> Of woman in me. Now from head to foot
> I am marble-constant; now the fleeting moon
> No planet is of mine. (V. II. 237–40)

It is not simply feminine inconstancy that Cleopatra rejects here, but also Egyptian fluidity and flux, and, associating herself with an image of statuesque constancy, announcing her masculine suicidal resolution, Cleopatra adopts the resolute solidity of an iconic self-image; whereas Antony's cloud pictures shifted and dislimned, Cleopatra is aesthetically stabilized as marble-constant. Her act of effacement perpetuates her myth, her remembrance, ergo her identity; the stony fixity of the statue has bolted up change, shackled her image for ever, but equally it has promoted endurance beyond her temporal span. Elsewhere she announces that 'I am again for Cydnus, | To meet Mark Antony' (ll. 227–8), suggesting that her end completes a return to where her love began, on the river of Cydnus where Enobarbus watched as she captivated his general; here is the final preposterous temporal involution, an ending presaging a beginning. This is politic—as Caesar knows, 'by some mortal stroke | She do defeat us' (V. I. 64–5)—but this is loving: 'The stroke of death is as a lover's pinch, | Which hurts, and is desired' (V. II. 289–90). In death she is ideal, immortal, cold as marble, but she is warm, earthly: 'she looks like sleep, | As she would catch another Antony | In her strong toil of grace' (ll. 340–1). She dies with nothing of woman in her (ll. 237–8), but she dies a mother: 'Dost thou not see my baby at my breast, | That sucks the nurse asleep?' (ll. 303–4). She dies resolute, with firm resolve, but as she dies the world dissolves around her: 'Dissolve, thick cloud, and rain' (l. 293).

The suicidal impulse, seen as a form of self-assertion grounded in self-negation, matches and surpasses the model of the Roman wanting desire, a love founded on lack: in self-slaughter, Antony and Cleopatra redeem this model of desire so the dependence of gain upon loss, love upon lack, is rewritten as an act of total self-effacement that leads to absolute mutual gain.

CLEOPATRA. As sweet as balm, as soft as air, as gentle—
O Antony! — Nay, I will take thee too.
        [*She applies another asp*]
    What should I stay— [*Dies*]
CHARMIAN. In this wide world? So, fare thee well. (V. II. 305–8)

And, in the unfinished line and the move beyond, the move away from this wide world which that verbal open-endedness figures, Cleopatra escapes, transcends, finds the Senecan open door and employs the Stoic key. And, back in the wide world and the actuality of historical report, Octavian permits the completion of their Egyptian monument, allows exotic romance, sets them up as icons of tragic passion, connotatively Eastern and foreign, clearly no threat to Roman power and supremacy figured in the mausoleum of Augustus situated back in Rome, 'at the heart of the empire'.[62] The symbolism of this pair of buildings, delineating both private triumph and political defeat, finally encapsulates the paradoxical connotations of Roman and erotic self-slaughter.

[62] Valerie M. Hope, 'Contempt and Respect: The Treatment of the Corpse in Ancient Rome', in ead. and Eireann Marshall (eds.), *Death and Disease in the Ancient City* (London, 2000), 104–27 at 116.

6

Renaissance Attitudes to Self-slaughter

In the second sub-circle of the seventh circle of Hell live Dante's self-murderers. The Italian poet's treatment of suicide stands as a productive point of transition in the changing moral conceptions of self-harm. Among the suicides in the *Inferno*'s thirteenth canto the poetic keynote is of constraint and bondage, the overriding atmosphere one of terrifying restriction:

> I heard cries of woe on every side but saw no
> person uttering them, so that all dismayed I stood
> still.
> My belief is that he believed that I must believe
> that so many voices, among those thickets, came
> forth from people hidden from us.[1]

Surrounded on every side, Dante and Virgil enter a landscape described in extraordinarily contorted constructions, 'expressive', as Durling and Martinez suggest, 'of the problematic of suicide'.[2] The convolutions of assumption in line 25—where belief is predicated upon belief predicated upon belief—risk losing the reader in what Leo Spitzer describes as a 'hopeless entanglement in a verbal thicket', only succeeding in obscuring observed reality behind a confusion of subjective perspectives.[3] If the travellers in Hell are disorientated by the cacophonous voices of untraceable speakers, the reader of the *Inferno* is equally

---

[1] Dante Alighieri, *The Divine Comedy*, ed. and trans. Robert M. Durling, notes Durling and Ronald L. Martinez, 3 vols. (Oxford, 1996), *Inferno*, XIII. 22–7.
[2] Ibid., 25–7 n.
[3] Leo Spitzer, 'Speech and Language in *Inferno* XIII', *Italica*, 19 (1942), 81–104 at 96.

assailed, equally distracted. As we first hear the voices of the suicidal souls, Dante initiates a linguistic set-piece, sending the poetic voice into these paroxysms of introversion and verbal entanglement. That 'my belief is that he believed that I believe' presents a causal progression with a familiar crumple in contingency, a confusion of cause with effect, beginnings with endings. The verbal tendency for a line to turn in upon itself and enact a double bind or linguistic preposterous inversion imposes containment and enforces a rigorous restriction on both the characters and verse: 'inflamed against me all spirits; and those inflamed | inflamed Augustus' (ll. 67–8). This, for Dante, is suicidal: 'My spirit, at the taste of disdain, believing by | death to flee disdain, made me unjust against my just | self' (ll. 70–2).

The fissure between 'me unjust' and 'my just self' offers another instance of potential obscurity via verbal recurrence, more violence of similarity, more words undoing themselves in repetition. The Italian configuration is dense: 'ingiusto fece me contra me giusto'. The forms of 'just' in epaneleptic relation enclose the self-destructive paregmenonic, 'me against me'. As the translators confirm, the line 'condenses and almost spatializes the self-division of the suicide', with *contra* standing as the 'symbol of the counter-natural' (l. 72[n]) the pivot of an antagonistic line, while the word-stems counteract around it, 'suggest[ing] the outrage wrought by the one half of the human soul against the other'.[4] As before in the case of Lucrece, we recall the Augustinian condemnation of suicide that holds the suicide of an innocent more serious than that of one guilty of sin.[5] This is hard-line Augustinian opprobrium, 'for it is not just', as Dante insists, 'to have what one has taken from oneself'; what one has lost cannot be taken back, and uniquely Dante suggests that the souls of his suicides will, alone of all the damned, be refused the reunification of body and soul on Judgement Day.[6]

Having rejected the God-given hybrid of body and soul, the suicides have been punished with a new hybridity, acting as a sign of their sin.[7] In Hell, Dante's suicides are 'imprisoned spirit[s]' (l. 87), bound within

---

[4] Ibid., 96.
[5] Augustine, *The City of God*, trans. J. H., 2 vols. (London, 1890), I.
[6] Dante, XIII. 104–5; 103–8.
[7] Spitzer, 'Speech and Language', 87.

trees, locked into a new wooden corporeality, a new materiality that dictates their expression:

> Then I stretched out my hand a little before me
> and plucked a small branch from a great thornbush;
> and its stem cried out: 'Why do you split me?'
> . . .
> so from the broken stump came forth words and
> blood together. (ll. 31–3; 43–4)

The tale of Piero delle Vigne can only be heard through his wounds, his words only audible in conjunction with the shedding of blood through articulate wounds in 'punitive counterpart [to the] act of self-laceration': the self-murderers find expression in harm, their self-assertion necessitating self-destruction.[8]

Dante's canto is run through with these small symbolic punishments, verbal pinches, linguistic binds, constant reminders that the suicides have broken their bond with God by breaking the bond between body and soul. These passages are riddled with near-consonance, discordant antiphony, verbal dismemberment, and what Patricia L. MacKinnon describes as 'the lexical particles of negation [in] a conspicuous accumulation of negative clauses'.[9] 'They offer', concludes Spitzer, 'a sort of linguistic, or onomatopoeic rendition of the ideas of torture, schism, estrangement . . . bear[ing] in themselves the stamp of self-torture and self-estrangement, and ultimately of infructuous paradox.'[10] '[T]ronchi . . . monchi . . . ramicel . . . tronco . . . sciante . . . scerpi . . . scheggia rotta . . . Ruppi': the language of rupture accumulates while the suicides are bound ever more tightly, knotted, to their new material bodies:

> tell us how the soul is bound in these knots;
> and tell us, if you can, if anyone ever unties himself
> from such limbs. (ll. 88–90)

The suicidal souls have failed to find liberation. While they may express themselves through gashes, and be defined almost exclusively in terms of breakage and violent separation, it is precisely the liberation of broken

---

[8] Ibid., 91.

[9] Patricia L. MacKinnon, 'The Analogy of the Body Politic in St. Augustine, Dante, Petrarch, and Arioso' (Ph.D. diss., University of California, Santa Cruz, 1988), 62.

[10] Spitzer, 'Speech and Language', 95.

bonds that they are ultimately denied. Dante's construction of a textured language of suicidal paradox, entwined violence, this constricting bind of poetic form, his 'consummately mannered formulation', articulates both the suicidal urge for enfranchisement and the inevitability of imprisonment.[11] The self-slaughterer dreams of liberation into infinite space, but is bound to bad dreams.

1. GUILTY DOTH KILLING OF HIMSELF MAKE HIMSELF: RENAISSANCE SUICIDE

So some ... in fury, but most in despaire, sorrow, feare, and out of the anguish and vexation of their soules, offer violence to themselves.... They can take no rest in the night, nor sleepe, or if they doe slumber, fearfull dreames astonish them.[12]

In 1601, Hamlet has bad dreams. His monologue's dialogic question— to be or not to be (III. 1. 56)—can figure as the governing enquiry behind the following discussion of Renaissance conceptions of suicide. Hamlet's lines, seemingly initiating a sequence of binary possibilities set up from this initial dichotomy of being and not being, positive and negative, in fact proceed only to balance negative with negative: slings and arrows against seas of troubles. Being equates to 'suffer[ance]' (l. 57), to the 'pale cast of thought' (l. 85), and to 'bear[ing]' (l. 70), while not to be is to 'take arms' (l. 59), 'oppos[e]' (l. 60), 'fly' (l. 82), finding 'resolution' (l. 84) in an 'enterprise...of great pitch and moment' (l. 86). While the Everlasting has fixed his canon against self-slaughter (I. 11. 131–2), Renaissance dramatists, poets, and essayists typically allow this association of self-destruction with active agency, self-assertion, and resolute determination. But, in the works of later treatise writers, responding to the perceived lenience of Renaissance artists and intellectuals and their correlation of self-slaughter with 'the name of action' (III. 1. 88), we see how this suicidal 'resolution' can be 'sicklied o'er with the pale cast of thought' (ll. 84–5), revoked, and forbidden. We see how a 'nobler' (l. 57), classically inflected resolution interacts with Christian 'conscience' (l. 83).

---

[11] MacKinnon, 'The Analogy of the Body Politic', 77.
[12] Burton, *The Anatomy of Melancholy*, ed. Faulkner, Kiessling, and Blair, i. 431.

'Many and Strange are the Delusions and Evil Suggestions of the Prince of Darkness',[13] and accordingly suicide is understood by Christian commentators as a damnable action, prompted by the enticements of the devil who has the 'power | T'assume a pleasing shape' (II. ii. 552–3) and 'tempt [his victim] toward the flood', drawing his prey to 'the dreadful summit of the cliff' before assuming his true 'horrible form' to deprive man's 'sovereignty of reason, | And draw [him] into madness' (I. iv. 69–74): 'He had a thousand noses, | Horns whelked and waved like the enragèd sea. | It was some fiend' (*Lr.*, IV. v. 70–2). The fear of satanic temptations and the 'desperation' (l. 75) they promote, unnerves Horatio on Elsinore's battlements, and excuses Gloucester's leap at Dover. 'Resist the Devil with the Word', the afflicted are advised, just as Christ resisted when Satan 'tempted [him] to cast himself down from a Pinacle'.[14] Horatio's distrust of the ghost is substantiated by Ezra Pierce's description of despair-inducing visitation, where 'the frightful Shade puts on a pleasing Vizard, and appears to him *sub umbra boni*'.[15]

Indeed, Hamlet's contemplation of self-inflicted quietus seems to lie latent in the suicide debate (either as influence or simply because of a shared literary-historical inheritance), so Pierce's *Discourse of Self-Murder* of 1692 sounds disconcertingly Shakespearean when asking: 'will it not be better for our quiet and security, to pass into the sweetness of Nothing, than to remain a being torn and dissipated with care and concernment?'[16] Equally, Mary Sidney's 1592 translation of Philippe de Mornay's 1576 'Discourse of Life and Death' provides unremitting shocks of recognition (here I intersperse de Mornay and adapted Hamlet):

Follow the one way [*to be*], or follow the other [*not to be*], he must either subject himselfe to a tyrannicall passion [*and by opposing end himself*], or undertake a weery and continuall combate [*suffering the slings and arrows of outrageous fortune*], willingly cast himselfe to destruction [*to die, to sleep*] ... Loe here the young man, who in his youth hath drunke his full draught of the [*uses of this*]

---

[13] Anon., *Sad and Dreadful News from Dukes-place near Aldgate; or, a True Account of a Barbarous and Unnatural Self-Murther Commited by Dorcas Pinkney* (London, 1686), 1.

[14] Owen Stockton, *Counsel to the Afflicted; Or, Instruction and Consolation for such as have Suffered Loss by Fire...Occasioned by the Dreadful Fire in the City of London of the Year 1666* (London, 1667), 222.

[15] Pierce, *A Discourse of Self-Murder*, 11.

[16] Ibid., 7.

worlds vaine and deceivable pleasures, [is] overtaken by them with such a dull heavines, and astonishment [*until he loses all his mirth*], as drunkards the morrow after a feast [*a wassail, a funeral, or a wedding*]: either so out of taste [*that man delights him not*], that he will no more . . . he feeles himselfe so weery [*flat and stale*], and with this continuall conflict so brused and broken [*so whipped and scorned*], that either he is upon the point to yeeld himselfe, or content to dye, and so acquit himselfe [*making his quietus with a bare bodkin*].[17]

Were it not for his conscience ('a perpetually tormenting executioner', de Mornay agrees), Hamlet might 'fly' (III. i. 83) from the 'civill warre within our selves: the flesh against the spirite, passion against reason, earth against heaven, the worlde within us fighting . . . the world', but this conflict is 'evermore so lodged in the bottome of our owne hearts, that on no side we can flie from it'.[18] No matter if we '[r]etire our selves into our selves, we find it there as incleane as any where', as bad dreams invade even the smallest nutshell.[19] As Milton's Satan and Marlowe's Mephastophilis also discover, 'every where we finde our selves' beset by 'a continual warfare', disturbed by 'the debates a man feeles in him-selfe'.[20] Hamlet, it is clear from these insistent echoes, articulates this extremely contentious and absolutely contemporaneous debate.

Part of the complexity of Hamlet's characterization resides in how close he comes to fulfilling a type, confirming period expectations of the melancholic, or assuming the mantle of the insane. When he exclaims 'break, my heart, for I must hold my tongue' (I. ii. 159), he signals the desperate corporeal dislocation of a man 'divided, and at enmity against himself', and, throughout his campaign of cerebral vengeful action he seems 'in a strange manner [to have become] both the active and passive subject of his own action', partly instigating resolute action but prone to contemplation of suicidal 'dissolution'.[21] The tension between the cerebral and corporeal, or the immaterial (solute mental matter) and material (resolute physical form), is encapsulated in his wonderfully ambiguous desire to 'melt, | Thaw and resolve [his solid flesh] into a

---

[17] Philippe de Mornay, 'A Discourse of Life and Death', trans. Mary Sidney Herbert, in *The Collected Works*, ed. Margaret P. Hannay, Noel J. Kinnamon, and Michael G. Brennan, 6 vols. (Oxford, 1998), i. 229–54, 115–27.

[18] Ibid., 498–502.

[19] Ibid., 512–13.

[20] Ibid., 534.

[21] Pierce, *A Discourse of Self-Murder*, 30.

dew' (ll. 129–30) where 'resolve' becomes part of the process not of firm vengeful activity but of liquefaction: Hamlet, to continue appropriating from Pierce, 'separate[s] himself so preposterously', but is too frightened to 'send one part of himself [i.e. his soul], to inherit no . . . mercy [while allowing the body] to be exposed like the interment of some viler Creature, and to be denied [like Ophelia] the decencies of a common obsequy'.[22]

Robert Burton's influential *Anatomy of Melancholy* gestures towards a range of responses to suicidal behaviour. Displaying fashionable contemporary contempt for life's 'squalid, ugly, and . . . irksome daies', typical of the new melancholic vogue for which Burton himself can be held accountable, his text is both censorious of suicide and quietly sympathetic.[23] The melancholic madness, 'the very seedes of fire', seldom causes death, Burton explains, except when the melancholics 'make away themselves', which is 'a frequent thing', and 'the greatest, most grievous calamity, and the misery of all miseries'.[24] Yet elsewhere, Burton pities the suicidal madmen, who find themselves 'beside themselves for the time'.[25] As Rowland Wymer has discussed, the link between melancholy and suicide is a period commonplace, their inextricability affirmed by descriptions of melancholy that disclose its innate violently geminative dynamic:[26] 'My fancie makes me make my selfe, unto my selfe a scorne', the dedicatory verse for Nicholas Breton's *Melancholike Humours* attests, invoking the standard emblem of suicide, the Christ-like 'kind life-rendering pelican' (IV. v. 146), only to emphasize the egocentricity of his selfish sorrow:

> The Pelican, that kils her selfe, her young ones for to feede,
> Is pleas'd to dy, that they might liue, that suck when she doth bleede:
> But, while I in those cares consume, that would my spirit kill,
> Nought liues by me, when I must die, to feede but sorrowes will.[27]

---

[22] Pierce, *A Discourse of Self-Murder*, 30.
[23] Burton, *The Anatomy of Melancholy*, i. 431.
[24] Ibid., 430.
[25] Ibid., 438.
[26] Wymer, *Suicide and Despair*.
[27] Nicholas Breton, *Melancholike Humours* (London, 1600), 18. See the 'kinde Pelican' in George Wither, *A Collection Of Emblemes, Ancient and Moderne* (London, 1635), 154.

Just as the solitary subject is frequently described (after Aristotle) as having 'something that is either *Savage*, or *Divine*, in their Composition', the 'melancholick man', Thomas Walkington explains, is 'either angel of heauen or a fiend of hell: for in whomsoeuer this humour hath dominion, the soule is either wrapt vp into an *Elysium* and paradise of blisse by a heauenly contemplation, or into a direfull hellish purgatory by a cynicall meditation'.[28] Clearly steeped in this kind of rhetoric, the speeches of Shakespeare's meditative Dane are suffused with the rhetoric of suicidal 'melancholy' (III. i. 159); while initially uncertain whether his ghostly father is 'a spirit of health, or goblin damned, | Bring[ing] airs from heaven or blasts from hell' (I. iv. 40–1), Hamlet ultimately relocates conflict 'within' (I. ii. 85). If melancholy 'causeth men to bee aliened from the nature of man', Hamlet articulates a similar dislocation from a nature grown 'rank and gross' (I. ii. 136), and if it causes men 'wholy to discarde themselues from all societie',[29] Hamlet has similarly 'of late... lost all my mirth, forgone all custom of exercises' (II. ii. 280–1): 'Now I am alone' (l. 501).

Accordingly, John King, Bishop of London, laments that the suicidal mind is 'most distrustfull... suspecting it selfe', depicting the suicide not as having the heroic self-sufficiency of the Stoic wise man, but as suffering the plurality of the distracted, feeling what Thomas Browne describes as 'a Hell within my selfe, [where] *Lucifer* keeps his Court in my breast, [and] *Legion* is revived in me'.[30] It is this discrepancy between Stoic self-sufficiency and Christian 'hell within [the] selfe' that underscores Renaissance attitudes towards self-murder: temptation comes from Stoicism, caution from Christianity. Hamlet is caught between the potential quietus his bare bodkin would allow, the Senecan desire to avoid the oppressor's wrong, the whips and scorns of time, and his Christian suspicion that he should bear those ills, grudgingly accept his fardels, and be remembered in orisons rather than a Senecan revenge tragedy. What is Hamlet reading, other than word words words? Like

---

[28] Jeremy Collier, *Essays upon Several Moral Subjects* (London, 1700), 51; T[homas] W[alkington], *The Optick Glasse of Humors; or, The Touchstone of a Golden Temperature* (London, 1607), 64.

[29] Walkington, *The Optick Glasse*, 68.

[30] John King, *Lectures Upon Ionas: Delivered at Yorke in the Year of our Lord 1594* (London, 1618), 189; Thomas Browne, *Religio Medici and Other Works*, ed. L. C. Martin (Oxford, 1964), 49.

his precursor Hieronimo in Kyd's *Spanish Tragedy*, it could as easily be the Bible as *Agamemnon*.[31]

A text such as Philip Sidney's *Old Arcadia* discloses the prevalence of a sixteenth-century suicide debate, demonstrating how suicidal models of melancholic 'self-detestation', amatory sacrifice, Stoic assertion, and damnable desperation can compete for precedence within a single text.[32] Dangerous isolationism—epitomized by Basilius' retreat from the world, where he 'subject[s him]self to solitariness'—is forced hospitably to accommodate intrusive and divisive outsiders, just as the composed single state of mind is forced into 'dangerous division' by the love-sick host's 'incorporati[on]' of desire: 'my life within itself dissolve[s]', a lover will complain, adding 'I am divided in myself; how can I stand? I am overthrown in myself.'[33] 'Gaoler I am to myself, prison and prisoner to mine own self': the text repeatedly attests to the dangerous 'mutual working' of love's pharmaceutical invasion (the curative poison, the poisonous remedy) into the confines of a distracted individual.[34] Love of the beloved 'strange guest' both perfects the subject and disturbs the equilibrium of self-possession, spoiling the security of a retreat 'myself into myself' when the 'unfortunate guest [arrives] to draw me from myself' with the hostile invasion of 'unkind kindness': 'in myself yourself true love doth plant'.[35]

> Echo, what do I get yielding my sprite to my griefs?   Griefs.
> What medicine may I find for a pain that draws me to death?   Death.
> O poisonous medicine![36]

Death is the poisonous medicine for the medicinal poison of love, and deadly suicide the apt cure for self-division.

The introspective repining lover is subject to the self-gratification of narcissine grief—'in wat'ry glass my watered eyes I see'—and the pastoral landscape is enlisted to support his fragile dividuality with its reciprocating kind response: 'my secret woes, | With flamy breath do issue oft in sound . . . [and] doth with echo's force rebound | And make

---

[31] Kyd, *The Spanish Tragedy*, III. xiii. 1–44.
[32] Philip Sidney, *The Old Arcadia*, ed. Katherine Duncan-Jones (Oxford, 1985), 243.
[33] Ibid., 13; 305; 18; 56; 160.
[34] Ibid., 78; 93.
[35] Ibid., 97; 83; 87; 206.
[36] Ibid., 141.

me hear the plaints I would refrain: | Thus outward helps my inward griefs maintain.'[37] The demystification of the pastoral landscape is guaranteed once its responsiveness is revealed as ascribable to a projected egotism; pastoral values of natural kindness are undermined as they are appropriated by the self-absorbed elite, 'wrapped in foggy mist | Of . . . self-love', who invade this formerly bucolic Arcadia.[38] The reciprocal dynamic is shown to be no more than the self-perpetuation of 'self-destructi[ng]' narcissistic emotivity: 'the more I plain, I feel my woes the more', each lover complains as 'he heaps in inward grief that most destroys him'.[39] The 'sweet doubling' of lovers is uncomfortably correlated with a devaluing association with narcissism—'he had lifted up his face to glass himself in her fair eyes'—articulated in bathetic geminative and chiastic rhetoric—'And sorrow feed, feeding our souls with sorrow'—and the self-sacrifice of desire is repeatedly understood in relation to overindulgent self-slaughter: 'if I must die, who can be fit executioners as mine own hands which, as they were accessories to the fact, so in killing me they shall suffer their own punishment?'[40]

Suicide is understood as an affectation of self-infatuated youth. Pyrocles and Philoclea conduct an exhaustive and impressively informed suicide debate. The jejune and Narcissus-like Pyrocles rehearses a series of standard Stoicisms—'an assured tranquillity shuns the greater [evils] by valiant entering into less'—together with theologically specious quibbles that wilfully misread biblical injunction: 'Neither be offended that I do abandon this body, to the government of which thou hadst placed in me, without thy leave, since how can I know but that thy unsearchable mind is I should so do, since thou hast taken from me all means longer to abide in it?'[41] Philoclea, equally well informed, rebuts his logic—'other wise men say that killing oneself is but a false colour of true courage'—and expresses Augustinian argumentation to counter his Classical claims: 'God hath appointed us captains of these our bodily forts.'[42]

---

[37] Ibid., 104.
[38] Ibid., 130.
[39] Ibid., 129; 133.
[40] Ibid., 168, 247, 252.
[41] Ibid., 257; 253. Pyrocles is, like Narcissus, 'of such a cheerful favour as might seem either a woman's face on a boy or an excellent boy's face in a woman' (p. 326).
[42] Ibid., 255.

I have long learned to set bodily pain in the second form of my being.

is his boast.

A virtuous man ... is never to do that which he cannot assure himself is allowable before the everlasting rightfulness, but is rather to think ... pains or not pains ... to be nothing in regard of an unspotted conscience.

is her reply, surprisingly alive to the nuances of contemporary debate.

God have made us masters of ... our own lives ... do you not think?

he attempts. She replies:

No, certainly do I not.[43]

The discussion prefigures the romance's courthouse conclusion, evaluating the competing claims of self-ownership, social responsibility, and divine ordinance: to commit suicide would be to 'prejudicate' God's determination and to indulge in an act of juvenile narcissine self-destructive reflection born of a self-indulgent pastoral eroticism. As the text reawakens from its conceited 'Pastoral' illusion, Euarchus the judge, 'orderer of present disorders', administers his 'cure' of stringent reciprocity; coming as a 'stranger' but being 'engrafted' into the body politic he is the aggressive pharmaceutical remedy, re-establishing 'laws of hospitality' while administering medicine to the poisoned host: 'let us restore unto us our prince by duly punishing his murderers', is Philanax's pharmacal prescription.[44] Although the text ultimately sidesteps the enforcement of like-for-like punishment, there is a pervasive and persuasive sense that judicial rationality must be seen to supersede the empassioned but self-destructive irrationality of erotic indulgence. Just as Philoclea disabuses the emotive loving illogic of the suicidal Pyrocles, the text comes to renounce the trivial concerns of cheapened pastoralism. Erotic suicide or desperate heroism is emphatically allied to old-world naivety and offered as a nadir of its narcissine emotiveness.

    Equally, philosophical representations of suicide divide or continually waver between endorsements of suicidal dignity or honour, and condemnations of shame and despair.[45] Pierre Charron may confess to

---

[43] Ibid., 257–8.
[44] Ibid., 315; 313; 314; 338.
[45] Wymer, *Suicide and Despair*, 2.

writing 'a sort of Stoical Rant'—his Senecan influence clear in talk of
how 'the Soul is fetter'd, and coop'd up in Prison' and of how we have
'the Keys in our own hands'—but ultimately will conclude that to
'desire and pursue Death is very criminal . . . the blackest Ingratitude
to God'.[46] Alongside arguing that, in relation to Cato, there are
incidents in life 'worse and much more formidable than Death: Such
as a Man had better die than continue under', Charron condemns acts
of self-slaughter as 'the Vicious Extremes of Weakness and Want of
Virtue'.[47]

Suicide becomes the front line for Christianity's conflict with Classical
philosophy, whose attitudes towards 'this wickedness' proved tenacious
throughout the period and well into the eighteenth century.[48] Consequently, condemnatory confrontation with the 'many false and foolish
notions of courage, greatness and honour' of the Stoics is unequivocal
only in the minority of cases, although the literature of the period is well
aware that '[y]ourself to kill yourself were such a sin | As most divines
hold deadly'.[49] Sir Thomas Browne's coinage of the word 'suicide' in the
Religio Medici seeks to avoid the connotations of violent and murderous
criminality implicit in 'self-murther' and 'self-slaughter'. Like Burton,
Browne recognizes that there is 'no happinesse within this circle of flesh',
and so resorts to a familiar philosophical consolation:

There is no misery but in himselfe where there is no end of misery; and so
indeed in his own sense, the Stoik is in the right. Hee forgets that hee can die
who complains of misery, wee are in the power of no calamitie while death is in
our owne.[50]

Conversely, his condemnation of those who 'so highly extoll the end
and suicide of *Cato*' sees the essayist seeking to establish new heroes
to counter those of antiquity; 'religion', he says, 'hath taught us a
noble example', for 'all the valiant acts of *Curtius, Scevola* or *Cordus*,

---

[46] Charron, *Of Wisdom*, II. ii. 8; 9; II. xi. 16; 12.
[47] Ibid., II. xi. 16; 5.
[48] Isaac Watts, 'A Defence Against the Temptation to Self-Murder', in *Sermons,
Discourses and Essays on Various Subjects*, 6 vols. (London, 1753), ii. 364.
[49] Ibid., 362; Chettle, *The Tragedy of Hoffman*, III. ii. 1330–1.
[50] Browne, *Religio Medici*, 42.

do not parallel or match that one of Job'.[51] Christianity fights to
establish its own role models and ideals, forbearance usurping the place of
sufficiency. As the Christian commentators condemn Stoic teaching, they
sabotage its vocabulary, finding 'noble' examples of non-Roman suffer-
ance.

In its development into a major world religion, Christianity, faced
with the glamorization of martyrdom, found it expedient to condemn
suicide as sinful: '[n]othing is more damnable, nothing more
vngodly'.[52] Accordingly, St Augustine categorically condemns the 'volun-
tary butchery' of self-murder and attacks the philosophical source of
Classical acceptance.[53] Indeed, it is Augustinian anti-classicism that
Renaissance writers struggle to incorporate into what are frequently
otherwise neoclassical texts, and there are often incongruous acknow-
ledgements of the saint employed to suppress a latent paganism that
threatens to surface. In Augustine's discussion of Cato's suicide, he
undertakes an aggressive reinterpretation of classical texts, an act of
moral translation; 'rather dejected, than magnanimous' is his conclusion
on Cato.[54] Turning Stoicism's doctrine against itself, countering heroic
action with patient suffering, Augustine locates the inherent contradiction within Senecan views on self-murder, defining an integral paradox
in Stoicism itself: the private man can only define himself in terms of
public display, so even in incarceration, Seneca's death requires an
audience, becoming an iconic, ideological, and public action. Consequently, Augustine turns the heroic good death into vain sin, 'being a
Roman' becoming synonymous with being 'covetous of glory'.[55] Equally,
Aquinas's Augustinian discussion adopts a metastatic method of
refutation first to recall and then repudiate the Stoic position. Before
declaring self-slaughter 'completely wrong for three reasons', Aquinas
has recited in terms of high-Stoicism why a 'person may . . . legitimately
kill himself': 'no noble and courageous act is illicit', he has argued;
therefore, 'suicide is not illicit'.[56] The Stoic position once established is

---

[51] Ibid., 41–2.
[52] William Vaughan, *The Golden-Groue* (London, 1600), sig. E[r].
[53] Augustine, *The City of God*, 1. 23.
[54] Ibid., 1. 22.
[55] Ibid., 1. 18.
[56] Thomas Aquinas, 'Injustice', in *Summa Theologiae*, 60 vols. (London, 1974), 38.
33; 31; 33.

then deconstructed: '[t]his is, however, not true courage, but, on the contrary, softness of spirit, i.e. the inability to bear penal afflictions'.[57] Cato and the models of Classical antiquity, icons in their prison cells, are thus dismissed as if by their own hands.

The metastatic skills of anti-suicide moralizers are exemplified in their adoption and reimplementation of the vocabulary and rhetorical tactics of suicide oratory: 'Whoever kills himself is guilty of homicide: and so much the more guilty doth that killing of himself make himself.'[58] In AD 400, the phrasal circuitry of suicidal gemination entails tight escalation (so much the more) of self-enclosed, therefore self-induced, sinful guilt, connoting in verbal microcosm the escalations of cyclic suicidal violence. By obeying the 'reflexive logic of suicide', Augustine is formative in fashioning a linguistic model governed by the 'reflexive mechanism of violence implicit in suicide'.[59]

[May] Gods Image at Gods Image strike?[60]

The self-slaughterer is, we are repeatedly told, a dangerously antisocial individual, advised, in John Sym's cautionary *Lifes Preservative Against Self-Killing*, to 'make use of the more publicke helps and assistance of the *Church*'.[61] Henry Fedden sees suicide as the 'most extreme act of individualism', a misplaced assumption of self-authority that seeks to circumvent state ownership and God's power to forgive with a 'precipitate' act that leaves himself no time for repentance or absolution between 'the bridge and the brooke, the knife and the throte': 'It is ... very perilous because it leaves no time for repentance.'[62] So Sym's complaint that 'a *self-murderer*, erects a counterwork of *creation*, and *use* of things against *God*' directly takes issue with the self-slaughterer's arrogant assumption of an excessive agency.[63] 'Man *cannot* have the *Original Propriety of himself*', agrees John Adams in his

[57] Ibid., 37.
[58] Augustine, *The City of God*, 1. 16.
[59] MacKinnon, 'The Analogy of the Body Politic', 80; 87.
[60] William Denny, *Pelecanicidium; or The Christian Adviser Against Self-Murder* (London, 1653), 23.
[61] Sym, *Lifes Preservative Against Self-Killing*, 324.
[62] Henry Romilly Fedden, *Suicide: A Social and Historical Study* (London, 1938), 27; Burton, *The Anatomy of Melancholy*, 431; 438; Aquinas, 'Injustice', 35.
[63] Sym, *Lifes Preservative*, 184.

1699 response to the publication of John Donne's *Biathanatos*, 'because he could not make himself, nor can he be ever so derelinquished or forsaken by the great Cause of his Being, as to remain independent and absolute'.[64] Explicitly, this is self-sufficiency, the cornerstone of Stoicism, under attack, its pretension to independent absolutism rejected.

In 1618, George Strode, in *The Anatomie of Mortalitie*, defines suicide as 'a sinne most horrible and fearefull, [which] breaks the bonds of God and Nature, and this no Beast (be it never so savage and cruell) will do'.[65] Strode's objection—'monstrous, barbarous, and most unnaturall for one to laye violent hands upon himselfe'—insistently worries at the 'monstrous pride' implicit in the self-murderer's decision that 'he hee will not be at all, unlesse hee may be as hee list himself, he will not submit himself to Gods will'.[66] Strode cannot stand the wilful impertinence of self-slaughter—'Diddest thou appoint the beginning of thy owne life; Diddest thou fashion and quicken the flesh in thy mothers wombe?'—it being explicitly the assumption of agency that he finds so offensive: 'didst thou make thy self', William Denny asks the self-slaughterer, 'if not. Submit!'[67] We should, Strode pleads, desire to 'bee a Patient, not an Agent, a Sufferer, not a Doer in this businesse'.[68] A similar frustration, recalling Alain de Lille's disgust at the sexual impropriety of men of 'two declensions . . . push[ing] the laws of grammar too far', surfaces in William Fenner's later sermon against *Wilfull Impertinency; The Grossest Selfe-Murder.*

two contrary wills can never stand together. No, if thy will be contrary to Christ, Christs Will, wil be contrary to thine; if thy will be to do that which will offend him, his Will will be to doe that which will vex thee; . . . if any man wil come after me, let him deny himself.[69]

---

[64] John Adams, *An Essay Concerning Self-Murther* (London, 1700), 5.
[65] George Strode, *The Anatomie of Mortalitie* (London, 1618), 244.
[66] Ibid., 244; 245.
[67] Denny, *Pelecanicidium*, 16.
[68] Strode, *The Anatomie of Mortalitie*, 259; 256.
[69] Alanus de Insulis, *De planctu naturae*, trans. D. M. Moffat, in *The Complaint of Alain de Lille* (New York, 1908), 3. William Fenner, *Wilfull Impertinency* (London, 1648), 114. Fenner occasionally employs a dialogue device, allowing the wilful impertinent his own voice, figuring a self-division close to schizophrenic: 'So thou dost murder thy selfe, nay more *thy best selfe; thou makest thy away thy soule.* Be vext then with thy wicked will, what a madde man am I? . . . So thou art wilfull, and thou wilt do thus; Oh

The convolutions deliberately undercut and undermine, enacting the interplay of contrary wills, running contorted threads of literal contrariness into structure, mapping opposition of 'Will' to 'wil', 'Christ' to 'thee', 'his' to 'thine', escalating, through this gratuitous sequence, to the final effacement of 'him' denying 'himself'. If the self-slaughterer wants to privilege his will, his self, the sermonizer will give it him, over and over, verbally overwhelming him in the repetition, feeding the appetite till it sickens and so dies. There is something in this excess that suggests pollution, something in the ungoverned verbal surfeit that echoes the sermonizer's conclusion: 'so thou corruptest thy selfe, thy will corrupteth it selfe'.[70] Again it is the retreat to a single state, a solitary place of will or selfhood, that paradoxically breeds legion. We must not retreat into the self but abandon it: 'humble thee, that thou mayest be driven out of thy selfe unto God'.[71]

Milton's *Paradise Lost*, a text structured around aggressive but formative opposition (where God requires an enemy, where Adam needs his Eve, and where so many descriptions are characterized by the oxymoronic chiaroscuro of contrast that the text burns with a bright darkness and a dark brilliance), also understands the narcissine or suicidal impulse to be driven by a damnable sense of self-ownership. With his 'unconquerable will', Satan, secure in the preposterous belief that 'the mind is its own place', disdains that governing dynamic of binary 'subjection' and asserts the 'presumptuous' claims of self-authorship in incremental tumbles of self-assertive rhetoric: assuming himself to be 'self-begot, self-raised, | By [his] own quickening power', Satan presumes to a dangerous individualism which will only lead to self-inflicted disaster, 'self-tempted, self-depraved'.[72] Mistakenly celebrating a subjectivity seemingly liberated from subjection, Satan fails to appreciate how God's universe is governed by interrelation, so every concept (for instance 'innocence') by etymological necessity only exists against its

---

do not do it, the Lord hath forbidden thee? Nay but I will do it. Thus thou art wilfull, and thou wilt to Hell' (pp. 102–3).

[70] Ibid., 102.

[71] Ibid., 70.

[72] John Milton, *Paradise Lost*, ed. Alastair Fowler (London, 1971), I. 106; 254; IV. 50; II. 522; III. 122; V. 860–1; III. 130.

binary opposite in a relationship of mutual subjection (so 'innocence', meaning 'not nocent' as Milton is demonstrably aware, only exists as a state of not-guiltiness).[73] Equally, Milton confirms that any permitted notion of individualism must be acknowledged as predicated upon the requisite sense of 'not dividual', and indebted to a 'subjected' inter-action with the divine.[74] The subject cannot escape these subjectifying structures, finding not liberation from his denominated role as other ('Satan' literally denoting 'adversary') but only 'hell within him, for within him hell | He brings': 'Which way I fly is hell; my self am hell' is the revelation of the self-reliant, self-subjected subject who internal-izes this 'hateful siege | Of contraries' only to find individualist self-reflection to be synonymous with self-division.[75] '[A]ll good to me becomes | Bane', the lonely Satan concedes when coveting the 'sweet interchange' of Eden's responsive natural world, thereby admitting the pharmaceutical poisonous potential within what he had thought to be a medicinal state of independence, a pharmacal paradox made manifest in that 'cure of all', the deadly apple.[76]

So, this is a text where even etymological structure insists on recipro-cation, where identity is demonstrably dependent, where the preposter-ous dynamic is first associated with Satan's egotistical assertions of auto-progeniture but later redeemed by association with predestination (your end, determined from your very beginning), and where self-admiration is damned in its association with Sin-ful incest ('thy self in me thy perfect image viewing | Becamest enamoured').[77] And so, this is equally a text predisposed to associating self-assertion with both narcissism and self-slaughter. Eve's narcissine impulse—'as I bent down to look, just opposite, | A shape within the watery gleam appeared | Bending to look on me . . . with answering looks | Of sympathy and love'—is the antith-esis to Adam's laudable self-denial—'I fell | Submiss: he reared me'—and disturbs the individuate identity of the first couple, destroying the integrity of their '[c]ollateral love':[78]

> I espied thee [Adam], fair indeed and tall,
> Under a platan, yet methought less fair,

---

[73] John Milton, *Paradise Lost*, ed. Alastair Fowler (London, 1971), IX. 186.
[74] Ibid., IX. 155.   [75] Ibid., IV. 20; 75; IX. 121–2.
[76] Ibid., IX. 122–3; 115; 776.
[77] Ibid., II. 764–5.   [78] Ibid., IV. 460–2; VIII. 315–16; VIII. 426.

Less winning soft, less amiably mild,
Than that smooth watery image; back I turned . . . (IV. 477–80)

This is far from the licensed narcissism typically accorded to God, whereby 'seeing God hath created vs to his image and likenesse, it cannot bee but that he loueth his image and similitude in vs, and vs also in respect of that, as it were himselfe'.[79] Maggie Kilgour's translation of Pierre de Marbeuf's poetry demonstrates how geminative rhetoric can be redeemed in relation to the 'fundamentally narcissistic [quality of] God's self-love':

> In this crystal [i.e. the creation] you gaze at yourself,
> Great God, perfect Narcissus,
> And yourself in yourself admire,
> Amorous of your object.[80]

However, in rejection of God's kindness, Eve's narcissism first suggests her propensity for self-destructive self-directed action, later realized in the 'defaced, deflowered, and now to death devote[d]' couple's suicidal 'resolution'.[81]

Their sympathetic self-destruction—'How can I live without thee . . .'—seeks to reinstate a loving but costly responsivity—'how forgo | Thy sweet converse, and love so *dearly* joined'—and provides geminative glue to their newly fractured, disjointed state (cut off from God): 'flesh of flesh, | Bone of my bone thou art, and from thy state | Mine never shall be parted, bliss or woe'.[82] The demands of incorporated identity dictate their mutual death as the reciprocal dynamic impels Adam towards the self-destructive reciprocal gesture of biting the apple, which he does to meet the responsibility of responding to Eve (they are both 'engag[ed] to emulate'[83]) and which he justifies with all the self-defeating logic of Satan's deluded isolationism:

> So forcible within my heart I feel
> The bond of nature draw me to my own,

---

[79] Peter de la Primaudaye, *The Second Part of the French Academie*, trans. n.k. (London, 1594), 279.
[80] Kilgour, '"Thy Perfect Image Viewing"', 308.
[81] Milton, *Paradise Lost*, IX. 901; 907.
[82] Ibid., IX. 908–9 (emphasis added); 914–16.
[83] Ibid., IX. 963.

My own in thee, for what thou art is mine;
Our state cannot be severed, we are one,
One flesh; to lose thee were to lose my self. (IX. 956–9)

Sharing the poisonous medicine of the apple equates to an act of sympathetic suicide, responding to the dictates of 'one heart' and 'one soul in both' with 'one guilt, one crime'.[84] As they bite, the eyebeams fly, darting 'contagious fire' as the reciprocal motif fuses them indivisibly in 'mutual guilt', entwining them in the reflexive completion of total and terrible occlusion: 'he on Eve | Began to cast lascivious eyes, she him | As wantonly repaid; in lust they burn'.[85] They are 'both in subjection now' but only to 'sensual appetite', as 'discord' shakes their 'inward state[s] of mind' and their interdependence is revealed as an excessive exclusivity.[86]

The eye to eye, hand in hand, flesh to flesh response has been revealed as dangerous involution, comparable to the 'hiss for hiss' response of the metamorphosed fallen angels, caught in their 'horrid sympathy' and cut by their own dust.[87] As Book X moves towards Eve's contemplation of suicide, Milton prepares the semantic ground, studding the verse with violent signs of destructive response: all is 'fierce reflux . . . redound . . . reduce . . . resign . . . render back | All I received . . . reproved, retort' until the acceptance that 'be it so, for I submit, his doom is fair, | That dust I am, and shall to dust return'.[88] All rhetorical response, so redolent of the false economy of Satan's self-evaluation or the self-reflection of Eve, now resounds with 'double terror' and the fountains, hillocks, dales, and bowers of a lost Eden withhold their kindly echoes from the deservedly isolated couple.[89] Finally, the 'dreadful revolution' of self-inflicted guilt comes 'thundering back' on Adam's 'defenceless head', as he feels not his isolation from the world but the weight of absolute responsibility for his selfish actions: 'on me, me only, as the source and spring | Of all corruption, all the blame lights due'.[90] The geminative structure, replayed in Eve's 'me me only just object of his ire', is indicative of a suicidal egocentricism that 'refutes | That [Divinely gifted] excellence' of

---

[84] Ibid., IX. 967; 971.
[85] Ibid., IX. 1036; 1043; 1013–15.
[86] Ibid., IX. 1128–9; 1124–5.
[87] Ibid., X. 518; 540.   [88] Ibid., X. 739–70.
[89] Ibid., X. 850; 860–2.   [90] Ibid., X. 814–15; 832–3.

life, attempts to 'evade | The penalty pronounced', and wilfully seeks to forestall the 'vengeful ire' of divine justice:[91]

> Then both our selves and seed at once to free
> From what we fear for both, let us make short,
> Let us seek death, or he not found, supply
> With our own hands his office on our selves;
> Why stand we longer shivering under fears,
> That show no end but death, and have the power,
> Of many ways to die the shortest choosing,
> Destruction with destruction to destroy. (X. 999–1006)

Eve's 'vehement despair', resorting to Seneca's catalogue of the 'many ways to die', attempts a preposterous evasion, seeking destructively to destroy destruction, necessitating a division of the single subject into passive innocent and aggressive nocent. Self-slaughter represents the final untenable resource of the self-perpetuated and defeated, a pharmacal (dis)solution to the now incurable disease that is life.[92]

Paradise Lost presents a sustained advocation of human/divine indivisibility, entailing a critique of troublingly tempting self-reflection, complicated by Milton's characteristic rhetorical insistence upon the interrelation of opposites (hence his predilection for the Satanic double negative, where in Hell every positive depiction can only be articulated via a 'not un-' or 'not in-' construction). Simply, the subject (or any knowable quality) is forced into relation beyond itself, and any attempt to substitute that extraspective interaction with an introspective self-response—even if that private relation is between the author and his idolatrous textual mirror—is as roundly condemned as the damnable act of suicide. Milton, as his commonplace book makes clear, is indebted to both Dante and Sidney, but later commentators, such as John Adams in his turn-of-the-century *Essay Concerning Self-Murther*, reserve Milton, this '*Excellent Author of our own*', for particular approval.[93] Not only does Milton caution against self-slaughter, he himself, although beset by blindness, resists Stoic temptation and refuses to pander to self-indulgent despair; whereas, a Stoic, as 'they do', may

---

[91] Ibid., 936; 999–1006.
[92] Ibid., X. 1007; 1005.
[93] Adams, *An Essay*, 111.

regard the loss of a bodily sense as an indication of corporeal redundancy and respond to the failure of a faculty with resigned resolution:

> Shall [blindness] be taken for a certain Sign of being past doing good? And consequently *a reasonable Plea* for Self-murther; and shall *that* be *acted accordingly?* Had it been so always, how much Instruction and Delight wou'd Mankind have been depriv'd of... had *Milton* done so, the World had lost that *admirable Poem.*[94]

Like Milton, Adams describes suicide as a 'refus[al] to submit to the Will of God', both 'Injuring our Neighbour, and encouraging others to do so'; this is a crime, Adams succinctly states,

> for this is the destruction of God's *particular Propriety*, the *Positive Renouncing that End* for which he gives Man Life; the doing what is *destructive* to *Civil Society*, the *Overthrowing the Laws both of God and Man;* to Rebel against Providence, and break out into Eternity.[95]

The rebel angel, and perhaps even the perpetrators of the recent self-slaughtering English civil war, receive Adams's condemnation; '*Self-murther* is the doing all this', he concludes, 'and what is still *more,* the doing it *wilfully* and *advisedly* and therefore what Punishment shall be due to it?'[96]

Adams's is a common critique, for suicide 'is an offence against God, against the King, and against Nature'; there is, William Denny announces, 'a Publicke Right in Every Man, | That Life He neither may dispose; nor can'.[97] What is destructive to God's creation, the commentators insist, is '*destructive to the very Being* of *Society*', and society therefore punishes the self-slaughterer as best it can:[98]

> CLOWN. Here lies the water—good. Here stands the man—good. If the man go to this water and drown himself, it is will he, nill he, he goes—mark you that. But if the water comes to him, and

[94] Ibid., 313; 111.
[95] Ibid., 314.
[96] Ibid.
[97] Michael Dalton, *The Countrey Justice* (London, 1630), 235; Denny, *Pelicanicidium*, 16.
[98] Adams, *An Essay*, 25.

drown him, he drowns not himself. Argal, he that is not guilty
of his own death shortens not his own life.

OTHER.   But is this law?

CLOWN.   Ay marry is't, crowner's quest law.

OTHER   .... she should have been buried out o' Christian burial.

(*Ham.*, V. i. 13–21)

As Elsinore's gravediggers are aware, both legally and theologically,
distinction was made between felonious and unfortunate death.[99] The
felo de se or 'felon of himself' was one of those who wilfully sought their
'own salvation' (ll. 1–2), and was punishable by law as a sane man
exercising illegal choice: 'He is a *Felo de se* that doth destroy himself out
of a premeditated hatred against his own life, or out of a humor to
destroy himself [and] forfeits all his Goods and Chattels to the King.'[100]
As Henry Hammond makes clear, canon and scriptural law combine to
make suicide a legal 'crime, as contrary to the sixt Commandment'.[101]
A non compos mentis verdict could, however, be recorded in such cases
where symptoms of insanity, and therefore diminished responsibility,
could be evidenced: 'Divided from herself and her fair judgement'
(IV. v. 84), Ophelia, although her 'death was doubtful' (V. i. 194),
would have been deemed non compos mentis. Local juries, largely
comprised of men from the same parish as the deceased, potentially
neighbours of the surviving family, had, until the reign of Henry VIII,
been recording non compos mentis verdicts to allow the suicide's
property to be inherited by the family:

[The coroners] were so full of pitty as to exempt the dead body from that
sentence to which those who do destroy themselves are lyable, for he was not
buried in the High-way, he had no stake plated with Iron thrust through his
body to terrifie all passengers from committing such a black and desperate act,
but ... he was civilly buried.[102]

---

[99] See James V. Holleran, 'Maimed Funeral Rites in *Hamlet*', *ELR*, 19 (1989),
65–93, and Michael MacDonald, 'Ophelia's Maimèd Rites', *SQ*, 37 (1986), 309–17.
[100] Edmund Wingate, *Justice Revived* (London, 1661), 68.
[101] Henry Hammond, *To the Right Honourable, The Lord Fairfax* (London, 1649),
9–10.
[102] Anon., *A Sad Caveat to all Quakers Not to Boast any more that they have God
Almighty by the Hand, when they have the Devil by the Toe* (London, 1657), 11.

Cumulatively, however, between 1485 and 1660, only 2 per cent of
verdicts passed were non compos mentis acquittals, 95 per cent of the
decisions being of felo de se, as new governmental stricture and rewards
of one mark for each coroner who recorded a decision of felo de se were
quickly to create one of the most punitive periods in suicide's legal
history.[103]

'This point calls for *great humiliation*': the social and moral un-
acceptability of suicide is economically re-enforced as members of
a community and family lose wealth to the crown.[104] While Burton is
concerned that 'we ought not to bee so rash and rigorous in our
censures', commentaries emphasize a moral obligation for both canon
and civil law to provide a perceptible 'public mark of abhorrence',
something cautionary to 'leave a print or badge of their prophanesse
behind them';[105] 'She should', Ophelia's churlish Priest argues in
defence of her 'maimèd rites' (V. I. 186), 'in ground unsanctified have
lodged | Till the last trumpet. For charitable prayers, | Shards, flints, and
pebbles should be thrown on her' (ll. 196–8). By the 1660s, the more
brutal punishments of the suicide's corpse were less stringently enforced, so it is 'a pity', according to Watts, who complains during a
period of relative lenience, that the practice of staking the corpse at the
crossroads 'has been omitted of late years by the too favourable sentence
of their neighbours on the jury, who generally pronounce them distracted'.[106] 'Put him in a hole', urges Fenner, 'drive a stake through his body,
set a Monument of shame on him.'[107] Dalton's instructions to the
Justices of the Peace on the treatment of the corpse, which is to be
'drawne out of the house, &c. with ropes, by a horse, to a place
appointed for punishment, or shame, where the dead body is hanged
upon a Gibbert' are unashamedly designed to invoke 'the terror of
others'.[108] So while Burton and Browne may complain of 'hard
censures', talk of mitigation, and ask the reader to 'pity the mercifull

---

[103] Michael MacDonald and Terence R. Murphy, *Sleepless Souls* (Oxford, 1990), 16.
[104] Fenner, *Wilfull Impertinency*, 97.
[105] Burton, *The Anatomy of Melancholy*, 438; Watts, *Sermons*, 368; Strode, *The Anatomie of Mortalitie*, 267.
[106] Watts, *Sermons*, 368.
[107] Fenner, *Wilfull Impertinency*, 102.
[108] Dalton, *The Countrey Justice*, 236.

intention of those hands that doe destroy themselves', Isaac Watts, insistent on ascribing a social stigma, emphasizes the 'odium, . . . scandal and everlasting shame you bring upon your name and character . . . a reproach that spreads wide among the kindred of the self-murtherer'.[109] As Maurice Bloch and Jonathan Parry conclude in their discussion of mortuary ritual, the suicidal individual is 'regarded with such incomparable horror that the soul may forever be excluded from the society of the dead and must wander the earth a lonely and malignant ghost, while the corpse may not be accorded the normal rites of disposal'.[110] Ophelia's botched rites demonstrate comparative lenience.

Strode's writing is fervent in its desire to isolate the potentially polluting filthy, bestial self-murderer and distance him from both companionship and humanity: 'If any will be beastly, let him be beastly alone. The fillthie person and beastly man shall not have me for a companion.'[111] Accordingly, the state, from the legal to the linguistic level, isolates the self-slaughter. Henry's one mark coroner's reward suggests not an attempt genuinely to assess, but rather speaks of the need to locate difference, to cut the suicide off from familial ties and community support. The state's desire to create 'a felon of himself', to identify an isolated individual while simultaneously appropriating his property, facilitates segregation. The self-sufficiency of self-slaughter is accentuated, emphasized as an aspect of the suicidal identity until pronominal gemination runs through these texts in long strands of 'himself upon himself', 'himself against himself' rhetorical construction; this insistence upon the self, even the self-owned 'himself', becomes part of the anti-suicide writers' strategy to isolate the self-sufficient self-slaughterer. Rather than admit the self-slaughterer into the public, the commentators will insist upon what is now a dreadfully solitary individualism. The political, governmental desire to ostracize has been made linguistically manifest.

---

[109] Burton, *The Anatomy of Melancholy*, 438; Browne, *Religio Medici*, 49; Watts, *Sermons*, 368. See Maurice Bloch and Jonathan Parry, 'Introduction', in Maurice Bloch and Jonathan Parry (eds.), *Death and the Regeneration of Life* (Cambridge, 1982), 1–45 at 41; Arnold van Gennep, *The Rites of Passage*, trans. Monika B. Vizedom and Gabrielle L. Cafee (London, 1960); Ruth Richardson, *Death, Dissection and the Destitute* (London, 1987).
[110] Bloch and Parry, 'Introduction', 16.
[111] Strode, *The Anatomie of Mortalitie*, 267.

Legal severity, according to Donne, is indicative of 'the propensnesse of that people at that time to that fault', necessitating what Robert N. Watson describes as 'the extraordinary punitive attitudes towards suicide in sixteenth and early seventeenth century England' that he sees to 'suggest a terrible anxiety about the surrender of the self', but which equally reflect a concomitant anxiety concerning presumption of agency.[112] Consequently, these theological social commentaries are not without a trace of hysteria: 'I . . . stand Amazed at the Steam of so much Humane Bloud, running in streams, and the open Veins dayly bleeding of so many Christians, as is continually shed.'[113] These texts reflect an appreciable pragmatic concern that 'great numbers may make themselves away', which 'by Example and Custom may grow still greater and greater, till the Publick is weaken'd', putting a 'check and stop' 'upon all Business, and Trade, Trust in one another'.[114] Without the threat of punitive measures, authority is left with no weapons against a tide of antisocial unrest: to licence death is to licence anarchy and 'then what meanes our Pillaries and Gallowes, &c and other punishments upon Malefactors?'[115] So if suicide, as Belsey suggests, allows an illusory triumph that 're-establishes the sovereign subject', seemingly representing 'the crowning affirmation of the supremacy of the self', allowing the subject to be 'momentarily absolute', in so doing it fashions a moment of such epitomized individuality that it becomes 'a threat to the control of the state': 'they will not be oblig'd to any Duty . . . but wou'd Rob, Ravish, Murther'.[116]

There is unease in the lectures and commentaries, a concern that even in writing on the subject the evil may be propagated and normalized through discourse. Consequently, an apparent apologist like John Donne is seen to play a deadly role, condoning the streams of blood, promoting private response over public responsibility to the detriment of all. For every John King, who thinks it a topic 'not unmeet to be considered', preferring the tongue to the knife—some, 'instead of

---

[112] John Donne, *Biathanatos: A Declaration of that Paradoxe or Thesis, that Selfe-homicide is not so Naturally Sinne, that it may never be Otherwise* (London, 1644), 93; Watson, *The Rest is Silence*, 4.

[113] Denny, *Pelicanicidium*, sig. A5ʳ.

[114] Adams, *An Essay*, 28.

[115] Fenner, *Wilfull Impertinency*, 24.

[116] Ibid., 125; Adams, *An Essay*, 26.

sharpnes of wit, have used the sharpnes of knives, and other bloody
instruments to decide it'—we find a Richard Capel, who worries that
'perhaps such things printed hath been an occasion to cause some spirits
to presume, of which in our parts we have had too many black examples
of late [and] many strange doctrines now adayes'.[117] Capel's suspicion is
that 'it had been better for them and others not to have sent [such ideas]
abroad the world in print' as he 'would men would not make halters for
mens consciences'.[118] The texts themselves, it seems, can actively
participate in self-murther; the debate itself is imbued with suicidal
tendencies: 'Should the positions printed by some of late, grow common, and take hold of the hearts of men, I fear me where there is one
who makes himself away, there would be an hundred.'[119]

2. BY HIMSELF, UPON HIMSELFE: JOHN DONNE'S *BIATHANATOS*

To what purpose should a Christian cite the heathens to justify that which the
scripture forbids?[120]

Donne's *Biathanatos: A Declaration of that Paradoxe or Thesis, that Selfe-
homicide is not so Naturally Sinne, that it may never be Otherwise,* is
debatably the first work in English to excuse self-slaughter and is the
focus of later commentators' distaste.[121] Writing 'lest the Frequency of
such Actions might in time arrogate a Kind of Legitimation by Custom', the anti-suicide commentators legitimate their treatises precisely
as attempts to redress the balance, answering those who 'plead Authority
from some late-publisht *Paradoxes,* That Self-homicide was Lawfull'.[122]
To perpetuate Stoic tolerance is, argues John Adams, to assert 'the

[117] King, *Lectures Upon Jonas,* 183; Richard Capel, 'An Apology', in *Tentations: Their Nature, Danger, Cure* (London, 1659), 272–87 at 278–9.
[118] Capel, ibid., 279–80.
[119] Ibid., 284.
[120] Watts, *Sermons,* 362.
[121] Sprott cites the 1578 pro-suicide manuscript dialogue, 'Whether it be damnation for a man to kill himself', found amongst John Harrington's papers in the British Museum as a thirty-year antecedent to *Biathanatos.* S. E. Sprott, *The English Debate on Suicide from Donne to Hume* (La Salle, Ill., 1961), 15.
[122] Denny, *Pelicanicidium,* sigs. A5ʳ⁻ᵛ.

Agreeableness of the Argument to the present Age': an agreeableness that it is his duty to denounce.[123]

Donne, whose 'sickly inclination' predisposes him to compassion, equally sees the propensity of the present age towards self-violence, including those 'Preaching and Chatechizing' who have 'wrastled, and fought with their naturall appetite, and tamed them to a perplexity, whether it might be done or no'; they struggle to 'induce amongst us' the fear of self-immurement 'because we exceeded in that naturall desire of dying so'.[124] Written in 1608 but only published posthumously in 1644 during what Sprott describes as a mild suicide epidemic in Puritan circles, Donne cannot have fully anticipated the extent to which his argument would prove agreeable to its new civil-war-torn context.[125]

Fighting the 'tyranny of... prejudice', Donne employs the terms of the 'natural', thus countering the Augustinian 'unnatural' brand, in an act of humanist conflation—natural as rational—until 'all the precepts of Naturall Law, result in these, *Flye evill, seek good.* That is, doe according to Reason.'[126] Fedden, in his socio-historical study of suicide, proposes that 'reason, like isolation, leads to an increase in suicide, for reason sees a variety of situations in which death is preferable to a painful or dishonourable life', and accordingly Donne's reason is customarily expressed in neat intricacies of enclosed logic—'what could kill the world, but it selfe, since out of it nothing is'—that locate us in a world of near-suicidal natural paradox.[127]

Donne's method employs paradox as part of his relativist agenda, playing one commentator against another, view against view, so as effectively to flatten the terms and efface the universalist objectivity of Scripture, quoting Puritanical commentators in a profusion of theoretical concord and discord:

Donne employed the commonplaces of the debate on suicide as they had appeared for centuries and were currently flourishing in Continental commentaries on Scripture, law, and casuistry, cited them purposefully in a profusion of

[123] Adams, *An Essay*, 41.
[124] Donne, *Biathanatos*, preface; 87; 91.
[125] Sprott, *The English Debate*, 56.
[126] Donne, *Biathanatos*, 26; 45.
[127] Fedden, *Suicide*, 77; John Donne, *Paradoxes and Problems*, ed. Helen Peters (Oxford, 1980), 2.

paradoxical disagreement, persistently oppugned one with the other, and concluded as a humanist that individual reason or conscience might convey the divine summons and not make cowards of us all.[128]

From this confusion comes the individual voice, self-ratified. And this confusion and profusion becomes, in a sense, the legitimation for *Biathanatos*. Answering the too fervent zeal and 'reprehension of others', Donne proceeds via paradox to truth, 'the best way [being] to debate and vexe' the matter.[129] With a metastatic method similar to that of Aquinas, Donne moves through his antagonist's position before locating himself, seemingly validated via opposition. So he begins a representative section by agreeing that the self-murderer 'steals from the Universe, or from the State, to which his service is due, one person, and member of the body'.[130] This staple Augustinian statement is followed by the familiar elision between the secular and sacred—'he userps upon the right of God'—and denouncement of wilful assertion: 'the passage from this life to the next, bee not generally left to our freewill, and no body be properly Lord of his own Life'.[131] 'Yet . . .': having acknowledged the limitations of the will, ceding self-possession to the Divine, having rehearsed an encapsulation of the standard anti-suicide stance, Donne turns on 'yet' to reveal his Senecan rebuttal: '*Though we have not* Dominium, *we have* Usum, *and it is lawfull for vs to loose that, when we will.*'[132] Via the sacred and politic tone of 'Dominium', the legalese of '*lawfull*', the loosening of life's bonds, Donne reinstates the self-murderers into each discourse previously denied to them, returning to the loaded '*when we will*', a final assertion of individual agency and the primacy of will.

Often, the text rehearses prescribed positions, both Senecan and scriptural. '[W]hensoever any affliction assailes me', he confesses in the mode of Cato or Seneca, 'mee thinks I have the keyes of my prison in mine owne hand, and no remedy presents it selfe so soone to my heart, as mine own sword'.[133] But significantly, in a work pertaining to condemnation of Augustinian severity, Donne locates his argument biblically, within the terms of Christianity. *Biathanatos* tests Christian

[128] Sprott, *The English Debate*, 24–5.
[129] Donne, *Biathanatos*, preface.
[130] Ibid., 111.   [131] Ibid., 112.
[132] Ibid.   [133] Ibid., preface.

stringency as Augustine had done Stoicism, from within, testing the efficacy of its medicine with poisonous purpose:

> may [not] I, when I am weather beaten, and in danger of betraying that precious soule which God hath embarqued in me, put off this burdenous flesh, till his pleasure be that I shall resume it? For this is not to sinck the ship, but to retire it safe Harbour, and assured Anchor.[134]

Where Burton worries that the self-slaughterer may act 'as *Æsopes* fishes, [as] they leap from the frying-pan into the fire it selfe',[135] *Biathanatos* maintains that suicide signifies a retreat from potential sin. Donne's insistence that 'there is no external act naturally evil, and that circumstances condition them, and give them their nature' discloses a governing relativism: 'in applying moral theology to different cases, both Catholic and Protestant casuists had always been guided by the idea that the moral props of any act are always rooted in its motivation rather than its outward form'.[136] 'Wee may safely inferre', says Donne, 'that nothing which we call sinne, is so against nature, but that it may be sometimes agreeable to nature.'[137] The text ultimately exposes the impossibility of all-encompassing evaluation by locating division, and by admitting paradox, legitimizing moral self-legislation: 'a private man is Emporer of himselfe'.[138]

In typically paradoxical, potentially self-defeating summation, Donne compares his authorial task to that of the Satanic serpent who opened Eve's eyes to the human reality of a fallen world: 'And as the eyes of *Eve* were opened by the taste of the Apple . . . [s]o the digesting of this may, though not present faire objects, yet bring them to see the nakednesse and deformity of their owne reasons.'[139] This analogy encapsulates the complexity, entirely unacknowledged by its literalist detractors, of Donne's innately suicidal text. While scorning the deformity of the zealous sermonizers' dogmatic reason, Donne potentially undermines the radical humanism he appeared to expound. To digest the apple of

---

[134] Donne, *Biathanatos*, 110–11.
[135] Burton, *The Anatomy of Melancholy*, 431.
[136] Wymer, *Suicide and Despair*, 17.
[137] Donne, *Biathanatos*, 37.
[138] Ibid., 47.
[139] Ibid., preface.

Biathanatos would open one's eyes but occasion one's fall. Conversely, we may not see pleasant things (what we see are fallen realities) but at least we see things for what they are beyond the savage purity of idealism. Donne equates the false logic of the sermonizers with a pre-fallen sight, allowing the implication that only if they consume *Biathanatos* will they see their former innocent purity to be a form of stringent deformity. These discordant convolutions suggest that Donne is alive to a human existence that is far from Edenic, and understands how an excessively pious perception, one that pretends to Edenic insight, becomes deformed and untenable in a fallen world. But the comparison that allies Donne with the selfish wilful presumption of a Satanic claim for self-begotten agency threatens to discredit the entire preceding text. Donne allows his paradox to pause on its axis, balanced between pharmacal possibilities: he presents suicide as life's medicine; he quietly acknowledges the poisonous nature of the knowledge *Biathanatos* imparts. He advocates ambiguity in both acknowledging human imperfection and the severity of absolutism, but deftly concedes the deception implicit in his seemingly clear-sighted leniency. Importantly, the contemporary reception of Donne's text ignores the self-aware suicidal contradiction at the core of *Biathanatos*, seemingly intent on resolving its pharmaceutical paradox into a merely poisonous simple.

Although elsewhere, in order to condemn the 'sicknesse and . . . medicine' of Catholic martyrdom ('how hungrie of poison, how Ambitious of ruine, how pervious an penetrable to all meanes of destruction are you?'), Donne explicitly denounces suicide, the delicacy of his position is ignored.[140] *Biathanatos* is principally responsible, after its mid-century publication, for an explosion of anti-suicide commentaries, sermons, and lectures, many of which attempt to unpick his logic, some of which dismiss his arguments, but all of which Donne, in his preface, proclaims himself invulnerable to. The suicide debate unfolds in earnest, and, as it does so, the rhetorical display begins, and the ingenious tactics of the suicidal polemic become more marked.

'If then reasons which differ from me, and my reasons be otherwise equall, yet theirs have this disadvantage, that they fight with themselves,

---

[140] John Donne, *Pseudo-Martyr*, ed. Anthony Raspa (Montreal, 1993), 15. 7; 23. 1–2.

and suffer a Civill Warre of contradiction.'[141] Donne's concluding comments in *Biathanatos*, read alongside his dedicatory verses to Sir Edward Herbert, seek to forestall the anticipated condemnations of his paradox, while disclosing an authorial unease as to the stability of the suicide debate. Suicide, say Michael Neill, Margaret Higonnet, and Rosalie L. Colie, is a paradox: it is, Colie concludes, 'the paradox of self-contradiction at its irrevocable extremity'.[142] Donne's pro-suicide rhetoric is, as his full title insists, precisely constructed on a framework of unresolved paradox. There is an undisputed congruence between the subject of Donne's work and the linguistic conceits he employs in the process of justification, a congruence which Donne clearly believes has, if badly handled, the potential to cripple the suicide orator. Those who attempt to differ, he says, find themselves at a disadvantage to him, their tracts more likely than his to fall foul of the suicidal logic of the self-defeating paradox, to fight with themselves, or suffer a civil war of contradictory logic. Meanwhile, Donne's work, which 'hath inough perform'd it wch it undertooke, both by Argument and Example', 'shall not therefore kill ittselfe; that is, not bury itselfe'.[143] Less than a decade after *Biathanatos*'s publication, however, Richard Capel, citing 'Dr. *Donns* Book', suggests that anyone who argues that 'a man may die in self-murther, and final impenitency and yet die in Christ' is in fact arguing 'such a piece of Divinity as clearly destroys it selfe; for, what is it that makes us fall from Christ, and from Grace but sin?'[144] There is therefore a potential in these intricately woven arguments, complex discussions, counter-discussions, and paradoxical displays, for authorial self-murder. The author at the beginning of his book, as Charles Blout describes,

enters either with an Halter about his Neck, submitting himself to his Readers Mercy whether he shalt be hang'd or no; or else in a huffing manner he appears

---

[141] Donne, *Biathanatos*, 214.

[142] Michael Neill, 'Ford's Unbroken Art: The Moral Design of *The Broken Heart*', *MLR* 75 (1980), 249–68 at 261; Margaret R. Higonnet, 'Suicide as Self Construction', in M. Gutwirth et al. (eds.), *Germaine de Staël: Crossing the Borders* (New Brunswick, NJ, 1991), 69–81 at 69; Rosalie L. Colie, *Paradoxia Epidemica: The Renaissance Tradition of Paradox* (Princeton, 1966), 486.

[143] Donne, *Biathanatos*, ed. Sullivan, appendix A, 249.

[144] Capel, *Tentations*, 280; 279.

with the Halter in his hand, and threatens to hang his Reader, if he gives him not his good Word.[145]

The philosophical and theological reactions to *Biathanatos* (appearing largely mid- to late seventeenth century) habitually seek to turn their opponent's arguments upon themselves, to read self-destruction into opposing arguments, and to use a text against itself, fighting an argument via adoption of its own methods. Donna Hamilton, in her discussion of Protestant controversies, explores in detail how a 'particular controversy appropriated the idioms and arguments of the other side', and here the habits of appropriation that Hamilton notes are peculiarly apt.[146] To adapt Blout's image, these authors appear in a decidedly huffing manner, threatening to hang John Donne, using the logic of *Biathanatos* against itself, making it a halter against its author. Even the geminative figure is appropriated, used itself against itself. The poisonous text must become its own medicine.

'*It is therefore high time that the danger of this desperate, devilish and damnable practice be plainly and fully set out*':[147] John Sym's 1637 Anglican treatise, *Lifes Preservative Against Self-Killing*, the first published text solely concerned with suicide, is, as Michael MacDonald observes, 'marbled with paradoxes'; 'an unyielding opponent of self-murder, Sym was actually prepared to be more tolerant in practice than many of his contemporaries'.[148] The arguments that Sym propounds are largely standard, the usual complaint being, as Aristotle, Augustine, and Aquinas have rehearsed before them, that 'by killing himselfe, a man wrongs *God, himselfe*, the *Church* and *Commonwealth*, in bereaving them of that service and good which they all might have by his life'.[149] Equally, like his contemporaries, Sym makes a distinction between felo de se and non compos mentis, 'because [in the case of the latter], they are not properly so much *agents*, as *sufferers*'.[150] But Sym's expression of almost

[145] Charles Blout, *The Two First Books of Philostratus: Concerning the Life of Appollonius Tyaneus* (London, 1680), sig. A2^r.

[146] Donna B. Hamilton, *Shakespeare and the Politics of Protestant England* (Lexington, Ky., 1992), p. x.

[147] William Gouge, 'To the Christian Reader', in Sym, *Lifes Preservative*, prefatory matter.

[148] MacDonald and Murphy, *Sleepless Souls*, p. xliv.

[149] Sym, *Lifes Preservative*, 81–2.

[150] Ibid., 172.

puritanical zeal (his Anglicanism having a Puritan inclination) combines both his sensible awareness of the secular causes of self-murder and a genuine fear that it is he who, in a sense, is being asked to commit an act of near *necessitas*. On occasion the minister of Leigh's religious intransigence landed him in serious trouble with the government and its new canonical legislature, as he regarded injunctions concerning vestments and ceremony as effecting an enforced idolatry, a spiritual self-murder. '[C]orrupt doctrine, and evill examples', Sym cautions, 'doe draw others with them to perdition' and '*self-soule-murder*'.[151] Perhaps as a consequence, Sym's tract can be both hugely polemic and subtly understanding. The text's characteristic modes of expression are exemplified in instances of circuitous logic: 'For, *self-murder* being *death*, and *death* being onely a *privation*, it cannot be knowne what it is but by the knowledge of *life*, which is its contrarie.'[152] At such moments, where layers of contrary predication seem to hang on a central privation or absence, Donne's rival indeed seems to 'suffer a Civill warre of contradiction'. But Sym's argument, presumably in part owing its structural paradox to *Biathanatos*, finds tolerance via paradox, so he can work through to the lenient suggestion that '[t]here is nothing absolutely *evill*, neither is there a *meere evill* subsisting by it selfe, but in that which is good'.[153]

Somewhere within this apparent tolerance, however, is the suggestion of something a little more vehement: 'good', in these terms, has the potential to act as a breeding ground for evil, which only exists within it, displaying a fear of integral corruption that is more fully articulated in Sym's description of the suicidal disposition:

Mans life is loseable by two sorts of *meanes. First, internall,* arising from, and within a mans selfe, that kills him, as the worme that breeds of, and in the tree, and destroyes it: so in mans bodie doe distempers and diseases breed of, and from it selfe.[154]

Man's life, Sym implies, is beset by this internal suicidal predilection, something insidious in the 'carnall reason' of a 'corrupt nature'.[155] Or

[151] Ibid., 45; 58.   [152] Ibid., 2.
[153] Ibid., 3.   [154] Ibid., 44.   [155] Ibid., 179.

rather, corrupt*ed*, in this case 'by the *Stoicks*' as much as by 'the *devill*', whose powerful instigation 'workes and injects into the minds of men... such self-killing *resolutions*'.[156] In this depiction of paradoxically corrupting self-sufficiency (feeding its own flame), Sym begins to adopt a familiar linguistic model, building almost spatial inverse patterns into the lines, tucking progression into itself; so we have movement 'arising from' to 'within', that 'breeds of, and in', as the distempered self 'breed[s] of, and from it selfe'. Simply, Sym's text, so reliant on the workings of self-involved paradox, begins to bind itself up in the tight pronoun clusters, patterned verbal reflections, and convoluted locution of a suicide/suicidal text.

First we see isolated instances:

So, in *Self-murder*, as it is murder, an *Innocent*, (never deserving of himselfe that himselfe should kill himselfe,) is slaine: the *Actor* whereof hath no authority, nor calling over himselfe so to doe: seeing, no man can be both *superiour* and also *inferiour* to himselfe.[157]

Donne, excusing the act of 'perplexitie', enjoys the confusion of an act where 'we cannot properly work upon our selves, because in this act, the same partie must be agent and patient, and instrument'.[158] But Sym feels this impropriety deeply. Faced with the perplexing doubleness of superior and inferior, or acting agent and innocent subject, within the single self, confronting the 'division and enmity' within the man who is both '*active* and *passive subject*' of his own *action*', Sym finds an unstoppable linguistic multiplicity that grimly parallels the manifold nature of the suicidal subject: 'himselfe... himselfe should kill himselfe... himselfe... himselfe'.[159] Suicide is an act of disastrous self-reflection, 'the greatest act of hostility in the world' when a man 'bound to preserve *himselfe*, reflects upon *himselfe*, to destroy himselfe'.[160] And, as Sym divides the self, showing how the self-slaughterer 'reflects and returnes upon himselfe, in an *act* of the greatest hostility', he forces the words to reflect back upon themselves, with a deliberately exaggerated aggression: 'by himselfe, upon himselfe... a contrary *act*'.[161] If 'by unitie, things are preserved' and if 'individuals are principally one', then the division

---

[156] Ibid., 179; 184; 247.   [157] Ibid., 49.
[158] Donne, *Biathanatos*, 116; 118.   [159] Sym, *Lifes Preservative*, 54.
[160] Ibid., 53.   [161] Ibid., 160; 161.

of the individual 'against themselves' occasions a large-scale natural catastrophe ('the world cannot stand... things shall cease to be true'), as well as a microcosmic psychic perversion ('the horribleness whereof is so monstrous').[162]

Sym allows us to feel this monstrosity infiltrating the text, corrupting it, causing these extraordinary moments of textual entwine. This following passage is, I am suggesting, very deliberately uncomfortable; we should feel this as jarring, as both a shock and as a textual deformity. So one response to Denny's despairing 'canst Thou Self from Self divide?' would seem to be Sym's gratuitously aggressive self-divisions, which make it clear that an attempt to do so only leads to something near horrific.[163] His reasoning runs as follows:

We are carefully to cleave to *God* for preservation, praying him not to give us up to our *selves*...

The single self is inadequate: there is a doubleness in 'cleaving' that speaks of our need to abandon our isolation and find preserving duality through amalgamation with God.

who are mercilefly cruell to our *selves*, when wee fall into our owne hands...

But the inadequate single self is in fact riven—our selves cruel to our selves—as oxymoron (merciful cruelty) creeps in.

for the nearer that any are linked and knit together in condition, or affection, the more desperately *opposite* they are, when they fall into division...

Indeed, it is the intrinsic unity of the single self (its nearness to itself, how close it is knit) that, paradoxically, occasions the violence of division; what had been 'like' are now desperately opposed, falling into division as self-sufficiency becomes self-destructive.

... because of the want of a fit *medium* or *mediatour* of reconciliation, betweene a *mans selfe* and *himselfe*: what meane is there, either to keepe himselfe from himselfe, or to reconcile himselfe to himselfe, when himselfe is fallen out into murderous resolutions against himselfe?[164]

---

[162] Ibid., 54.   [163] Denny, *Pelicanicidium*, 24.
[164] Sym, *Lifes Preservative*, 57.

Without God to come between the self and self, proximity has become fractious (violent, breached), as Sym subtly conflates self-isolation with self-destruction while indulging in the most violent oratorical sequence of paregmenonic escalation. The overwhelming self-signifiers reveal only want, presenting an absorption that binds the self into dangerous proximity with itself, a sinfully excessive autonomy like that of those who 'looke not out or beyond themselves', who 'cannot but sinke under their owne burden'.[165] Sym connects a limited paucity with an excessive overloading: 'himselfe... himselfe from himselfe... himselfe to himselfe... himselfe... against himselfe', but still, just himself. You can, as Isaac Watts suggests, be 'too much alone': solitary yet excessive.[166] It is, says Sym, 'monstrous that *one* should be *two*; and that *division* should be in unity', and, in this verbal proliferation we feel the monstrosity of this multiplicity.[167] Denny's query signals a suicidal numerical confusion where 'fight not Two, but One', while the one refracts, acts back upon its self.[168]

> Wu't thou Keep 'sizes in thy self? Act all?
> Be Judg? Be Jury? Party Criminall?
> Accuser? Jayler? (All unfit to do)
> And must thou be the cursed Hangman too?[169]

In what is becoming a characteristic tactic, Denny overloads the self, giving it too many parts to play, simultaneously congesting his verse with rhetorical enquiry, so self, stanza, and metre all strain against an uncomfortable overcapacity.

This legalese is directly revisionary: Donne, for whom 'any man may be the Bishop & Magistrate to himselfe', questions that 'because Judges are established, Therefore no man should take dominion over himselfe', asking who 'is judge of sinne, against which no civill law provides, of which there is no evidence? May not I accuse, and condemne my selfe to my selfe, and inflict what penance I will?'[170] It is part of Donne's mode to elide the distinction between Civil and Natural Law, internalizing the structures and figures of judicial rule and putting them under the

---

[165] Ibid., 219.   [166] Watts, *Sermons*, 377.
[167] Sym, *Lifes Preservative*, 190.   [168] Denny, *Pelicanicidium*, 24; 15.
[169] Ibid., 15.   [170] Donne, *Biathanatos*, 48; 61–2.

auspices of 'conscyence' and private 'Law'.[171] While Donne finds
sufficiency between the bourns of 'my selfe to my selfe' to offer the
generous capacity for individuate agency, both Sym, in his appropriation and exaggeration of the same device, and Denny, in his legalistic
reprisal and his impossibly accumulating judicial functions, repackage
sufficiency as inadequacy, generosity as paucity. 'My selfe to my selfe'
offers tidy encapsulation, a potential space of perfect self-affirmed identity formation where 'we are our selves sufficient to doe all Offices; . . .
delivered from all bondage, and restored to our naturall libertie'.[172]
'[H]imselfe . . . himselfe from himselfe . . . himselfe to himselfe . . . himselfe . . . against himselfe' offers only confusion, obscurity via surfeit.

So, here, at what is perhaps simultaneously both an acme and nadir of
geminative involution, as Sym plays a word back and forth against itself,
making rhetoric 'unnaturall and monstrous' in its sufficiency and destructive surfeit, I shall focus the discussion further, from a figure to a
single word from Sym's passage, a word with its own internal and
integral division, and a Roman word redeemed by the moralists: 'resolution'.[173] ' *Thirdly,* a *self-murderer* is *constant,* or rather *obstinate,* in his
resolution.'[174] This word, a keynote of neo-Stoic descriptions of suicidal
constancy, is the site for an aggressive Christian requisition of a Roman
vocabulary. Throughout descriptions of Stoic suicides, the firm resolution of the self-slaughterer was idealized, glorified as a key virtue of the
self-sufficient wise man and the heroic self-murderer. So the Donne
of the *Paradoxes* has recourse to 'our Valiants' who 'offer our brests to
the canons mouthe, yea to our swords points', and to him 'this seemes a
brave, a fiery sparkling, and a climbing resolution', even if it cannot
quite obscure a 'cowardly, an earthly, and a grovelling Spiritt' beneath
the heroic gloss.[175] So likewise Burton cannot hide his admiration for
one who 'was resolved voluntarily by famine to dispatch himselfe, to be
rid of his paine . . . *with a setled resolution hee desired againe.* . . . And so
constantly died.'[176] '[B]ut these', he reminds himself, 'are false and
Pagan positions, prophane Stoicall Paradoxes, wicked examples, it
bootes not what Heathen Philosophers determine in this kinde,
they are impious, abominable, & upon a wrong ground.'[177] The later

---

[171] Ibid., 45.   [172] Ibid., 107.   [173] Sym, *Lifes Preservative,* 283.
[174] Ibid., 187.   [175] Donne, *Paradoxes,* 9.
[176] Burton, *The Anatomy of Melancholy,* 436.   [177] Ibid., 437.

Christian commentators, in their attacks on *Biathanatos*, are glad to acknowledge the connotative correlation of self-slaughter and 'resolve', talking of the '*stiffnesse of purpose, and resolution* of committing self-murder', but couching it in especially gruesome terminology. Suicide is, says Denny, 'a Resolution in a desperate Madnesse to throw our selves headlong into Perdition'.[178] Denny's emotive employment of the word forcibly promotes analogy between what Sym calls 'inimicall and unnaturall resolutions' and despair, asking, 'Can dire Resolves help?' and allowing the preposterous paradox, can 'Scabs cure a Wound?'[179] Affirming the association by using the paradox, Denny exaggerates the grotesque and emphasizes the absurdity. George Strode, writing years earlier in 1618, has done his bit to pick at and unpick the loaded vocabulary of self-murther:

Where is thy wisedome that resolvest so foolishly? thy Justice to resolve so injuriously, thy love to God . . . that [thou] dost resolve so hatefully. . . . Did ever man conclude and resolve in any thing then thou doest in this . . . and most hatefully thou proceedest against God and thy selfe in this resolution. . . . I hope that the thing that thou art resolved to doe, will appeare so foule and odious before thee, that thy resolution will alter and vanish away.[180]

From excessive repetition to nothing, the verbal overwhelming resolves itself and vanishes away.

But 'perhaps', suggests Isaac Watts, the self-slaughterer 'has not resolution enough to endure'.[181] Watts engages Stoic ideals from within, lightly denying the ancient philosophers an emblematic signifier just as he, in passing, adopts and reapplies high-Stoic phraseology when suggesting that 'the infinite wisdom of God, may open a door of escape'.[182] Suddenly, it is not the wise man who must be constant in his resolve, but the Christian man who must 'dwell upon [Scripture] with a resolute constancy'.[183] 'A resolute constancy': in a line, Watts appropriates two focal terms, defying hundreds of years of entrenched connotation. This is a characteristic of all these anti-suicide treatises, which quietly invoke and deny Stoicism, as in Sym above, where the self-murderer is '*constant*', or, rather,

---

[178] Sym, *Lifes Preservative*, 320; Denny, *Pelicanicidium*, sig. A5ᵛ.
[179] Sym, *Lifes Preservative*, 322; Denny, *Pelicanicidium*, 3.
[180] Strode, *The Anatomie of Mortalitie*, 258–9.
[181] Watts, *Sermons*, 358.
[182] Ibid., 373.   [183] Ibid., 378.

he is '*obstinate*, in his resolution'. 'Resolution is the fixing of courage': the language, back in Denny, sounds Stoic—'vigor of fortitude . . . valiant Courage . . . to suffer . . . and undergo . . . undaunted'—but is now resolutely Christian, the 'strength of Faith'.[184]

Denny, more than any other commentator, forces the language and ideology of Donne and the Stoics back upon themselves as he goes about the creation of a model of 'Christian Resolution'.[185] So if Donne can claim 'a private man is Emporer of himselfe', Denny offers the reader the opportunity to reject self-slaughter, cleave to God, and then '[t]hou maist become Master of thy Self', a 'Master but of One Resolution!'[186] And so, in this final escalation of emphatic linguistic appropriation, Denny steals suicide from the self-slaughterer:

Resolve, thou wilt not goe into that bad Company! . . . Resolve, to deny thy Heart . . . ! Resolve to say but One Prayer! . . . Resolve to say it humblie! In thy Heart! Resolve to do it humblie! Resolve, as much as possibly thou canst, to think of Nothing then, but God, and thy prayer! And thy self in it to Him! Conceive it is the Sacrifice of thy Soul! . . .

And in this sacrifice we see the first signs of the final requisition:

Who shall deliver me from the body of this Death! . . . Resolve . . . ! Strike thy Breast! That thy rockie Heart may be Mollified.[187]

'Strike thy brest!' is Denny's first explicit call for an alternative model of suicide—'Take up thine Arms then!'—a model of theological self-slaughter:

Come hither, Backsliding Man! Here is thy nearest way; and thy best Death. And since nothing would down with thee, but Death, thou shalt have enough of self-killing. . . . Thou must kill thy self all over. The Dagger, or the like strikes but at a Part; This strikes at all. Mortifie the Flesh! and the sinful Members thereof! and thou offerest a Sacrifice; and committest not a Murder. . . . Draw thine Affections off from the World! And thou hast drawn a Dagger against Temptations. Fast! and thou starvest thy worser self. Fast![188]

---

[184] Denny, *Pelicanicidium*, 172.   [185] Ibid., 185.
[186] Ibid., 192.   [187] Ibid., 192–3.
[188] Denny, *Pelicanicidium*, 193; 250–1. The backsliding man refers to Proverbs 14: 14, a passage Thomas Hooker also refers to in his description, dealt with in more detail later, of the self-loving man: 'onely a Back-slider in heart shall be fill'd with his own wayes'. Thomas Hooker, *Heautonaparnumenos* (London, 1646), 21.

Promoting 'the mortification of thy sinful Flesh' over 'the destruction of thy human Body', the 'holy Sword' over the self-murderer's halter, Denny describes the Christian best death—'th'art a dead man'—as a self-killing, a murder of corporeal identity.[189] Sym's text, like Denny's, enforces the separation of spiritual and corporeal man precisely in order to facilitate this violent acting-back upon the self, to 'destroy our *self-old-man*' [i.e. the devil or sin], a part of ourselves whom we should kill, paradoxically, in order not to kill ourselves: 'if we doe turne the edge of our spirituall sword to slaughter it, with the lusts thereof, we shall be diverted, not onely from unjustly killing of *others*, but much more from *killing* our selves'.[190] In both Sym and Denny, suicide has murdered suicide: 'thou shalt have enough of Self-killing, even to wearinesse'.[191]

The self-slaughterer's resolution has been requisitioned, leaving him with nothing but what Sym describes as 'the dissolution of his personall *subsisting*'.[192] From a position of fixed resolution, it is the self-slaughterers who have come to dissolution as they 'violently dissolve themselves' in a 'death of *dissolution*'.[193] This is the movement of *Hamlet*, where suicidal 'resolution' (III. i. 84) becomes sicklied over, and the solid flesh melts, thaws, and 'resolve[s] itself into a dew' (ll. 129–30), in a line where, as I have argued, resolve no longer connotes firmness or fixity, but liquefaction and fluidity.

There has been in the sermonizers' calls for mortification a recourse to the preaching rhetoric of martyrdom. Clement Cotton's *Mirrour of Martyrs*, published in 1639, calls for the martyr-hopeful to be 'well exercised in the continuall practice of mortification', declaring that the 'mortified man is the likeliest to make a Martyr'.[194] While the proximity of martyrdom to suicide clearly worries a number of our sermonizers, the theological recuperation of the language of suicide facilitates the safe use of the tenor of martyrdom, allowing writers to enjoy its undoubtable emotive efficacy in sanitized form. Death is a powerful preaching tool,

---

[189] Denny, *Pelicanicidium*, 251.
[190] Sym, *Lifes Preservative*, 56.
[191] Denny, *Pelicanicidium*, 251.
[192] Sym, *Lifes Preservative*, 58.
[193] Ibid., 164; 166.
[194] Clement Cotton, *The Mirrour of Martyrs: The First and Second Part* (London, 1639), sig. A5^r.

spiritual suicide even more so, and rather than condemn and efface all trace of self-murder, the sermonizers and tract writers work with it, making its potential poison work medicinally for them. It is possible, in an act of impressive near paradox, to present spiritual suicide, or the mortification of the flesh, as the actual solution to what Lewis Bayly in 1616 depicts as the essentially suicidal nature of man: 'Thinke with what a *body of sinne* thou art loaden', he insists; think 'what great *civill warres* are contained in a *little world*; the *flesh fighting against the spirit: passion* against *reason*'.[195] The human condition is in a state of perpetual self-aggression, continually deferred self-murder. In revealing the typical association with civil war and self-slaughter, Bayly also reveals how thin the line between mortification and self-murder can become: the '*one* onely meane' that 'remaines to end this conflict' is '*Death*: which (in Gods appointed time) will separate thy *spirits* from thy *flesh*: the *pure* and *regenerate* part of thy soule, from that part which is *impure* and *unregenerated*'.[196] Bayly's parenthetical aside offers quick reassurance among an increasingly impassioned polemic that momentarily threatens to sound more like the call to arms, bridge, or rope of Seneca than the disapproving caution of Augustine. Suicide, condemned and dismissed as a particularly unattractive aspect of a degenerate classical culture, is nevertheless, in its safely spiritualized manifestation, as prevalent as ever: its keywords, argumentative models, and rhetorical habits, clearly dramatic and undoubtedly still charged with the aggressive visceral power of their former setting, are kept alive by the writers who seek to challenge them.

3. OUR SELVES AGAINST OUR SELVES: PROTESTANT SELF-SCRUTINY

I. What is selfe?
When a man placeth a kinde of supremacy or excellency in himselfe, or any other thing hee doth or hath besides Christ . . . that is self.[197]

---

[195] Lewis Bayly, *The Practice of Pietie* (London, 1616), 746.
[196] Ibid., 746–7.
[197] Thomas Hooker, *The Christians Two Chiefe Lessons, Viz. Selfe-Deniall, And Selfe-Tryall* (London, 1640), 35.

Thomas Hooker's conception of an over-indulgent subject, self-sufficient to a fault, is typical of a theology that, occasionally uncomfortably, tempers mild humanism with harsh self-stricture, and fledgling individualism with stringent self-denial. He that 'workes all of himselfe, and for himselfe', and they who make 'their own persons the end of their actions',[198] practise a sinful self-absorption, an excessive inclusivity, intriguingly described in what is by now instantly recognizable as the distinct vocabulary of the anti-suicide debate. Intriguing, because the end result of Hooker's argument is precisely a violent self-destruction: 'Self-denyall is a speciall meanes to fit the soule for suffering. Therefore these two goe hand in hand, he that is a self-denyer, will be a cheerfull sufferer.'[199] The geminative construction (of himselfe, for himselfe) and the condemnation of the occupation of simultaneously active and passive subject positions are, as we have seen, primary features of the aggressive backlash against *Biathanatos*, but here they take their place in the rhetoric of puritanical self-immolation, a habit of thought that had, paradoxically, been blamed for a 1640s epidemic of despairing, apparently reprobate, Protestant suicides.[200] The pressure of predestination anxiety, provoking a coruscating self-contemplation, is frequently cited as a cause of religious despair, for 'as the sword taken at the wrong end is readie to wound the hand of the taker . . . the doctrine of predestination being preposterously conceived, may through the fault of the conceiver procure hurt':[201] 'that Studious Youngster [was] found hang'd in his Study, supposed by the direction of his Finger on the sacred Text, to be driven thereto by the terror of the Predestinarion Opinion'.[202] Perhaps, if we are to credit these often partisan accounts, the presence of suicide tropes in the vocabulary of abjection is unusually pertinent, morbidly germane to preaching that is seen to have significantly contributed to the creation of a culture of suicide.

The introspection of the English Protestants, 'retiring into our selves and checking our hearts', seeks to 'raise our selves against our selves',

---

[198] Ibid., 40.
[199] Ibid., 86.
[200] See H. C. Erik Midelfort, 'Religious Melancholy and Suicide: On the Reformation Origins of a Sociological Stereotype', in Andrew D. Weiner and Leonard V. Kaplan (eds.), *Madness, Melancholy, and the Limits of the Self* (Madison, Wis., 1996), 41–56.
[201] T. Bright, *A Treatise of Melancholy* (London, 1613), 245.
[202] Pierce, *A Discourse of Self-Murder*, 23.

ridding 'our selves [of] the greatest enemies to our selves'.[203] Richard
Kilby's note to the printer at the start of his confessional tract, *The
Burden of a Loaden Conscience*, first insists upon the retention of '*I am*',
which he refuses to have replaced by the mitigating past-tense '*I was*',
then announces that it is '*very needfull for a man to know what he is*', and
that '*I know none but myself*', before explaining that '*I judge none but my
self, because I fear the Judgment of God*'.[204] Here we see the Protestant
progression, first towards the self, subjecting the self to a rigorous
examination, and then beyond itself to God; introspection leads away
from the self, moving from '*I am*' to '*I . . . would perswade People to fear
God*', from *I* to *God*.[205] The dialogic conscience becomes, in the words
of Charles Taylor, 'the "space" in which we come to encounter God, in
which we effect the turning from lower to higher', a transition demanding what Peter Iver Kaufman recognizes as a kind of 'bruising self-
exploration', an aggressive introspection.[206] While setting out his stall
against suicidal despair ('it is better to be a living dog, than a dead
Lion'), the Reverend Richard Greenham understands both the sinful-
ness of self-absorption—'every sinner is condemned in himselfe, or by
himselfe'—while advocating the pharmaceutical scouring of self-
judgement: 'this is', he explains, 'a medicine whereby if we profit, it is
bitter and wholesome as the treacle: but if we doe not, it is a poison
bitter and deadly'.[207] Clearly, the emphatic insistence on self-scrutiny
does not, as a matter of consequence, result in essentialist or Cartesian
subjectivity or in a prototype modern self-consciousness. Rather, the
inward gaze seeks to look beyond the selfish concerns of the individual:
'Thus to seeke our selves is to deny our selves, and thus to deny our
selves, is truly to seeke our selves.'[208] This reflexive language is double-
edged. It is both mimetically indicative of the '*excellency of the soule, that
can reflect upon it selfe*', and simultaneously recalls the reflexive dynamic

[203] Richard Sibbs, *The Soules Conflict With It Selfe, and Victory Over It Selfe by Faith*
(London, 1636), prefatory matter; 110; 77.
[204] Richard Kilby, *The Burden of a Loaden Conscience* (London, 1699), prefatory
matter.
[205] Ibid.
[206] Taylor, *Sources of the Self*, 140; Peter Iver Kaufman, *Prayer, Despair, and Drama*
(Urbana, Ill., 1996), 139.
[207] Richard Greenham, *The Works*, ed. H. H. (London, 1612), 656; 657; 672.
[208] Sibbs, *The Soules Conflict*, 145.

of self-slaughter: 'The gate, the [entrance] of Religion, is narrow; we must strip our selves of our selves before we can enter.'[209]

Textual reflexivity literalizes the self-reflection being promoted. John Abernethy describes, in a section that thirty years after Kepler still shows the lingering imaginative legacy of extramissive ocular theory, how our 'speculatiue beames' should be 'reflected on our selues' until 'we should behold, contemplate and study our selues (which is both great Philosophy, and a beginning of Theology)'.[210] At the heart of the Protestant faith is self-reflection. Abernethy worries that these beams may, in sinful times, be 'farre more darkened' than they ought, fearing that 'those ascending beames, that shall penetrate vnto God [are] wonderfully weakened, that they cannot attaine to their highest zenith: and [are] strangely stopped, by the interposition of so many clouds', or that they may 'in the very Christalline humour of the minde so suffocate that now man is become darknesse in abstract'.[211] The 'blindnesse of the mind' that concerns Abernethy is 'not only a simple priuation of the knowledge of our selues, but also a wilfull want of that meditation upon our selues'.[212] In a set-piece analogy that borrows much from the outmoded eye-emitted ray paradigm, Abernethy rails against the dulled faculty of the mind, impaired in reason, understanding, and judgement, that is 'vnwilling to return their owne beames by a kinde of reflection: whereby a man might behold and contemplate himselfe'.[213] This visual reciprocation has learnt the anatomic lessons of ocular theory and now conducts its 'kinde' reflections internally, where the to-and-fro movement of beams now occurs entirely within the mind of the self-scrutinizing Protestant. Reflection has been internalized: the movement from extramission to intromission has come to this. What was scientific fact is now pure metaphor, and what was by definition external has moved to the new psychic interior. This is critical, not merely because it finally shows how a scientific metaphor has been subsumed into a whole new model of thought, but also because it illustrates how self-to-self reflection has

---

[209] Ibid., 68; 140.
[210] John Abernethy, *A Christian and Heavenly Treatise: Containing Physicke for the Soule* (London, 1630), 19.
[211] Ibid., 19.
[212] Ibid., 21.
[213] Ibid., 21.

now become the cornerstone of theological ontology: 'Begin, and acquaint thy selfe, with thy selfe.'[214]

This sense of ontologic duality within the single subject is indebted to Augustine, whose two books of soliloquies have the dialogic form of what Marshall Grossman describes as an 'inward dialogue that begins with a division of self that is at once the cause and effect of a movement toward self-knowledge'.[215] 'I asked myself questions and I replied to myself, as if we were two, reason and I, whereas I was of course just one', explains Augustine, and 'as a result I called the work *Soliloquies*'.[216] Grossman, with post-Lacanian inflection, distinguishes between 'the "I" that speaks and the "I" that is bespoken; . . . the subject of the enunciation and the subject of the utterance', seeing the subject 'irreducibly double-entrapped in its own verbal mirror': 'there suddenly spoke to me—what was it? I myself or someone else, inside or outside me? (this is the very thing I would love to know but don't)'.[217] Augustine toils to know God, to recognize God's operation within his own faculty of reason, to interact with this second extrinsic yet internalized self who allows 'ontogenesis' (the construction of a subjectivity dependent on divine in-dwelling) through a kind of 'anticipatory retrospection', as he narrates the earlier development of a spiritual identity that anticipates fulfilment.[218] Conflict is crucial for the confessional Augustine, whose sense of ontological structure includes a vicious in-fighting: 'the self which willed to serve was identical with the self which was unwilling', he admits, adding, with a characteristic grammatical knowingness, 'it was I' (Henry Chadwick's translation of the *Confessions* is faithful to Augustine's insistence on applying singular forms to plural states, enforcing the indivisibility of his spiritual individuality, and capturing that sense of structural 'conflict with myself').[219] Augustinian gemination—'a struggle of myself against myself' or a soliloquized dialogue 'with myself to myself'—is an integral part of his attempt to 'reject my own will and to desire [God's]', allowing self-abjection and a perpetual recourse to the

---

[214] Ibid., 27.
[215] Grossman, *The Story of All Things*, 57.
[216] St Augustine, *Soliloquies and Immortality of the Soul*, trans. Gerald Watson (Warminster, 1986), 1. 4.
[217] Ibid., 1. 23.
[218] Grossman, *The Story of All Things*, 63; 58.
[219] St Augustine, *Confessions*, trans. Henry Chadwick (Oxford, 1991), 148.

rhetoric of self-denial to result in divinely informed self-knowledge: 'I am ashamed of myself and reject myself'; 'I do not know myself'; therefore 'what I know of myself I know because you grant me light'.[220] The Augustinian autobiographical project is a sustained denial of authorship, a redirection of authority.

Therefore, while self-formation operates with an internally relational dynamic, it is important to appreciate the inadequacy of the private self and acknowledge the presence of God operating privily in one of these dual subject positions:

Wee see likewise hence a *necessity of having something in the soule above it selfe, it must be partaker of a diviner nature than it selfe.* . . . Therefore we must conceive in a godly man, a double selfe, one which must be denied, the other which must denie.[221]

Sibbs's anatomy of human duality, rather than intensifying an emphasis on subjective agency, incorporates (quite literally) the divine into the self. This first self figures as a lack, which the second self (divinely informed) redeems. We are, says Sibbs, 'never our selves perfectly till we have wholly put off our selves', and 'nothing should be at a greater distance to us, than ourselves'.[222] We recognize a geminative dynamic resurfacing from earlier discussion that once again reveals the moment of attainment to be a moment of loss, affirming reflection of self to self to be a catastrophe of integral, self-perpetuated violence. A moment of self-sufficiency becomes a recognition of worthlessness—'a good man is wiser than *himselfe*, holier than himselfe, stronger than himselfe, there is something in him more than a man'—and the introspective Protestant is caught up in a reflexive double bind of the type that Giles Firmin complains is 'enough to sink a poor Christian', and that even Abernethy admits is a dangerously paradoxical entanglement:

But, O too heauie distress (said one) If I looke into my selfe, I suffer not my selfe: If I looke not into my selfe, I know not my selfe: If I looke into my selfe, my face affrighteth me: If I consider not my selfe, my damnation deceiueth me:

[220] Ibid., 152; 160; 155; 179; 182.
[221] Sibbs, *The Soules Conflict*, 110.
[222] Ibid., 111.

If I see my selfe, it is horrour intolerable: If I see not my selfe, it is death intolerable. And it is a rare thing to find a man that seeth himselfe rightly.[223]

It is a rare thing to find a man who sees anything through this confusion, and who can succeed with his 'owne reflected beames to see and know it self'.[224] Ultimately, these writers agree that the only true form of reflection is the kindliness of God, and the only true self is one that has ceded responsibility even for the linguistic subject position, the locale of self: 'what is he in himselfe? (a worm) What within himself? (a [c]reature of evil.)'[225] Theological gemination strives to share the quality of '*Faith*', which Sibbs describes as '*nothing else but a spirituall eccho, returning that voice back againe, which God first speakes to the soule*'.[226]

It is no wonder that this rhetoric of self-abjection, coupled with what John Stachniewski describes as the fear of reprobation—which he sees as creating a nation of 'quaking obsessives' and which Firmin blames for creating an atmosphere in which those who have 'lost their assurances' merely 'lye bemoaning themselves in their dark desertions'—frequently leads to the violence of self-slaughter.[227] Henry Jessey's account of the despair of that 'Empty Nothing Creature', Sarah Wight, a woman terrified that she is 'damn'd already' and convinced that she is 'Castaway, a Reprobate, walking daily in the midst of fire and brimstone, as one in Hell already', unsurprisingly contains numerous references to how 'shee oft attempted wickedly to destroy her selfe, as by drowning, strangling, stabbing, seeking to beat out her braines, wretchedly bruising, and wounding her self'.[228] Suicidal rhetoric, it seems from this kind of fashionably hyperbolic discourse, is an extreme by-product of the admission that if '*you see your selfe nothing; and see all fulnesse in Christ, you are the neerest to comfort . . . you must be lost in your selfe, that*

---

[223] Ibid.; Giles Firmin, *The Real-Christian; or, A Treatise of Effectual Calling* (London, 1670), 207; Abernethy, *A Christian and Heavenly Treatise*, 26.

[224] Abernethy, ibid., 27.

[225] Ibid., 30.

[226] Sibbs, *The Soules Conflict*, 480.

[227] John Stachniewski, *The Persecutory Imagination: English Puritanism and the Literature of Religious Despair* (Oxford, 1991), 22; Firmin, *The Real-Christian*, 206.

[228] Henry Jessey, *The Exceeding Riches of Grace Advanced By the Spirit of Grace, in an Empty Nothing Creature, viz M^{ris} Sarah Wight* (London, 1647), 7–9. The argument in this text between Mistresses A and S demonstrates just how near to being vogue suicide has become and how fashionable melancholy has become.

you may be found in him.[229] So, Foucault, turning his attention towards the 'technologies of the self' in his later work ('the history of how an individual acts upon himself'), argues that Classical instruction in self-care is suppressed in favour of a 'tradition of Christian morality which makes self-renunciation the condition for salvation', where 'to know oneself was paradoxically the way to self-renunciation', and therefore '"Know thyself" has obscured "Take care of yourself" because our morality... insists the self is that which one can reject.'[230] Suicide is so anomalous to Christian doctrine precisely because it implicates a violent self-care, a renunciation that is in fact an intense involvement. True renunciation does require a penitential martyrdom, involving 'violent rupture and dissociation', a 'refusal of self', a 'breaking away from self', a 'self-revelation [that] is at the same time self-destruction': 'At their parting, for a farewell, Mris A. said, I think I shall perish ere I see you againe.'[231]

4. MY SELF, MY SELF, MY SELF BETRAY: GEORGE GOODWIN'S *AUTO-MACHIA*

I sing my Self; my Civill-Wars within.[232]

George Goodwin, a staunch anti-Papist, can be taken quite as literally as Montaigne when the French philosopher claims to *essai* himself; Goodwin sings himself, not simply making manifest an internal discordance, but allowing geminative rhetoric to structure ontological awareness and provide structure for formative reflexivity.[233] His is a rhetorical display of ipseic fracture and division of unprecedented ferocity. *Auto-Machia* offers both an aesthetic commentary on an ontic state, and a commentary upon its own poetic production: as its keynote we can take the couplet, 'Concording Discord kils mee; and again, | Discording

---

[229] Ibid., 47.

[230] Foucault, 'Technologies of the Self', 19; 22.

[231] Ibid., 43; Jessey, *The Exceeding Riches of Grace*, 47; 44. See Wymer, *Suicide and Despair*, 16.

[232] George Goodwin, 'Auto-Machia', in Guillaume Du Bartas, *His Divine Weekes, and Workes; with, A Compleate, Collection of all the Other Most Delightfull Workes*, trans. Josuah Sylvester (London, 1641), 566–7, l. 7.

[233] Montaigne, *Essais*, sig. A6ᵛ; see George Goodwin, *Babels Balm*, trans. John Vicars (London, 1624).

Concord doth my Life sustain' (ll. 185–6). The poem itself is both constructed from, and sustained by, discordance, which increasingly threatens its own complete deconstruction. With epizeuxis in extremis, Goodwin sings himself and exemplifies Francis Barker's claim that 'this world achieves its depth not in the figure of interiority by which the concealed inside is of another quality from what is external, but by a *doubling of the surface*.[234] While figures that pertain to interiority dominate this poem—the *I*, and *myself*—their failure to disclose psychological depth is increasingly apparent; the self is encountered entirely on the level of surface, in the dense gloss of reflexive pronouns that Goodwin lays over his text, and literally in the doubling of surface figured in the rhetoric of repetition.

If Stephen Greenblatt is correct in his assertion that, during the period, 'inwardness is a psychological state (and hence subjective) and [increasingly becomes] a spiritual condition (and hence objective)', then Goodwin's *Self-Conflict of a Christian* occupies an intricate position between these two binaries.[235] A poem of spiritual self-analysis finds itself characterized by both the subjective tone of self-assessment and the spiritual objectivity against which that assessment is made; in other words, it looks within, keeping one eye beyond itself, judging itself in terms both subjective and objective. Equally, while the poem's preoccupation with interiority 'bespeaks withdrawal', this remains an 'insistently public' interiority, 'a discursive inwardness . . . dependent not only upon language but upon an audience'.[236] The audience is introjected within *myself*, the self-assessing *I*, and is a graphically displayed, mimetically structured discursive and desperate inwardness.

The anxiety of the potentially reprobate clouds the clarity of his constant self-scrutiny: the closer the scrutiny, the more panic obscures. We witness the complicated interaction of a theological emphasis on 'the perpetual distrust of "interior" motivation' and 'an equal fascination with the "inner" voice of conscience', an uncomfortable combination that breeds a palpable disgust with the poet's compulsive self-absorption.[237]

[234] Francis Barker, *The Tremulous Private Body: Essays on Subjection* (London, 1984), 28.

[235] Stephen Greenblatt, *Renaissance Self-Fashioning* (Chicago, 1980), 126.

[236] Ibid.

[237] Sawday, 'Self and Selfhood in the Seventeenth Century', 31.

The familiar conflation of internal conflict with civil war makes both clear correlatives to self-murder. Goodwin's '*daily* Duel', his '*continuall Strife*', will not cease '*till I end my Life*' (ll. 9–10). Reading through the ambiguity of this line, we allow both the possibility of 'until I die', and, more pertinently, 'until I kill myself', with its suggestion of agency, self-murder. In fact the *Self-Conflict of a Christian* can conclude in a moment of self-violence '*not onely Mine*' but '*every One*'? when the '*Triumphant Captaine, Glorious* Generall' furnishes the poet with arms and '*in* This Conflict, *make*[s] *Mee conquer* Mee' (ll. 11; 12; 17–20). Here is the recognizable tenor of spiritual self-slaughter, a rejection not just of the body but of the wilful self, the agency of Mine, the sufficiency of the human One, and the active Me. Goodwin alludes to a stock motif of suicide debate: the soldier who should not desert his post unless his general calls him (of course, Augustinians never hear the call too early, while Senecans hear it almost continually). Called by God, the Christian can resolve his civil war, preposterously turn *Mee* upon Mee, only when confident of Heavenly Love (l. 16).

But while he remains cleaved to this earth, Goodwin's Christian is trapped within the self-civil-war, '[w]ith and against my self', caught in a state of self-surfeit: 'I both | Too-love my Self, and yet my self I loath' (ll. 16; 23–4). Geminative structure often works as visual emulation of psychic division, and Goodwin explicitly employs the model as the point of departure for what follows; a poem of crafted 'Confused Method', a sustained paradoxical display, it fractures from this point, escalating in monosyllabic tumbles of over-sustained oxymoron as the poet '[t]ransports mee to the Contrary' (ll. 156, 89). There is both impossibly tight economy and gratuitous excess as he continues:

> I joyne, I jar:
> I burn, I freeze; I fall downe, I stand fast:
> Well-ill I fare; I glory though disgrac't:
> I die alive: I triumph, put to flight;
> . . .
> I strike, and stroake my selfe: I, kindly-keen,
> Work mine own woe, rub my gall, rouz my spleen. (ll. 26–34)

The poem is constructed from these examples of extreme foreshortening, where 'Well-ill' and 'die alive' graphically constrict the interstitial space between words, making the verse itself uncomfortably restricted, repeatedly catching up the reader in flurries of Petrarchan antitheses and self-effacement: 'O! how I like, dis-like, desire, disdain; | Repell, repeal, loath, and delight again! | . . . | I will, I nill; I nill, I will' (ll. 169–73). Poetic time is, in like manner, crumpled to 'To-Day, to-Morrow; this, that, Now, Anon' (l. 43). And, as the above quotation indicates, these violent antitheses resolve themselves in moments of self-violence that verge on self-gratification, striking and stroking, rubbing and rousing. This is too kindly, too self-involved. '[K]indly-keen': the alliterative and unusually hard velar plosives make the line itself too kind, too implicated within its own workings. The comfort of self-absorption and the potential ideal of self-sufficiency, the conflicted Christian is telling us, is a tempting but gratuitous 'Self-soothing' gratification, a 'pleasing Torment, a tormenting Pleasure' (ll. 181; 162). Distanced from the life of the spirit, the sheer vitality (and sexuality) of his secular single self is ultimately indicative only of a spiritual death; thus, he dies alive, every act of will figuring only as nil. As the pronouns multiply, '[i]n divers *Factions* I my Self divide' (l. 39) until the tenability of the single self is itself so threatened that number is slain, all quantitative value collapses to 'All, Nothing, crave I; Ever Never-one' (l. 44). Sense suffers such ellipsis, phrasal construction undergoes such telescopic reduction, that the line becomes tight with internal relations and counter-relations, each word both calling up (so 'All' is matched by 'Ever', and 'Nothing' by 'Never'), while denying another ('Nothing' counters 'All', and 'Never' 'Ever'). What results is an unachieved I, a Never-one, that craves recognition or substance, a this or that, a time to be either 'Now' or 'Anon', but that perishes, undoing itself: 'Alive I perish, and my Self undo; | Mine eyes (Self-wise) witting and willing too' (ll. 65–6).

   Both witting and willing (again it is wilfulness that induces such guilt), Goodwin's conflicted Christian is caught in a suicidal bind, between the perimeters of self and self, a circuitous self-implication that inevitably recalls a narcissine speculation:

> Sick to my Self I run for my reliefe;
> So, Sicker of my *Physicke* than my *Grief:*
> For, while I seek my swelting Thirst to swage,
> Another Thirst more ragingly doth rage. (ll. 67–70)

These lines are so self-involved that at times a word can only regenerate itself, a line can only progress via replication, and nothing now seems capable of seeing beyond the confines of itself. 'Sick' only gets 'Sicker', and thirst 'ragingly doth rage'; the phrase surely takes its force from signification's inadequacy, expressing rage as rage with no other word able or available to intensify the sense. Rage is both itself and yet 'more' than itself. The movement is almost centrifugal, and, increasingly, it is preposterous: qualities begin to feed back into themselves, acting simultaneously as product, catalyst, and initiator.

We can feel the narcissistic dynamic coming to the surface, for example in the sense of the pharmaceutical physic, becoming gradually more explicit as he continues: 'While burnt to death, to coole mee I desire; | With flames, my flames; with Sulphur quench I fire' (ll. 71–2). This is the chronologically confused preposterous logic of the Narcissus myth, feeding one's flame, a cyclic escalation that now speaks, in this Christian context, of a latent threat in spiritual introspection and the dangers of looking only inwards for spiritual physic:

> Thus am I cur'd, this is my common ease;
> My *Med'cine* still worse than my worst Disease:
> My Sores with Sores, my wounds with wounds I heal,
> While to my Self, my Self I still conceal. (ll. 75–8)

Layering flames on flames, sores on sores, and wounds on wounds, Goodwin brings us to the first pronoun epizeuxis, reflexive and as a superfluous nominative, in 'to my Self, my Self I still conceal'. Here the self that is concealed is not only figured forth, but doubly so, its hidden interiority both displayed and denied in what is explicitly a word game, a language pattern, so convoluted on the level of text that all depth is insistently horizontal, while vertical depth, a movement down towards the interior, is actually impeded by surface overactivity. '[I]f the text cannot dramatize this interiority', to rehearse Barker, 'it can at least display its impossibility': my Self, my Self I still conceal.[238]

If 'character is a kind of language, and language is a kind of action', as Edward Burns has argued, Goodwin's ontic character is delineated by gemination, his action necessarily suicidal.[239] 'Constructed in these purposive linguistic praxes, in this rhetoric', Burns continues, 'interiority

---

[238] Barker, *The Tremulous Private Body*, 37.

[239] Edward Burns, *Character: Acting and Being on the Pre-Modern Stage* (London, 1990), 90.

is in itself a series of rhetorical strategies.'[240] The linguistic quality of a rhetorically constructed interiority is so insistent in this poem that the reader is made to feel the extent to which the subject is caught up, figured and effaced by, the poem's rhetorical models of expression:

> My Self at once I both displease and please:
> Without my Self, my Self I fain would seaze:
> For my too much of mee, mee much annoyes:
> And my Self's Plenty my poor Self destroyes. (ll. 187–90)

The multiple germinations—'my Self, my Self', and 'mee, mee'—speak of the impossibility of seizing a self that is paradoxically less present the more that it figures, a self that threatens to slip through the text's web of over-signification, and speaks of a superfluity, an over-representation.

Jonathan Sawday cautions the modern critic concerned with 'self-hood' that, in the Renaissance, 'the word [self] was anchored, in a theological sense, to an entirely negative set of ideas... [being] a token of the spiritually unregenerate individual, in thrall to the flesh rather than the spirit'.[241] This negative token betrays self-absorption and to find it employed only in relation to itself affirms this unfavourable anchor. My self, my self: again in Barker's terms, while gesturing towards a place for subjectivity, the 'promised essence remains beyond the scope of the text's signification' (while, in this case, being exasperatingly over-represented), 'marking out the site of an absence it cannot fill'.[242] There is an excess of plenty and a central paucity playing off against each other in these lines, a sense of paradoxical full absence that is well described by Terry Eagleton's formulation of a modern subjectivity that seems equally applicable to these constructions of its early modern precursor. Eagleton talks of a subject, 'its feet planted on nothing more solid than itself', whose 'defiant boast ("I take value from myself alone!")' is simultaneously 'its catastrophe ("I am so lonely in this universe!")'.[243] As Arthur Kirsch explains, this kind of poetic 'narcissism results in a sense only of the loss of the self, because a self that encompasses everything cannot be defined by anything, and is indeed

[240] Edward Burns, 92; 142.

[241] Sawday, 'Self and Selfhood in the Seventeenth Century', 30.

[242] Barker, *The Tremulous Private Body*, 37.

[243] Terry Eagleton, 'Self-Undoing Subjects', in Roy Porter (ed.), *Rewritting the self: Histories from the Renaissance to the Present* (London, 1997), 262–9, at 266.

defined by nothing'.[244] This subject, exhibiting 'certain manic-depressive symptoms, as it veers wildly between self-abasement and self-aggrandizement',[245] could boast to be, as Goodwin's speaker shortly does, 'Hermaphrodite in minde, | . . . (at once) Male, Female', displaying the complete sufficiency of an autonomous subject, all at once, a wealthy self (ll. 192–3). Yet, facing his catastrophe, complaining '[w]retch that I am' (l. 196), the self seems poor. But I am applying Eagleton's model primarily for what comes next: 'its existence a perpetual irony', he continues, '[the subject] leaves itself with no alterity in whose mirror it might confirm its own identity'.[246] Although this is clearly Lacanian in tenor, the 1641 text displays, in the multiple examples of pronoun repetition and reflection which follow, the conflicted Christian's search (my Self I would seize) for some form of affirming reflection (my Self, my Self), an ultimately futile search (my too much of me), leaving the subject only able to 'now confer value upon itself' (me, me much annoys).[247] Having no criteria beyond itself by which to assess itself, the subject is subject to a 'pointless form of narcissism, and though this subject is all knowing, the last thing it can know is itself'.[248] Identity in this text is therefore both susceptible to radical poverty and crippling overdetermination.

As Goodwin continues, his poem implicates itself still further with this paradoxical dynamic of oscillatory presence and absence:

> Who seeks mee in mee, in mee shall not finde
> Mee as my Self. (ll. 191–2)

Me in me in me not me: convoluted staccato clumps of pronouns in near complete linguistic paroxysm fashion an ontological state not merely in conflict but envisaged in bouts of what is simultaneously suicidal self-reflection and complete narcissistic self-absorption. Simply looking at the lines leaves the impression of an isolated other (the 'Who' that seeks is almost effaced by 'Mee . . . mee . . . mee . . . Mee') and an

---

[244] Kirsch, 'Macbeth's Suicide', 289. Michael Neill describes something similar when he talks of 'paradoxy [that] can express both annihilating self-contradiction and mysterious transcendence'; *Issues of Death: Mortality and Identity in English Renaissance Tragedy* (Oxford, 1997), 363.

[245] Eagleton, 'Self-Undoing Subjects', 266.
[246] Ibid.   [247] Ibid.   [248] Ibid.

equally solitary but endlessly refracted self, a self that ultimately even succeeds in incorporating that near-insignificant other:

> *Hermaphrodite* in minde,
> I am (at once) Male, Female, Neuter: yet
> What-e'r I am, I am not mine, I weet:
> I am not with my Self as I conceive. (ll. 192–5)

Any chance of fertility, of progression beyond the single/multiple self, is merely in mind alone, an introspective fantasy of sexual mutuality which, while moving through the reproductive pairing of Male and Female, results in neuter, a non-sexual neutered nothing. That keynote of Renaissance assertion, the 'I am', is couched on both sides by indeterminacy ('What-e'r I am') and negation ('I am not . . . I am not'), and comes only to the denial of generative potential. Not with himself as he conceives (a pun activated by its sexual context), the poet is unproductive both in sexual and aesthetic authorship. The poem's undercurrent of disgust briefly surfaces in this non-conception, this sterile voice.

As the poem concludes, Goodwin's verse exhibits the conflicted Christian's self, unloaded, unpacked, and finally unpicked in a rhetorical display seemingly as extravagant as the verse form can take. Gemination has never been so structurally self-destructive:

> Wretch that I am, my Self my Self deceive:
> Unto my Self, my Self my Self betray. (ll. 196–7)

The unique triple repetition, packed together, cannot be read with epizeuxis's handbook sense of escalation: this is diminution, signifying less and less with each incidence. To appropriate a phrase from Patricia Fumerton, 'it was as if the self were chasing its self-image endlessly'.[249] Having become linguistically protean, Goodwin's speaker succumbs to a verbal manifestation of Paul Delany's 'destructive schizophrenia':[250]

> I from my Self, banish my Self away:
> My Self agrees not with my Self a jot,

---

[249] Patricia Fumerton, *Cultural Aesthetics: Renaissance Literature and the Practice of Social Ornament* (Chicago, 1991), 129.

[250] Paul Delany, *British Autobiography in the Seventeenth Century* (London, 1969), 12.

Knowes not my Self: I have my Self forgot:
Against my Self, my Self move jarres unjust:
I trust my Self, and I my Self distrust:
My Self I follow, and my Self I fly:
Besides my Self, and in my Self, am I. (ll. 198–204)

This is the language both of insanity (being out of one's mind), fury and melancholy (being beside oneself), self-love (I follow and fly), and self-slaughter (against oneself), all senses which, in these the final lines, fuse in a phrase that encapsulates this study: 'My Self am not my Self, another same; | Unlike my Self, and like my Self I am: | Self-fond, Self-furious' (ll. 205–7). Goodwin cures narcissism with poisonous self-violence. Every self is paired with a self that denies, distrusts, and destroys it.

We recall what Michael Schoenfeldt has described as the 'tension between self-assertion and submission' that governs the period's devotional verse.[251] We recall Donne's demand to be broken, burned, imprisoned, and enthralled: the demand of the self-banished subject to be made new in the cathartic fire of violent divine invasive in-dwelling, to be made chaste by divine ravishing assault.[252] In Goodwin's geminative crescendo, we sense the fervour of something approaching religious '*Raptures* and *Extasies*', which, in the words of the Reverend Edward Reynolds, 'raise and ravish the Soul with the sweetness of extraordinary contemplations, wherein a man is, as it were, carried *out of himself*'.[253] If the 'Root of every mans love unto himself, is that *Unity* and *Identity* which he hath with himself', we feel, in Goodwin's pronominal proliferation, both a desperate attempt to interrelate that produces merely endless refraction, and simultaneous horror at the destruction of the 'simplicity of . . . Being'.[254] If 'the more *Simple* and *One* [we are], the more like [we are] the Fountain of Being', Goodwin's near-neurotic repetition seems to both aspire to and short-circuit this simplicity while grotesquely convoluting the licensed ontological intra-action of *Amor Concupiscentiæ*: 'a *Circular love*, that which begins and ends in a *Man's*

[251] Michael C. Schoenfeldt, '"Respective Boldnesse": Herbert and the Art of Submission', in Mary A. Maleski (ed.), *A Fine Tuning* (New York, 1989), 77–94 at 82.

[252] John Donne, 'Holy Sonnet 14', in *The Complete English Poems*, 314–15.

[253] Edward Reynolds, 'A Treatise of the Passions and Faculties of the Soul of Man', in *The Works* (London, 1679), 613–780 at 616.

[254] Ibid., 640.

self, when his affection having gone forth to some object, doth again return home, and loves it not *directly* for any *absolute* goodness which it hath in its self, but as it is conducible'.[255] Reynolds describes a connotatively extramissive spiritual love of 'mutual sympathy', of 'sweet subordination of things each to other', where 'similitude is the ground of Love', and it is this sympathetic mutuality that Goodwin craves, as he mimetically constructs lexical kindness in each line of chiasmatic rigour, but which has been superseded by unkind reciprocation, by violent geminative response.[256]

Making itself heard throughout these final lines is the voice of what Debora Shuger describes as the pneumatic self: 'not a "thing" or agent or individuality but the locus of presence . . . not a bounded *ego* but a space—a void, if you like—where God comes (or does not come)'.[257] The self, understood in these terms, is something akin to a desire, an emptiness that craves fulfilment through the presence of God, and it is this craving that exists as an undercurrent in discussions of mortification, denying the self, making space for God's presence, for when, in the words of Jacob Bauthumley, 'God spiritually discovers himself'.[258] Pneumatic, oscillatory, with absence and presence in constant concomitant interaction, the self is paradoxically most fulfilled when empty, most affirmed when denied; 'the locus of the sacred shrinks to the private spaces of the psyche, which remains permeable to presence but also tormented by a sense of desolation', and yet this anguish, Shuger explains, 'discloses the indwelling of grace as it carves out the centre of the self, creating the neediness only it can fill'.[259] Goodwin's text—throughout which his invocations and denials of self play back and forth—fashions this pneumatic self, lacking sufficiency, 'open to the crisis of desolation'.[260] The self is emphasized, overemphasized,

---

[255] Ibid., 643.
[256] Ibid., 638; 637; 638.
[257] Debora Kuller Shuger, *Habits of Thought in the English Renaissance: Religion, Politics, and the Dominant Culture* (Toronto, 1997), 100.
[258] Jacob Bauthumley, 'The Light and the Dark Sides of God', in *A Collection of Ranter Writings from the Seventeenth Century,* ed. Nigel Smith (London, 1983), 262. Nigel Smith describes how 'an "inner self" was defined and explored for the sake of the divine working within it' (p. 18).
[259] Shuger, *Habits of Thought,* 118.
[260] Ibid., 257.

revealed as lacking; in turn the lack is emphasized, asked to be filled, but, in its moment of self-fondness and self-fury, Goodwin's text can only fulfil Shuger's definition of the unfulfilled; '[t]he pneumatic self is not only permeable to presence but constituted by it', she concludes, and 'when presence is deferred, it collapses into suicidal chaos'.[261] Sawday's description of the linguistic token 'self' finds the word signalling only 'an absence of God, a state of spiritual isolation, rather than the presence of reflective enquiry', and indeed it is, in Goodwin's verse, the very presence of the reflective, and verbally reflecting enquiry, that fashions that integral isolated absence.[262] Each personal pronoun, in reflection and repetition, is far from what Charles Taylor describes as a feature of ontological certainty, but perhaps figures as a fraught gesture towards what he describes as the 'radical reflexivity' of the modern.[263]

Only able to figure, in Eagleton's terms, as 'some kind of empty excess', once this subject is enunciated, 'in some usable image', it 'ceases in that moment to be itself'.[264] Eagleton talks of a 'vaunted liberty which is also a sort of vacancy . . . a mere pregnant silence or enigmatic cipher', and while 'Self' in this text is far from silent, its ciphers more insistent than enigmatic, the subject still potentially 'slips through the net of language'; and while not just 'leaving the merest spectral trace of itself behind', the superfluity of traces speaks just as clearly of the vacancy at the heart of this text.[265] We could apply Belsey's formula, 'the subject . . . is a chimera, an effect of language', but alongside the qualification that this chimera is the subject of very real aspiration; ipseic idealism in this period—often articulated as nostalgia for a lost plenitude or faith for future fulfilment—is as voluble as its unachievable object is inexpressible (is it that Renaissance desire for subjectivity works with the same faith-based aspirational structure—craving fulfilment—as language's integral dynamic of longing? Certainly, to deny Renaissance subjectivity because it was found wonting/wanting would be as reductive as to deny signifiers existed just because they were not referents).[266]

---

[261] Ibid., 101.
[262] Sawday, 'Self and Selfhood in the Seventeenth Century', 30.
[263] Taylor, *Sources of the Self,* 133; 177.
[264] Eagleton, 'Self-Undoing Subjects', 266.
[265] Ibid.
[266] Catherine Belsey, *The Subject of Tragedy: Identity and Difference in Renaissance Drama* (London, 1985), 54. My discussion deliberately falls short of a Lacanian

But what we have seen here usefully correlates to Katherine Eisamann Maus's description of Renaissance dramatic culture, one in which, she says, 'truth is imagined to be inward and invisible, and in which playwrights seem perversely to insist upon parading the shortcomings of their art, theatrical representation becom[ing] subject to profound and fascinating crises of authenticity'.[267] Reapplied to poetics, Maus's depiction of truthful representation in crisis encapsulates what is fundamental to Goodwin's compulsive repetition. The shortcomings of the sign, the signification of interiority, the integral 'truth' that Goodwin's text and limited vocabulary ineffectually grasps at, are indeed paraded with merciless regularity in a surfeit of increasingly self-effacing referents, referring only to something that is both beyond and yet which ultimately tightens the perimeters of the text. Semiotic urgency, a reiterative but forever frustrated drive beyond representation to the primacy of presentation, correlates to the compulsion towards 'that within'. The impulsion to introspect is clear; the seeming wont or vacancy impels desire for plenitude. Throughout this study we have felt the ipseic urge respond to a wonted responsion; we have seen the introjection of reflexivity as a response to the denial of affirmation elsewhere. The spiritual subject wonts divine indwelling just as the lover craved an incorporated beloved, or just as the newly isolated seeing subject found herself alone and unacknowledged. The ipseic structure is precisely of a hungry vacancy or a demand for response: later second-order awareness of a desire for desire, or consciousness of consciousness, should be understood as awareness of the ipseic primacy of process, not attainment. Geminative structures, instant repetition of self to self, provide structures of nascent

telescopic collapse, which would now assert that subjectivity was not just *like* language, but *was* language; there can be synonymity without absolute identification. See Mikkel Borch-Jacobsen, 'The Freudian Subject, from Politics to Ethics', in Eduardo Cadava, Peter Connor, and Jean-Luc Nancy (eds.), *Who Comes after the Subject?* (New York, 1991), 61–78. 'The subject continues to subsist in the representation of its lack, in the closed combinative of signifiers in which it stubbornly continues to self-represent itself, always vanishing but always, upon its disappearance, re-emerging' (p. 64). This conception of subjectivity as a response to its own concomitant creation of lack (an absence calls up a presence which collapses to create an absence which calls up a presence which collapses to . . .) therefore understands ipseic re-presentation (Vor-stellen) as a preposterous endeavour.

[267] Katherine Eisamann Maus, *Inwardness and Theater in the English Renaissance* (Chicago, 1995), 32.

'radicalism' (in Taylor's terms) where the desire for subjectivity dictates a self-subjection that is necessarily preposterous as the end of this process is the process, the drive towards being the very structure of identity. Early modern identity is structurally preposterous, formed from a circuitry of unsatiable wont. Narcissism, and similar self-directed actions, appear in response to a perceived lack of reciprocity, and are condemned partly for the blatancy with which they exhibit a common need, partly for their historic preposterousness; self-gemination may be a Cartesian medicine but in a period coming to terms with a movement away from responsive indivisibility, it is punished as a poisonous excess, an unwelcome guest. To locate absence at the heart of early modern ipseic discourse is simply to identify the wont that is circuitous geminative ipseity, a self-perpetuating discourse of intrasubjection that myself myself legitimates.

Consequently, as Maus concludes, 'inwardness, inaccessibility, all seem to lose their authenticity as soon as they are advertised to or noted by another'.[268] Authenticity (being autocratic self-authorization, etymologically speaking) should not be mistaken for substance-seeking essentialism, and thereby could not be displayed like a trophy or a quantity, but as a process could be heard in the echo between words or in the vacancies that impel these narratives of self. There is ipseic desire and Narcissus exhibits its endless involution; there is an aggressive desire for agency and the self-slaughterer enacts its pharmaceutical excesses; there is a need for validated indwelling and the penitent articulates that ongoing irresolvable process of self-contemplation and denial: but nowhere could there be more than a depiction of wont, the charting of a process of what could be mistaken for discovery but which is intrinsically explorative: 'The student of inwardness—playwright, inquisitor, or critic—annihilates the material, like a physicist who explodes subatomic particles in order to reveal the structure they supposedly used to possess.'[269]

Goodwin's explosion of reflexive and self-reflexive pronouns articulates the circuitry of endlessly geminative and regeminating preposterousness, his valueless self becoming an inescapable constraint, one which he cannot live without, or outside of, fashioning a divided but intervoluted individual, defined in terms only of itself, and lonely in this universe:

---

[268] Ibid., 33.
[269] Ibid.

... and thus, Wayward Elf,
I cannot live with, nor without my Self.
FINIS. (ll. 207–8)

Goodwin's double-bind, expressed in a lexical failure to do without 'Self', dictates almost total poetic paralysis, bringing him to a FINIS that acknowledges the impossibility of poetic progression. The poem enacts what Elsner has described, in relation to Ovid's Narcissus, as an 'objectification of self [that] turns the subject into an object and results in an absorbed paralysis of self, a self-absorption whose only end is death'.[270] 'Subjectivity, objectified' becomes, as perhaps Hamlet is forced to concede, 'feminized, infantalized, passive', and paused.[271]

But for Goodwin, failure of the self was always the intended aim. As Abernethy has predicted, these moments of absolute self-doubt are themselves the closest the Christian poet could come to the actualization of a redeemable subjectivity, responsive to the in-coming of grace. Alan Sinfield suggests that Renaissance poetry represents a 'project for actualizing interiority', displaying an 'incoherence that makes the self aware of itself, that sets it to work on the endlessly deferred task of discovering coherence'.[272] To adjust Sinfield's argument, Goodwin's text, garrulously proclaiming the subject's incoherence, not only makes the self aware of itself, but more importantly, makes the self aware of the inadequacy of itself, readying itself for the passive task of accepting a divinely induced coherence. The failure to signify coherent inwardness could in fact be read as an acknowledgement of incoherence, and work towards the task of discovering or admitting God's cohering presence. While this study repeatedly throws up conceptions of identity that discover that the ontological epiphany is also a nadir (the narcissist's realization; the suicide's death), it could be that in the case of George Goodwin the process is reversed, that the moment of loss is, precisely, the moment of gain. Allowing this, the final *Self* of *Auto-machia*, could, of all its multiple appearances in the poem, be the one time that *Self* not only signifies back to Goodwin, but outwards and inwards to God:

I cannot live with, nor without my Self.

---

[270] Elsner, *Roman Eyes*, 148.   [271] Ibid.
[272] Alan Sinfield, *Faultlines: Cultural Materialism and the Politics of Dissident Reading* (Oxford, 1992), 160; 161.

Conclusion
Othello's Suicides

So with prayers I leave you, and must try
Some yet unpractic'd way to grieve and die.[1]

If the scorned Aspatia of Beaumont and Fletcher's *Maid's Tragedy*
wishes to find some new way to express her suicidal grief she could do
no better than look around her on the early modern stage, littered with
the bodies of resolute Romans, desperately distracted melancholics,
the entwined corpses of young lovers, and the mutilated cadavers of
self-slaughtering avengers. Early modern drama incorporates suicide
as an integral aspect of its broader consideration of humanist self-
determination, trying out the possibility of self-authored action, testing
the inextricability of our dependence upon a presiding deity. Elsewhere,
suicide is the natural conclusion to a romantic narrative, encapsulating
the self-effacement implicated in loving another and the dissolution of
erotic consummation, or offering an image of delicate but absolute
geminative reciprocation. In suicide, the loving couple expresses their
mutual self-sacrifice and interdependence, while the solitary subject
appropriates its reflexive activity in tragically limited imitation of their
indivisible double identity.

Revenge tragedy in particular is driven by a suicidal impetus: 'Revenge
proves . . . its own executioner.'[2] Even to accept the responsibility for
revenge is to be complicit with one's violent conclusion, as D'Amville

---

[1] Francis Beaumont and John Fletcher, *The Maid's Tragedy*, ed. Howard B. Norland
(Lincoln, Nebr., 1968), II. i. 119–20.
[2] John Ford, *The Broken Heart*, in *The Selected Plays*, ed. Colin Gibson (Cambridge,
1986), IV. i. 139.

discovers to his cost in *The Atheist's Tragedy* by accidentally 'strik[ing] out his own brains', and suicidal endings are particularly apt for a genre driven by retribution, violent reprisal, aggressive in-kind response, and the reciprocation of death for death: '*Whether we fall by ambition, blood, or lust*', almost any tragedian should agree, '[*l*]*ike diamonds, we are cut with our own dust*'.[3] Seneca's catalogue of available suicidal options is surpassed as the stage self-slaughterers line up their 'guns and knives, | Swords, poison, halters, and envenom'd steel', their 'burning Coales and Cordes, | Aspes, Poysons, [and] Pistols'.[4] While the penknife, advocated by both Hieronimo and *The Changeling's* De Flores, seems the most appropriate implement for a self-authored end—'here's my penknife.... It is but one thread more... and now 'tis cut'—there can be no denying the 'cunning' of *The Broken Heart's* Orgilus, whose blood-letting mechanism slowly drains him dry.[5] Suicidal figures in Fletcher's canon, meanwhile, are almost competitive in their numerous attempts at the 'good death': in *The Fair Maid of the Inn* a sequence of stage directions evidences an unseemly struggle as Clarrisa '*offers to kill herself*', before Mentivole '*snatches away her knife, and sets it to his own breast*'.[6]

Playwrights diagnose social disease, prescribe the cathartic cure of remedial violence, dispense a pharmaceutical purgative localized in the figure of the revenger, and then dispense with the agent of their poisonous medicine, lest the vaccination become a plague. The pharmacal metaphor is a constant throughout the genre, where, for instance, the source (a king) is poisoned, and corruption runs through the arteries of the body politic, until the avenger, like a hectic in the blood, purifies the pestilence with his own aggressive remedy; a true antibody, the

---

[3] Cyril Tourneur [?], *The Atheist's Tragedy*, in *The Plays of Cyril Tourneur*, ed. George Parfitt (Cambridge, 1978), V. II. 235; Webster, *The Duchess of Malfi*, V. v. 72–3.

[4] Christopher Marlowe, *Dr Faustus*, ed. Roma Gill (London, 1989), VI. 21–3; Du Bartas, *Divine Weekes*, trans. Sylvester, I. 375; Rowland Wymer, *Suicide and Despair*, also recites these grim arsenals, see p. 23. He also provides an extended discussion of suicide in tragedy.

[5] Kyd, *The Spanish Tragedy*; Thomas Middleton and William Rowley, *The Changeling*, ed. N. W. Bawcutt (Manchester, 1998), V. III. 173; Ford, *The Broken Heart*, V. II. 150.

[6] Francis Beaumont and John Fletcher, *The Fair Maid of the Inn*, in *The Dramatic Works in the Beaumont and Fletcher Canon*, ed. Fredson Bowers (Cambridge, 1996), x, V. I. 9.

revenger emulates the illness, operates with comparable cruelty, and is either tainted by the sickness he seeks to cure, or finds himself a carrier of the contagion he was prescribed to purge. He is a course of treatment; he is the illness. His suicide is self-medication, and self-administered. *The Maid's Tragedy* displays the full potential of pharmaceutical suicide. The lascivious Evande, infected by a moral 'plague' via intercourse with the 'surfeited foul body' of her adulterous King, seeks to cure her 'contagious name' and 'leprous' reputation, to 'purge [her] sickness' with the twin 'physic[s]' of revenge and subsequent suicide.[7] But her cuckolded husband Amintor will not accept her murderous remedy—'disease [is] thy nature'—and will not play host to her infectious presence: 'Take me home', she begs to no avail.[8] Meanwhile, Aspatia, successful in her intention to discover new suicidal practice, achieves erotic consummation with suicidal ingenuity; dressing as a man, she provokes her former lover into delivering a fatal blow, inviting death from the source of her amatory infection. In killing her, Amintor cures her; in wounding her, he heals the wound of desire: 'well' one minute and 'wondrous sick' the next, a 'kind of healthful joy wanders within [her]', as her blood slips out.[9] As the play descends into a self-inflicted bloodbath—both Amintor and his perfect friend Melantius feel the responsibility of suicidal response ('I will not leave this act unsatisfied, | If all that's left in me can answer it')—we see once more the amatory unification achieved in sympathetic suicide.[10] We see how love could, in the words of Othello, kill with a kiss, and how loving suicide could be dedicated, in the words of Desdemona, to a kind lord and thereby seek to reinstate that lost kindness.

But Iago has forcefully supplanted Desdemona in Othello's affections. Likewise, as Melantius pushes aside the corpse of Aspatia to insert himself into the 'kind' arms of his 'friend Amintor', we sense the competing claims of masculine kinship that contest and strive to be the dominant model for mutual identity, reacting aggressively to the counter claims of heterosexual partnership: 'Here's to be with thee,

---

[7] Beaumont and Fletcher, *The Maid's Tragedy*, V. i. 92; 57; IV. i. 58; 198; 59; V. i. 53.

[8] Ibid., V. iii. 135; 157.

[9] Ibid., 211; 222; 212.

[10] Ibid., 195–6.

love', Amintor exclaims, expiring with Aspatia in his arms; 'Amintor, give a word | To call me to thee', Melantius begs, reasserting the claims of masculine amity and displacing his rival.[11] While Beaumont and Fletcher elide the possibility of a perfect homoerotic tableau—Melantius' death is delayed beyond the curtain-fall—they allow Amintor a final dying word to his male alter idem: 'let me give up my soul | Into thy bosom'.[12] As is often remarked, this *Tragedy* seems only tangentially the *Maid's*: but similarly I would not ascribe it to *The Mistress* either; rather, I read this play as *The Friends' Tragedy*. Iago might agree. The multivalent motif of self-slaughter can, it is clear, become a site of contested values, where narrative meaning and symbolic action are fraught and fought over, where death is read, reread, authored, and rewritten. 'Who is the author of this tragedy?' each play enquires, 'O who has done this deed?' (V. II. 124); the response is cacophonous, each victim laying desperate claim to self-affirming self-murder: 'I myself' (l. 125).

1. I MYSELF: THE SUICIDE(S) OF OTHELLO (AND DESDEMONA)

The sympathetic suicides of Romeo and Juliet and Antony and Cleopatra stand as romantic ideals; they are monuments of star-crossed reciprocal love the like of which can only be briefly glimpsed in the tragic love story of Othello and Desdemona, whose tale fleetingly appears to be ending with the suicide of a similarly 'ill-starred wench!' (V. II. 270):

EMILIA. O, who hath done this deed?
DESDEMONA. Nobody; I myself. Farewell.
      Commend me to my kind lord. O farewell! *she dies.* (V. II. 124–6)

Why does Desdemona claim to have committed suicide and excuse her 'kind lord'? To understand, it is necessary to return to the vocabulary of reciprocation, and examine the language of kindness in *Othello*.

It is against a world of divided duty and 'mangled matter' (I. III. 171) that Othello and Desdemona perceive their love, a love which privileges patterns of reciprocation over the confusion of Venetian racism (which

---

[11] Ibid., V. I. 260; 259; 244; 256–7.   [12] Ibid., 271–2.

muddies Othello's spotless self-image), martial discord, and natural tempest, which answers the threat of division and flux with the stability of give and take: 'I do love thee; and when I love thee not, | Chaos is come again' (III. III. 91–2). It is the language of love, typified by motifs of repetition and echo, that is looked to in order to provide balance in an increasingly unbalanced world: 'came [your love] by request and such fair question | As soul to soul affordeth?' (I. III. 113–14). When Othello describes how 'I did thrive in this fair lady's love, | And she in mine' (ll. 125–6), he speaks a recognizable rhetoric of erotic love, where, as previously described, separate pronouns encounter each other in increasing proximity, and where the mutual love of the couple circumscribes a self-enclosed perpetuating dependence. Othello knows this:

> But that I love the gentle Desdemona,
> I would not my unhousèd free condition
> Put into circumscription and confine
> For the sea's worth. (I. II. 25–8)

Circumscription and confining appear to be restrictive for this free spirit, but behind the machismo is a kinder secondary sense. The sea that Othello mentions may be suitable imagery for his expansive, wild condition, and yet the sea is also the primary archetypal image of 'desperate' (II. I. 21), 'dangerous' (l. 46) mutability and uncontrolled, 'indistinct' (l. 40) matter that the period's imaginative lexicon can offer. Love for Desdemona provides a safe confine, a loving circumscription into which she binds Othello, and so the dangerous flux is gently answered: 'Tempests themselves, high seas, and howling winds | . . . do omit | Their mortal natures, letting go safely by | The divine Desdemona' (ll. 68–73). 'If after every tempest come such calms', Othello says on seeing her ashore, '[m]ay the winds blow till they have wakened death' (ll. 177–8).

Indeed, it is in the calm after the storm that Othello makes his case for complete loving isolation and mutual exclusivity:

> If it were now to die,
> 'Twere now to be most happy; for I fear
> My soul hath her content so absolute
> That not another comfort like to this
> Succeeds in unknown fate. (II. I. 181–5)

Death, almost craved, has been brought into the confines of the loving relationship, becoming part of its content, in lines not undercut by but rather quietly aware of the fragility of these contained loving environs. And, when Desdemona succeeds in introducing fertile increase and progression into their loving entwine—'our loves and comforts should increase, | Even as our days do grow' (ll. 186–7)—they have almost achieved the ideal of self-satisfying but productive erotic love. Their sexual deaths, full of the vitality of 'love's quick pants' (l. 80), bring the lovers to a climactic near-suicidal state—a grammatical stop rather than Hamlet's musical rest—that captures an almost Egyptian sense of gratuitous repletion:

> I cannot speak enough of this content;
> It stops me here; it is too much of joy.
> *They kiss.*
> And this, and this, the greatest discords be
> That e'er our hearts shall make. (II. i. 188–91)

Othello's lines delineate a loving relation both complete in itself, contented and end-stopped, and endlessly outdoing itself with 'too much' joy, both perfect and perfectly destructive. So a kiss—'and this, and this'—beats a neat rhythm, a give and take, a little moment of harmonious reciprocation, creating only a happy discordance in their beating hearts. They are, as Iago sees, 'well-tuned now', and he can set about unsettling their stability and introducing discordance into the harmonious reciprocation of a loving couple: 'But I'll set down the pegs that make this music | As honest as I am' (ll. 191–3).

The play's language of romantic reciprocation breaks down: 'My lord is not my lord' (III. iv. 118), Desdemona announces, employing the linguistic patterns of mutuality but only to acknowledge how they are failing. A 'strange unquietness' (l. 127) begins to take over, displacing the kind and natural language of love with new 'unkindness' (l. 146), new unnaturalness. The language of love is not only displaced by a disproportionate language of jealousy, but it also has its characteristics subverted; the thousand thousand kisses of Romeo and Juliet mutate into Othello's estimate that Desdemona is 'O, a thousand thousand times [worse]' (IV. i. 181). So, emerging from behind the fixing figures of amorous exchange is a new language of confusion and distemper; succinctly, Iago has 'puddled' Othello's 'clear spirit' (III. iv. 137) until

he could chop Desdemona 'into messes' (IV. i. 188).
covered in his inebriation, behind a regimented exterior is a .
nothing distinct. Nothing, that is, except the ideal of romai
Desdemona, and ultimately Othello, continually seek to re-esı

> Unkindness may do much,
> And his unkindness may defeat my life,
> But never taint my love. (IV. ii. 158–60)

'This is', writes Rowland Wymer, 'a tragedy of love as much as anything else and the participants can be seen as tragic lovers rather than as murderer and victim.'[13]

The final suicide scenes of *Othello* attempt to write the couple back into the systems of kindness and reciprocation that Iago's machinations have untuned. Just as we saw in *Romeo and Juliet* and *Antony and Cleopatra*, there is an attempt made by the dying lovers to conceptualize themselves as literal manifestations of the romantic model. Initially, there is something savagely ironic about Othello's adoption of the 'dying kiss' motif: 'One more! one more!' he says, '[b]e thus when thou art dead, and I will kill thee | And love thee after. One more, and this the last. | So sweet was ne'er so fatal' (V. ii. 17–20). The confusion of the sweet and fatal only occludes the grim reality of his actions, actions that seek to appropriate the old fond paradoxes and by-the-book kisses of Petrarchan desire in order to establish some system, some meaningful order: 'Thy bed, lust-stained, shall with lust's blood be spotted' (V. i. 36). This is not apt or fit: his sorrow that 'strikes where it doth love' (V. ii. 22) is rather a perversion of an erotic metaphor. His calls for peace, and for her to 'be still!' (l. 46), simply figure as increasingly distasteful takes on stock lyric images of 'smooth . . . monumental alabaster' (l. 5): 'Ha! No more moving? | Still as the grave' (ll. 94–5). But as she reclaims her murder as an act of self-slaughter Desdemona repositions herself back into the role of star-crossed heroine, back into a romance tragedy tradition. Commending herself to her 'kind' lord (l. 126), she presents the opportunity for a kindly conclusion, playing the first part in a sequence of mutual suicide. There is 'no way but this',

[13] Wymer, *Suicide and Despair*, 92.

as, in his final lines, Othello returns to the balanced patterns of reciprocation, and, allying himself with the lineage of Amintas, Romeo, and Cleopatra, adopts his new role, the loving self-slaughterer:

> I kissed thee ere I killed thee: no way but this,
> Killing myself, to die upon a kiss. (V. II. 354–5)

However, against the loving aspiration towards sympathetic, climactic, sexualized suicide, Shakespeare places the intractable silence of a diffidently unresponsive Iago. In this juxtaposition perhaps we should read an acknowledgement comparable to that made by Venus at the death of Adonis. The archetypal values of reciprocation—loving response, responsive identity—come face to face with a disconcerting sense of guarded privacy. Venus, finding herself in a world where eyes no longer reflected and ocular intromission had replaced the reciprocation of eyebeam exchange, was forced to confront the unkindness of the introspect; Othello and Desdemona, while desperately attempting to join the sympathetic lineage of Antony and Cleopatra, Pyramus and Thisbe, Romeo and Juliet, are equally faced with an aggressively introspective individual, uninterested in reciprocation, refusing to participate:

> From this time forth I never will speak word. (V. II. 301)

2. I AM A DRUNKARD:
THE DISSOLUTION OF CASSIO

Previously, I cited Nicolaus de Cusa's suggestion that we should understand the subjective quality of vision, so that seeing 'snow through a red glass' we would attribute the 'redness not to the snow, but to the glass'.[14] De Cusa's pair of red spectacles introduced the rose-tinted glasses of young lovers, while John Abernethy's depiction of darkly introspective religious despair described a vision characterized by its isolation: a vision not merely distorted but blind.[15] If the rosy glow of extramissive loving vision sought to bind couples together in entwines

---

[14] Cit. Freedman, *Staging the Gaze*, 17.
[15] Abernethy, *A Christian and Heavenly Treatise*, 19.

of optic beams, Abernethy's self-speculating eyes saw only the solitude of the godless individual, lost in his spiritual darkness. Now, I shall obey Nicolaus de Cusa once more, taking his recognition of mediated outlook and adding to it more pairs of tinted corneas. Now, red, black, and green eyes will see with a vision far less innocent than those looking-glasses of lovers, with a vision distorted by fury, melancholy, or jealous apprehension. Ironically for a play preoccupied with ocular proof, the eyes of *Othello* are rarely reliable, seldom unmediated. When Iago is your friend, your second-self, the recipient of your confession, the medicine for your sickness, when he kneels beside you in pseudo-marital union, and stages the world for your credulous inspection, you only see through his devilish dark eyes. An Iago in(tro)jected is a suicidally poisonous medicine.

Discussing 'those in whom a mellancholly temper prevaileth', Richard Sibbs remarks that 'their spirits . . . were died black', and explains in terms similar to Nicolaus's that

as we see where there is suffusion of the eye by reason of distemper of humours, or where things are presented through a glasse to the eye; things seeme to be of the same colour: so, whatever is presented to a melancholly person, comes in a darke way to the soule.[16]

Othello, blinded and made monstrous in his adoption of the green eyes of jealousy, sees through similarly tinted, or tainted, eyes, introspecting false signs that travel down 'a darke way to [his] soule'. Seeing only through the eyes of that false alter-idem Iago, Othello's jealousy fractures and disrupts his vision, speech, and identity. As civil war led to self-slaughter in the plays of mutual suicide, here jealousy provides the governing tenor of self-destructive violence:

> O beware, my lord, of jealousy:
> It is the green-eyed monster which doth mock
> The meat it feeds on. (III. iii. 167–9)

In *Othello*'s depiction of jealousy, we see the final manifestation of the preposterous dynamic, a movement previously associated with narcissism and suicide, and now with jealousy. Its self-sustaining covetous cycle, where the sufferer consumes himself, creates 'a monster | Begot

[16] Sibbs, *The Soules Conflict*, 21; 22.

upon itself, born on itself' (III. IV. 155–6) with a dangerously self-perpetuating sense of self-sufficiency: they are 'jealous for they're jealous' (l. 154). Othello's paradoxical defence, 'to be once in doubt | Is once to be resolved' (III. III. 181–2), makes clear that the self-perpetuating cycles of jealousy will come to a suicidal culmination: for the jealous, a flicker of doubt occasions an absolute resolute certainty yet initiates self-destructive dissolution. But while born of a self-defeating jealousy, the protagonists' deaths seek to re-establish the tenor of mutual self-sacrifice, clinging to the imaginative vestiges of a loving world, seemingly nostalgic for its rose-tinted spectacles.

One further pair of coloured eyes provides a point of entry into this discussion: these are red eyes, but not the red fiery eyes of the angry Coriolanus (*Cor.*, V. I. 64) or the lustful fires of Tarquin (*Luc.*, 1353). These are the red eyes of the drunkard: 'give me a cup of sack to make my eyes look red' (*1H4*, II. IV. 317). Abernethy condemns 'The Passion of Drunkennesse' with the sort of a dubious explanation only possible in an era where extramissive correspondence is still latent and discernible in folklore or traditional sayings: 'The drunken eyes looketh upon the wine when it is red, and begetteth rednesse of eyes by tarrying too long at it.'[17] Looking through the eyes of his drunkards, Shakespeare sees how 'sweet, and contagious' (*TN*, II. III. 49) intoxication has infectious potential, making the seeing subject see double, offering an alternative dissolute identity that divides a man like Cassio from that 'immortal part of myself' (II. III. 243). Drunkenness, the 'quick sand' into which Lepidus sinks (*Ant.*, II. VII. 55), is to the unfortunately weak-stomached Cassio a catastrophically 'distempering draught' (I. I. 100). Although only 'few men rightly temper with the stars' (*3H6*, IV. VI. 29), to know one's temper as Prince Hal always does (*H5*, V. II. 139), or to keep one's temper 'constant' as Coriolanus (*Cor.*, V. II. 88), 'comfortable' as Timon cannot (*Tim.*, III. IV. 65), or 'still' (*TNK*, IV. II. 28), is to fit or snugly inhabit one's character, achieving stability within oneself. One's 'temper' is one's personality, but to temper is also to fit, to match, to join, or tune. And so, in Shakespeare's amalgamating usage, to temper is to occupy oneself, to align oneself harmoniously with one's stars or predestined character, or to liken to one's own temperament or

---

[17] Abernethy, *A Christian and Heavenly Treatise*, 506.

temperance.[18] Michael Schoenfeldt lists it as one of the words in the Renaissance 'earlier lexicon of self': we know when Lear is mad because, losing his temper, he cannot 'keep in temper' (*Lr.*, I. v. 38); we know when Macbeth is beyond himself with anger when he 'cannot buckle his distempered cause within' (*Mac.*, V. II. 15); or when Romeo is beyond himself with love when he wears a 'distempered head' (*Rom.*, II. III. 33).[19] Of all Shakespearean characters, it is the apparently insane Hamlet who is most frequently said to be distempered (*Ham.*, II. II. 55; III. II. 305; III. IV. 122). If to be tempered is to fit or be contained comfortably within oneself, to be distempered is to suffer some internal discordance, disrupting one's relationship with oneself. It is in the company of the madman, the furious man, the distracted lover, all those who may fall into Shuger's category of 'hypertrophied subjectivity', that Shakespeare places the drunk and his literally dissolute identity.[20] Confused with alcohol, divided from his tongue, and an inebriated step outside himself, the drunkard and his stomach, as Stephano discovers, cannot be constant: 'Prithee, do not turn me about' (*Tmp.*, II. II. 115–16). Consequently, Shakespeare's treatment of the effects of the 'distempering draught' repeatedly insists on a psychic division, a mismatch within the drunken self, raising 'war between him and his discretion' (*Ant.*, II. VII. 9–10). Cassio knows it. The drink 'dislikes me' (II. III. 39), he says: it makes him unlike himself; it dis-likes him.

Lepidus' acknowledgement that 'I am not so well as I should be', followed by his comically confident assertion, 'but I'll ne'er out' (*Ant.*, II. VII. 29), suggests that indeed the inebriated old man is 'out' of himself, divided into the drunken *I* and the sober *I* that he 'should be'. Finding that 'mine own tongue | Splits what it speaks', he comes to sound increasingly like the distempered Hamlet, admitting that the drunken 'wild disguise hath almost | Anticked us all' (ll. 118–19). Hamlet, in his antic disposition, adopts a second identity, one behind which he hides, multiplying ontologically and verbally to evade Claudius' politic and linguistic control. And so, Lepidus' intoxication

---

[18] *OED*, s.v. 'Temper', n. II. 9; v. II. 9; v. I. 13; II. 3. See *Tmp.*, II. I. 43.

[19] Michael Schoenfeldt, 'The Matter of Inwardness: Shakespeare's Sonnets', in James Schiffer (ed.), *Shakespeare's Sonnets: Critical Essays* (London, 1999), 305–24 at 305.

[20] Debora Kuller Shuger, 'Subversive Fathers and Suffering Subjects: Shakespeare and Christianity', in Donna B. Hamilton and Richard Strier (eds.), *Religion, Literature, and Politics in Post-Reformation England, 1540–1688* (Cambridge, 1996), 46–69.

provides an echo, his identity becoming antic, becoming dangerously protean. There are, in inebriated ramblings, moments where discordance in language signals a deeper discordance in identity, where an antic tongue discloses an antic self-division: a Caliban becomes, when tipsy, a 'Cacaliban', linguistically self-replicating as his psychic coherence is challenged by his drink (*Tmp.*, II. ii. 184). As with Lepidus' split tongue, this self-division is most obvious on the level of language. Made to 'discourse fustian' with his 'own shadow' (II. iii. 257), Cassio, once a most 'sufficient man' (III. iv. 87), has drunk himself into duality, and is left amazed 'that men should put an enemy in their mouths to steal away their brains', and submit themselves to a dreadful and degrading self-assault: 'That we should with joy, pleasance, revel and applause transform ourselves into beasts!' (II. iii. 265–7). Verbal escalation, indicative of a psychic multiplication and an uncontrollable superfluity, is intoxication's rhetorical motif: 'so light, so drunken, and so indiscreet an officer. Drunk! And speak parrot! And squabble! Swagger! Swear?' (ll. 256–7). Fustian drunken bombast is exactly a superfluity of signifiers, a babble of syllabic repetition, verbal parrot-like proliferation. Finally, with a familiar inward turn, Cassio comes to 'despise myself' (l. 272), and, '[u]nfit for mine own purpose' (III. iii. 33), becomes capable of turning in disgust upon the self that no longer fits his own self-conception. In Cassio's world of moral absolutes, geminative self-iteration equates to an unkind fracture.

In Shakespeare's 'dissolute . . . crew' (*R2*, V. iii. 12) 'given to . . . taverns, and sack, and wine' (*Wiv.*, V. v. 142), we see how any notion of the fixed, firm resolute self has been abandoned by those, like Falstaff, who are men 'of continual dissolution' (III. v. 116). This dissolution, of course, is suicidal: 'a drunkard, through love to his belly, inflameth & indurates his liver: ingendereth an atrophy or hydropsie, and so killeth himselfe':[21]

OLIVIA.   What's a drunken man like, fool?

CLOWN.   Like a drowned man, a fool, and a madman: one draught above
heat makes him a fool, the second mads him, and a third
drowns him. (*TN*, I. v. 107–10)

---

[21] Abernethy, *A Christian and Heavenly Treatise*, 156.

Indeed drunkenness follows a familiar pattern: those 'who want but a wide wombe to their wanton will, to excell the capacity of a Caske' find that in this 'overcoming [they] are overcome'.[22] I have previously called this rhetorical movement the narcissistic dynamic, identified it also as a suicidal progression, and in each case shown how attainment preposterously outdoes itself, and how, in Eagleton's terms, boast turns to catastrophe.[23] In overcoming, the narcissist, the suicide, and now the drunk are all overcome.

Falling prey to the mistaken assumptions of inebriation, Cassio tries, more than any other Shakespearean drunk, to keep things fitting—'Do not think . . . you must not think . . . '(II. iii. 97; 101–2); to keep things in their right order—'this is my ancient'; and tries desperately to remain like himself—'this is my right hand, and this is my left hand'. Yet, his increasingly determined assertions are predicated upon intoxicated assumptions:

Do not think, gentleman, I am drunk; this is my ancient, this is my right hand, and this is my left hand. I am not drunk now, I can stand well enough, and I speak well enough. (II. iii. 97–9)

Grasping for self-control—'I am . . . I am not . . . I can'—Cassio's toil is characteristic of a play in which all the major protagonists similarly struggle. The drunken dislocation of identity, where alcohol fractures the speaker and disrupts the single-state of man, exposes the underlying ipseic tendency of the play. We see in *Othello* how a rhetoric of self-division which will come to define later Cartesian self-definition is experienced only as an assault on each character's naive sense of absolute and indivisible simple subjectivity ('simple' in one of its early modern senses, connoting singularity). Act II, Scene III may play a raucous variant of the 'Othello music' in the drunken songs, 'barbarous brawl[s]' (l. 153), and 'clamour' (l. 212) of drunkenness, but the sense of self-division suffered here by Cassio is comparable to that inflicted upon Othello, Roderigo, and ultimately Desdemona. Those who are in this 'vile brawl distracted' (l. 236)[24] have suffered the distraction of 'the devil drunkenness' (l. 270), until 'a sensible man' has 'by and by'

---

[22] Ibid., 428.
[23] Eagleton, 'Self-Undoing Subjects', 266.
[24] *OED*, s.v. 'Distract', v. 1. trans.

become 'a fool, and presently a beast!' (ll. 278–9), until 'I am not drunk' has become 'I am a drunkard' (ll. 276–7): 'I remember a mass of things, but nothing distinctly' (l. 263). Cassio experiences the disruption of what he had thought to be a distinct stable identity predicated on definitive concepts. In drunkenness, he finds only a threatening 'mass of things', nothing distinct, nothing but a slippery identity; he is, in this way, no Toby Belch who, in apt drunken simplicity, belches (*TN*, I. v. 100). This new 'I am' is indicative of Cassio's problem, merely setting up a new single-state definition in answer to protean flux: 'I am a drunkard. Had I as many mouths as Hydra, such an answer would stop them all' (ll. 276–8). There is, however, no such 'stop' while Iago works his turns.

It is 'the damnèd slave' (V. ii. 289) Iago who works his self-confessed devilry (II. iii. 317–20) like wine: 'O thou invisible spirit of wine, if thou hast no name to be known by, let us call thee devil!' (ll. 257–9). Iago works with something akin to the spirit of drunkenness, invisibly inducing psychic discord. So, while Cassio is driven to confusion—'O strange!'—Iago can answer his complaint that '[e]very inordinate cup is unblessed, and the ingredience is a devil' (ll. 279–80) with the reassurance that 'good wine is a good familiar creature, if it be well used' (ll. 281–2). Wine is this devil's familiar, and he can use it well. Iago is no drunk, but, while everyone around him struggles to keep hold of themselves, to locate themselves according to their 'virtue', 'reputation', or 'occupation', he is peculiarly able to adapt himself to a model of identity best represented by another Renaissance declaration of inebriation:

Constancy it selfe is nothing but a languishing and wauering dance. I cannot settle my obiect; it goeth so vnquietly and staggering, with a naturall drunkennesse. I take it in this plight, as it is at th'instant I ammuse my selfe about it. I describe not the essence, but the passage . . . from minute to minute. My history must be fitted to the present. I may soone change, not onely fortune, but intention. It is a counter-roule of divers and variable accidents, and irresolute imaginations, and sometimes contrary.[25]

---

[25] Montaigne, *Essais*, trans. Florio, 451.

Montaigne's conception of subjectivity, which Hugh Grady describes as a new stage in ipseic development and Thomas Greene describes as a 'doctrine of inconsistency', is one that Iago, unlike any other of the dramatis personae in the play, is comfortable with.[26] He goes with a natural drunkenness, celebrating his ability to distemper and distract, and proudly adopts the hypertrophied subjectivity of the proto-modern. Wine is his familiar because while those around him—Othello, Rodrigo, Cassio—are thrown into turmoil by the disruption of their settled natures (respectively by jealousy, love, and wine), Iago can 'take it in this plight' just as it is in any given moment. He passes, like Montaigne, from minute to minute, or as Pierre Charron puts it, 'upon the Float'.[27] As Montaigne warns us in his essay on drunkenness, there is 'as much diversity in [vice] as in anything else'.[28] Montaigne's 'register of varied and changing occurences' depicts an irresolute and contradictory identity, an identity that can 'fluctuate and flutter [with] driftings and evasions', a 'mode of consciousness characterized by an ever-shifting point of view'.[29] 'Whether I am different myself, or whether I take hold of my subjects in different circumstances and aspects' sounds to Grady less like 'the essentialist Roderigo [and, I would add, Othello and Cassio] than the anti-essentialist Machiavel Iago'.[30] Intro-spected gemination, the definitive feature of Cartesian self-affirmation, is, as has been evidenced throughout this study, experienced first as a threat, an assault upon an identity formerly predicate upon reciprocation but now dislocated by scepticism. The reflex response of seventeenth-century texts is first towards resistance, so, as Sawday admits, 'it is', for example, 'difficult to resist the sense that Milton is ... trying to quieten Descartes'.[31] Before philosophical rehabilitation as a remedial restorative of self-knowledge and localized self-certainty, self-reflection is condemned

---

[26] Hugh Grady, *Shakespeare, Machiavelli, and Montaigne: Power and Subjectivity from Richard II to Hamlet* (Oxford, 2002); Thomas Greene, 'The Flexibility of the Self in Renaissance Literature', in Peter Demetz, Greene, and Lowry Nelson, Jr. (eds.), *The Disciplines of Criticism: Essays in Literary Theory, Interpretation, and History* (New Haven, 1968), 241–64 at 259.

[27] Charron, *Of Wisdom*, ii, II. 6.

[28] Montaigne, *Essais*, 187.

[29] Greene, 'The Flexibility of the Self', 259; Robert Ellrodt, 'Self-Consciousness in Montaigne and Shakespeare', *SS*, 28 (1975), 37–50 at 43.

[30] Grady, *Shakespeare, Machiavelli, and Montaigne*, 123.

[31] Sawday, 'Self and Selfhood in the Seventeenth Century', 46.

as narcissistic, self-defeating, idolatrous, and satanic, as if culture compulsively punishes a model of subjectivity that arrives like a poison. Similarly, Othello is unwitting host to a hostile Iago-infection.

'I will incontinently drown myself' (I. III. 301): there are two ways to read Roderigo's incontinent threat. The editorial choice has been towards 'straightaway' or 'at once', but the second available sense of 'incontinent', connoting 'loosely', 'unable to contain', even 'evacuation', is more useful, being symptomatic of the language of the scene, and the language of suicide. Roderigo threatens to act out of continent, out of constraint, without restraint, in so doing allying self-slaughter with a strain of imagery in the play that signals division, confusion, and mess. Throughout, we are constantly aware of the threat of indistinction: Cassio discovered it in drunkenness; now Roderigo seeks it in suicide. Cassio, a man whose essentialist notion of himself was founded upon his '[r]eputation, reputation, reputation . . . the immortal part of myself' (II. III. 242–3), is easy prey to Iago's divisive tactics, and Roderigo, a similarly single-faceted character, is as easily confounded:

> RODERIGO. I confess it is my shame to be so fond, but it is not in my
> virtue to amend it.
> IAGO. Virtue? A fig! 'Tis in ourselves that we are thus and thus. (I. III.
> 311–13)

It is in relation to incontinent suicide, an act that he describes as 'clean out of the way' (l. 346), that Iago propounds his theory of self-sufficient interiority, predicated accordingly on self-love: 'I never found a man that knew how to love himself' (l. 308). Throughout his Act I, Scene III speeches, Iago, comparing the body of man to a garden and his will to the gardener who tends and nurtures himself, employs a language of containment and mutability. The gardening will can either plant 'one gender of herbs', he explains, or 'distract it with many' (l. 316). Iago's suggestion is that Roderigo, looking to some preconceived virtue, plants only one herb, while he, a master of distraction, can contain division and difference. Where, with characteristic simplicity, Roderigo sees 'love', monolithic and absolute, Iago sees a 'sect or scion' (l. 324) of 'raging motions . . . carnal stings . . . unbitted lusts' (ll. 322–3), an assortment of multiple emotions. This is what he holds 'in'. Literal suicide, for the self-displacing Iago, is out of the way, a bestial failure to love oneself, to keep one's myriad nature within. Roderigo is correct; to drown himself would be incontinent, a shameful failure to keep within himself.

Only Iago would understand Montaigne's ontological drunkenness, employing a multiply shifting self as an advantage in a play-world where everyone else has not suspected that ipseity may have this multiplicity, and where characters discover to their costs—like the love-addled Roderigo, the divided Othello, and the drunken Cassio—that their selves are liable to refract, distract, and distemper. 'The worst state for a man', as Montaigne warns, can be 'when he loses all control of himself',[32] but Iago, willingly adopting a position of radical ontological uncertainty, claims 'I am not what I am' (I. i. 66). In so doing, he suicidally subverts the basic but principal grammatical clause of subjectivity: 'I am'.

3. I AM NOT WHAT I AM: IAGO'S SUICIDAL SILENCE

The Law of the Command of Unity, was to knowe one, and only one (God.) Man will know more than one; know himself in a state of division; here creeps in sin, and brings man from his uprightness.[33]

While *Othello*'s composition pre-dates many of the theological texts previously discussed, the language of the play shares comparable concerns; the language of a theologically understood ontology impacts upon the dramatic vocabulary of self-awareness. Joseph Salmon, a Ranter but despite his radicalism expressing a typical Protestant theme, sees God alone as 'simple, single, uncompounded'; compared to God, the only 'pure individual self' (in its Trinitarian sense), man is dangerously prone to sinful division and the contrary impulses of the will and flesh.[34] While being considerably more extreme in his puritan zeal, Salmon follows the standard Protestant chronology of salvation, with grace coming only by way of a frequently desperate but ultimately redemptive fall. ''Twas given to me', he says, 'that I might drink,

---

[32] Montaigne, *Essais*, 382.
[33] Joseph Salmon, 'Heights in Depths and Depths in Heights', in Smith (ed.), *A Collection of Ranter Writings*, 221.
[34] Ibid., 222.

I drank, that I might stumble, I stumbled, that I might fall: I fell, and through my fall was made happy.'[35] The division that Cassio, and Othello in his turn, experience resonates with a commonplace theological correlation of the divisive quality of sin or temptation. If God is 'not the Author of division', but rather 'the divider is the Divel, [and] the division is sin'[36] it is tempting to draw a comparison with the dividing, mangling Iago, 'that demi-devil' (V. ii. 298) of *Othello*, a self-confessed '[a]uthor of division', working under the '[d]ivinity of hell' (II. iii. 317). As the dramatis personae divide and suffer their psychic fractures, 'here creeps in sin'.

Salmon's allusion is to 1 Corinthians—'For God is not *the author* of confusion, but of peace'—and Iago's claim that 'I am not what I am' (I. i. 66) demands to be read in the light of another passage in 1 Corinthians that has generated a tradition of similarly phrased assertions.[37] Within his discussion of self-division and heavenly unity, the Ranter arrives at this statement of authorial intent:

To declare to all men what I now am, onely in what *I* am not: ... *I* now am made to speak, because *I* am almost weary of speaking, and to informe the world that silence has taken hold of my spirit. Come then, O my Soule, enter thou into thy Chamber, shut thy doores about thee, hide thy selfe in silence for a season till the indignation bee blown over.[38]

In his commentary on this passage, Nigel Smith draws a distinction between the italic *I* and the roman I, as Salmon differentiates between the man who writes, who therefore is still grudgingly bound to the world of the flesh, and the I who retreats, sublimating himself figuratively and literally under the surface of the text.[39] Declaration, speech, informing, and writing are made analogous to the sinful body of man—they are the outward mode—while the absence of expression, the silent *I*, is allowed to slip away into a cloister of soulful privacy, a hidden interiority. The *I* therefore gestures beyond the text, to a non-signifiable

---

[35] Ibid., 215.
[36] Ibid., 222.
[37] *The Geneva Bible* (Geneva, 1560; repr. Madison, Wis., 1969), 1 Corinthians 14: 33.
[38] Salmon, 'Heights in Depths', 206.
[39] Nigel Smith, *Perfection Proclaimed: Language and Literature in English Radical Religion, 1640–1660* (Oxford, 1989), 36.

silent self, hidden and discrete, while the worldly I remains only to speak of what it is not. Self-reflexive action leaves a negated I, only defined in terms of its failure, a kind of empty I, absent from God. In short, the *I* is keen to depart from the I and looks for new residence in what it is not (i.e. the divine): clearly *Hamlet* could be given a similar synopsis. The subject of the utterance is near worthless, while the utterance itself longs only to be silent; the text and its author speak themselves out, hoping to become not I or 'my' but 'Thine in Silence', in a form of narrative suicide or, to make the *Hamlet* analogy explicit, a 'rest' (V. II. 337).[40]

Salmon's reasoning travels this way because, ultimately, as Smith points out, the self can only be 'realised in terms of the *Bible* [so eventually] "I am" is adopted by the self to emphasise the total negation of ego in the presence of Scripture'.[41] Here is the progression, all in the words of that 'lump of sinne and uncleannesse' D. R., as reported by Vavasor Powell: 'I thought my selfe to be something', but 'when being seriously weighed' by 'calling my selfe to a strict examination' 'I became nothing', 'finding my selfe out of Christ' and 'having often had thoughts of destroying my self', discovering 'an emptinesse in my selfe' 'and a greater fulnesse in the Creator'.[42] D. R. concludes: 'I am, in and through Gods free grace, what I am; not for any thing in me, or that I could do; but as in [1 Corinthians 15: 10].'[43] This is key: the biblical passage referred to in these theological writings, the source for their expressions of 'I am', is not always, as most modern editors assume when Shakespeare makes similar assertions, the Exodus passage, referred to by Jacob Bauthumley when he says 'thou art pleased to give thyself that Title, I am',[44] but rather the Corinthians passage spoken by St Paul. And there is a crucial distinction between the two:

[40] Salmon, 'Heights in Depths', 206.
[41] Smith, *Perfection Proclaimed*, 36.
[42] Vavasor Powell, *Spirituall Experiences, of Sundry Beleevers* (London, 1652), 113; 115; 116; 118.
[43] Ibid., 125. Powell's text actually says Titus 4: 5, but Nigel Smith (while attributing the passage to Henry Walker) suggests this is a false reference to the Corinthians passage (p. 36).
[44] Jacob Bauthumley, 'The Light and the Dark Sides of God', in Smith (ed.), *A Collection of Ranter Writings*, 232.

And God answered Moses, I AM THAT I AM. Also he said, Thus shalt thou say unto the children of Is[r]aél, I AM hathe sent me unto you. (Exodus 3: 15)

But by the grace of God, I am that I am: and his grace which is in me, was not in vaine: but I laboured more abundantly then they all: yet not I, but the grace of God which is in me. (1 Corinthians 15: 10)

On the one hand, the ultimate expression of divine agency, on the other, an acknowledgement of complete subjection: the apostle's assertion, 'I am that I am', defines not an asserted ego, but rather the absence of independent agency, the dominance of God's grace, and the acceptance that the affirmation *I am* requires the qualification 'I am . . . yet not I'; 'I', as Paul says earlier in Corinthians, 'know nothing by my self'.[45] The divine 'I AM', a statement that delineates both a private and omnipotent identity, stands in complete antithesis to the acknowledgement of mortal 'subjection'.[46] As K. Go explains, it is this second passage, read out annually on 'xj. Sunday after Trinitie' as set out by the *Book of Common Prayer*, that would have been more frequently heard in turn-of-the-century church services.[47] Go's re-evaluation of Shakespeare's Sonnet 121 signals the consequences of hearing 'I am' instead of '*I AM*'; 'the poet's words', he concludes, 'may no longer be taken, as they were by Pequigney, for a "ringing declaration of moral independence" which "affirms the principle that the individual's conscience is the final arbiter of what is right or wrong for him."'[48] 'I am' should therefore be undercut by the biblical admission of subservience (*subject*ivity), that 'I am . . . not I'. But neither do we need, as perhaps Go's note implies, to abandon hearing an echo of Exodus in the phrase; we seem to have a neatly double-edged declaration that both signals the absolute power and the subjection of the *I*: a not unfamiliar duality of affirmation and negation.

If we then apply this double echo to the lineage of self-asserting Shakespearean bastards, we hear Falconbridge's claim that 'I am I, howe'er I was begot' (*Jn.*, I. i. 175) with increased disquiet, his individualism adopting both the words of God and subverting the words of the

---

[45] 1 Corinthians 4: 4.
[46] Ibid., 9: 27.
[47] K. Go, '"I am that I am" in Shakespeare's "Sonnet 121" and 1 Corinthians 15:10', *N&Q*, 49/2 (2002), 241–2.
[48] Ibid., 242. Cit. Pequigney, *Such is My Love*, 100.

blessed penitent. Don John's multiple assertions—'I cannot hide what I am' (*Ado*, I. III. 10); 'I am a plain-dealing villain' (l. 32); 'let me be that I am' (l. 36)—equally play false notes on St Paul's self-effacing humility. Each of these assertions, including Edmund's own 'I should have been that I am . . .' speech (*Lr.*, I. II. 115–16), seeks to isolate a bastard—for all three are illegitimate—from his familial inheritance, or set him up in pure self-relation, cut off from family, society, and the divine. Consequently, the 'misbegotten devil Falconbridge' (*Jn.*, V. IV. 4), Edmund, conceived under the dragon's tail (with its satanic connotations), and Don John with 'the devil my master' (*Ado*, III. III. 155), are all connotatively allied to *Othello*'s devilish Iago: 'O damned Iago!' (V. I. 62). What we hear is a strong *I*, not the self-effacing first-person pronoun of Salmon or St Paul, but an *I* that will not look beyond itself, that knows no other referent but itself, self-divided only in order to be self-referential, seemingly fitting all the criteria of the sinful, duplicitous self-willed man, and revelling in it.

'I am not what I am' in fact works in an almost identical fashion to Salmon's 'I now am, onely in what *I* am not', in the sense that Iago's statement, like that of the Ranter, seeks to signify beyond the text (Salmon's to the hidden secrets of the soul, or to the *I* that is God: Iago's to something more like a second unsoundable self separate from his external persona). Particularly peculiar to Iago's statement, setting it apart from Hamlet's expressions of similar sentiment, is the complete integral negation involved in the line; his construction not equating to 'I am not what I *seem* to be', Iago is simply not what he is. In what Greenblatt calls a phrase of 'hypothetical self-cancellation', Iago has gone 'beyond social feigning', working through a discourse of 'seeming' (I. I. 61) and 'shows of service' (l. 52), far beyond the ontological construction that St Paul requested from God, to a moment of absolute controlled indeterminacy.[49] From this position he can as easily say 'I am your own for ever' (III. III. 480), as 'I follow but myself' (I. I. 59), as easily say 'I am a very villain' as 'I am a very villain else' (IV. I. 122).

It is his easy adoption of multiple roles, his ability to lay claim—I am—to a variety of names and natures, that makes Iago the representative of a successfully unstable self-geminating identity, cheerfully an-

---

[49] Greenblatt, *Renaissance Self-Fashioning*, 235–6.

nouncing his textual annihilation. It is on this level that Iago attacks his victims, leaving them in self-doubt—'Am I that name? (IV. II. 117)—or in refracted confusion: 'He's that he is; I may not breathe my censure | What he might be. If what he might he is not, | I would to heaven he were' (IV. I. 261–3). This is murder on the level of pronoun, because although Iago himself can cope with saying 'I am not what I am', Othello simply cannot be 'that he is' when subjected to similar treatment; what he 'might be' is almost hopelessly lost. Ultimately, throughout the play we repeatedly hear that '[m]y lord is not my lord' (III. IV. 118), or 'I am sure I am none such' (IV. II. 122), but Iago alone celebrates sceptical solipsism. Indeed, of all the suicides in the play, perhaps Iago's narrative self-cancellation—'I never will speak word' (V. II. 301)— comes closest to self-assertion, 'preserving inviolate the mysteries of the self', fulfilling the potential for self-effacement signalled in this 'I am not' statement.[50] His is a preposterous subjectivity, not quite thinking itself into thoughtful being, but affirming itself in negation, negatively asserting itself in a loud silence: he is the exponent of self-perpetuating ipseity before such a thing is deemed philosophically or morally legitimate, while such introjected gemination speaks only of satanic self-subjection.

Iago's lexical self-slaughter—a sinister parallel of Hieronimo's heroic self-silencing in Kyd ('I have no more to say')—is a malign triumph of isolationist self-sufficiency.[51] 'My death', as Webster's Flamineo announces, 'shall serve mine own turn', and Iago announces his place in this lineage of Renaissance dramatic self-assertive self-slaughterers, serving his own evil turn on their declarations of ultimate suicidal agency; his silence is, for example, comparable to Flamineo's announcement that 'I am i'th'way to study a long silence', similarly claiming that 'at myself I will begin and end'.[52] Iago becomes a dangerously self-possessed agent in a play desperate for loving, mutual union. Amongst the reciprocating suicides of this study, Iago's silence stands defiant as an act of malicious individualism; a man, as Montaigne would say, must 'sequester and recover himselfe from himselfe', and accordingly Iago 'depend[s]' upon

---

[50] Neill, *Issues of Death*, 365.
[51] Kyd, *The Spanish Tragedy*, IV. IV. 152.
[52] John Webster, *The White Devil*, ed. Christina Luckyj (London, 1996), V. VI. 50; 201; 256.

himself.[53] While 'he that was Othello' (V. ii. 281) is left pleading to be spoken of 'as I am' (l. 338), still grasping at verbally defined identity—'here I am' (l. 281)—Iago, the demi-devil, has (to misappropriate and taint the vocabulary of Salmon) become weary of speaking, informed the world that silence has taken hold of him, entered into his own chamber, shut the doors about him, and hidden himself in silence 'till the indignation bee blown over': he enters the little room 'not to pray' (l. 302) like perhaps Donne would (in his stanzaic room), but, like Montaigne and Descartes in their respective chambers, to be alone with himself.

When Charles Taylor describes an expansion in available conceptions of selfhood—accrued from, amongst others, Augustine, Descartes, and Montaigne—he charts an incremental supplementation; a model of self-scrutiny that looked inward for signs of the divine was increasingly asked to negotiate with, or incorporate, a new radically reflexive self whose second-order introspection sought to privilege the self-subjectifying operation of individuality. And, while being wary of a general critical tendency that compulsively identifies the crisis point of epistemological change, it is clear that Iago's transition away from the mortal self-abjection implicit in the divine instruction 'I AM THAT I AM', to his counter-claim, 'I am not what I am', and his final retreat within a silent self, follows Taylor's conception of ontological history. In Iago, we hear a wilful subversion of theological reflexivity, and begin to hear something much more akin to the voice of Michel de Montaigne. There is a crucial discrepancy between the following expressions of interiority, from Abernethy and the sceptical neo-Stoic (and hence extravagantly self-sufficient) Montaigne, respectively, that illustrates Taylor's variant models of individuality. Abernethy insists on indivisible union with God, achieved via self-denying self-attentiveness: 'Gather thy selfe unto thy selfe; and shut up thy selfe, within thy selfe, examine, search, know thy selfe. Let the studie of thy selfe, be true, long, daily, serious, attentive.'[54] In contrast, Montaigne, and an equally amused Iago, can claim an individuality born of interiorized self-gemination: '*I turne my sight inward, there I fix it, there I ammuse it.*'[55] Iago, like the introspec-

---

[53] Montaigne, *Essais*, 119.
[54] Abernethy, *A Christian and Heavenly Treatise*, 29.
[55] Montaigne, *Essais*, 371.

tive Adonis who looked away from his goddess, fixes his attention within and will not disclose his secrets easily, especially not when faced with the crude torture implements of the old somatic regime.

While, in the silence of an Iago or a Hamlet, we hear echoes of what Philip Davis describes as 'the creation of that sense of separatedness out of which comes the consciousness of individuality as an inward dimension',[56] it is equally important to understand how Iago perverts and pollutes pre-existing structures of ipseic indivisible interdependence. Iago's final act of introversion may be a harbinger of what is conservatively felt as a dangerous isolationist tendency in ontological development, but his actions more demonstrably threaten to undermine available models of mutuality. He embodies a contemporary unease concerning the limitations of double-self, turning division into distraction, and entering into reciprocal relations to manipulate the precariously dependent identities of those around him. He is the poisonous *alter idem.* He ruins responsiveness.

4. PREPOSTEROUS SUBJECTS

As previously discussed in relation to the indivisible friendship of Cassius and Brutus, the friend or second self provides the reciprocation fundamental to individuate identity. The reflection of friend to friend, taken to its nadir in the self-admiration of Narcissus, is integral to this sense of responsive ipseity: '*As face answereth to face in water, so the heart of man to man*'.[57] As Bacon describes, the friend is crucial to ipseic health:

We know Diseases of Stoppings and Suffocations are the most dangerous in the body, and it is not much otherwise in the Mind: You may take *Sarza* to open the Liver, *Steel* to open the Spleen, *Flowr* of *Sulphur* for the Lungs . . . but no Receipt openeth the Heart but a true Friend, to whom you impart Griefs, Joyes, Fears, Hopes, Suspicions, Counsels, and whatsoever lieth upon the Heart to oppress it in a kind of Civil Shrift or Confession.[58]

---

[56] Philip Davis, *Sudden Shakespeare: The Shaping of Shakespeare's Creative Thought* (London, 1996), 45.

[57] Reynolds, 'A Treatise of the Passions and Faculties of the Soul of Man', in *The Works*, 613–780 at 640.

[58] Francis Bacon, 'Of Friendship', in *Essayes and Counsels*, 145–6.

'A Principal *Fruit* of *Friendship* is', Bacon explains, 'the Ease and Discharge of the Fulness and Swellings of the Heart, which Passions of all kinds do cause and induce.'[59] Just as the constipated blocked body requires purgation, the suffering of an oppressed mind or a bruised heart must be alleviated by the ministrations of medicinal friendship and remedied with reciprocation. 'Eaten up with passion' (III. iii. 392), sick with jealousy, Othello is infected with the 'forkèd plague' (l. 278) of a cuckold's anxiety, his forehead aching both with the pressure of his trammelled thoughts and the imagined press of his new-grown horns. Seemingly incapable of finding release, his bosom 'swell[s]' with the venom of 'aspics' tongues' (ll. 450–1), his blood burns 'like the mines of sulphur' (l. 330), his untranquil mind causing him to 'tremble', to 'shake', to 'foam . . . at the mouth', until he *falls in a trance* (IV. i. 38–52). Having 'garnered up his heart' (IV. ii. 56) so tightly that his 'bloody passion shakes [his] very frame (V. ii. 44), Othello, as Bacon has prescribed, desperately needs a 'true Friend', a 'Civil Shrift', an opportunity for 'Confession'. Yet what the play provides is merely the misconstrued confession of a true councillor—'[Cassio] hath confessed' (l. 67)—the enforced confession of an innocent—'confess thee freely of thy sin' (l. 53)—and the poisonous attentions of a dissembler mistaken for a 'Good friend' (IV. ii. 149); a politic flatterer is fatally conceived of as 'My friend, [the] honest, honest Iago' (V. ii. 153). Here, the medicinal friend, whose ministrations should offer remedy to both body and mind, offers only poison, metaphorically plaguing the body with pestilence, rubbing its angry pustules (see V. i. 11–12), and practising a cruel and invasive physic: 'Work on, | My medicine, work!' (IV. i. 42–3).

The friend, the second self, should act as the 'self compos'd', taking the division of a distempered subject and recomposing it, turning the threat of difference into the comfort of 'correspondencie and relation that begetteth . . . true and mutually-perfect amities':

Friendship . . . makes two as it were *One*, but so as the *Communication* is hereby increased: for who can doubt disclosing what troubles or perplexes him to one *so much himself*? 'tis but appealing from my *distemper'd* self, to my self *compos'd*, all the difference is for my advantage.[60]

---

[59] Ibid., 145.
[60] Wither, *Friendship*, 9.

In making himself indispensable to Othello—'nothing else than a *second selfe*, and therefore as individuate as man from himselfe'—Iago simply spoils this system of ipseic generosity, showing how non-autonomous identity is painfully susceptible to attack.[61] By providing opportunity for a troubled soul to 'freely and safely dilate it self', a good friend should be a good physic, an 'Antidote [or] ointment', 'the medicine of life',[62] but Iago pours only 'pestilence into [Othello's] ear' (II. III. 323).

> The Moor already changes with my poison:
> Dangerous conceits are in their natures poisons,
> . . .
> . . . [they] act upon the blood,
> [and b]urn like the mines of sulphur. (III. III. 326–9)

While the 'true friend serves for a healthfull medicine', the false flatterer 'is a sweet poison'.[63]

Accordingly, while depriving Othello of his 'tranquil mind' (III. III. 349), Iago creates a need for his friendly machinations, 'poison[ing Othello's] delight' (I. I. 69), and then offering attentive cures and remedies (II. I. 283; I. I. 35), prescribing his patients the medicine for the poison he himself administers; 'Not poppy nor mandragora, | Nor all the drowsy syrups of the world, | Shall ever medicine thee to that sweet sleep | Which thou owed'st yesterday' (III. III. 331–4). Driving out Desdemona, Iago insists on Othello's absolute dependency, and consequently, his total malleability. The 'faithfull friend' becomes 'as a mans own self', 'knit [together] in Conjunction', until as the 'two several Bodies . . . meet in one Mind' they become, as Francis Bacon describes, 'married and joined in one Manner of Disposition . . . fast locked in a League of Love'.[64] Playing the part of the second self, Iago inhabits the minds and effects the dispositions of his victims; he is the 'individuate

---

[61] Richard Brathwaite, *The English Gentleman* (London, 1630), 293. Masten, *Textual Intercourse*, 32.

[62] Wither, *Friendship*, 12.; Cicero, *The Booke of Freendship*, trans. Harrington, 1; Plutarch, *The Philosophie*, 91.

[63] Grey Bridges, *A Discourse Against Flatterie* (London, 1611), 112.

[64] Bacon, 'Of Friendship', 156; Dorke, *A Tipe or Figure of Friendship*, sig. A4ᵛ; Bacon, 'Of Friendship', 253; 254.

companion' who can 'knit unto you, as if he were individually united to your selfe', until he is 'therefore impossible to be divided from you, as you from your selfe'.[65]

To appreciate and avoid this threat, one should not look for response elsewhere, but look to oneself:

> Therefore consider well thy selfe with thy selfe, & let us not bee such fooles as to judge of our selves by the opinion of others, within thy selfe behold well thy selfe, an if thou art then give no credence to others . . . let your owne conscience be your owne praiser.[66]

This catoptric self-speculation cannot be condemned as narcissistic: it is the 'remedy' of self-geminative individualism.[67] Where Adonis merely demurred, privileging an introspective retreat over extramissive responsiveness, Iago participates to pervert, appropriates what he sees as hopelessly naive, and reveals the inadequacy of an out-dated model of subjectivity. In his narrative suicide, his self-inflicted silence, Iago finally removes himself from the circulation of responsivity, leaving the ipseic earth scorched behind him.

Shakespeare's nostalgic vision sees Iago and his egotistic solipsism as a threat to the kind couple, and as a challenge to indivisible individualism. Charles Taylor's account of ipseic development moves towards what Jonathan Sawday has described as the Cartesian 'self-reflective machine', in which subjectivity is increasingly understood, in Manfred Frank's terms, as the 'auto-reflexivity of thinking'.[68] 'Apperception', as Frank describes this second-order ipseic structure, comes to the fore in Cartesian notions, here described by Mikkel Borch-Jacobson, of 'the auto-foundation or auto-positioning of a subject presenting itself to itself as consciousness'.[69] This self-speculating subject—indebted to its uncelebrated Ovidian predecessor—is now permitted to ask what Jaś Elsner has described as Narcissus' forbidden enquiry: 'what happens when you

---

[65] Brathwaite, *The English Gentleman*, 297; 299.

[66] Bridges, *A Discourse*, 134–5.

[67] Ibid., 137.

[68] Taylor, *Sources of the Self*; Sawday, 'Self and Selfhood', 47; Manfred Frank, 'Is Self-Consciousness a Case of Presence à soi? Towards a Meta-Critique of the Recent French Critique of Metaphysics', in David Wood (ed.), *Derrida: A Critical Reader* (Oxford, 1992), 218–34 at 223.

[69] Borch-Jacobsen, 'The Freudian Subject', 63.

objectify yourself?'[70] 'I resolved to make my studies within myself', Descartes' self-subjecting subject announces, 'to discourse with myself about my own thoughts.'[71] Despite living in 'the most frequented cities', he can therefore be all-one, living 'a life as solitary and retired as though I were in the most remote deserts'.[72]

'I'd like to argue that there is something very valuable which has emerged from this development', Taylor cautiously concludes, 'that something has been gained in our self-interpretations.'[73] And in the radical uncertainty of Cartesian thought there will emerge valuable knowledge—'I am, I exist'—amongst systematic doubt.[74] As William Cornwallis's essays indicate, there is something almost Hegelian about the early-modern ability to incorporate contradiction:

> I still contradicted my self, attempted nothing [but] in the end I found my self... [my soul's] motions, my own memory & bookes have done something.... I am my selfe still, though the world were turned with the wrong side outward.[75]

For the 'right managing of our selves' in a world losing faith with friendship, 'self observation' makes 'an excellent counsellor', since 'no words, no works, no passion, no Patience comes from us, that turn not back their heads to looke upon [their] Author'; the offspring of our actions 'all resemble the Father, and cast backe upon us the true reflection of our Selves'.[76] Montaigne knows that his 'essential forme is fit to communication', that he is 'all outward and in apparance, borne for society and vnto friendship', but by appropriating the geminative structures of reciprocal identity and relocating them within, by 'retir[ing] my affections and redeem[ing] my thoughts vnto my selfe',

---

[70] Elsner, *Roman Eyes,* 136.

[71] René Descartes, 'Discourse on the Method of Rightly Directing One's Reason and of Seeking Truth in the Sciences', in *Philosophical Writings,* trans. and ed. Elizabeth Anscombe and Peter Thomas Geach (London, 1970), 6–57 at 14; 15.

[72] Ibid. 30.

[73] Charles Taylor, 'The Person', in Michael Carrithers, Steven Collins, and Steven Lukes (eds.), *The Category of the Person* (Cambridge, 1985), 257–81 at 281.

[74] René Descartes, 'Meditations on First Philosophy', in *Philosophical Writings,* 59–124 at 69.

[75] William Cornwallis, *Essayes* (London, 1600), sig. B1^v–5^v.

[76] Ibid., sigs. D3^r; B2^{r-v}.

he can find the 'solitude that I love and commend'.[77] Accordingly, the self-geminative subject integrates 'alienation [and] extraneousness', articulating its sense of what Jean-Luc Nancy describes as a 'proper being-outside-of-itself' to give early indication that 'the logic of the *subjectum* is a grammar' that allows the subject to reappropriate to itself 'in advance and absolutely, the exteriority and the strangeness of its predicate': myself myself can love, and himself himself can kill.[78] The early modern narcissist and suicide are, albeit reductively, working with a grammar of self-subjection that will be their fleeting triumph, their eventual downfall, but their lasting legacy.

This over-assertive subject regards it as a weakness to countenance that it may not be 'its own subject, [or that] it does not rest upon itself, [or become] its own foundation'; faced with this anxiety, Sylviane Agacinski suggests, 'it would have to duplicate itself, like the [Cartesian] philosophical subject that redoubles itself into an empirical and a transcendental subject',[79] or, I would add, like the self-slaughterer or self-lover. So self-destruction is the dangerous product of self-absorption, and, as Bacon attests, 'the sting and remorse of the mind accusing it selfe doubleth all adversitie'; the doublings of self-involvement can be 'deadly inwards and suffocat[ing]' for 'if the evill bee in the sence and in the conscience both, there is a gemination of it'.[80] As Taylor nostalgically acknowledges, 'I also think that something has been lost in the interiorisation, particularly an understanding of being an interlocutor'.[81]

The connection between the suicide and the narcissist is that they embody and prefigure the kind of radically reflexive activity that will become central to philosophical constructions of ipseity. Both proffered as cautions against a rising recourse to self-geminative models of identity, they become increasingly empty as threats, increasingly resonant as precursors. The involutions, the recoils, the turns that these two figures serve upon themselves will not always be thought so preposterous.

---

[77] Montaigne, *Essais*, 461.

[78] Jean-Luc Nancy, 'Introduction', in Cadava et al. (eds.), *Who Comes*, 1–8 at 6.

[79] Sylviane Agacinski, 'Another Experience of the Question, or Experiencing the Question Other-Wise', in Cadava et al. (eds.), *Who Comes*, 9–23 at 16.

[80] Francis Bacon, *Essayes* (London, 1597), sigs. G1^V–2^V.

[81] Taylor, 'The Person', 281.

Narcissine rhetorical structures, chiasmatic and reflexive, intricate in their involutions, will not always be condemned as suicidal: or rather, reflexive models of self-subjection, self-gemination, and self-absorption will not always be castigated as excessive self-adoration or violent self-slaughter. If the Renaissance takes exception to narcissine ipseic structures, they nevertheless become the rule (I am reminded of Michel Jeanneret's description of Montaigne's fascination with the 'division and disturbance within himself' as both a 'crisis' and 'the birth certificate of the *Essays*').[82] Renaissance treatments of suicide and narcissism fail to prevent an introspective turn; indeed that introspection becomes an increasingly 'legitimate action, the quest . . . [to] coincide with [one]self'.[83] Perhaps, to forget that 'individual' once meant 'indivisible' is to ignore the caution articulated in early modern depictions of the self-lover and self-murderer; 'without relation, we are loveless, speechless, witless'.[84] Or perhaps, the assumption of self-division, the promotion of self-subjection, presupposes that interlocution should occur within and that we are willing to listen to a dialogue of one, and that such a dialogue need not be narcissistic, need not be punished: 'I see in us only one thing in us which could give us good reason for esteeming ourselves', Descartes will conclude, 'namely the exercise of our free will and the control we have over our volitions [which] renders us in a certain way like God by making us masters of ourselves.'[85]

Perhaps this has proven, as Shakespeare's Venus seemed to predict, a sad story:

One story about modernity would identify it with the apprehension of the self's autonomous grounding. . . .[But] there is nothing to *guarantee* the modern self—nothing, that is, except its abandonment, in the mode of reflection or of delirium, of all external guarantees. . . . The very strength of the modern self is its weakness, just as its weakness is the ultimate source of its strength.[86]

---

[82] Michel Jeanneret, *Perpetual Motion: Transforming Shapes in the Renaissance from da Vinci to Montaigne*, trans. Nidra Poller (London, 2001), 99.

[83] Ibid., 160.

[84] Nuttall, 'Ovid's Narcissus and Shakespeare's Richard II', 148.

[85] René Descartes, 'The Passions of the Soul', in *The Philosophical Writings*, trans. John Cottingham, Robert Stoothoff, and Dugald Murdoch, vol. 1 (Cambridge, 1985), 325–404 at 386.

[86] Connor, 'The Modern Auditory I', 203.

So every friendship essay describes the death of the friend, and every dead friend, every lost response, is an acknowledgement of a loss of faith; the reciprocation must be found elsewhere. Adonis has looked away, Echo departed, Iago fallen silent, and the world of generous reciprocity is itself acknowledged as a narcissistic and self-destructive dream. To predicate one's identity upon the response of an unresponsive world, as Venus discovered, is to be Sir George Rodney, denied a kind response, and driven to a preposterous conclusion:

And when he had sent [his verses] to her, as a sad *Catastrophe* to all his *Miseries*, he ran himself upon his Sword, and so ended that life which he thought death to injoy.[87]

---

[87] Wilson, *The History of Great Britain*, 258.

Bibliography

Primary Works

A., H., *The Scourge of Venus; or, The Wanton Lady. With the Rare Birth of Adonis* (London, 1613).

Abercromby, David, *Academia Scientiarum* (London, 1687).

Abernethy, John, *A Christian and Heavenly Treatise: Containing Physicke for the Soule* (London, 1630).

Adams, John, *An Essay Concerning Self-Murther* (London, 1700).

Alanus de Insulis, *The Complaint of Alain de Lille*, trans. D. M. Moffat (New York, 1908).

Anon., *Narcissus: A Twelfe Night Merriment Played by Youths of the Parish at the College of S. John the Baptist in Oxford, A.D. 1602* (London, 1893).

——., *A Sad and Dreadful Account of the Self-Murther of Robert Long, alias Baker* (London, 1685).

——., *A Sad Caveat to all Quakers Not to Boast any more that they have God Almighty by the Hand, when they have the Devil by the Toe* (London, 1657).

——., *Sad and Dreadful News from Dukes-place near Aldgate; or, a True Account of a Barbarous and Unnatural Self-Murther Commited by Dorcas Pinkney* (London, 1686).

Aquinas, Thomas, *Commentary on the Nicomachean Ethics*, trans. C. I. Litzinger (Notre Dame, Ind., 1964).

——, *Summa Theologiae*, 60 vols. (London, 1974).

Aristotle, *Metaphysics X–XIV: Oeconomica, and Magna Moralia*, ed. and trans. G. Cyril Armstrong (Cambridge, Mass., 1947).

——, *Nicomachean Ethics*, trans. Terence Irwin (Indianapolis, Ind., 1985).

Arius Didymus, *Epitome of Stoic Ethics*, ed. Arthur J. Pomeroy (Atlanta, Ga., 1999).

Augustine, *The City of God: De Civitate Dei*, trans. J. H., 2 vols. (London, 1890).

——, *Confessions*, trans. Henry Chadwick (Oxford, 1991).

——, *Soliloquies and Immortality of the Soul*, trans. Gerald Watson (Warminster, 1986).

B., J., *An English Exposition* (London, 1616).

B., M., *The Triall of True Friendship; or Perfit Mirror, wherby to Discerne a Trustie Friend from a Flattering Parasite* (London, 1594).

Bacon, Francis, *Essayes* (London, 1597).

—— *Essayes and Counsels: Civil and Moral* (London, 1664).

—— *Sylva Sylvarum; or, A Naturall Historie* (London, 1628).

—— *The Wisedome of the Ancients*, trans. Arthur Gorges (London, 1619).

Barksted, William, *Mirrha the Mother of Adonis; or, Lustes Prodegies* (London, 1607).

Barrough, Philip, *The Method of Phisick* (London, 1583).

Bayly, Lewis, *The Practice of Pietie* (London, 1616).

Beaumont, Francis, *The Dramatic Works in the Beaumont and Fletcher Canon*, ed. Fredson Bowers (Cambridge, 1996).

—— *Salmacis and Hermaphroditus* (London, 1602).

—— and Fletcher, John, *The Maid's Tragedy*, ed. Howard B. Norland (Lincoln, Nebr., 1968).

Beedome, Thomas, *Poems, Divine and Humane* (London, 1641).

B[lount], T[homas], *Glossographia; or, A Dictionary* (London, 1661).

Blout, Charles, *The Two First Books of Philostratus: Concerning the Life of Appollonius Tyaneus* (London, 1680).

Brandon, Samuel, *The Virtuous Octavia, 1598* (Oxford, 1909).

Brathwaite, Richard, *The English Gentleman* (London, 1630).

—— *The Golden Fleece* (London, 1611).

—— *The Honest Ghost* (London, 1634).

Breme, Thomas, *The Mirror of Friendship* (London, 1584).

Breton, Nicholas, *Melancholike Humours, in Verses of Diverse Natures* (London, 1600).

Bridges, Grey, *A Discourse Against Flatterie* (London, 1611).

Bright, T., *A Treatise of Melancholy* (London, 1613).

Brinsley, John, *Ludus Literarius; or, The Grammar Schoole* (London, 1612).

Brooke, Arthur, *The Tragicall Historye of Romeus and Iuliet* (London, 1562).

Browne, John, *Myographia Nova; or, a Graphical Description Of All The Muscles in the Humane Body, As Arise In Dissection* (London, 1698).

Browne, Thomas, *Religio Medici and Other Works*, ed. L. C. Martin (Oxford, 1964).

Burton, Robert, *The Anatomy of Melancholy*, ed. Thomas C. Faulkner, Nicolas K. Kiessling, and Rhonda L. Blair, 6 vols. (Oxford, 1989).

Callistratus, *Descriptions*, trans. Arthur Fairbanks (London, 1931).

Calvin, John, *The Institution of Christian Religion* (London, 1561).

Capel, Richard, *Tentations: Their Nature, Danger, Cure* (London, 1659).

Cartwright, William, *Comedies, Tragi-comedies, with other Poems* (London, 1651).

Chapman, George, *Ovid's Banquet of Sence, and . . . The Amorous Contention of Phillis and Flora* (London, 1595).

—— *Petrarchs Seven Penitentiall Psalmes* (London, 1612).

Charron, Pierre, *Of Wisdom*, trans. George Stanhope, 3 vols. (London 1707).

Chester, Robert, *Loves Martyr; or, Rosalins Complaint: With its Supplement, Diverse Poeticall Essaies on the Turtle and Phœnix by Shakespeare, Ben Jonson, George Chapman, John Marston, etc (1601)*, ed. Alexander B. Grosart (London, 1878).

Chettle, Henry, *The Tragedy of Hoffman*, ed. J. D. Jowett (Nottingham, 1983).

Churchyard, Thomas, *Churchyard's Challenge* (London, 1593).

—— *A Sparke of Frendship and Warme Goodwill* (London, 1588).

Cicero, *The Booke of Freendship*, trans. John Harrington (n.p., 1550).

—— *De natura deorum*, trans. H. Rackham (London, 1951)

—— *De Officiis*, trans. Walter Miller (London, 1913).

—— *Letters to Atticus*, ed. and trans. D. R. Shackleton Bailey, 4 vols. (Cambridge, Mass., 1998).

—— *On Stoic Good and Evil: 'De Finibus Bonorum et Malorum Liber III' and 'Paradoxa Stoicorum'*, trans. M. R. Wright (Warminster, 1991).

—— *On the Ideal Orator (De oratore)*, ed. and trans. James M. May (Oxford, 2001).

—— *Tusculan Disputations I*, ed. and trans. A. E. Douglas (Warminster, 1985).

A Collection of Ranter Writings from the Seventeenth Century, ed. Nigel Smith (London, 1983).

Collier, Jeremy, *Essays upon Several Moral Subjects* (London, 1700).

—— *Miscellanies Upon Moral Subjects* (London, 1695).

Conti, Natale, *Mythologies: A Select Translation*, trans. Anthony DiMatteo (London, 1994).

Cornwallis, William, *Essayes* (London, 1600).

Cotgrave, Randle, *A Dictionarie of the French and English Tongues* (London, 1611).

Cotton, Clement, *The Mirrour of Martyrs: The First and Second Part* (London, 1639).

Cowper, William, *Myotomia Reformata; or, A New Administration of all the Muscles of the Humane Bodies* (London, 1694).

Cushman, Robert, *A Sermon Preached at Plimmith in New-England* (London, 1622).

Dalton, Michael, *The Countrey Justice* (London, 1630).

Daniel, Samuel, *Delia and Rosamund* (London, 1592).

—— *The Whole Workes of Samuel Daniel* (London, 1623).

Dante Alighieri, *The Divine Comedy*, ed. and trans. Robert M. Durling, notes by Durling and Ronald L. Martinez, 3 vols. (Oxford, 1996).

Davies, John, *Nosce teipsum* (London, 1599).

—— *Wittes Pilgrimage* (London, 1605).

Day, Angel, *The English Secretorie* (London, 1614).

Day, John, *The Knave in Graine* (London, 1640).

Denny, William, *Pelecanicidium; or The Christian Adviser Against Self-Murder* (London, 1653).

Descartes, René, *Philosophical Writings*, trans. and ed. Elizabeth Anscombe and Peter Thomas Geach (London, 1970).

—— *The Philosophical Writings of Descartes*, trans. John Cottingham, Robert Stoothoff, and Dugald Murdoch, vol. 1 (Cambridge, 1985).

Digrassi, Giacomo, *His True Arte of Defence* (London, 1594).

Donne, John, *Biathanatos*, ed. Ernest W. Sullivan II (London and Toronto, 1984).

—— *Biathanatos: A Declaration of that Paradoxe or Thesis, that Selfe-homicide is not so Naturally Sinne, that it may never be Otherwise* (London, 1644).

—— *The Complete English Poems*, ed. A. J. Smith (Harmondsworth, 1971).

—— *Paradoxes and Problems*, ed. Helen Peters (Oxford, 1980).

—— *Pseudo-Martyr*, ed. Anthony Raspa (Montreal, 1993).

Dorke, Walter, *A Tipe or Figure of Friendship* (London, 1589).

Drayton, Michael, *The Poems of Michael Drayton*, ed. John Buxton, 2 vols. (London, 1953).

Dryden, John, *Of Dramatic Poesy and Other Critical Essays*, ed. George Watson, 2 vols. (London, 1962).

—— *Sylvæ; or, the Second Part of Poetical Miscellanies*, in *The Works of John Dryden*, ed. Earl Miner, 20 vols. (Berkeley, 1969), iii. 2–90.

Du Bartas, Guillaume, *His Divine Weekes, and Workes; with, A Compleate, Collection of all the Other Most Delightfull Workes*, trans. Josuah Sylvester (London, 1641).

Edwards, Thomas, *Cephalus and Procris; and, Narcissus (1595)*, ed. W. E. Buckley (London, 1882).

Empedocles, *The Extant Fragments*, ed. M. R. Wright (London, 1995).

Epictetus, *A Stoic and Socratic Guide to Life*, trans. A. A. Long (Oxford, 2002).

Epicurus, *The Philosophy of Epicurus: Letters, Doctrines, and Parallel Passages from Lucretius*, trans. George Strodach (Easton, 1963).

Eramus, 'The Letter of Friendship', in *Collected Works*, ed. J. K. Sowards, 40 vols. (Toronto, 1985), xxv. 203–5.

Euclid, *The Elements of Geometrie*, trans. Henry Billingsley (London, 1570).

Fenner, William, *Wilfull Impertinency; The Grossest Selfe-Murder* (London, 1648).

Ficino, Marsilio, *Commentary on Plato's Symposium on Love*, trans. Sears Jayne (Dallas, Tex., 1985).

Firmin, Giles, *The Real-Christian; or, A Treatise of Effectual Calling* (London, 1670).

Fisher, Samuel, *The Rustick's Alarm to the Rabbies* (London, 1660).

Ford, John, *The Selected Plays*, ed. Colin Gibson (Cambridge, 1986).

Fraunce, Abraham, *The Third Part of the Countesse of Pembrokes Yvychurch: Entituled Amintas Dale* (London, 1592).

Gale, Dunstan, *Pyramus and Thisbe* (London, 1617).

Galen, *On the Usefulness of the Parts of the Body*, trans. Margaret Tallmadge May, 2 vols. (Ithaca, NY, 1968).

—— *On the Doctrines of Hippocrates and Plato*, trans. Phillip de Lacy (Berlin, 1984).

Garnier, Robert, *The Tragedie of Antonie*, trans. Mary Sidney Herbert (London, 1595).

The Geneva Bible: A Facsimile of the 1560 Edition (Geneva, 1560; repr. Madison, Wis., 1969).

Glanvill, Joseph, *Plus Ultra; or, The Progress and Advancement of Knowledge Since the Days of Aristotle* (London, 1668).

—— *Essays on Several Important Subjects in Philosophy and Religion* (London, 1676).

Golding, Arthur, *see Shakespeare's Ovid.*

Goodwin, George, 'Auto-Machia: Or The Selfe-Conflict of a Christian', in Du Bartas, 566–7.

—— *Babels Balm*, trans. John Vicars (London, 1624).

Gouge, William, 'To the Christian Reader', in Sym, prefatory matter.

Greenham, Richard, *The Works*, ed. H. H. (London, 1612).

H., T., *A Looking-Glasse for Women* (London, 1644).

Hakewill, George, *The Vanitie of the Eye* (Oxford, 1615).

Hammond, Henry, *To the Right Honourable, The Lord Fairfax, and His Councell of Warre: The Humble Addresse of Henry Hammond* (London, 1649).

Hart, Alexander, *Alexto and Angelica* (London, 1640).

Heath, Robert, *Clarastella* (London, 1650).

Hedley, Thomas, *Judgement of Midas* (London, c.1552).

Hooker, Thomas, *The Christians Two Chiefe Lessons, Viz. Selfe-Deniall, And Selfe-Tryall* (London, 1640).

—— *Heautonaparnumenos* (London, 1646).

Hopkins, John, *Amasia; or, The Works of the Muses*, 3 vols. (London, 1700).

Horace, *The Odes of Horace in English Verse*, trans. various (London, 1929).

Huloet, Richard, *Abecedarium Anglicolatinum* (London, 1552).

Hutchinson, Lucy, *Translations of Lucretius: De rerum natura*, ed. Hugh de Quehen (London, 1996).

Jacoby, Felix, *Die Fragmente der griechischen Historiker*, vol. 1 (Leiden, 1957).

Jessenius, Joannes, *Præs; Universalis humani corporis contemplatio* (Wittenberg, 1598).

Jessey, Henry, *The Exceeding Riches of Grace Advanced By the Spirit of Grace, in an Empty Nothing Creature, viz M^{ris} Sarah Wight* (London, 1647).

Jordan, Thomas, *Love's Dialect* (London, 1661).

Kepler, Johannes, *Optics: Paralipomena to Witelo and Optical Part of Astronomy*, trans. William H. Donahue (Santa Fe, 2000).

Kilby, Richard, *The Burden of a Loaden Conscience; or, The Penitent Confession of a Clergy-Man* (London, 1699).

King, John, *Lectures Upon Jonas: Delivered at Yorke in the Year of our Lord 1594* (London, 1618).

Kyd, Thomas, *The Spanish Tragedy*, ed. J. R. Mulryne (London, 1989).

Lodge, Thomas, *Scillaes Metamorphosis* (London, 1589).

Lucretius, *De rerum natura IV*, ed. and trans. John Godwin (Warminster, 1992).

—— *An Essay on the First Book of T. Lucretius Carus*, De Rerum Natura, trans. John Evelyn (London, 1656).

—— 'The Fourth Book Concerning the Nature of Love', trans. John Dryden, in *The Poems of John Dryden*, ed. Paul Hammond, 5 vols. (London, 1995), ii. 332–44.

Lynche, Richard, *Diella* (London, 1596), repr. in *Seven Minor Epics*, ed. Miller.

Marandé, Leonard de, *The Judgment of Humane Actions*, trans. John Reynolds (London, 1629).

Marlowe, Christopher, *The Poems*, ed. Millar Maclure (London, 1968).

—— *Dr Faustus*, ed. Roma Gill (London, 1989).

—— and Chapman, George, *Hero and Leander* (London, 1598).

Marston, John, *Antonio and Mellida*, ed. W. Reavley Gair (Manchester, 1991).

—— *Antonio's Revenge*, ed. G. K. Hunter (London, 1966).

—— *The Poems of John Marston*, ed. Arnold Davenport (Liverpool, 1961).

Martial, *Epigrams*, ed. and trans. D. R. Shackleton Bailey (Cambridge, Mass., 1993).

Middleton, Thomas, *The Ghost of Lucrece* (London, 1600).

—— *The Wisedome of Solomon Paraphrased* (London, 1597).

—— and Rowley, William, *The Changeling*, ed. N. W. Bawcutt (Manchester, 1998).

Milton, John, *Paradise Lost*, ed. Alastair Fowler (London, 1971).

Miscellaneous Antiquities, ed. Horace Walpole (London, 1772).

Montaigne, Michel de, *Essais*, trans. John Florio (London, 1613).

More, Henry, *Divine Hymns* (London, 1706).

Mornay, Philippe de, 'A Discourse of Life and Death', trans. Mary Sidney Herbert, in *The Collected Works*, ed. Margaret P. Hannay, Noel J. Kinnamon, and Michael G. Brennan, 6 vols. (Oxford, 1998), i. 229–54.

Narrative and Dramatic Sources of Shakespeare, ed. Geoffrey Bullough, 8 vols. (London, 1964).

Nashe, Thomas, *The Works of Thomas Nashe*, ed. Ronald B. McKerrow, 5 vols. (Oxford, 1966).

Ovid, *The Fable of Ovid Treting of Narcissus*, trans. T. H. (London, 1560).

—— *The Heroicall Epistles of the Learned Poet Publius Ovidius Naso*, trans. George Turberville (London, 1567).

—— *The Love Poems*, trans. A. D. Melville (Oxford, 1990).

—— *Metamorphoses I–IV*, ed. and trans. D. E. Hill (Warminster, 1985).

—— *Metamorphoses*, trans. A. D. Melville (Oxford, 1986).

—— *Metamorphoses: 1–5*, ed. with commentary by William S. Anderson (London, 1989).

—— *Ovids Metamorphosis English'd, Mythologiz'd, And Represented in Figures*, trans. George Sandys (London, 1640).

—— *Ovid's Metamorphosis: Translated by Several Hands*, trans. Pittis and Bridgwater (London, 1697).

—— *Shakespeare's Ovid; being Arthur Golding's Translation of the Metamorphoses*, ed. W. H. D. Rouse (London, 1904).

Painter, William, *Rhomeo and Julietta*, in *The Second Tome of the Palace of Pleasure* (London, 1567), 234–62.

Peacham, Henry, *The Garden of Eloquence* (London, 1577).

Petrarca, Francesco, *Petrarch in English*, ed. Thomas P. Roche, trans. various (London, 2005).

Pettie, George, *A Petite Pallace of Pettie: His Pleasure* (London, 1576).

P[hilipot], T[homas], *Self-Homicide-Murder; or, Some Antidotes and Arguments . . . Against that Horrid and Reigning Sin of Self-Murther* (London, 1674).

Philostratus, *Imagines and Callistratus*, trans. Arthur Fairbanks (London, 1931).

P[ierce], E[zra], *A Discourse of Self-Murder, Lately Written, and now Published as a Disswasive from so Horrid a Thing* (London, 1692).

Plato, *Alcibiade*, trans. Chantal Marboeuf and Jean-François Pradeau (Paris, 1999).

—— *Complete Works*, ed. John M. Cooper, trans. various (Indianapolis, Ind., 1997).

—— *Phaedo*, trans. David Gallop (Oxford, 1975).

—— *Phaedrus*, trans. Christopher Rowe (London, 2005).

—— *Timaeus and Critias*, trans. A. E. Taylor (London, 1929).

Platter, Felix, *Observationum, in hominis affectibus plerisque, corpori et animo* (Basle, 1641).

Pliny the Younger, *Letters*, trans. William Melmoth and W. M. L. Hutchinson (London, 1915).

Plotinus, *Collected Writings*, trans. Thomas Taylor (Frome, 1994).

Plutarch, *the Philosophie; commonlie called The Morals*, trans. Philemon Holland (London, 1603).

—— *Shakespeare's Plutarch: The Lives of Julius Caesar, Brutus, Marcus Antonius, and Coriolanus in the Translation of Sir Thomas North*, ed. T. J. B. Spencer (Harmondsworth, 1968).

Porta, John Baptista, *Natural Magick* (London, 1658).

Powell, Vavasor, *Spirituall Experiences, of Sundry Beleevers* (London, 1652).

Primaudaye, Peter de la, *The Second Part of the French Academie*, trans. n.k. (London, 1594).

Prior, Matthew, *Dialogues of the Dead and Other Works in Prose and Verse*, ed. A. R. Waller (Cambridge, 1907).

Puttenham, George, *The Arte of English Poesie* (London, 1589).

Puede-ser, Diego, 'To My Worthy and Much Esteemed Friend, Sir Thomas Richardson, Knight', in Fernando de Rojas, *The Spanish Bawd* (London, 1631), prefatory matter.

Reynolds, Edward, *The Works* (London, 1679).

Reynolds, Henry, *Mythomystes: Wherein a short survey is taken of the nature and value of true poetry and depth of the ancients above our moderne poets. To which is annexed the tale of Narcissus briefly mythologized* (London, 1632).

Robinson, Clement, *A Handful of Pleasant Delights (1584)*, ed. Hyder E. Rollins (Cambridge, 1924).

Sackville, Thomas, and Norton, Thomas, *The Tragedie of Gorbuduc* (London, 1565).

Saviolo, Vincentio, *His Practice* (London, 1595).

Seneca, *Four Dialogues*, ed. C. D. N. Costa (Warminster, 1994).

—— *Letters from a Stoic: Epistulae Morales ad Lucilium*, trans. Robin Campbell (Harmondsworth, 1969).

—— *Moral Essays*, trans. John W. Basore, 3 vols. (London, 1928).

—— *Naturales Quaestiones*, trans. Thomas H. Corcoran, 2 vols. (London, 1972).

—— 'On Mercy', in *Moral and Political Essays*, ed. and trans. John M. Cooper and J. F. Procopé (Cambridge, 1995), 117–64.

—— *The Workes of Lucius Annaeus Seneca, both Morall and Naturall*, trans. Thomas Lodge (London, 1614).

Seven Minor Epics of the English Renaissance (1596–1624), ed. and introduced by Paul W. Miller (New York, 1977).

Shakespeare, William, *Antony And Cleopatra*, ed. David Bevington (Cambridge, 2005).

—— *As You Like It*, ed. Michael Hattaway (Cambridge, 2000).

—— *Coriolanus*, ed. Lee Bliss (Cambridge, 2000).

—— *Hamlet*, ed. Philip Edwards (Cambridge, 2003).

—— *1 Henry IV*, ed. H. Weil and J. Weil (Cambridge, 2007).

—— *Henry V*, ed. Andrew Gurr (Cambridge, 2005).

—— *3 Henry VI*, ed. Michael Hattaway (Cambridge, 1993).

—— *Julius Caesar*, ed. Marvin Spevack (Cambridge, 2003).

—— *King John*, ed. L. A. Beaurline (Cambridge, 1990).

—— *King Richard II*, ed. Andrew Gurr (Cambridge, 2003).

—— *Love's Labours Lost*, ed. H. R. Woudhuysen (Oxford, 1998).

—— *Macbeth*, ed. Albert Braunmuller (Cambridge, 2008).

—— *The Merchant of Venice*, ed. M. M. Mahood (Cambridge, 2003).

—— *The Merry Wives of Windsor*, ed. David Crane (Cambridge, 1997).

—— *A Midsummer Night's Dream*, ed. R. A. Foakes (Cambridge, 2003).

—— *Much Ado about Nothing*, ed. F. H. Mares (Cambridge, 2003).

—— *Othello*, ed. Norman Sanders (Cambridge, 2003).

—— *Pericles*, ed. Doreen DelVecchio and Antony Hammond (Cambridge, 1998).

—— *The Poems*, ed. John Roe (Cambridge, 2006).

—— *Romeo and Juliet*, ed. G. Blakemore Evans (Cambridge, 2003).

—— *The Sonnets*, ed. G. Blakemore Evans (Cambridge, 2006).

—— *The Taming of the Shrew*, ed. Ann Thompson (Cambridge, 2003).

—— *The Tempest*, ed. David Lindley (Cambridge, 2002).

—— *Timon of Athens*, ed. Karl Klein (Cambridge, 2001).

—— *Titus Andronicus*, ed. Alan Hughes (Cambridge, 2006).

—— *The Tragedy of King Lear*, ed. Jay L. Halio (Cambridge, 2005).

—— *Troilus and Cressida*, ed. Antony Dawson (Cambridge, 2003).

—— *Twelfth Night*, ed. Elizabeth Story Donno (Cambridge, 2004).

—— *The Two Gentlemen of Verona*, ed. Kurt Schlüter (Cambridge, 1990).

—— *Two Noble Kinsmen*, ed. Lois Potter (Oxford, 1996).

—— *The Winter's Tale*, ed. Susan Snyder and Deborah T. Curren-Aquino (Cambridge, 2007).

Sheppard, S[amuel], *Epigrams Theological, Philosophical, and Romantick*, 6 books (London, 1651).

Shirley, James, *Narcissus; or, The Selfe-Lover* (London, 1646).

Sibbs, Richard, *The Soules Conflict With It Selfe, and Victory Over It Selfe by Faith* (London, 1636).

Sidney, Philip, *The Old Arcadia*, ed. Katherine Duncan-Jones (Oxford, 1985).

Smith, John, *Mystery of Rhetoric Unveiled* (London, 1665).

Spenser, Edmund, *Amoretti and Epithalamion* (London, 1595).
—— *The Faerie Queene*, ed. A. C. Hamilton (London, 1977).
Stockton, Owen, *Counsel to the Afflicted; Or, Instruction and Consolation for such as have Suffered Loss by Fire . . . Occasioned by the Dreadful Fire in the City of London of the Year 1666* (London, 1667).
Stoicorum Veterum Fragmenta, ed. Joannes Arnim, 4 vols. (Leipzig, 1905).
Strode, George, *The Anatomie of Mortalitie* (London, 1618).
Suetonius, *History of Twelve Caesars*, trans. Philemon Holland (London, 1606).
Sym, John, *Lifes Preservative Against Self-Killing; or, An Useful Treatise Concerning Life and Self-Murder*, ed. Michael MacDonald (London, 1988).
Tacitus, *The Annals of Imperial Rome*, trans. Michael Grant (London, 1996).
Tasso, Torquato, *Aminta English't*, trans. Henry Reynolds (London, 1628).
Tourneur, Cyril, *The Plays of Cyril Tourneur*, ed. George Parfitt (Cambridge, 1978).
Turberville, George, *Epitaphes, Epigrams, Songs and Sonnets* (London, 1567).
Valerius Maximus, *Memorable Doings and Sayings*, ed. and trans. D. R. Shackleton Bailey (Cambridge, Mass., 2000).
Various, *A General Collection of Discourses of the Virtuosi of France, upon all Sorts of Philosophy, and other Natural Knowleg*, trans. G. Havers (London, 1664).
Vaughan, William, *The Golden-Groue* (London, 1600).
Vesalius, Andreas, *On the Fabric of the Human Body*, trans. William Frank Richardson, 2 vols. (San Francisco, 1999).
Vicary, Thomas, *The Anatomie of the Bodie of Man*, ed. F. J. Furnivall and Percy Furnivall (London, 1888).
Virgil, *The Aeneid*, trans. C. Day Lewis (Oxford, 1986).
—— *Eclogues*, trans. W. L. Gent (London, 1628).
W[alkington], T[homas], *The Optick Glasse of Humors; or, The Touchstone of a Golden Temperature* (London, 1607).
Warner, William, *Albions England* (London, 1612).
[Watson, Thomas], *The Lamentations of Amintas for the Death of Phillis*, trans. Abraham Fraunce (London, 1588).
Watts, Isaac, *Sermons, Discourses and Essays on Various Subjects*, 6 vols. (London, 1753).
Webster, John, *The Duchess of Malfi*, ed. John Russell Brown (Manchester, 1997).
—— *The White Devil*, ed. Christina Luckyj (London, 1996).
Weever, John, *Faunus and Melliflora* (London, 1600).
Whitney, Geffrey, *A Choice of Emblemes* (Leiden, 1586).
Wilson, Arthur, *The History of Great Britain: Being the Life and Reign of King James the First* (London, 1653).

Wilson, Thomas, *The Arte of Rhetorike* (London, 1553).

Wingate, Edmund, *Justice Revived* (London, 1661).

Witelo, *Witelonis Perspectivae*, trans. A. Mark Smith (Wrocław, 1983).

Wither, George, *A Collection Of Emblemes, Ancient and Moderne* (London, 1635).

—— *Friendship* (London, 1654).

Wright, Thomas, *The Passions of the Minde in Generall* (London, 1630).

Secondary Works

Adelman, Janet, *Suffocating Mothers: Fantasies of Maternal Origins in Shakespeare's Plays* (London, 1992).

Agacinski, Sylviane, 'Another Experience of the Question, or Experiencing the Question Other-Wise', in Cadava et al. (eds.), 9–23.

Altman, Joel B., '"Preposterous Conclusions": Eros, *Enargeia*, and the Composition of *Othello*', *Representations*, 18 (1987), 129–57.

Andrews, John F. (ed.), Romeo and Juliet: *Critical Essays* (London, 1993).

Barkan, Leonard, *The Gods Made Flesh: Metamorphosis and the Pursuit of Paganism* (London, 1986).

Barker, Francis, *The Tremulous Private Body: Essays on Subjection* (London, 1984).

Bartsch, Shadi, *The Mirror of the Self: Sexuality, Self-Knowledge, and the Gaze in the Early Roman Empire* (Chicago and London, 2006).

Bate, Jonathan, *Shakespeare and Ovid* (Oxford, 1993).

Beare, John I., *Greek Theories of Elementary Cognition: From Alcmaeon to Aristotle* (Oxford, 1906).

Belsey, Catherine, 'Cleopatra's Seduction', in Terence Hawkes (ed.), *Alternative Shakespeares*, vol. 2 (London, 1996), 38–62.

—— *Desire: Love Stories in Western Culture* (Oxford, 1994).

—— 'The Name of the Rose in *Romeo and Juliet*', in White (ed.), 47–67.

—— *The Subject of Tragedy: Identity and Difference in Renaissance Drama* (London, 1985).

Bloch, Maurice, and Parry, Jonathan (eds.), *Death and the Regeneration of Life* (Cambridge, 1982).

Borch-Jacobsen, Mikkel, 'The Freudian Subject, from Politics to Ethics', in Cadava et al. (eds.), 61–78.

Braden, Gordon, 'Beyond Frustration: Petrarchan Laurels in the Seventeenth Century', *Studies in English Literature, 1500–1900*, 26 (1986), 5–23.

Brennan, Teresa, and Jay, Martin (eds.), *Vision in Context: Historical and Contemporary Perspectives on Sight* (London, 1996).

—— '"The Contexts of Vision" from a Specific Standpoint', ibid., 217–30.

Burns, Edward, *Character: Acting and Being on the Pre-Modern Stage* (London, 1990).

Bush, Douglas, *Mythology and the Renaissance Tradition in English Poetry* (New York, 1963).

Cadava, Eduardo, Connor, Peter, and Nancy, Jean-Luc (eds.), *Who Comes after the Subject?* (New York, 1991).

Callaghan, Dympna C., 'The Ideology of Romantic Love: The Case of *Romeo and Juliet*', in ead., Lorraine Helms, and Jyotsna Singh (eds.), *The Weyward Sisters: Shakespeare and Feminist Politics* (Oxford, 1994), 59–101.

Charnes, Linda, *Notorious Identity: Materializing the Subject in Shakespeare* (Cambridge, Mass., 1993).

Clark, Stuart, *Vanities of the Eye: Vision in Early Modern European Culture* (Oxford, 2007).

Colie, Rosalie L., *Paradoxia Epidemica: The Renaissance Tradition of Paradox* (Princeton, 1966).

Connor, Stephen, 'The Modern Auditory I', in Porter (ed.), *Rewriting the Self*, 203–23.

Cornford, Francis M., *Plato's Cosmology* (London, 1935).

Cracy, Jonathan, *The Techniques of the Observer: On Vision and Modernity in the Nineteenth Century* (Cambridge, Mass., 1992).

Craig, Horace S., *The Duelling Scenes in Shakespeare* (Berkeley, 1940).

Danby, John F., '*Antony and Cleopatra*: A Shakespearean Adjustment', in John Drakakis (ed.), Antony and Cleopatra: *New Casebooks* (Basingstoke, 1994), 33–55.

Davies, Jon, *Death, Burial and Rebirth in the Religions of Antiquity* (London, 1999).

Davis, Lloyd, '"Death-Marked Love": Desire and Presence in *Romeo and Juliet*', *SS*, 49 (1996), 57–67.

Davis, Philip, *Sudden Shakespeare: The Shaping of Shakespeare's Creative Thought* (London, 1996).

Delany, Paul, *British Autobiography in the Seventeenth Century* (London, 1969).

Dent, Robert W., *Shakespeare's Proverbial Language: An Index* (Berkeley, 1981).

Derrida, Jacques, 'The Politics of Friendship', *Journal of Philosophy*, 85 (1988), 632–44.

Dollimore, Jonathan, *Radical Tragedy: Religion, Ideology and Power in the Drama of Shakespeare and his Contemporaries* (Brighton, 1984).

Donaldson, Ian, *The Rapes of Lucretia: A Myth and its Transformations* (Oxford, 1982).

Dubrow, Heather, *Echoes of Desire: English Petrarchism and its Counterdiscourses* (Ithaca, NY, 1995).

Eagleton, Terence, *Shakespeare and Society: Critical Studies in Shakespearean Drama* (London, 1970).

—— 'Self-Undoing Subjects', in Porter (ed.), 262–9.

Ellrodt, Robert, 'Self-Consciousness in Montaigne and Shakespeare', *SS* 28 (1975), 37–50.

Elsner, Jaś, *Roman Eyes: Visuality and Subjectivity in Art and Text* (Princeton, 2007).

Enterline, Lynn, *The Tears of Narcissus: Melancholia and Masculinity in Early Modern Writing* (Stanford, 1995).

Evans, Robert O., *The Osier Cage: Rhetorical Devices in* Romeo and Juliet (Lexington, Ky., 1966).

Fedden, Henry Romilly, *Suicide: A Social and Historical Study* (London, 1938).

Ferry, Anne, *The "Inward" Language: Sonnets of Wyatt, Sidney, Shakespeare, Donne* (Chicago, 1983).

Fichter, Andrew, '*Antony and Cleopatra*: "The Time of Universal Peace"', *SS*, 33 (1980), 99–111.

Fineman, Joel, *Shakespeare's Perjured Eye: The Invention of Poetic Subjectivity in the Sonnets* (Berkeley, 1986).

Foster, Donald W., '"Against the Perjured Falsehood of Your Tongues": Frances Howard on the Course of Love', *ELR*, 24 (1994), 72–103.

Foucault, Michel, *The Order of Things: An Archaeology of the Human Sciences* (Abingdon, 2002).

—— 'Technologies of the Self', in Martin et al. (eds.), 16–49.

Fowler, Don, *Roman Constructions: Readings in Postmodern Latin* (Oxford, 2000).

Frank, Manfred, 'Is Self-Consciousness a Case of Presence à soi? Towards a Meta-Critique of the Recent French Critique of Metaphysics', in David Wood (ed.), *Derrida: A Critical Reader* (Oxford, 1992), 218–34.

Frankfurt, Harry G., 'Freedom of the Will and the Concept of a Person', *Journal of Philosophy*, 68 (1971), 5–20.

Freedman, Barbara, *Staging the Gaze: Postmodernism, Psychoanalysis, and Shakespearean Comedy* (Ithaca, NY, 1991).

Fumerton, Patricia, *Cultural Aesthetics: Renaissance Literature and the Practice of Social Ornament* (Chicago, 1991).

Fuseli, Henry, *Lectures on Painting: Delivered at the Royal Academy* (London, 1830).

Garrison, Elise P., *Groaning Tears: Ethical and Dramatic Aspects of Suicide in Greek Tragedy* (Leiden, 1995).

Gil Harris, Jonathan, '"Narcissus in thy Face": Roman Desire and the Difference it Fakes in *Antony and Cleopatra*', *SQ*, 45 (1994), 408–25.

—— 'Atomic Shakespeare', *SS*, 30 (2002), 47–51.

Gill, Christopher, *Personality in Greek Epic, Tragedy, and Philosophy: The Self in Dialogue* (Oxford, 1996).

—— *The Structured Self in Hellenistic and Roman Thought* (Oxford, 2006).

Go, K., '"I am that I am" in Shakespeare's "Sonnet 121" and 1 Corinthians 15:10', *N&Q*, 49 (2002), 241–2.

Grabes, Herbert, *The Mutable Glass: Mirror-Imagery in Titles and Texts of the Middle Ages and English Renaissance*, trans. Gordon Collier (Cambridge, 1982).

Grady, Hugh, *Shakespeare, Machiavelli, and Montaigne: Power and Subjectivity from Richard II to Hamlet* (Oxford, 2002).

Greenblatt, Stephen, *Renaissance Self-Fashioning: From More to Shakespeare* (Chicago, 1980).

Greene, Thomas, 'The Flexibility of the Self in Renaissance Literature', in Peter Demetz, Thomas Greene, and Lowry Nelson, Jr. (eds.), *The Disciplines of Criticism: Essays in Literary Theory, Interpretation, and History* (New Haven, 1968), 241–64.

Gregerson, Linda, *The Reformation of the Subject: Spenser, Milton, and the English Protestant Epic* (Cambridge, 1995).

Griffin, Miriam, 'Philosophy, Cato, and Roman Suicide', *Greece and Rome*, 33 (1986), 64–77 and 192–202.

—— *Seneca: A Philosopher in Politics* (Oxford, 1976).

Grossman, Marshall, *The Story of All Things: Writing the Self in English Renaissance Narrative Poetry* (Durham, 1998).

Hadzsits, George Depue, *Lucretius and his Influence* (London, 1935).

Halio, Jay L. (ed.), *Shakespeare's Romeo and Juliet: Texts, Contexts, and Interpretation* (Newark, Del., 1995).

Hamilton, Donna B., *Shakespeare and the Politics of Protestant England* (Lexington, Ky., 1992).

Hammond, Paul, 'The Integrity of Dryden's Lucretius', *MLR*, 78 (1983), 1–23.

—— 'Marvell's Sexuality', *Seventeenth Century*, 11 (1996), 87–123.

Hardie, Philip, *Ovid's Poetics of Illusion* (Cambridge, 2002).

Harris, William V., *Restraining Rage: The Ideology of Anger Control in Classical Antiquity* (Cambridge, Mass., 2001).

Higonnet, Margaret, 'Speaking Silences: Women's Suicide', in Susan Rubin Suleiman (ed.), *The Female Body in Western Culture: Contemporary Perspectives* (Cambridge, Mass., 1986), 68–83. *The Tragicall Historye*

—— 'Suicide as Self Construction', in M. Gutwirth et al. (eds.), *Germaine de Staël: Crossing the Borders* (New Brunswick, NJ, 1991), 69–81.

Hillman, David, and Mazzio, Carla (eds.), *The Body in Parts: Fantasies of Corporeality in Early Modern Europe* (London, 1997).

Hillman, Richard, *Self-Speaking in Medieval and Early Modern English Drama: Subjectivity, Discourse and the Stage* (Basingstoke, 1997).

Hollander, John, *The Figure of Echo: A Mode of Allusion in Milton and After* (Berkeley, 1981).

Holleran, James V., 'Maimed Funeral Rites in *Hamlet*', *ELR*, 19 (1989), 65–93.

Holmer, Joan Ozark, '"Draw, if You be Men": Saviolo's Significance for *Romeo and Juliet*', *SQ*, 45 (1994), 163–89.

Hope, Valerie M., 'Contempt and Respect: The Treatment of the Corpse in Ancient Rome', in ead. and Marshall, Eireann (eds.), *Death and Disease in the Ancient City* (London, 2000), 104–27.

James, Heather, 'Ovid and the Question of Politics in Early Modern England', in Yvonne Bruce (ed.), *Images of Matter: Essays on British Literature of the Middle Ages and Renaissance* (Newark, Del., 2005), 92–122.

Jardine, Lisa, *Still Harping on Daughters: Women and Drama in the Age of Shakespeare*, 2nd edn (New York, 1983).

Jeanneret, Michel, *Perpetual Motion: Transforming Shapes in the Renaissance from da Vinci to Montaigne*, trans. Nidra Poller (London, 2001).

Jonas, Hans, *The Phenomenon of Life: Toward a Philosophical Biography* (New York, 1966).

Kaufman, Peter Iver, *Prayer, Despair, and Drama: Elizabethan Introspection* (Urbana, Ill., 1996).

Kelly, Colleen, 'Figuring the Fight: Recovering Shakespeare's Theatrical Swordplay', in John W. Frick (ed.), *Theatre and Violence* (Tuscaloosa, Ala., 1999), 96–108.

Kilgour, Maggie, '"Thy Perfect Image Viewing": Poetic Creation and Ovid's Narcissus in *Paradise Lost*', *Studies in Philology*, 102 (2005), 307–39.

Kirsch, Arthur, 'Macbeth's Suicide', *ELH*, 51 (1984), 269–96.

Lacan, Jacques, *Écrits: A Selection*, trans. Alan Sheridan (London, 1977).

Langer, Ullrich, *Perfect Friendship: Studies in Literature and Moral Philosophy from Boccaccio to Corneille* (Geneva, 1994).

Lanham, Richard, *Motives of Eloquence: Literary Rhetoric in the Renaissance* (New Haven and London, 1976).

Leggatt, Alexander, *Shakespeare's Political Drama: The History Plays and the Roman Plays* (London, 1988).

Levenson, Jill, '"Alla Stoccado Carries it Away": Codes of Violence in *Romeo and Juliet*', in Halio (ed.), 83–96.

Levin, Harry, 'Form and Formality in *Romeo and Juliet*', in Andrews (ed.), 41–53.

Lezra, Jacques, *Unspeakable Subjects: The Genealogy of the Event in Early Modern Europe* (Stanford, 1997).

Lindberg, David C., *Theories of Vision from Al-Kindi to Kepler* (Chicago, 1976).

Lobanov-Rostovsky, Sergei, 'Taming the Basilisk', in Hillman and Mazzio (eds.), 194–217.

Long, A. A., *Stoic Studies* (Cambridge, 1996).

—— 'Thinking and Sense-Perception in Empedocles: Mysticism or Materialism?', *Classical Quarterly*, 16 (1966), 256–76.

Lowenstein, Joseph, *Responsive Readings: Versions of Echo in Pastoral, Epic, and the Jonsonian Masque* (New Haven, 1984).

Lyne, Raphael, *Ovid's Changing Worlds: English Metamorphoses, 1567–1632* (Oxford, 2001).

MacDonald, Michael, 'Ophelia's Maimèd Rites', *SQ*, 37 (1986), 309–17.

—— and Murphy, Terence R., *Sleepless Souls: Suicide in Early Modern England* (Oxford, 1990).

McGuire, Donald T., *Acts of Silence: Civil War, Tyranny, and Suicide in the Flavian Epics* (Hildesheim, 1997).

MacKinnon, Patricia L., 'The Analogy of the Body Politic in St. Augustine, Dante, Petrarch, and Arioso' (Ph.D. thesis, University of California, Santa Cruz, 1988).

Martin, L. C., 'Shakespeare, Lucretius, and the Commonplaces', *Review of English Studies*, 21 (1945), 174–82.

Martin, Luther H., Gutman, Huck, and Hutton, Patrick H. (eds.), *Technologies of the Self: A Seminar with Michel Foucault* (Amherst, Mass., 1988).

Martindale, Charles (ed.), *Ovid Renewed: Ovidian Influences on Literature and Art from the Middle Ages to the Twentieth Century* (Cambridge, 1988).

—— and Martindale, Michelle, *Shakespeare and the Uses of Antiquity: An Introductory Essay* (London, 1990).

Masten, Jeffrey, *Textual Intercourse* (Cambridge, 1997).

Maus, Katherine Eisaman, *Inwardness and Theater in the English Renaissance* (Chicago, 1995).

Melville, Stephen, 'Division of the Gaze, or, Remarks on the Color and Tenor of Contemporary "Theory"', in Brennan and Jay (eds.), 101–16.

Midelfort, H. C. Erik, 'Religious Melancholy and Suicide: On the Reformation Origins of a Sociological Stereotype', in Andrew D. Weiner and Leonard V. Kaplan (eds.), *Madness, Melancholy, and the Limits of the Self* (Madison, Wis., 1996), 41–56.

Miles, Geoffrey, *Shakespeare and the Constant Romans* (Oxford, 1996).

Miller, J. Hillis, *Versions of Pygmalion* (Cambridge, Mass., 1990).

Neill, Michael, 'Ford's Unbroken Art: The Moral Design of *The Broken Heart*', *MLR*, 75 (1980), 249–68.

—— *Issues of Death: Mortality and Identity in English Renaissance Tragedy* (Oxford, 1997).

Nordlund, Marcus, *The Dark Lantern: A Historical Study of Sight in Shakespeare, Webster, and Middleton* (Goteburg, 1999).

Novy, Marianne L., ' "And You Smile Not, He's Gagged": Mutuality in Shakespearean Comedy', *Philological Quarterly*, 55 (1976), 178–94.

Nuttall, A. D., 'Ovid's Narcissus and Shakespeare's Richard II: The Reflected Self', in Martindale (ed.), *Ovid Renewed*, 137–50.

Oakley-Brown, Liz, *Ovid and the Cultural Politics of Translation in Early Modern England* (Aldershot, 2006).

—— 'Translating the Subject: Ovid's *Metamorphosis* in England, 1560–7', in Roger Ellis and Liz Oakley-Brown (eds.), *Translation and Nation: Towards a Cultural Politics of Englishness* (Clevedon, 2001), 48–84.

Parker, Patricia, *Literary Fat Ladies: Rhetoric, Gender, Property* (London, 1987).

—— *Shakespeare from the Margins: Language, Culture, Context* (Chicago, 1994).

—— 'Virile Style', in Louise Fradenburg and Carla Freccero (eds.), *Premodern Sexualities* (London, 1996), 199–222.

—— and Freccero, Carla (eds.), *Premodern Sexualities* (London, 1996).

Pearcy, Lee T., *The Mediated Muse: English Translations of Ovid, 1560–1700* (Hamden, Conn., 1984).

Pearlman, E., 'Shakespeare at Work', *ELR*, 24 (1994), 315–42.

Pequigney, Joseph, *Such Is my Love: A Study of Shakespeare's Sonnets* (Chicago, 1985).

Pittenger, Elizabeth, 'Explicit Ink', in Parker and Freccero (eds.), 223–42.

Plass, Paul, *The Game of Death in Ancient Rome: Arena Sport and Political Suicide* (Madison, Wis., 1995).

Porter, Roy (ed.), *Rewriting the Self: Histories from the Renaissance to the Present* (London, 1997).

Regan, Mariann Sanders, *Love Words: The Self and the Text in Medieval and Renaissance Poetry* (Ithaca, NY, 1982).

Richardson, Ruth, *Death, Dissection and the Destitute* (London, 1987).

Rist, J. M., *Stoic Philosophy* (Cambridge, 1969).

Ryan, Kiernan, *Shakespeare* (Basingstoke, 1989).

Sambursky, S., *Physics of the Stoics* (London, 1959)

Sawday, Jonathan, *Engines of the Imagination: Renaissance Culture and the Rise of the Machine* (London, 2007).

—— ' "Mysteriously Divided": Civil War, Madness, and the Divided Self', in Thomas Healy and Jonathan Sawday (eds.), *Literature and the English Civil War* (Cambridge, 1990), 127–43.

—— 'Self and Selfhood in the Seventeenth Century', in Porter (ed.), 29–48.

Schoenfeldt, Michael C., 'The Matter of Inwardness: Shakespeare's Sonnets', in James Schiffer (ed.), *Shakespeare's Sonnets: Critical Essays* (London, 1999), 305–24.

—— '"Respective Boldnesse": Herbert and the Art of Submission', in Mary A. Maleski (ed.), *A Fine Tuning: Studies in the Religious Poetry of Herbert and Milton* (New York, 1989), 77–94.

Shannon, Laurie, *Sovereign Amity: Figures of Friendship in Shakespearean Contexts* (Chicago, 2002).

Shoaf, R. A., *Milton: Poet of Duality. A Study of Semiosis in the Poetry and the Prose* (London, 1985).

Shuger, Debora Kuller, *Habits of Thought in the English Renaissance: Religion, Politics, and the Dominant Culture* (Toronto, 1997).

—— 'Subversive Fathers and Suffering Subjects: Shakespeare and Christianity', in Donna B. Hamilton and Richard Strier (eds.), *Religion, Literature, and Politics in Post-Reformation England, 1540–1688* (Cambridge, 1996), 46–69.

Simon, Gérard, 'Behind the Mirror', *Graduate Faculty Philosophy Journal*, 12 (1987), 311–50.

Sinfield, Alan, *Faultlines: Cultural Materialism and the Politics of Dissident Reading* (Oxford, 1992).

Smith, Nigel, *Perfection Proclaimed: Language and Literature in English Radical Religion, 1640–1660* (Oxford, 1989).

Snow, Edward, 'Language and Sexual Difference in *Romeo and Juliet*', in Andrews (ed.), 371–401.

Snyder, Susan, 'Ideology and the Feud in *Romeo and Juliet*', *SS*, 49 (1996), 87–96.

Sonnino, Lee A., *A Handbook to Sixteenth-Century Rhetoric* (London, 1968).

Spitzer, Leo, 'Speech and Language in *Inferno XIII*', *Italica*, 19 (1942), 81–104.

Sprott, S. E., *The English Debate on Suicide from Donne to Hume* (La Salle, Ill., 1961).

Stachniewski, John, *The Persecutory Imagination: English Puritanism and the Literature of Religious Despair* (Oxford, 1991).

Taylor, A. B., 'Two Notes on Shakespeare and the Translators', *Review of English Studies*, 38 (1987), 523–6.

Taylor, Charles, 'The Person', in Michael Carrithers, Steven Collins, and Steven Lukes (eds.), *The Category of the Person: Anthropology, Philosophy, History* (Cambridge, 1985), 257–81.

—— *Sources of the Self: The Making of the Modern Identity* (Cambridge, 1989).

Therbon, Göran, *The Ideology of Power and the Power of Ideology* (London, 1980).

Timonen, Asko, *Cruelty and Death: Roman Historians' Scenes of Imperial Violence from Commodus to Philippus Arabs* (Turku, 2000).

Tissol, Garth, *The Face of Nature: Wit, Narrative, and Cosmic Origins in Ovid's Metamorphoses* (Princeton, 1997).

Van Gennep, Arnold, *The Rites of Passage*, trans. Monika B. Vizedom and Gabrielle L. Cafee (London, 1960).

Van Hoorn, Willem, *As Images Unwind: Ancient and Modern Theories of Visual Perception* (Amsterdam, 1972).

Vernant, Jean-Pierre, *Mortals and Immortals: Collected Essays*, ed. Froma I. Zeitlin (Princeton, 1991).

Vinge, Louise, *The Narcissus Theme in Western European Literature up to the Early Nineteenth Century* (Lund, 1967).

Watson, Robert N., *The Rest is Silence: Death as Annihilation in the English Renaissance* (Berkeley, 1994).

Weber, Samuel, *Return to Freud: Jacques Lacan's Dislocation of Psychoanalysis*, trans. Michael Levine (Cambridge, 1991).

Whigham, Frank, *Ambition and Privilege: The Social Tropes of Elizabethan Courtesy Theory* (Berkeley, 1984).

White, R. S. (ed.), Romeo and Juliet: *Contemporary Critical Essays* (Basingstoke, 2001).

Williams, Raymond, *Keywords: A Vocabulary of Culture and Society* (Bungay, 1976).

Wymer, Rowland, *Suicide and Despair in the Jacobean Drama* (Brighton, 1986).

Index